Global Governance and Regulation

With a diverse group of contributors from law, business and the social sciences, this book explores the line not only between order and disorder in global affairs, but also chaos and control, continuity and change, the core and the margins. The key themes include: global crises and the role of international law, norms and institutions; the challenge of pluralism to regulatory clarity; and critical assessments of taken-for-granted systems and values such as capitalism, centralised government, de-militarisation and the separation of powers. The book divides into two key parts. The first part, 'Conceptions', considers the diverse way in which order/disorder can be conceived in global governance and regulation. The second part, 'Case Studies', groups chapters around five topic areas: citizens, capitalism, conflict, crime and courts. The authors here build on the themes presented in the first part by embedding them within specific areas of international regulation, such as international criminal law, maritime law or finance regulation; jurisdictions and regions, such as Australia, Canada, China, Japan and South Asia; and subject matter, such as water resources, citizenship, statelessness and public interest litigation. This blend of contemporary subject matter, empirical studies, multi-disciplinary perspectives and academic theories provides a comprehensive analysis to current and emerging debates in the broader global community. In utilising interdisciplinary studies to draw out common issues and alternative solutions, the book will appeal to a wide readership among academics and policy-makers.

Leon Wolff is Associate Professor of Law, Queensland University of Technology, Brisbane. He is founding Co-Director of the Australian Network for Japanese Law (ANJeL), former Co-Coordinator of the Transnational, International and Comparative Law and Policy (TICLP) Network, and Director of the Asia-Pacific Legal Institute of Australia (APLIA). His research expertise lies in Japanese law and society, where he has written widely on sexual harassment, litigiousness and popular culture, the judiciary, public law reforms, corporate governance and employment relations in Japan. His most recent publication is the co-edited book *Who Rules Japan? Popular Participation in the Japanese Legal Process* (Edward Elgar, 2015).

Danielle Ireland-Piper is Associate Professor of Law, Bond University, Gold Coast, and Co-Director of the Transnational, International and Comparative Law and Policy (TICLP) Network. Her areas of interest and publication are international law, comparative constitutional law and human rights. Her latest publication is *Accountability in Extraterritoriality: A Comparative and International Law Perspective* (Edward Elgar, 2017). She was a Chevening Scholar at the University of Cambridge and holds a PhD from the University of Queensland.

Law, Ethics and Governance Series
Series Editor: Charles Sampford
Director, Institute for Ethics, Governance and Law,
Griffith University, Australia

Recent history has emphasised the potentially devastating effects of governance failures in governments, government agencies, corporations and the institutions of civil society. 'Good governance' is seen as necessary, if not crucial, for economic success and human development. Although the disciplines of law, ethics, politics, economics and management theory can provide insights into the governance of organizations, governance issues can only be dealt with by interdisciplinary studies, combining several (and sometimes all) of those disciplines. This series aims to provide such interdisciplinary studies for students, researchers and relevant practitioners.

Recent titles in this series:

Rethinking International Law and Justice
Edited by Charles Sampford, Spencer Zifcak and Derya Aydin Okur
ISBN 978-1-4724-2668-0

International Rule of Law and Professional Ethics
Edited by Vesselin Popovski
ISBN 978-1-4724-2803-5

Responsibility to Protect and Sovereignty
Edited by Charles Sampford and Ramesh Thakur
ISBN 978-1-4094-3782-6

Protection of Refugees and Displaced Persons in the Asia Pacific Region
Edited by Angus Francis and Rowena Maguire
ISBN 978-1-4094-5540-0

Intellectual Liberty
Natural Rights and Intellectual Property
Hugh Breakey
ISBN 978-1-4094-4711-5

Health Workforce Governance
Improved Access, Good Regulatory Practice, Safer Patients
Edited by Stephanie D. Short and Fiona McDonald
ISBN 978-1-4094-2921-0

Global Governance and Regulation

Order and Disorder in the 21st Century

Edited by
Leon Wolff and Danielle Ireland-Piper

Routledge
Taylor & Francis Group
LONDON AND NEW YORK

First published 2018
by Routledge

2 Park Square, Milton Park, Abingdon, Oxfordshire OX14 4RN
52 Vanderbilt Avenue, New York, NY 10017

Routledge is an imprint of the Taylor & Francis Group, an informa business

First issued in paperback 2020

British Library Cataloguing-in-Publication Data
A catalogue record for this book is available from the British Library

Library of Congress Cataloging-in Publication Data
Names: Wolff, Leon, 1969– editor. | Ireland-Piper, Danielle, editor.
Title: Global governance and regulation : order and disorder in the 21st century / Leon Wolff, Danielle Ireland-Piper.
Description: Abingdon, Oxon ; New York, NY : Routledge, 2017. | Includes bibliographical references and index.
Identifiers: LCCN 2016052679 | ISBN 9781472489012 (hardback) | ISBN 9781351734011 (web pdf) | ISBN 9781351734004 (epub) | ISBN 9781351733991 (mobipocket)
Subjects: LCSH: Law and globalization. | International law and human rights. | International organization. | International and municipal law. | World politics—21st century.
Classification: LCC KZ1268 .G55 2017 | DDC 341—dc23
LC record available at https://lccn.loc.gov/2016052679

ISBN: 978-1-4724-8901-2 (hbk)
ISBN: 978-0-367-59356-8 (pbk)

Typeset in Galliard
by Apex CoVantage, LLC

Contents

Figures and Tables

Figures

Tables

Contributors

Syed Ali Abbas is a PhD candidate and Adjunct Tutor in International Business, Bond University, Gold Coast.

Victoria Schnure Baumfield is Assistant Professor of Law, Bond University, Gold Coast and a PhD candidate in Law at the University of Queensland. Her current research interests include corporate governance, the accountability of government entities, corporatisation and privatisation, particularly in the area of public utilities.

Narelle Bedford is Assistant Professor of Law, Bond University, Gold Coast. She researches Australian administrative law with interests in State tribunals, vexatious litigants, access to justice, and the intersection between administrative law and sports law. She is Deputy Director of the Transnational, International and Comparative Law and Policy (TICLP) Network.

Susan Bird is Lecturer, School of Business and Law, Central Queensland University, Melbourne. Bird's current research interests are the connections between law and geography, anarchy and property, and free speech in neo-colonial spaces.

Lisa J. Bonin is Teaching Fellow, Bond University, Gold Coast. Her interests include advocacy and access to justice. Before emigrating to Australia, Lisa Bonin practiced as a litigator for seven years at McCarthy Tétrault, a top-tier Canadian law firm.

Anthony E. Cassimatis is Professor of Law, University of Queensland, Brisbane. He is the Director of the Centre for Public, International and Comparative Law at the University of Queensland and is the chairperson of the Australian Red Cross's International Humanitarian Law Committee for Queensland. Anthony is the author or co-author of four books and numerous articles and book chapters on public international law, administrative law and legal advocacy.

Jonathan Crowe is Professor of Law, Bond University, Gold Coast. He is also the President of the Australasian Society of Legal Philosophy and Co-Director of the Transnational, International and Comparative Law and Policy (TICLP) Network. He has published widely on the relationship between law and ethics, particularly the nature of legal obligation and the role of ethics in legal reasoning. He is currently completing a book on the natural law tradition in ethics and jurisprudence.

Malcolm Davis is Senior Analyst, Australian Strategic Policy Institute, Canberra. He was previously a Post-Doctoral Research Fellow in China-Western Relations in the Faculty of Society and Design, Bond University, Gold Coast (2012–2016) and he retains an Honorary Assistant Professor position in the Faculty.

Maziar M. Falarti is Honorary Research Fellow in International Relations, Bond University, Gold Coast. His research interests are in indigenous political systems and models, international relations, economic blocks and integration and historiography, particularly in the Malay-Indonesian World, East & Southeast Asia, Indian Ocean themes, South Asia and the Islamic World in general. His most recent book is *Malay Kingship in Kedah: Religion, Trade, and Society* (Rowman & Littlefield, 2012).

Madhav Gautam is Assistant Protection Officer at United Nations High Commissioner for Refugees, Damak, Nepal. He has 13 years' experience in the areas of human rights, gender mainstreaming, and civilian, refugee and child protection in armed conflicts and post-conflict situations. He was awarded the Honour of Jana Sewa Sri Padak in 2012 by the President of Nepal for his contribution to the field of human rights protection and promotion in Nepal.

Umair Ghori is Assistant Professor of Law, Bond University, Gold Coast. His primary area of research is international trade and investment laws (particularly from the Asian developing country perspective) with secondary interests in international law and human rights. He is the author of *Global Textiles and Clothing Trade: Trade Policy Perspectives* (Kluwer, 2012). He is Deputy Director of the Transnational, International and Comparative Law and Policy (TICLP) Network.

Douglas Guilfoyle is Professor of Law, Monash University, Melbourne. He researches and teaches in the fields of public international law, international criminal law, and the law of the sea. He is the author of *Shipping Interdiction and the Law of the Sea* (Cambridge University Press, 2009) and numerous articles on maritime security, naval warfare and Somali piracy.

Sanzhuan Guo is Lecturer in Law, Flinders University, Adelaide. Her research interests include history and theory of international law, nationality and statelessness, and international human rights law. Her latest book is *Comparative Studies on the Effectiveness of National Human Rights Institutions* (Law Press, 2013).

Danielle Ireland-Piper is Associate Professor of Law, Bond University, Gold Coast, and Co-Director of the Transnational, International and Comparative Law and Policy (TICLP) Network. Her areas of interest and publication are international law, comparative constitutional law and human rights. Her latest publication is *Accountability in Extraterritoriality: A Comparative and International Law Perspective* (Edward Elgar, 2017). She was a Chevening Scholar at the University of Cambridge and holds a PhD from the University of Queensland.

Eve Massingham is Regional Legal Adviser for the Nairobi Regional Delegation of the International Committee of the Red Cross. She has worked in the field of international humanitarian law for ten years with the International Red Cross and Red Crescent Movement and has published a number of book chapters and articles on international humanitarian law. She has a PhD from the University of Queensland, Brisbane.

Jodie O'Leary is an Assistant Professor at the Faculty of Law, Bond University, Gold Coast, and a PhD Candidate at the School of Regulation and Global Governance (RegNet), Australian National University, Canberra. She researches criminal law and international criminal law. Her doctoral thesis is on 'Holding Security Sector Institutions Accountable for International Crimes'.

Louise Parsons is Assistant Professor of Law, Bond University, Gold Coast. Her research interests include banking law, especially central banking, the regulatory architecture for financial stability and cryptocurrencies; remedies in private law; international arbitration; and legal education.

Leon Wolff is Associate Professor of Law, Queensland University of Technology, Brisbane. He is founding Co-Director of the Australian Network for Japanese Law (ANJeL), former Co-Coordinator of the Transnational, International and Comparative Law and Policy (TICLP) Network, and Director of the Asia-Pacific Legal Institute of Australia (APLIA). His research expertise lies in Japanese law and society, where he has written widely on sexual harassment, litigiousness and popular culture, the judiciary, public law reforms, corporate governance and employment relations in Japan. His most recent publication is the co-edited book *Who Rules Japan? Popular Participation in the Japanese Legal Process* (Edward Elgar, 2015).

Preface

Global Governance and Regulation—A Dreamscape

Leon Wolff

> 'Chaos was the law of nature; Order was the dream of man' (Henry Adams, 1974, p. 451).

"All the world's a stage," penned Shakespeare in his play *As You Like It* (Shakespeare, 1988, 2.7.1). So, too, in this book, the globe is our stage. But our "players", rather than men and women, are Regulation and Governance. I capitalise these terms because they serve as our book's central characters. They personify two distinct but interlinked concepts (Trubek and Trubek, 2006, pp. 543–44); they serve both as sites of scholarship as well as realms of practice (see, eg, Kingsford-Smith, 2012, pp. 378–80) and, despite different disciplinary bases, they share a joint concern for power and control.

Governance and Regulation are characters with a rich back-story. This is especially so in the literature on international and transnational law (see, eg, Djelic & Sahlin-Andersson, 2006; Head, Mann & Kozlina, 2012). Invariably, scholars tie them together when discussing international issues. Examples include *Transnational **Governance**: Emerging Models of Global Legal **Regulation*** (Head, Mann & Kozlina, eds, 2012, emphasis added); and *The Politics of **Regulation**: Institutions and Regulatory Reforms for the Age of **Governance*** (Jordana & Levi-Faur, eds, 2006). This book does so, too. The difficulty, however, in doing so is that Governance and Regulation have an unsettled relationship: do they stand in a relationship of harmony, rivalry or transformative co-existence (see, eg, Trubek & Trubek, 2006)?

In large part, this problem is less about the relationship *between* Governance and Regulation and more about their relationship *with* a third character: Law. Under some conceptions, Regulation is the concern of legal scholars; Governance, social scientists (see, eg, Chhotray & Stoker, 2008). Yet, this over-simplifies. Regulatory Studies, as O'Leary observes (Chapter 14 this volume), although a way of "thinking about law", "does not understand law as the primary or only solution to regulatory problems" (citing Simm, 2011, p. 476); rather, it is just one element among a number of regulatory resources (Parker, Scott, Lacey & Braithwaite, 2004, p. 1). Likewise, Governance, as the study of how power is exercised and coordinated among a "wide range of state, non-state and supranational actors" (Scott, 2004, p. 145), sees state law as relevant, albeit not necessarily central, in this process. Law, in short, can be "hard" or "soft", "centred" or "de-centred" (Kingsford Smith, 2012, pp. 386–87; Parker, 2002, p. 16).

Likewise, authors in this volume vest Law with different identities and functions in their chapters. In some accounts, Law is the *protagonist*. It is a hero, achieving qualified success despite the nightmarish problems it confronts (Cassimatis, Chapter 2). It is an adventurer, consistently evolving and changing over time, yet consistently aspiring to unity

(Crowe, Chapter 3). It is a champion of the powerless, giving small States flexible dispute resolution machinery to keep in check the territorial ambitions of the powerful over the oceans (Guilfoyle, Chapter 11). It is a detective, finding within the text of international and comparative law solutions to the threat of State-endorsed citizenship-stripping (Ireland-Piper, Chapter 6), proposals for third-party States to commit more meaningfully to prevent post-conflict, cross-border humanitarian abuses (Massingham, Chapter 13), ideas for improving citizens' access to the courts to ensure State accountability (Bonin and Bedford, Chapter 15) and clues for strengthening regulation of valuable resources such as water (Baumfield, Chapter 9). It is an unreliable narrator, narrating a positive body of jurisprudence criminalising serious international crimes yet transmitting multiple (not necessarily coherent) messages about their regulatory scope and nature (O'Leary, Chapter 14). In other accounts, Law is the *antagonist.* It is a villain, conspiring to keep the Rohingya people stateless and desperate due to the combined failures of the domestic law citizenship and the international law of nationality (Guo and Gautam, Chapter 7). It is an anti-hero, rendering military courts in Pakistan a necessary stop-gap to the problem of terrorism due to the inefficacy of domestic judicial and law enforcement institutions (Ghori, Chapter 16); or keeping alive the threat of another global financial crisis due to incomplete reforms to domestic and international financial regulatory architecture (Parsons, Chapter 10). In yet other accounts, Law is a *non-character.* In the normative world order, for example, it is Western Liberalism, not Law itself, that needs protection against the rogue activities of illiberal States (Davis, Chapter 5). In the uneasy peace between India and Pakistan, it is foreign military aid and mutual armament, not Law, that secures peaceful co-existence (Falarti and Abbas, Chapter 12).

This apparent tension among the characters of Governance, Regulation and (when invoked) Law, however, masks what unifies them. It is this: *they all dream of order.* Crowe (Chapter 3) makes this claim explicitly for Law. Law's dream of order inheres in its language, imagery, norms and institutional design, he argues. This is also evident in the way Law, whether international or domestic, structures itself into a system – an order. But Governance and Regulation also dream this dream. Governance, for example, is the study of collective decision-making. It explores the processes, structures and frameworks by which stakeholder interests are asserted, coordinated and managed in economic, social or economic spheres of human activity (Chhotray & Stoker, 2008, pp. 3–6). The goal of Governance, in short, is to equip reformers and policy-makers with the conceptual tools to interpret and improve policy outcomes – a single, coherent, organised result. Regulation, too, is also outcome-oriented. It seeks to direct resources across a "spectrum of legality" (Kingsford Smith, 2012, p. 378) – from the authoritative force of State law to the normative influence of markets, organisational culture and ethics (Kingsford Smith, 2012, pp. 378–79) – to resolve problems. Its aim, therefore, is to shape a desirable order.

This shared dream is the thematic thread that ties together this collection of essays. Our contributors were invited to consider the extent to which, if any, the "dream" of global order is actuality. This might suggest three possible answers: the world is ordered, disordered or somewhere in between. Yet drawing on their distinctive disciplinary expertise, case studies and methodologies, our contributors generated a far richer array of insights. For some, the dream order is alive, expressing cautious optimism about our global future (Bonin & Bedford, Cassimatis, O'Leary); for others, it is about to degenerate into a nightmare (Davis). For some, international law is a source of ideas to craft solutions to improve humanity's lot (Massingham); for others, it is to urge responsibility

(Ireland-Piper) or to laud inaction (Guo & Gautam). For some, disorder is evidence of regulatory or governance failure (Parsons, Baumfield); for others, chaos is worth celebrating (Bird). For some, global order and disorder are in a constant state of flux, yet their fluid, adaptive, dynamic natures are a source of strength and hope (Crowe, Guilfoyle); for others, global dysfunction offers pragmatic possibilities for peaceful order (Abbas & Falarti, Ghori).

The diversity of our contributors' scholarly traditions, backgrounds and topical interests might explain this range of conclusions. Many of our contributors hail from legal backgrounds, with expertise in international law (Cassimatis, Ghori, Guilfoyle, Guo, Ireland-Piper, Massingham, O'Leary), comparative law (Baumfield, Bedford, Bonin, Parsons, Wolff) or legal theory (Bird, Crowe). Others come from the humanities or social sciences, including experts in International Relations and Policy Studies (Davis, Falarti) and International Business (Abbas). Some, including the co-editors, have interdisciplinary training and focus. Our contributors come from different national and cultural backgrounds: Canada (Bonin), China (Guo), Iran (Falarti), Nepal (Gautam), Pakistan (Ghori and Abbas), South Africa (Parsons) and the United States (Baumfield). The contributors' subject matter is sweeping, encompassing economic activity (such as water regulation, international finance and employment), social justice and human rights (including international humanitarian law, the plight of Stateless peoples and international crimes), military problems (such as foreign military aid and military courts) and political issues (citizenship-stripping legislation and citizens' rights to challenge executive over-reach). And the canvass upon which our contributors depict global order varies: from global approaches (for example, O'Leary on international criminal law and Massingham on international humanitarian law) and regional analyses (for example, Falarti & Abbas and Guo & Gautam on South Asia) to comparative studies (Bedford & Bonin on Australia and Canada) and single-jurisdiction case studies (Baumfield and Bird on Australia, Ghori on Pakistan, Wolff on Japan).

This book owes its origins to the first international conference hosted by the Transnational, International and Comparative Law and Policy (TICLP) Network on 7–8 August 2015. TICLP, established in November 2014 at the Faculty of Law, Bond University, also had a dream – a unified scholarly commitment to a research agenda into global issues but through an open network that welcomes interdisciplinary collaboration and cross-fertilisation of ideas. Although originally created to cater to the growing number of Bond legal scholars pursuing global research agendas, its mission at the outset was also to reach out and welcome researchers from non-law backgrounds with a similar international outlook. This context explains why many of our contributors are (or were) from Bond University. In law, these include researchers in International Law (Crowe, Ireland-Piper, Ghori and O'Leary), international trade law (Ghori), public law (Bedford, Crowe, Ireland-Piper and O'Leary); comparative law (Baumfield, Bedford, Bonin, Parsons and former colleague Wolff) and legal theory (Crowe); in the humanities and social sciences, researchers in International Business (Abbas) and International Relations (former colleague Davis). Although anchored at Bond University, however, TICLP has a broader reach. Its membership, like its non-Bond contributors (Bird, Cassimatis, Davis, Guilfoyle, Gautam, Guo, Wolff), come from universities and organisations across Australia and the world.

The co-editors extend their gratitude to all the authors who expended time to make this book project a reality. Governance, Regulation and Law might be the characters in this book. But it is our contributors who brought these characters to life.

References

Adams, H. (1974). *The education of Henry Adams* (Ernest Samuel, Ed.) Boston, Massachusetts: Houghton Mifflin. (Original work published 1918).

Chhotray, V. and Stoker, G. (2008). *Governance theory and practice: A cross-disciplinary approach.* London and New York: Springer.

Djelic, M. & Sahlin-Andersson, K. (2006). A world of governance: The rise of transnational regulation. In Djelic, M. and Sahlin-Andersson, K. (Eds.). *Transnational governance: Institutional dynamics of regulation* (pp. 1–28). Cambridge: Cambridge University Press.

Head, M., Mann, S. and Kozlina, S. (2012). Introduction: The significance and problems of transnational governance. In Head, M., Mann, S. & Kozlina, S. (Eds.), *Transnational governance: Emerging models of global legal regulation* (pp. 1–12). London & New York: Routledge.

Head, M, Mann, S. and Kozlina, S. (Eds.). (2012). *Transnational governance: Emerging models of global legal regulation.* London & New York: Routledge.

Jordana, J & Levi-Faur, D. (Eds.). (2004). *The politics of regulation: institutions and regulatory reforms for the age of governance.* Cheltenham: Edward Elgar.

Kingsford Smith, D. (2012). Governing the corporation: the role of 'soft regulation'. *University of New South Wales Law Journal, 35(1),* 378–403.

Parker, C. (2002). *The open corporation: Effective self-regulation and democracy.* Cambridge & New York: Cambridge University Press.

Parker, C., Scott, C., Lacey, N., & Braithwaite, J. (2004). Introduction. In Christine Parker, C., Scott, C., Lacey, N. and Braithwaite, J. (Eds.). *Regulating law* (pp. 1–2). Oxford: Oxford University Press.

Scott, C. (2004). Regulation in the age of governance: The rise of the post-regulatory state. In Jordana, J. and Levi-Faur, D. (Eds.). (2004). *The politics of regulation: institutions and regulatory reforms for the age of governance* (pp. 145–174). Cheltenham: Edward Elgar.

Shakespeare, W. (1988). Wells. S & Taylor, G. Eds. *The Oxford Shakespeare: the complete works.* Oxford and New York: Clarendon Press.

Simm, G. (2011). International law as a regulatory framework for sexual crimes committed by peacekeepers. *Journal of Conflict and Security Law, 16(3)*, 473–506.

Trubek, D.M. & Trubek, L.G. (2006). New governance and legal regulation: complementarity, rivalry, and transformation. *Columbia Journal of European Law, 13(3)*, 539–564.

Acknowledgements

This book was compiled in the traditional lands of the Yugambeh people. To that end, the editors acknowledge these traditional custodians and offer respect to elders past, present and emerging.

We are indebted to our publisher, and particularly to Alison Kirk, Ruth Noble and Alfred Symons, for their patience and kind assistance.

We are grateful to our authors for their ideas, perseverance and good spirits. We also thank the Faculty of Law at Bond University for their support of the conference in which this collection was born and both Bond University and the Queensland University of Technology for funding research assistance.

We thank a number of research assistants for their time and energy, including Mikayla Briar-Mills, Jake Buckingham, Ngaire King, Amy Kosa and Paul Perovic.

Finally, we acknowledge those whose lives have been forever altered by the events referred to throughout this book.

Leon Wolff and Dr Danielle Ireland-Piper

1 Introduction

Global Order/Disorder

Leon Wolff and Danielle Ireland-Piper

This book interrogates the relationship between *order/disorder* in global affairs. We use a slash (/) to separate these two concepts exactly for the reasons writing stylists loathe it. As Garner complains, the slash is "unfit" for formal writing "because it is inherently ambiguous: its function may be conjunctive <secretary/treasurer> or disjunctive <a buy/sell decision>" (Garner, 2002, p. 50). We agree – but that is our point. *Order* and *disorder*, as our contributing authors make clear, may be conjunctive, disjunctive or possibly something in between. The slash, here, is not an "abomination" of style (Garner, 2002, p. 50); it is a precise illustration of the complexity of their conceptual interaction.

For example, are *order* and *disorder* antonyms, representing contrasting poles in global governance and regulation, opposite extremes between structural integrity and disassembled rubble? Or are they more like neighbours, linking arms in partnership (albeit not always happily) as the world confronts inevitable change and navigates itself through the challenges? Or, more radically, are they one and the same – within order, there is disorder; within disorder, there is order – like a stained-glass window that may be viewed either as a single piece of art or as multiple fragments of coloured pieces? In normative terms, too, is order the ideal, disorder the nightmare? Or is order a false god, and disorder the surprising friend? Or should we strip away all normative presumptions and analyse them dispassionately for the role they place in shaping our world?

Linked to such complexities is the relationship between *governance/regulation*, the two intellectual tools scholars and policy-makers used to make sense of the world and fashion a better one. We also use a slash to divide them because, like order/disorder, they are distinct but overlap. If order/disorder describe the *state* of the world, governance and regulation refer to the *processes* by which the world enters that state or the *tools* by which it can be altered (eg, Trubek & Trubek, 2006; Kingsford Smith, 2012). Although different disciplines vest different intellectual meanings and functions to each (see Wolff, Preface), they are united in their goals. Together, they target the order/disorder dichotomy. Together, they observe the intersecting interests of global stakeholders – from nation-states, regional groupings and transnational businesses to NGOs and individual citizens. And together, they seek to coordinate the competing claims, harmonize the differences and curb the tensions (eg, Chhotray & Stoker, 2008, pp. 3–6). From law and policy to diplomacy and economic incentives, they deploy a range of resources to deliver their aims (Parker, Scott, Lacey & Braithwaite, 2004, p. 1). But, just as views on order/disorder vary as to the shape of the world, so, too, do views on the techniques required for coordinating and aligning stakeholder interests. Internationalists, for example, talk of universalism and relativism (eg, Gaubatz and MacArthur, 2001). Comparativists observe convergence and divergence (eg, Fauvarque-Cosson, 2001; Hansmann and Kraakman, 2001; Nottage and Wolff, 2005).

Transnationalists speak of "unity in diversity" (cf Ang, 2014). Globalization scholars speak of regulatory structures and their failings (Darian-Smith, 2000).

Little wonder, then, as Kennedy (2008, p. 828) observes, the global system is such a "mystery":

> How does it all work, how do all the pieces fit together? How is public power exercised, where are the levers, who are the authorities, how do they relate to one another? Are the worlds of politics, markets and cultural influence held together in a tight structure or is it all more loose and haphazard? Are there more than one global order – how much, in the end, is simply chaos, how much the work of an invisible hand?

The purpose of this collection of essays is to shed light on this mystery. Our approach to this task is unity/diversity. Once again, we deploy the slash (/). This is because we asked our authors to address a *single* theme: global order/disorder. Yet, at the same time, to generate a rich interdisciplinary dialogue, we drew on intellectual and professional expertise of a *diverse* group of contributors, whose chapters canvass a plurality of case studies, normative positions, background experiences and disciplinary traditions. The surprise – as symbolized by the slash – is that conceptions of global/order and perspectives on governance/regulation do not fall neatly in disciplinary piles. This is the richness that comes from interdisciplinary conversation. As Berman (2012, p. 57) suggests, "instead of insisting on a single set of authoritative norms, we can direct our attention to a more comprehensive investigation of how best to mediate the hybrid spaces where normative systems and communities overlap and clash".

Interdisciplinary approaches to complex global issues, of course, require little defence. After all, if national borders no longer constrain global issues, so too disciplinary borders should not trap scholarship addressing these problems (eg, Beck, 2016). Yet, as Joyner (2006, p. 248) observes in the context of International Law and International Relations, there is sometimes a reluctance to acknowledge alternative disciplinary frameworks:

> Academicians who study either international law or international politics share a dirty little secret: both groups know that the presence of international law is critical for international relations to occur, and both know that the practice of international politics is essential for international law to evolve and function. But each is reluctant to admit the necessity of the other.

This book, however, is not so reluctant.

As such, it is like a symphony: there is single musical idea, a richness of orchestration, occasional harmony and the cymbal-like clash of dissent and the drum-roll of disagreement. Consider, for example, the different disciplinary backgrounds and professional experiences of our authors, the ensemble of instruments they bring to ensure orchestral lushness in expressing the book's themes. Many of our contributors hail from the discipline of law (Baumfield, Bedford, Bird, Bonin, Cassimatis, Crowe, Gautam, Ghori, Guilfoyle, Guo, Ireland-Piper, Massingham, O'Leary, Parsons, Wolff). Others come from the social sciences, including international relations (Davis) and international business (Abbas, Falarti). In many cases, however, our contributors dip into interdisciplinary waters to make out their arguments: for example, political theory and social activism (Bird, Chapter 4), resource management and regulation (Baumfield, Chapter 9), financial governance and law (Parsons, Chapter 10), social conflict and international law (Guo & Gautam, Chapter 7; Falarati

& Abbas, Chapter 12; O'Leary, Chapter 14; Ghori, Chapter 16), Asian Studies and law (Wolff, Chapter 8) and theology and jurisprudence (Crowe, Chapter 3). The interdisciplinary training of many of our authors – Ireland-Piper, for example, has dual qualifications in law and international relations; Gautam, in law, political science and business – ensures that the book engages in cross-disciplinary dialogue.

Further, diverse topics and case studies provide the musical notation – and, therefore, melodic interest – on the symphony's score. Part I addresses larger conceptions of global order/disorder. Thus, Cassimatis (Chapter 2) evaluates the successes of international lawyering despite the challenges of a troubled world. Crowe (Chapter 3) tracks the philosophical history of law and its enduring dream of order. Bird (Chaper 4) explores the anarchist challenge to the political orthodoxy of democracy. Davis (Chapter 5) laments the decline of Western normative influence in international relations. Part II then delves into specific case studies. These cover citizenship-stripping through State "abuse" of extra-territorial jurisdiction (Ireland-Piper, Chapter 6); statelessness of the Rohingya Muslim minority in Myanmar and Bangladesh (Guo & Gautam, Chapter 7); life-long employment as mistaken exemplar of Japanese "progressive capitalism" (Wolff, Chapter 8); water regulation (Baumfield, Chapter 9) in Australia and the United Kingdom; continuing institutional fragility in the world's financial architecture despite the lessons of the Global Financial Crisis (Parsons, Chapter 10); maritime disputes and the robustness of international dispute resolution mechanisms (Guilfoyle, Chapter 11); the militarization of India and Pakistan and the implications for South Asian stability (Abbas and Falarti, Chapter 12); the social costs of regional conflict and whether international humanitarian law and international criminal law can provide better solutions to minimize these costs (Massingham, Chapter 13; O'Leary, Chapter 14); the role of public interest litigation in protecting against executive over-reach (Bonin & Bedford, Chapter 15); and an evaluation of the establishment of military courts as a temporary solution to the enduring problem of domestic terrorism in Pakistan (Ghori, Chapter 16).

This book project, however, is no mere intellectual exercise. It has real-world implications. As Annan (2002) points out, in an increasingly globalized and inter-connected world, "problems [are] without passports". For Weiss (2014, p. 1), the "urgent global problems" are "climate change, weapons of mass destructions (WMDs), terrorism, atrocities, financial volatilities, pandemics, and the list goes on". This book addresses many on Weiss's list: militarization and global conflict (Chapters 12, 13 and 14), the scourge of terrorism (Chapter 16) and global finance (Chapter 10). The book also explores other problems. For example, Guo and Gautam (Chapter 7) report on the plight of the Rohingya people, stateless in Myanmar, rejected as refugees by Bangladesh – a human tragedy under-reported in the Western media (New Matilda, 2015).

1. General themes

Our authors construct the order/disorder divide in three distinct ways. The most common is to define 'order' and 'disorder' in adversarial terms. For some, for example, 'order' represents a well-functioning and neatly structured system or configuration – such as a rules-based international relations order (Davis, Chapter 4), a stable financial system comprising complementary domestic financial institutions (Parsons, Chapter 10) or an effective treaty-based international dispute resolution system (Guilfoyle, Chapter 11). The antonym 'disorder', then, refers to instability or threats to structural integrity – such as the increasing assertiveness of China on the global stage and its disregard of certain international norms and rules (Davis, Chapter 4); incomplete and inconsistent reforms to domestic financial institutions and regulators in the world's major economies (Parsons, Chapter 10); and litigation by smaller States that could test the support of the treaty-based regime by larger, more powerful, States (Guilfoyle, Chapter 11). For others, 'order' is a metaphor for peace, mutual respect, social justice and appropriate exercise of legal powers. 'Disorder', on the other hand, refers to problems of world conflict (Cassimatis, Chapter 2; O'Leary, Chapter 14); humanitarian crises (Massingham, Chapter 13); domestic terrorism (Ghori, Chapter 16); statelessness (Guo & Gautam, Chapter 7) or abuse of the State's powers in exercise of its extra-territorial jurisdiction (Ireland-Piper, Chapter 6) or its executive policy-making and decision-making powers (Bonin & Bedford, Chapter 15). Yet another approach is to conceive of 'order' in terms of regulatory uniformity and coherence and 'disorder' as regulatory diversity – this is the contrast Baumfield (Chapter 9) builds into her comparative analysis of water regulation in Australia and comparator jurisdictions.

A second construct perceives 'order' and 'disorder' as inter-connected and complementary. Unlike a see-saw, 'order' and 'disorder' do not move in opposite directions but function together like links in a chain. Like a see-saw, however, they can achieve an equilibrium, with both 'order' and 'disorder' balancing one another through the tension of their equal forces. Falarti and Abbas (Chapter 12), for example, make the provocative case that mutual nuclear capability by neighbours India and Pakistan, made possible by military aid, is evidence of "good" regional governance. Although increasing militarization might suggest regional 'disorder', applying the first construct of order/disorder, the authors contend that it has actually brought stability and improved economic ties to South Asia. Likewise, Ghori (Chapter 16), in another challenging piece, offers a partial defence of the use of military courts in Pakistan to prosecute non-military personnel for terrorism-related crimes. Ghori acknowledges that this use of military courts to try such offences may offend the separation of powers doctrine and, in turn, suggest systemic dysfunction. However, he supports their temporary use because Pakistan's traditional law enforcement and judicial institutions have failed to protect the country against the evils of domestic terrorism. In both these chapters, what might appear as 'disorder' – regional armament and non-judicial tribunals – achieve the effect of balanced 'order'.

A third construct paints 'order' in ideational, philosophical or ideological terms. 'Order' is a dream, a vision or an orthodoxy. 'Disorder', however is not necessarily a contrast or a corollary. 'Order' exists in 'disorder'; disorder' in 'order: just as Yin exists in Yang, and vice-versa. For example, Crowe (Chapter 3) envisions 'order' as Law's dream of unity. However, true unity is impossible. This is not simply because law's norms, institutions and influences are 'multi-faceted'. More fundamentally, Law faces an internal contradiction between its impulse to control (to exercise power and assert authority) and its desire for cooperation (to express and promote peace, security and mutual human understanding). Bird (Chapter 4) sees 'order' as the prevailing orthodoxy of capitalist markets and centralized government. However, its contrast – anarchy – is not disorder but an alternative, more attractive, governance structure that celebrates communal sharing and non-authoritarian collectivism. Wolff (Chapter 8), similarly, examines the triumph of capitalism in global economic governance. Rather than searching for an alternative, however, he explores the diversity of institutional forms within global capitalism, focusing, in particular, on Japanese employment practice. He concludes that, despite hopes of a progressive or exemplary model, capitalism is beset by a pathological 'disorder': an inability to care.

Our authors express a range of normative positions on the order/disorder relationships. For example, Cassimatis (Chapter 2) sees the resilience of the international order, despite its fragmentation, through principled resolution of international disputes. Guilfoyle (Chapter 11) affirms the success of the Convention on the Law of the Sea in resolving maritime conflicts between states that are unequal in power. Massingham (Chapter 13) expresses hope that international humanitarian law contains, within its provisions, a way forward in limiting cross-border humanitarian crises. Bonin and Bedford (Chapter 15), in their comparative analysis of public interest litigation in Australia and Canada, see useful lessons on how to strengthen citizens' access to courts to curb the powers of their governments. So, too, Baumfield (Chapter 9), who regards diversity in the regulation of water as offering useful clues on future regulatory directions. By contrast, O'Leary (Chapter 14) is more guarded: international criminal law has had patchy success in its regulatory endeavours. Ireland-Piper (Chapter 6) – in the context of global challenges to nationality and identity, on the one hand, and national security, on the other – is sharply critical of legislative initiative to revoke citizens of their citizenship. This is a 'disordered' (or problematic) approach to jurisdiction under international law, she argues, because it threatens amicable international relations and undermines the realization of the right to nationality. Davis (Chapter 5) deplores the erosion of the liberal core to the international order. Yet Bird (Chapter 4) delights in anarchy – and sees real prospects for human advancement under an alternative regime.

In untangling order/disorder, conceptually and normatively, our authors journey through the domains of the international/domestic and the political/legal. These spaces also intersect in complex ways. The international/domestic interplay, for example, reflects the reality that municipal courts and political institutions play a substantial role in the development of not only their own legal culture and doctrine but also international law and politics more generally. This means, as Cassimatis (Chapter 2) observes, the international legal order is simultaneously integrated – and fragmented. Similarly, the legal/political analysis of global issues is an honest reflection of the symbiotic relationship between these two normative systems of power and control (see, eg, Lehmann, 2011). This is powerfully illustrated in the case studies on the Rohingya people by Guo and Gautam (Chapter 7), India-Pakistan relations by Falarti and Abbas (Chapter 12) and the use of military courts to prosecute civilians in Pakistan by Ghori (Chapter 16): all observe that the "grand narratives" of law, justice and peace do not neatly match the "messy reality" of global and local politics (Lehmann, 2011). This multi-focal, multi-dimensional view of the world deepens and diversifies the analysis of our book's themes. As the Sufi poet, Jalaluddin Rumi, once mused: "The truth was a mirror in the hands of God. It fell, and broke into pieces. Everybody took a piece of it, and they looked at it and thought they had the truth" (quoted in Siddiqui, 2014, p. 23). By picking up these different pieces of the 'mirror', our authors view governance and regulation of global order/disorder in all its reflective and refractive possibilities.

2. Book outline

This book divides into two parts. The first part (Chapters 2–5) takes a big-picture view of the order–disorder dynamic, painting ideas in broad brushstrokes across a wide geographical, historical or conceptual canvas. This includes the achievements of international lawyers across a diverse range of global conflicts in today's world (Cassimatis, Chapter 2); the historical journey of law in its hopeless "dream" of unity (Crowe, Chapter 3); anarchy as an alternative order to prevailing political democracy (Bird, Chapter 4) and the implications of a rising China to global governance and regulation (Davis, Chapter 5).

The second part (Chapter 6–16) contains more detailed case studies on specific areas of law, regional relations, human rights abuses or institutions. These case studies sub-divide into five categories: *citizens* (Ireland-Piper, Chapter 6; Guo & Gautam, Chapter 7), *capitalism* (Wolff, Chapter 8; Baumfield, Chapter 9; Parsons, Chapter 10); *conflict* (Guilfoyle, Chapter 11; Falarti and Abbas, Chapter 12; Massingham, Chapter 13; O'Leary, Chapter 14); and *courts* (Bonin & Bedford, Chapter 15; Ghori, Chapter 16).

2.1 Conceptions

The book opens with 'International Law and Governance in the 21st Century: Disorder and Order in a Fragmented World' (Chapter 2) by Anthony Cassimatis. In this chapter, Cassimatis tests the resilience of the international legal system in the face of contemporary global challenges. He relies on three cases studies to conduct this test: (i) the strength of human rights law to delimit anti-terrorist activities by States and inter-governmental organizations; (ii) the robustness of maritime dispute resolution to prevent powerful states encroaching on the territories of their smaller neighbours; and (iii) the respect world trade law has for non-trade welfare or moral considerations. A resilient system, he proposes, is a principle-based institutional and normative framework that can curb the excesses of the powerful, whether they be States, international actors or the orthodoxy of free trade. But, as Cassimatis admits, this is not an easy test to satisfy. For one, the system is fragmented, with different regulatory regimes – over maritime disputes, human rights and world trade, for example – operating concurrently. For another, the dualism of the system – under which local or regional courts can reach conflicting conclusions on issues compared to their international counterparts – can cause confusion over standards. However, in all three case studies, there is evidence that the system is working. Cassimatis attributes this to the pluralism of the international legal order and the principles that undergird resolution of regional and global disputes. Pluralism, Cassimatis concludes, ensures that alternative voices can "talk back" against powerful, hegemonic discourses, and principles ensure outcomes are never merely a function of raw power.

In 'Law's Movement' (Chapter 3), Jonathan Crowe explores law's oscillation between order and disorder. Although law "dreams" of unifying its human subjects, it vacillates between orderliness and disintegration because of a self-contained contradiction: it simultaneously seeks concord and control. Thus, law celebrates the *communal* – the shared human goals of peace, security and harmony; but, at the same time, it empowers the *individual* – diversity, self-actualization and individual will. Put differently, it seeks to express the shared values of human existence, yet also asserts authority and control when individual interests inevitably cause conflict and competition. For Crowe, the future of law lies in internalising its positive lessons of peaceful co-existence and mutual respect and discarding its function as a disembodied, externalized tool of command and authority. One possible vision of this future comes from the Christian tradition. Not only does Christianity provide a foundational set of moral ideas that inform the Western legal, social and cultural outlook, but its core lessons gain wider resonance when placed alongside other non-Western religions and secular perspectives.

In 'How Anarchy Can Order the World' (Chapter 4), Susan Bird endorses anarchy as an alternative system of political and economic governance to liberal democracies. Anarchy, Bird is quick to point out, is not lawless chaos. Instead, it is a communal, participatory form of governance. Whereas capitalism celebrates greed and corporate excess, anarchy is about equality, freedom and peace. Whereas modern democracies define property as private interests or assets, anarchy classifies property as "commons", public resources that should be shared and managed locally. Whereas liberal democracies impose centralized, top-down governments on society, anarchy creates vertical, self-contained communities which make their own rules consistent with their shared philosophies. Anarchy, Bird insists, is not simply a utopian dream. Instead, it is a viable form of organization. She identifies successful examples of modern anarchist practice in the Occupy, green governance and urban scavenging movements.

In 'The Rise of China and Global Disorder – Can "the Centre" Hold in the 21st Century?' (Chapter 5), Malcolm Davis expresses concern over the future of the Western global order. For Davis, a rules-based order is the centre of world peace and security. This centre is under threat of collapse, like a failed soufflé, with assaults coming from all directions. Although only one among a cast of characters (including Russia, the Islamic State and the anti-democratic elements in the Middle East), China, in Davis's view, poses a particular threat because of its mounting economic heft, rising military capability and unapologetically unilateral activities in the South China Sea.

2.2 *Case studies*

2.2.1 *Citizens*

Part II of the book explores the order/disorder tension in the context of four case studies: Citizens, Capitalism, Conflict and Courts.

Chapters 6 and 7 consider the first case study of citizens' rights from contrasting perspectives. In 'Nationality and Extraterritoriality: A Disordered Paradigm?' (Chapter 6), Danielle Ireland-Piper critically engages with the *purpose and scope* of the nationality principle of jurisdiction at international law. Specifically, Ireland-Piper considers whether the right of a State under international law to exercise extraterritorial jurisdiction on the basis of citizenship brings with it an obligation to do so in certain circumstances. If so, is revocation of citizenship on the basis of crimes committed extraterritorially an abdication of such an obligation? She undertakes this analysis in the context of legislation enacted in Australia (and elsewhere) revoking the citizenship of persons who take part in armed conflict overseas, other than in a formal military capacity. This 'Foreign Fighter' dilemma has, in particular, evoked the ire of the international community and raises questions as to traditional notions of national identity and the extent to which a State ought to be responsible for the conduct of its nationals overseas. Ultimately, she concludes that jurisdictional rights must come with jurisdictional responsibilities. In this way, Ireland-Piper seeks to restore balance to order/disorder in the legal frameworks on extraterritoriality.

In 'Stateless Rohingya in Bangladesh and Refugee Status: Global Order and Disorder under International Law' (Chapter 7), Sanzhuan Guo and Madhav Gautam criticize the *gap* – what they dub a legal "black hole" – between the rhetoric of international law and the practical reality for the stateless Rohingya Muslim minority. Guo and Gautam (Chapter 7) explore the suffering of the Rohingya people, one of the most persecuted minorities in the world (Amnesty International, 2015). The Rohingya are a Muslim minority in the Rhakine State, Myanmar; many, however, have been forced to re-settle in neighbouring Bangladesh. The Rohingya are stateless: they have no home or citizenship. Despite an implied right of nationality under international law, neither Myanmar nor Bangladesh grant them citizenship under their domestic legislative regimes. Despite guaranteed human rights under international law, registered Rohingya refugees in Bangladesh do not have the right to receive food, to pursue an education or to work and are restricted in their freedom of movement and marriage. Despite a right to be processed as refugees, more than 90% of Rohingya languish, undocumented, in unofficial camps. And despite a non-refoulement obligation, Bangladesh authorities have forcibly re-patriated Rohingya refugees back to Myanmar. Unless international law develops stronger enforcement mechanisms, the authors conclude, it will continue to fail the Rhongya people.

2.2.2 Capitalism

Chapters 8, 9 and 10 investigate different aspects of economic governance in the global capitalist order: employment rights (Chapter 8), resource management (Chapter 9) and global finance (Chapter 10).

In 'Caring Capitalism? The Case of Japanese Employment' (Chapter 8), Leon Wolff critically evaluates the extent to which Japanese-style capitalism – in particular, the guarantee of lifelong employment as a corporate governance practice – should be hailed as an exemplar of progressive capitalism. Capitalism, as Wolff notes, is the dominant model of economic governance globally. However, capitalism has varied institutional forms and is a socio-political system rather than a mere regime of accumulation. It makes sense, therefore, to investigate which, of capitalism's many types, best serves human society. Lifelong employment in Japan, hailed by many as a more 'human' form of capitalism, offers a good test of whether capitalism can be configured to be compassionate and caring. However, as Wolff submits, Japanese capitalism does not have a beating heart. Instead, an analysis of the legal regulation of employment rights in Japan reveals a dark side to lifelong employment's promise of employment stability to Japanese workers.

In 'Monopolisation, Market Liberalisation and Madness: Order and Disorder in Water Supply Governance' (Chapter 9), Victoria Schnure Baumfield analyses the evolution of water supply governance in Australia and compares it with the different regulatory models adopted in England, Wales and Scotland. Although water was originally supplied by the State, the growing acceptance of free-market principles has led to progressive waves of corporatization and privatization. Currently, however, there is no one regulatory template. In Queensland, Australia, multiple government-owned businesses supply water to consumers; in England, it is a multitude of profit-driven private-sector companies; in Wales, a single not-for-profit company that outsources its operations to several competing for-profit private companies; and, in Scotland, a single government-owned business with a consumer representative body entitled to participate in price reviews and spending decisions. This disordered diversity, argues Baumfield, is not necessarily a bad thing. Given local conditions and needs, there simply might not be a one-size-fits-all model; and, at any rate, the different models and experiences across the different jurisdictions offer "great learning opportunities" for future policy reform.

In 'Domestic Regulatory Architecture for the Protection of Financial Stability after the GFC: Global Order or Disorder?', Louise Parsons evaluates the effectiveness of reforms to domestic financial regulatory architecture in the aftermath of the Global Financial Crisis (GFC). Parsons argues that reforms to the 'disorder' created by the GFC might, in itself, be 'disordered'. Although G20 countries have made significant progress in adopting best practice recommendations for improving financial regulation, Parsons observes "slow pace of change in some countries" and significant "divergence in regulatory frameworks". In her view, surprisingly little has changed in the financial regulatory architecture in G20 countries since the GFC. While conceding that non-statutory and non-legal tools can assist in guiding domestic practices, Parsons still argues in favour of black-letter law regulation and concludes that the absence of express, clear and legislated mandates in some countries is problematic. For Parsons, increased legal regulation is the key to better global governance.

2.2.3 Conflict

In 'Governing the Oceans and Dispute Resolution: An Evolving Legal Order?' (Chapter 11), Douglas Guilfoyle brings his expertise on the law of the sea to consider whether or not creative litigation by small States against great powers risks undermining legal order by pushing dispute settlement bodies to adopt novel and unanticipated interpretations of the Convention. In his view, the argument is mistaken. After all, any legal order involving authoritative dispute settlement anticipates evolution through interpretation. His analysis engages with three recent arbitration proceedings pursuant to the *United Nations Convention on the Law of the Sea (UNCLOS)*: the case brought by the Netherlands against Russia regarding Greenpeace activists aboard the *MV Arctic Sunrise*; the case brought by Mauritius against the United Kingdom concerning the Chagos Archipelago; and the case brought by the Philippines against China regarding the South China Sea dispute. In light of these case studies, Guilfoyle suggests the UNCLOS system is adaptive enough to provide effective legal recourse for smaller states against great powers. In his view, this can be done without damaging the integrity of the Convention, a key legal component of maritime governance.

In 'Foreign Military Aid as Good Governance? – The Case of South Asia' (Chapter 12), Maziar M. Falarti and Syed Ali Abbas, in one of our more controversial chapters, consider the provision of foreign military aid to India and Pakistan. The authors observe that military aid has assisted India and Pakistan to become nuclear powers. However, rather than this being a cause for concern, they instead argue that there is evidence to suggest that this has *improved* relations between the two countries. In their view, bilateral trade has increased and armed conflict has de-escalated. They attribute these achievements to the 'stability/instability' paradox. Much like the order/disorder dichotomy, the stability/instability paradox tells of contrary and opposing forces pulling at one another and, in so doing, maintaining balance. In short, in their view, instability has the ability to bring about broader regional stability, which in turn has implications for global governance.

In 'The Obligation to Respect and to Ensure Respect for International Humanitarian Law: A Potential Source of Assistance in Combating Humanitarian Cross-border Challenges Created by Armed Conflict' (Chapter 13), Eve Massingham then turns to the question of law in armed conflict. Massingham, a scholar and practitioner with the International Committee of the Red Cross, considers the legal obligation to not only 'respect', but to 'ensure respect' for international humanitarian law. This obligation is codified in the Four Geneva Conventions of August 12, 1949 and the Additional Protocols of 1977 and 2005 and also forms part of customary international humanitarian law. She argues that the scope of the obligation to 'ensure respect' can apply to third states that are not technically a party to a conflict. The nature of the obligation, however, will vary in each circumstance. Such variance, in her view, depends on the capacity of the third State to influence the transgressor State or other actor. For Massingham, the interpretation and pursuit of this obligation has significant implications for cross-border conflicts.

In 'International Criminal Law as a Regulatory Tool' (Chapter 14), Jodie O'Leary observes the high instances of international crime worldwide. This leads her to question whether international criminal law, of which the International Criminal Court (ICC) and the *Rome Statute* are part, has been effective as a regulatory tool. In particular, she considers international criminal law as it relates to crimes of genocide, torture, crimes against humanity, war crimes and aggression. In identifying 'transparency' as the criteria by which to assess regulatory effectiveness, O'Leary concludes that while the ICC deserves credit for promoting transparency in international criminal law, combining both rules and principle-based standards in international criminal law offers a better solution.

2.2.4 Courts

In 'Access to Courts by Public Interest Groups Seeking to Challenge Government Decisions: A Comparative Analysis of the Modern Position in Canada and Australia' (Chapter 15), Lisa Bonin and Narelle Bedford make the case that global order need not depend only on international enforcement and accountability. To the contrary, in their view, meaningful redress of wrongs through public interest litigation by ordinary citizens and community organizations in domestic courts is a key element of global governance. This is particularly so given that decisions of domestic courts can have a normative effect on the development of international law (Ireland-Piper, 2017). Specifically, in their comparison of the law on public standing in Canada and Australia, Bonin and Bedford argue that meaningful redress of wrongs can be achieved through public interest litigation in domestic courts. This is because the costs of bringing legal challenges in courts are out of the financial reach of most individuals. Public interest standing, therefore, can play a tangible role in holding decision-makers to account. This is particularly so in circumstances where their exercise of power might otherwise remain unchallenged.

In 'Military Courts in Pakistan: A Critical Analysis' (Chapter 16), Umair Ghori assesses the desirability, or otherwise, of crimes relating to terrorist acts being prosecuted in military courts rather than civilian courts. The threats posed by modern terrorism are well accepted and widely analysed – particularly from Western perspectives. Ghori's contribution, however, considers the issue in the specific context of Pakistan. This is a useful case study because Pakistan is a densely populated country situated at a geo-strategic crossroads between East and West, North and South. Terrorism is a scourge in Pakistan. Between 2002 and 2011, Pakistan was the second most targeted country by terrorists after Iraq. In Ghori's view, moves by Pakistan to allow the prosecution of non-military offences in military courts is a necessary evil in the fight against terror – a short-term 'anti-biotic' solution to the systemic deficiencies in the Pakistani legal system. Although the integrity of the separation of powers and basic rule of law principles are important, so, too, is taking proactive steps to protect the security of the population.

Conclusion

The complex relationship between order/disorder has a parallel with the Chinese principles of *Yin/Yang*. The Yin/Yang philosophy teaches that 'all universal phenomena are shaped by the integration of two opposite cosmic energies' (Fang, 2011, p. 7). Where *Yin* represents yieldingness and submissiveness, *Yang* signifies unyieldingness and dominance (Chen, 2008, pp. 7–9). The Yin/Yang symbol is a circle divided into two equal halves by a curvy line, one side of which is black (Yin) and the other white (Yang) (Fang, 2011, p. 7). As Fang and Faure (2011, p. 325) observe, "there exists no absolute borderline between black (Yin) and white (Yang); a dot of black (Yin) exists in the white (Yang) and a dot of white (Yang) also exists in the black (Yin). The healthy development of universal phenomenon hinges upon a constant dynamic balance between Yin and Yang". In this way, each opposing force is interconnected with the other and each requires the other for its existence.

According to Li (1998, p. 416), this has three key implications: first, a "phenomenon or entity cannot be complete unless it has two opposite elements"; second, "opposite elements will mutually transform into each other in a process of balancing under various conditions"; and third, "two contrary . . . yet interdependent . . . elements exist as opposites in unity to mutually affirm . . . and mutually negate". Put another way, "opposites contain within them the seeds of the other" (Fang & Faure, 2011, p. 325). The Bhagavad Gita speaks of the '*dvandva*' – or duality – of the material world and urges us to accept and not be disturbed by such duality (Bhagavad Gita, Chapter 4, Verse 22).

Global order/disorder has this same interaction. The slash (/) between them neither divides nor unites; it signals complex co-existence. Order and disorder require a little of the other so as to function. Disorder needs order. Order needs disorder. The trick lies in getting the balance right. In the words of singer-songwriter Leonard Cohen (1992, 'Anthem', *The Future*):

> There is a crack in everything/That's how the light gets in.

References

Ang, I. (2014). Beyond unity in diversity: Cosmopolitanizing identities in a globalizing world. *Diogenes*, *60*(1), 1–11.

Annan, K.A. (2002). Problems without passports. *Foreign Policy*, *132*, 30–31.

Amnesty International (2015, October 7). Rohingya People: The most persecuted refugees in the world. Retrieved from: https://www.amnesty.org.au/rohingya-people-most-persecuted-refugees-in-world/.

Beck, R.J. (2016). Thinking beyond borders: Reflections no law and disciplinarity. In R.J. Beck (Ed.), *Law beyond borders: Thinking beyond borders* (pp. 3–30). New York: Palgrave Macmillan.

Berman, P. (2012). *Global legal pluralism: A jurisprudence of law beyond borders*. Cambridge: Cambridge University Press.

Chen, G. (2008). Bian (Change): A perpetual discourse of I Ching. *Intercultural Communication Studies*. *17*(4), 7–16.

Chhotray, V. and Stoker, G. (2008). *Governance theory and practice: A cross-disciplinary approach*. London and New York: Springer.

Cohen, L. (1992). Anthem. On *The Future* (Vinyl, LP, Album). Spain: Columbia.

Darian-Smith, E. (2000). Structural inequalities in the global legal system. *Law and Society Review*, *34*, *809*–828.

Fang, T. (2011). Yin Yang: A new perspective on culture. *Management and Organization Review*, *8*(1), 25–50.

Fang, T. & Faure, G. (2011). Chinese communication characteristics: A Yin Yang perspective. *International Journal of Intercultural Relations*, *35*, 320–333.

Fauvarque-Cosson, B. (2001). Comparative law and conflict of laws: Allies or enemies? New perspectives on an old couple. *American Journal of Comparative Law*, *49*(3), 407–428.

Ganguly, S. & Miliate, B. (2015, October 14). Refugees and neighbors: Rohingya in Bangladesh. Retrieved from: http://thediplomat.com/2015/10/refugees-and-neighbors-rohingya-in-bangladesh/.

Garner, B.A. (2002). *The redbook: A manual on legal style* (2nd ed.). St Paul, Mn: West.

Gaubatz, K.Y & MacArthur, M. (2001). How international is 'international' law? *Michigan Journal of International Law*, *22*(1), 239–282.

Hansmann, H. & Kraakman, R. (2001). The end of history for corporate law. *Georgetown Law Journal*, *89*(2), 439–468.

Ireland-Piper. D. (2017). *Accountability in extraterritoriality: A comparative and international law perspective*. London: Edward Elgar.

Joyner, C.C. (2006). International law is as international theory does? *American Journal of International Law*, *100*(1), 248–258.

Kennedy, D. (2008). The mystery of global governance. *Ohio Northern University Law Review*, *34*, 827–860.

Kingsford Smith, D. (2012). Governing the corporation: the role of 'soft regulation'. *University of New South Wales Law Journal*, *35*(1), 378–403.

Lehmann, K.E. (2011), Globalisation and foreign policy: Grand narratives vs. messy reality? *Global Studies Journal*, *4*(1), 97–108.

Li, P. (1998). Towards a geocentric framework of organizational form: A holistic, dynamic and paradoxical approach. *Organization Studies, 19*(5), 829–861.

New Matilda. (2015, May 26). 'There is no front door': Rohingya in Australia reject Abbott's attack. Retrieved from: https://newmatilda.com/2015/05/26/there-no-front-door-rohingya-australia-reject-abbotts-attack/.

Nottage, L. and Wolff, L. (2005). Corporate governance and law reform in Japan: From the lost decade to the end of history? In R. Haak & M. Pudelko (Eds.), *Japanese management: In the search for a new balance between continuity and change* (pp. 133–166). London and New York: Palgrave Macmillan.

Parker, C., Scott, C., Lacey, N., & Braithwaite, J. (2004). Introduction. In C. Parker, C. Scott, N. Lacey, & J. Braithwaite, J. (Eds.), *Regulating law* (pp. 1–2). Oxford: Oxford University Press.

Siddiqui, M. (2014). *Leading from the heart: Sufi principles at work.* Los Angeles: Sage.

Trubek, D.M. & Trubek, L.G. (2006). New governance and legal regulation: complementarity, rivalry, and transformation. *Columbia Journal of European Law*, *13*(3), 539–564.

Weiss, T.G. (2014). *Governing the world?: Addressing 'problems without passports'.* London and New York: Routledge.

Part I

Conceptions

2 International Law and Governance in the 21st Century

Disorder and Order in a Fragmented World

*Anthony E. Cassimatis**

International lawyers and policy makers have had much to cause them to despair in recent times: war, conflict and social upheaval in the Middle East and Africa; economic, political and social crises in Europe; territorial conflicts in the South China Sea; and challenges to fundamental legal standards (such as the prohibition of torture) from States that have been the traditional defenders of the post-war international legal order. Such crises and conflicts pose multiple challenges for, and to, international legal regulation. And yet, notwithstanding the obvious grounds for despair, various counter-developments (in the context of maritime disputes, human rights and trade) suggest that the prognosis for international legal regulation is not as dire as these examples might initially suggest. Although ongoing social, economic, political and legal interactions continue to throw up new conflicts and challenges, a range of different actors have deployed international law and legal institutions in innovative ways in response. Some of the international legal responses have been unexpected and in some cases surprising. International law's fragmented legal norms and institutions, long the source of anxiety, have provided novel and creative opportunities to avoid global disorder and lawlessness. International adjudication, offering opportunities for disparate voices to be heard and allowing for the imaginative use of traditional techniques, may be a cause for hope.

Images of disorder, chaos, fragmentation and destruction confront us on a daily basis. Beheadings and sexual slavery, openly acknowledged and gruesomely recorded and distributed via social media, are a reality in Iraq, Syria and Libya. Millions have been displaced as a consequence, with many seeking refuge in other States, risking their lives to find safety and prompting fear and uncertainty in places of refuge. The European Union appears to be in disarray on multiple fronts, while Russia is dismembering Ukraine before our very eyes. The annexation of Crimea has been followed by direct military support by Russia for rebels in Eastern Ukraine. China is frenetically constructing artificial islands in the South China/West Philippine Sea. China's so-called Nine Dash Line involves unprecedented claims in relation to waters claimed by a number of South East Asian States. Acts of torture and inhuman and degrading treatment have been openly acknowledged by the United States, most recently in the United States Senate Select Committee on Intelligence's summary report,

* I would like to express my sincere appreciation for the assistance I received in preparing this Chapter from Ms Catherine Drummond, from the participants at the inaugural conference of the Transnational, International and Comparative Law and Policy Network, and from the editors of this collection. I remain, however, entirely responsible for any remaining weaknesses in the Chapter.

formally released by the United States Congress in 2014. Details of United States interrogation practices have been known for years, and yet calls for prosecutions by United States authorities continue to go unheeded. And if that was not a sufficient basis for despair, in 2016 a United States presidential candidate has gone even further, openly calling for the wives and children of terrorists to be targeted and for the resumption of practices such as water-boarding. National regulatory autonomy has continued to be challenged by global corporations. Fundamental health policy reform in Australia was unsuccessfully challenged by a multinational tobacco corporation via a bilateral investment treaty between Australia and Hong Kong, and States sympathetic to tobacco interests continue to challenge Australia's reforms through the World Trade Organisation. At the same time, States have continued to negotiate new free trade agreements that include investor State dispute settlement provisions.

International lawyers and policy makers are assailed from all directions. The euphoria of the early years of the post-Cold War era is now replaced for many by a grinding despair. Increasing social, economic, political and legal integration, rather than being the apparent path to prosperity and peace, now, at least in some parts of Europe, looks to be a path to years of poverty and penury. The European Union itself appears at risk of disintegration.

And yet, notwithstanding the profound challenges confronting us and the disorder and despair, a counter-narrative can be offered. It is a tentative and contingent narrative; all might still be swept away. But this counter-narrative does not appear to be simply naïve idealism. It can be constructed from developments that are real and pragmatic. Increasing integration has the potential to offer novel opportunities for the weak to potentially constrain the more powerful. Opportunities appear to exist for international law, in its fragmentation, to be used in flexible and pragmatic ways. Fragmentation, long the source of fear and anxiety amongst international lawyers, is also a potential source of dynamism. Pluralism can lead to creative tension and openness; and international dispute settlement, that connects disparate areas of international law, is offering glimmers of hope in an otherwise bleak landscape.

To illustrate, this chapter will focus on international adjudication addressing three important threats to the international legal order: threats to international human rights standards; territorial conflicts that threaten to escalate into armed conflict; and challenges to national regulatory autonomy that have done much to damage the perceived legitimacy of international law. International adjudication in these areas, applying traditional techniques of international law that have become more sophisticated due to increasing legal integration, has offered creative opportunities for less powerful actors to seek principled resolution of international controversies. The adjudication in these areas illustrates the creative potential of the fragmented character of the international legal system.

1. Threats to international human rights standards

Responses by States to threats of terrorism have, paradoxically, themselves threatened fundamental legal principles. For example, the House of Lords and the Grand Chamber of the European Court of Human Rights each concluded that anti-terrorism measures adopted by the United Kingdom after September 11 violated human rights standards set out in the European Convention on Human Rights and Fundamental Freedoms (1951) (*A v United Kingdom*, 2009).

In some cases these threats to fundamental legal principles have been countenanced by intergovernmental institutions. The United Nations Security Council, for example, initially targeted individuals with sanctions under resolution 1267 of 15 October 1999 without even basic due process guarantees. National and regional legal systems, to their credit, have been used effectively to respond to these institutional threats. By its affirmation of dualism, which is often seen by international lawyers as a threatening source of legal fragmentation, the European Court of Justice ("ECJ") in the *Kadi* litigation (*Kadi and Al Barakaat International Foundation v Council of the European Union and Commission of the European Communities*, 2008; reaffirmed in *European Commission v Kadi*, 2013) struck down European Union measures designed to implement Security Council resolutions on the grounds that the European Union's implementing measures violated fundamental rights under European Union law. Within a short period of time after this litigation, a Security Council ombudsperson was appointed to review Security Council sanctions imposed on individuals and other entities. Sequence and cause must of course be distinguished, but a causal link between the ECJ's challenge to the Security Council and the creation of the office of Security Council ombudsperson seems difficult to deny.

More recently, the European Court of Human Rights, in the 2012 *Nada* litigation and the 2016 *Al-Dulimi* litigation, affirmed the continuing relevance of international human rights obligations notwithstanding Security Council resolutions (*Nada v Switzerland*, 2012; *Al-Dulimi and Montana Management Inc v Switzerland*, 2016). The European Court of Human Rights does not have the dualist option that was available to the ECJ in the *Kadi* litigation. The European Court of Human Rights is required to apply the *European Convention on Human Rights and Fundamental Freedoms* (1951), a treaty. The Convention is part of international law, and the European Court of Human Rights is part of the international legal system. The ECJ, by contrast, treats European Union law as a discrete legal system separate from international law, leaving the ECJ the dualist option of ignoring the "other" legal system in favour of European Union law, and it does not matter that that "other" law is international law, including the United Nations Charter and Security Council resolutions. The European Court of Human Rights, conceptually tied to the international legal system, does not have this option. But with apparent inspiration derived by the dualist defiance in *Kadi*, the European Court of Human Rights in *Nada* and *Al-Dulimi* invoked traditional legal principles of treaty interpretation applicable in cases of ambiguity to defend international human rights standards in the face of potential encroachment by the Security Council (eg. *Nada v Switzerland*, paras. 163–199).

Political and legal integration has also offered opportunities to respond to torture and cruel, inhuman and degrading treatment. In the recent European Court of Human Rights decisions in *El-Masri v Macedonia* in 2012 and *Al- Nashiri v Poland* in 2014, the so-called "CIA black-site cases", European States were held legally responsible for assistance given to the United States program of extraordinary rendition and interrogation (*El-Masri v Macedonia*, 2012; *Al-Nashiri v Poland*, 2014). Legal responsibility has been found, not just for the actions of Macedonian and Polish security officials. Macedonia and Poland have been held legally responsible for the acts of CIA agents outside of the territories of Macedonia and Poland (*El-Masri v Macedonia*, paras. 238–241; *Al-Nashiri v Poland*, paras. 453–458 & 517–518). State responsibility based on principles such as complicity has been invoked by the European Court of Human Rights (eg. *Al-Nashiri v Poland*, paras. 440–443). These formal judicial proceedings have produced formal judgments authoritatively chronicling disappearances, torture and ill treatment under the rendition program. The victims have also received monetary recompense.

European judicial institutions have thus offered victims of human rights violations opportunities to seek independent and rule-based resolution of disputes involving powerful actors (the United Nations Security Council and the United States) from outside Europe. Regional integration mechanisms, by focusing on the implementation of international standards at the regional and national levels (which has been the source of anxiety in relation to fragmentation of international law) have allowed for the avoidance of jurisdictional obstacles that would have confronted efforts to directly challenge the conduct of the United Nations or the United States. A similar dynamic is apparent in other areas of international controversy.

2. Territorial conflicts

I leave responses to international terrorism and turn to another bleak topic: territorial crises. Russia's dismembering of Ukraine has prompted unilateral economic sanctions by the United States and European Union States but little more. Whether those sanctions will help restore Ukraine's territorial integrity, at least in the short term, appears unlikely given Russia's unwillingness to reverse its policies towards Ukraine.

China's island building in the South China / West Philippine Sea has not even prompted sanctions. The Philippines, however, in 2013 commenced arbitral proceedings against China under Annex VII of the *Law of the Sea Convention*. The arbitral tribunal found that it had jurisdiction in 2015 (*Republic of Philippines v People's Republic of China*, 2015) and ruled on the merits of the Philippines' case in 2016 (*Republic of Philippines v People's Republic of China*). The point relevant to fragmentation is that Annex VII tribunals under the *Law of the Sea Convention* have jurisdiction to deal with the interpretation or application of the *Law of the Sea Convention*, not territorial claims. China refused to participate formally in the proceedings. The arbitral tribunal was nonetheless obliged to determine whether it possessed jurisdiction and then rule of the merits of the claims made by the Philippines. China had unofficially communicated its views on the jurisdictional issues. In its award on admissibility and jurisdiction of October 2015, the arbitral tribunal found that it did have jurisdiction in respect of a number of the claims made by the Philippines. In its decision on the merits, the tribunal ruled substantially in favour of the Philippines. China has indicated that it will not accept the tribunal's decision.

The potential for Annex VII of the 1982 *Law of the Sea Convention* to provide a basis for judicial settlement of disputes between States was illustrated earlier in 2015 by the arbitral award on the dispute between Mauritius and the United Kingdom on the United Kingdom's declaration of a marine protected area around the Chagos archipelago in the Indian Ocean (*Republic of Mauritius v United Kingdom of Great Britain and Northern Ireland*, 2015). While the arbitral award studiously avoided ruling directly upon territorial claims, Annex VII nonetheless provided opportunities for legal resolution of important aspects of the dispute between Mauritius and the United Kingdom.

The careful and detailed analysis of the drafting history of the relevant provisions of the 1982 *Law of the Sea Convention* by the arbitral body in the *Chagos Archipelago case* has influenced the more recent Philippines China dispute. (The tribunal in its jurisdictional ruling in the more recent arbitration relied, for example, on the *Chagos Archipelago decision's* interpretation of Article 283 of the *Law of the Sea Convention* – see *Republic of Philippines v People's Republic of China*, para. 333.) The analysis by the tribunal in the *Chagos Archipelago case* of other provisions of the 1982 *Law of the Sea Convention* was relied upon by the tribunal in the merits phase of the *Philippines China case*. (The tribunal in its ruling on the merits relied, for example, on the *Chagos Archipelago decision's* interpretation of Article 56 of the *Law of the Sea Convention* – see *Republic of Philippines v People's Republic of China*, para. 742.) The overlapping membership of the arbitral tribunals in the *Chagos Archipelago case* and the *Philippines China case* (Judge Rüdiger Wolfrum was a member of the tribunal in the *Chagos Archipelago case* and was a member of the tribunal in the *Philippines China case*) promoted legal consistency and coherence in the way that Lawrence Helfer and Anne-Marie Slaughter described in their seminal work on the concept of a global community of law (Helfer and Slaughter, 1997).

Of course, the finding of jurisdiction and the ruling on the merits in the *Philippines China case* might not affect China's behaviour in the region. But China has repeatedly claimed that its reclamation works are in conformity with international law. China is increasingly integrated into the global legal system through institutions such as the World Trade Organisation. The rulings in the *Philippines China case* have increased the potential costs for China of pursuing unilateral action. The plausibility of its claims that it is acting consistently with international law has been damaged and the bargaining positions of other States in the region have been enhanced by the rulings.

The reliance by the Philippines on third party dispute resolution, which was supported by other States in the region (Indonesia, Japan, Malaysia, Thailand and Vietnam had formal observer status in the arbitration), including Australia, might also influence third party dispute resolution of other disputes. Australia's advocacy of third party dispute resolution of competing claims in the South China / West Philippines Sea makes it more difficult for Australia to resist on any principled basis Timor Leste's efforts to submit the maritime delimitation of the Timor gap to third party adjudication. Australia withdrew its consent to the jurisdiction of the International Court of Justice to resolve maritime delimitation disputes involving Australia just prior to Timor Leste's independence in 2002. It will be difficult for Australia to place any meaningful pressure on China to submit China's maritime delimitation claims to independent third party adjudication while Australia refuses to consent to adjudication regarding its maritime boundaries with Timor Leste.

The *Chagos Archipelago case* and the *Philippines China case* again illustrate how increased international legal integration has permitted less powerful international actors to seek to resolve international controversies on a principled basis by relying on international adjudication. The *1982 Law of the Sea Convention*, notwithstanding jurisdictional limitations and the absence of enforcement mechanisms, has created opportunities for the principled resolution of disputes between States. That these opportunities for dispute resolution have not involved the International Court of Justice, relying instead on arbitrations, has prompted concerns regarding fragmentation. Nonetheless, the creative potential of dispute resolution under the *Law of the Sea Convention* may allow for the resolution of dangerous territorial conflicts.

3. Threats to national regulatory autonomy

A third area of bleakness is the diminishing regulatory autonomy of States. International legal regulation of trade and investment has been the source of controversy for many years. Infamously, the Appellate Body of the World Trade Organisation ("WTO") in its 1998 report in the *Beef Hormones case* suggested that the lives of 371 European women who might be afflicted by breast cancer as a consequence of imports of beef containing growth hormones would not justify restricting trade (*European Communities – Measures Concerning Meat and Meat Products (Hormones)*, 1998, para. 198). As Anne Orford observed: "[b]y implication, the deaths of this number of women would not justify enacting measures that could constrain the operation of the market or inhibit progress towards economic integration" (Orford, 2005, p. 191).

The image of trade technocrats discounting or dismissing democratically endorsed and serious public health concerns is disturbing to say the least. If one turns to the more recent litigation surrounding Australia's plain packaging laws for tobacco products, it seems that the High Court of Australia is also potentially unable to "inhibit the progress towards economic integration". Notwithstanding the High Court's decision in 2012 (*JT International SA v Commonwealth of Australia*, 2012) dismissing constitutional challenges brought on behalf of tobacco corporations, WTO proceedings have been pursued against Australia by Cuba, the Dominican Republic, Honduras and Indonesia (eg. *Australia – Certain Measures Concerning Trademarks, Geographical Indications and Other Plain Packaging Requirements Applicable to Tobacco Products and Packaging, complaint by Indonesia*, 2014).

But there are contra-indications even from within the WTO. The WTO's dispute resolution system has been open to national regulatory autonomy at the expense of trade. European measures restricting trade in products containing asbestos were successfully defended in 2001 (*European Communities – Measures Affecting Asbestos and Asbestos-Containing Products*, 2001). In 2014, European restrictions on trade in seal products, motivated by animal welfare concerns, were considered by the WTO Appellate Body (*European Communities – Measures Prohibiting the Importation and Marketing of Seal Products*, 2014). The Appellate Body applied an expansive approach to the public morals exception to trade liberalisation contained in Article XX(a) of GATT 1994. The Appellate Body was prepared to apply Article XX(a) to a complex regulatory instrument that sought to balance animal welfare considerations with competing rights of indigenous peoples to exploit seals. Though the Appellate Body found that the European measures, as initially drafted, could not be protected under Article XX(a) due to the operation of the Chapeau to Article XX, the Appellate Body did, however, suggest that relatively modest changes to the European measures could be made in order to gain protection under Article XX(a) (*European Communities – Measures Prohibiting the Importation and Marketing of Seal Products*, 2014, paras. 5.316–5.339).

Concerns nonetheless remain. Notwithstanding the preparedness to countenance complex regulatory measures that seek to balance competing non-trade policies, the Appellate Body did not engage with international instruments in the *Seal Products case* in the way that international instruments were considered in the earlier *Shrimp Turtle case* (*United States – Import Prohibition of Certain Shrimp and Shrimp Products*, 1998, para. 154). In *Seal Products*, for example, international instruments on the protection of the rights of indigenous peoples are nowhere to be found in the Appellate Body's analysis even though such instruments were formally raised by the European Union in the dispute (*European Communities – Measures Prohibiting the Importation and Marketing of Seal Products*, para. 2.101).

The *Seal Products case*, like the *Shrimp Turtle case* before it, demonstrates that dispute settlement mechanisms within the international trade law system are capable of accommodating national and regional regulatory measures notwithstanding that they involve restrictions on international trade. Concerns nonetheless remain regarding the weight that international trade law adjudication will give to non-trade law policies and standards. Such concerns have been prominent in the scholarship on the fragmentation of international law.

4. Integration, fragmentation and the rule of law

What do all these disparate developments suggest? It has been a decade since the International Law Commission ("ILC") working group report on the fragmentation of international law (*International Law Commission*, 2006). Fragmentation has prompted understandable concerns regarding systemic integrity of international law with broader implications for the rule of law internationally. But the ILC working group's report also acknowledged the creative potential of fragmentation within the international legal system. The working group's conclusions include the observation that:

> [t]he very effort to canvass a coherent legal-professional technique on a fragmented world expresses the conviction that conflicts between specialized regimes [such as trade, environmental protection or human rights] may be overcome by law, even as the law may not go much further than require a willingness to listen to others, take their points of view into account and to find a reasoned resolution at the end. Yet this may simply express the very point for which international law has always [existed]. The move from a world fragmented into sovereign States to a world fragmented into specialized "regimes" may in fact not at all require a fundamental transformation of public international law – though it may call for imaginative uses of its traditional techniques (*International Law Commission*, 2 para. 487).

The recent developments described above can be seen in this light. The ILC working group also emphasised the importance, in cases of inter-regime conflict where, for example, trade treaties come into conflict with environmental or human rights treaties, of ensuring that the "law-applier is an impartial third party that approaches the conflicting instruments from beyond the regimes of which the treaties are a part" (International Law Commission, 2006, para. 280). The sound of disparate voices in dispute resolution, which is a consequence of fragmentation, paradoxically creates a context in which it is possible to test the impartiality of "law appliers", whether they be judges of the European Court of Human Rights, arbitrators appointed under Annex VII of the Law of the Sea Convention or members of the WTO Appellate Body. The contingent choices made by such "law appliers" are clearer when alternative approaches have been openly explored in dispute resolution.

The powerful are normally resentful of legal constraint. Apologists for United States exceptionalism immediately after the end of the Cold War appeared to be engaged in a cynical attempt to avoid or remove legal constraints that the United States had previously accepted (eg. Bolton, 2001). But legal integration can be entangling even for the most powerful, especially if they possess a well-developed municipal conception of the rule of law. Apologists for United States exceptionalism had to engage in forms of elaborate contortionism in efforts to escape international legal obligations without also undermining United States constitutional references to treaties and United States legislative references to the Law of Nations. These references to treaties and the Law of Nations within United States municipal law reflected a commitment to international law assumed by the newly independent United States. That commitment could not be readily abandoned by these international legal sceptics, and they continued to have constraining effects in the era of a single super-power. In more recent times and in a more multi-polar world, representatives of the same super-power (including in the United States Department of Defence, a former hotbed of scepticism toward international law) now regularly invoke international law in defence, for example, of freedom of navigation and overflight in the South China / West Philippines Sea.

Oscillation between despair and optimism over time is common. Religious extremists in the Middle East appear to represent a threat to global legal regulation. But are these religious extremists really that different to past forms of barbarous radicalism such as that perpetrated by the Khmer Rouge in Cambodia in the 1970s. The International Committee of the Red Cross ("ICRC") is currently unable to operate in territory in the Middle East controlled by Daesh. The ICRC was unable to operate in Cambodia when it was under the Khmer Rouge (ICRC, 2009).

Perhaps oscillating periods of global despair and optimism will no longer be discernible. In our increasingly complex world, despair and optimism might be forced to constantly cohabit. But is that necessarily a bad thing? Periods of certainty are also often eras of hegemony. Whether such periods are welcomed or feared depends significantly on the attitude of, and relationship with, the hegemon. The complexity of a multipolar world might therefore be preferable.

So this tentative and contingent counter-narrative offers glimmers of hope. Increasing legal and political integration will continue to offer opportunities for applying constraints on the powerful. The powerful can be expected to respond as they always have, but their freedom of action appears constrained in fragmented and sometimes unexpected ways. International adjudication, offering opportunities for disparate voices to be heard and allowing for the imaginative use of traditional techniques, offers hope in an otherwise bleak landscape. The contingencies and limitations remain, however. Some areas of international regulation are not conducive to dispute resolution. Some non-State actors, for example, are unlikely to be the subject of dispute resolution.

James Crawford observed in 2012 that "the variety of roles and arenas of international law" is "often presented under the rubric of fragmentation, as if it were a problem newly discovered – as if the mirror of international justice has latterly been shattered into fragments large and small. . . . But in some sense international law has always been shattered; from the beginning it has been composed of different pieces that refract differentially. That can be a strength, not merely a weakness" (Crawford, 2012, p. 473).

References

A v United Kingdom (European Court of Human Rights, Grand Chamber, Application No 3455/05, 19 February 2009).

Al-Dulimi and Montana Management Inc v Switzerland (European Court of Human Rights, Grand Chamber, Application No 5809/08, 21 June 2016).

Al-Nashiri v Poland (European Court of Human Rights, Fourth Section, Application No 28761/11, 24 July 2014).

Australia – Certain Measures Concerning Trademarks, Geographical Indications and Other Plain Packaging Requirements Applicable to Tobacco Products and Packaging, complaint by Indonesia, WTO Doc WT/DS467/19 (27 October 2014).

Bolton, J. R. (2000). Is there really "law" in international affairs. *Transnational Law and Contemporary Problems, 10*, 1–47.

Crawford, J. (2012). International law as discipline and profession. *American Society of International Law Proceedings, 106*, 471–486.

El-Masri v The Former Yugoslav Republic of Macedonia (European Court of Human Rights, Grand Chamber, Application No 39630/09, 13 December 2012).

European Commission v Kadi (European Court of Justice, Grand Chamber, Joined Cases C-584/10 P, C-593/10 P & C-595/10 P, 18 July 2013).

European Communities – Measures Affecting Asbestos and Asbestos-Containing Products, WT/DS135/AB/R (12 March 2001).

European Communities – Measures Concerning Meat and Meat Products (Hormones), WT/DS26/AB/R, WT/DS48/AB/R (16 January 1998).

European Communities – Measures Prohibiting the Importation and Marketing of Seal Products, WT/DS400/AB/R, WT/DS401/AB/R (22 May 2014).

Helfer, L. R., & Slaughter, A-M. (1997). Toward a theory of effective supranational adjudication. *Yale Law Journal, 107*, 273–392.

International Committee of the Red Cross. (2009). *Cambodia: history of ICRC activities.* Retrieved from https://www.icrc.org/eng/resources/documents/misc/cambodia-history-091209.htm.

International Law Commission. (2006). *Fragmentation of International Law: difficulties arising from the Diversification and Expansion of International Law.* UN Doc A/CN.4/L.682.

JT International SA v Commonwealth of Australia (2012) 250 CLR 1.

Kadi and Al Barakaat International Foundation v Council of the European Union and Commission of the European Communities (2008) 47 International Legal Materials 923.

Nada v Switzerland, (12 September 2012), Application No 10593/08, European Court of Human Rights (Grand Chamber).

Orford, A. (2005). Beyond harmonization: Trade, human rights and the economy of sacrifice. *Leiden Journal of International Law, 18*, 179–213.

Republic of Mauritius v United Kingdom of Great Britain and Northern Ireland (Award) (Arbitral Tribunal constituted under Annex VII to the 1982 UN Convention on the Law of the Sea, 18 March 2015).

Republic of Philippines v People's Republic of China (Award on Jurisdiction and Admissibility) (Arbitral Tribunal constituted under Annex VII to the 1982 UN Convention on the Law of the Sea, 29 October 2015).

Republic of Philippines v People's Republic of China (Award on Merits) (Arbitral Tribunal constituted under Annex VII to the 1982 UN Convention on the Law of the Sea, 12 July 2016).

United States – Import Prohibition of Certain Shrimp and Shrimp Products, WT/DS58/AB/R (12 October 1998).

3 Law's Movement

*Jonathan Crowe**

Law oscillates. It exists in time and therefore in movement. Law changes, and this change marks the passage of time. Change possibly *is* time (Reichenbach, 1958; Grünbaum, 1963; cf. Smart, 1969). Law's movement, however, is not simply linear. It is not a one-way journey from A to B. It is, rather, an oscillation between centres of gravity. Law moves from A to B, then back to A again. Law returns. Law's oscillation takes many forms, but one of the most basic is the movement of law between order and disorder. Law seeks order, but social reality intrudes. Order becomes disorder.

It is this oscillation that lies at the heart of the essays in the present collection. Some of these essays explore forms of order; others, sources of disorder. Some explore the movement between these two centres of gravity. We have essays on the unstable nature of global order and the potential for disorder to give rise to new forms of ordering. The essays in this collection are themselves in movement. Their movement provides a prism for approaching and understanding law's movement. This is an important endeavour: as Michael Detmold reminds us, law's movement is the hardest thing for it to grasp (Detmold, 1991, 31).

Law's movement between order and disorder is also the movement of history. Leo Tolstoy famously shows us how the plans of the so-called great leaders are ultimately hostage to the whims and emotions of individual actors (Tolstoy, 2008). The world, after all, is a stage. There is no play without the players. A general may plan a battle, but the success of the campaign rests on the enthusiasm or fear of the soldiers. It is human to be enthusiastic or afraid. It is human to be carried away by the moment. It is also human, however, to seek patterns. The human micro-narrative of the battle becomes, inevitably, the grand meta-narrative of history.

We have learned to be incredulous of meta-narratives (cf. Lyotard, 1984, xxiv). However, a focus on the role of individuals in history does not preclude the observation of patterns in human conduct. Human destiny is shaped by biology and environment. These variables tend to produce shared elements of society and culture. Humans return, for reasons of psychology and culture, to certain recurring obsessions and themes. These are history's centres of gravity. History, then, is itself an oscillation where humanity moves from A to B, then back to A again.

This chapter will explore law's movement through engagement with key Western cultural narratives about the role of law in human communities. It will focus particularly on themes and images from the Christian tradition, given its foundational status in Western legal and social discourse. However, the ideas discussed in the essay have a more general application, which I

* I would like to thank Cicely Bonnin for invaluable discussion and research assistance. Thanks also to Danielle Ireland-Piper, Radha Ivory and Leon Wolff for their helpful and constructive comments.

illustrate through reference to Buddhist, Hindu and secular viewpoints. My main focus is on the nature of law, but I will also make some remarks about the notion of governance.

1. Law's dream of unity

Law dreams.[1] It dreams of calmness, harmony and order. Law's dreams are projected in its symbols, buildings, uniforms and language. Themis wields the scales of justice: everything is balanced. The courthouse is quiet, symmetrical, secure and ordered. The judge and the lawyers are sombre, anonymous professionals. The language of the law is measured and rational. Law is depicted as a complete and unified system of norms that offers determinate answers. It claims ultimate authority over all aspects of social life.

We might speak here of the role of the *legal imaginary* in shaping social discourse (cf. Crowe, 2015). Michèle Le Doeuff has written of the way in which images may serve as unacknowledged premises in philosophical arguments. Le Doeuff's idea of the *philosophical imaginary* relates to the device of 'thinking in images', whereby an image is used to flesh out an otherwise incomplete discussion (Le Doeuff, 1989, 2). Le Doeuff points out that images have traditionally been disregarded for the purposes of philosophical analysis. However, she argues that this overt disavowal of images obscures the important role they often play in philosophical discourse.

Law, similarly, sustains its overarching narrative of unity by means of its symbols and language. We can offer a genealogy of law's self-image by exploring its historical dimension. This historical aspect is best understood not as a linear narrative, but as an oscillation between order and disorder. We can see how law characteristically seeks order in the midst of disintegration. The most famous diachronic account of this feature of law in the Western legal imaginary is perhaps that found in the opening books of the Bible. All creation, we are told in Genesis, was originally unified (Genesis 1:2; see also John 1:1). All beings existed in a state of pre-reflective harmony with the world around them (Genesis 2:15–25).

Humans, however, were able to exercise their will to act contrary to harmonious existence with each other and the natural environment (Genesis 2:16–17). The realisation of this ability to act in ways contrary to peace and order gave rise to reflective consciousness and self-knowledge (Genesis 3:5). This, in turn, produced a rift between humans and the rest of creation. Shame and guilt arose from self-consciousness and alienated humans from themselves and each other (Genesis 3:7–10). The exponential growth of the human population and competition for prestige, honour and scarce resources gave rise to further possibilities for disharmony and violence (Genesis 4:3–9).

Humans became dispersed throughout the earth, forming larger and larger societies (Genesis 4:14–26, 9–10). The members of these groups were faced with the challenges of relating to each other and interacting with other groups. The diversity of human cultures and languages increased the difficulty of communication (Genesis 11:1–9). The pressures and temptations of social existence led individuals and sub-groups to rebel against the community order (Genesis 6:1–6, 11–12). Sects arose devoted to the pursuit of pleasure and false idols (Genesis 17:9–14; Exodus 32). The communal response to this challenge was to rely on the scaffolding of law in an attempt to connect members with their shared practices and values.

1 This kind of talk may seem mysterious, but it is not. Law dreams in the same way as it claims, demands and orders. The claims of law are claims made by legal officials on law's behalf. Likewise, the dreams of law are ideals and aspirations expressed on its behalf by officials and citizens. Cf (Gardner, 2006, 213).

Codes of law were promulgated and associated with detailed rituals for purification and atonement (Exodus 20–23; Leviticus 1–27). Law was placed upon law. The people were immersed in layers of communal practice to provide structure and strengthen their sense of belonging. Some laws sought to preserve physical health and social harmony in order to enable social co-existence under difficult conditions and ensure the survival of the group (see, e.g., Leviticus 11–15, 17:10–16, 18). Other laws created internal standards of excellence to facilitate a sense of social virtue and belonging (see, e.g., Exodus 25–30; cf. MacIntyre, 2007, 187; 1999, 77).

The law, however, led to its own challenges. Power accrued in members of the community who were blamed when things went badly (Numbers 11:1–15, 12, 14:1–12). Different forms of legal authority and governance were tried in response to different historical conditions (Exodus 18:18–26; Numbers 11:16–30). The most successful rulers were wise and humble and unified the people. However, all were fallible (see Crowe, 2016). The burden of the law was heavy on the people and their leaders. Its contribution to unity was tempered by periodic unrest and dissatisfaction. Even the best rulers doubted their own competence (see, e.g., Exodus 4:10; Numbers 11:14).

Law's reliance on centralised authority and communal acceptance of detailed rules and practices ensures that it oscillates between order and disorder. The people are fickle and impatient. They chafe under the yoke of the law. They seek satisfaction of their desires – and when the law does not offer this, they look elsewhere. The model of law as detailed communal rules does not teach people how to relate constructively to their desires but seeks to constrain and channel them through social norms. Law's instability stems from this basic tension between the rule-oriented nature of law and the unruly character of human striving.

2. Law's disintegration

Let us turn now to a more modern story. Twice in one lifetime the scourge of war brought untold sorrow to humanity (*Charter of the United Nations, 1945*, preamble). The aftermath of the First World War saw the creation of the League of Nations as a mechanism to preserve international peace (see Bendiner, 1975). The League itself comprised an Assembly, Council and Secretariat, along with the Permanent Court of International Justice and a range of other auxiliary bodies. The core aim of the League was the protection of peace and security, but it quickly came to encompass a vast bureaucracy.

The International Labour Organisation, the Health Organisation, the International Commission on Intellectual Cooperation, the Commission on Refugees and the Slavery Commission were among the bodies included under the League's auspices. Each of these entities had its own administrative structure. The Health Organisation, for example, encompassed a Health Bureau, a General Advisory Council and a Health Committee. An additional layer of governance was placed upon the existing states in the international community.

Law was laid upon law. However, the League of Nations failed in its central aim of protecting world security. The Axis powers withdrew from the League, precipitating the Second World War. The Second World War, in turn, was succeeded by a new endeavour to protect world peace: the creation of the United Nations. The stated focus of the United Nations was twofold: first, to preserve international peace and security and second, to protect the basic rights and freedoms enjoyed by all people by virtue of their humanity (*Charter of the United Nations, 1945*, art. 1).

The United Nations inherited and built upon the surviving League of Nations apparatus. The International Labour Organisation survived; the Health Organisation became the World Health Organisation; the International Commission on Intellectual Cooperation became the United Nations Organization for Economics, Science and Culture. The United Nations now has its own massive bureaucratic apparatus, layered upon not only the governments of nation states, but also increasingly complex regional organisations (see Steiner, Alston & Goodman, 2008, chs. 9–11).

The creation of the United Nations, along with the adoption of the Universal Declaration of Human Rights, inaugurated a new era of human rights discourse at the international level. Human rights, in this sense, are a shield that people may use against not only foreign states, but also their own governments. The discourse of human rights has therefore added another layer to the international legal order. International law is no longer merely about relationships between states: it also gives legal and moral standing to individuals (see Crowe & Weston-Scheuber, 2013, 123–26).

However, human rights discourse, as critics have noted, is a double-edged sword: rights can be used to protect the vulnerable but can also be wielded pre-emptively to keep other people's legal and moral claims at bay (Crowe, 2008, 327). Human rights 'concretise (and to a certain extent dilute) the ethical responsibility for a unique other into a wider moral feeling of duty' (Douzinas, 2000, 354). The layered nature of global governance introduces additional complexity into this system. Human rights enforcement depends in practice upon the political dynamics of state diplomacy, which in turn transforms human rights compliance into a form of political currency. Law refracts, but at its heart is the circulation of power that lends its norms practical force.

The United Nations, like all positive legal orders, refracts and circulates power. And, as such, its influence and stability waxes and wanes. The same story could, of course, be told about the European Union and other regional bodies. Law oscillates between unity and disintegration. Forms of governance assert themselves, only to be challenged by the unruliness of human desires and relationships. Empires come and go. International organisations grow exponentially and thereby breed dissenters and outcasts.

Law, as we have seen, dreams of unity. Legal systems claim to be comprehensive and authoritative within a given domain (Raz, 1979, ch. 2). The reality, however, is somewhat different. Modern law is multifaceted. Domestic legal orders contain a proliferation of regulatory norms and institutions as well as being supplemented by international law, transnational law, religious law, customary law and alternative dispute resolution (see Crowe, 2015). Legislation and judicial decisions give content to law, but they operate alongside principles, practices and conventions.

Law's fundamental claim to unity is no less evident internationally than at a local level: witness the rhetoric of the *United* Nations and the European *Union*. Law wants to be whole. And this is no surprise, since law is a human institution and the yearning for wholeness lies at the heart of human striving. At the most basic level, humans want to be whole. At the same time, however, they find themselves perpetually divided against themselves and one another by their competitive desires for power, glory and material possessions.

This dual character of human motivation represents the two faces of legal order. Law is both cooperative and competitive: it therefore carries within it dual tendencies towards wholeness and disorder. Humans, inevitably, are drawn together. They cannot help but recognise their common ground. The tension between unity and power leads to attempts – some more successful than others – to preserve unity through the use of power. Law seeks to overcome its disintegration quite literally through sheer force of will.

The attempt to preserve the rule of law through force, however, cannot mask the tension at the heart of human governance. It may not be doomed to outright failure, particularly at a local level. It is, however, doomed to tension – to an uneasy coexistence with itself. Law, like the humans who create and preserve it, is fundamentally divided. It seeks to serve two irreconcilable aims: unity and desire, peace and competition, harmony and will. Things, inevitably, fall apart. And this is the unerring pattern of human history.

3. Law's future to come

The biblical story of law's movement, as recounted above, culminates in the person of Jesus. The historical tension between the detailed scaffolding of the Mosaic law, with its complex communal practices of purification and atonement, and the unruly desires of the people finds its resolution in a radical jurisprudence of love. The first and preeminent commandment, according to Jesus, is to love your God with all your heart. The second commandment – entailed by the first – is to love your neighbour as yourself (Matthew 22:37–40; Mark 12:30–31; see also Luke 10:27).

The jurisprudence of love, Jesus teaches, is not a replacement for the old law so much as a restatement of its central purpose. He has not 'come to abolish the Law and the Prophets . . . but to fulfil them' (Matthew 5:17 ESV). Jesus's teaching, then, does not give us a new body of legal rules and regulations but rather suggests another way of understanding and approaching the existing legal order. It is a 'jurisprudence for adults', focused not on literal compliance with the rules but on grasping the rationale and movement behind them (Manderson, 2006, 200).

Jesus, then, draws out the underlying point of the Mosaic law. However, his teaching is not limited to supplementing rules with underlying principles. It has a far more radical dimension. Jesus supplements his restatement of the law in the two commandments on love with a series of exhortations about our attitude towards the law as a whole. The Sermon on the Mount presents these exhortations in the form of a series of further commandments, intertwined with parables to illustrate their significance and purpose.

The central exhortation of the Sermon on the Mount is to *be* the law by embodying love. The law, on this view, is not something to be obeyed or enforced. It is something you live. Those who 'mourn', those who 'hunger and thirst for righteousness', the 'merciful' and the 'peacemakers' embody the law and thereby fulfil it (Matthew 5:4–9 ESV). The essence of the commandments against murder and adultery, for example, lies not in refraining from certain specified acts and avoiding judgment but in cultivating inner freedom from anger and lust (Matthew 5:21–30).

The fulfilment of the law, in this sense, lies in an attitude of radical non-attachment to desires that may lead one away from love and towards anger, jealousy and other destructive emotions. The radical nature of this teaching is underscored by subsequent exhortations against pre-commitment and retaliatory violence. Do not take an oath, Jesus says, for the future is beyond your control (Matthew 5:33–37). The law is not a matter of swearing oaths and following them in a legalistic fashion, but rather embodying an open and loving attitude.

The law, understood in this way, cannot ultimately be fulfilled by reacting against evil on the model of 'an eye for an eye and a tooth for a tooth' (cf. Exodus 21:24; Leviticus 24:20; Deuteronomy 19:21). This punitive model of law fuels the oscillation between order and disorder by producing a cycle of anger and resentment among both lawbreakers and their victims. Rather, Jesus counsels, do not respond to evil by force (Matthew 5:39). The way to break law's cycle of violence is to cultivate non-attachment and compassion towards wrongdoers: 'love your enemy, do good to those who hate you' (Luke 6:27 ESV; see also Matthew 5:43–48).

Similarly, Jesus counsels his followers not to attach importance to their self-image when praying or fasting and not to pursue material wealth for its own sake (Matthew 6:5-21). Pride, envy and covetousness foster competitive attitudes that undermine social harmony and lead people to use the law for their own advantage. It is for this reason that Jesus says '[n]o one can serve two masters . . . You cannot serve [both] God and money' (Matthew 6:24 ESV). The attitudes embodied in pursuit of wealth are those that tend to undermine the law in the long run.

The Sermon on the Mount represents a thoroughly diachronic view of what it means to fulfil the law (Tolstoy, 1951, 119). A view of law as a set of rules backed by force may be motivated by a desire for peace, unity and human dignity. However, this conception of law holds the seeds of its own destruction. In the long run, force will be overthrown by force: 'all who take the sword will perish by the sword' (Matthew 26:52 ESV). A law embodied in loving non-attachment, by contrast, is a living law capable of stable existence: 'there is a future for the [person] of peace' (Psalm 37:37 ESV; see also Matthew 7:24–27).

Jesus's teaching, then, represents a kind of synthesis in law's dialectical movement between order and disorder. The resolution of this oscillation comes not through the use of force to compel compliance with the rules but through a kind of letting go. Our task is not to create and impose the law. We cannot ensure its fulfilment through force of will. Our task, rather, is to *be* the law by embodying the loving and compassionate attitude that lies at its core. We need to take a long-term view of law that understands its historical development and fixes its sights not on short-term solutions but on law's future to come.

4. Small governance

I have spoken about law's movement primarily in terms of texts and images from the Christian canon. However, the idea of a kind of law that transcends a rule-oriented outlook and focuses instead on radical non-attachment can also be found in other cultural and religious traditions. Buddhist and Hindu texts, for example, frequently contrast ritualistic and rule-bound approaches to religious observance with meditative or ascetic practices that help promote non-attachment to prestige, merit and other worldly concerns.

The Buddha, for example, counsels us not to be distracted by the dual temptations of sensory pleasure, on the one hand, and obsessive self-mortification, on the other. The body, consciousness and sensations, the Buddha says, are constantly burning with passion and desire (*Ādittapariyāya-sutta*, trans. Rahula, 1974, 95–6). However, ritual devotion can become its own form of attachment that frustrates the search for enlightenment. True enlightenment comes from a Middle Path that avoids the extremes of both indulgence and self-annihilation (*Dhammacakkappavattana-sutta*, trans. Rahula, 1974, 92–3).

The wise person, the Buddha teaches, strives to become dispassionate with respect to body, thoughts and senses. 'Being dispassionate, [she] becomes detached; through detachment, [she] is liberated' (*Ādittapariyāya-sutta*, trans. Rahula, 1974, 96-7; see also *Udumbarika-sīhanāda-sutta*, trans. Walshe, 1987, 394). This liberation, in turn, brings realisation of the futility of human striving: 'what has to be done is done, there is no more left to be done on this account' (*Ādittapariyāya-sutta*, trans. Rahula, 1974, 97). The enlightened one, free of competitive urges, can then be 'compliant, gentle and humble'; her 'thoughts of boundless love [may] pervade the whole world . . . without any obstruction, without any hatred, without any enmity' (*Metta-sutta*, trans. Rahula, 1974, 97).

Similar themes can be found in the Hindu canon. The *Muṇḍaka Upaniṣad*, for example, emphasises the dangers of strict ritualism or an overt emphasis on accruing merit. Those who focus on sacrifices and gifts as signs of their piety are mired in ignorance and futility; they can never enjoy their good works, since they must always engage in further rituals to store up more virtue (1.2.8–10, trans. Olivelle, 1998, 441). A wise person, by contrast, is 'free from passion and tranquil', focusing on a reality beyond 'austerities or rites' (3.1.8, 3.2.5, trans. Olivelle, 1998, 451, 453).

The *Bhagavad Gītā* similarly emphasises the need to carry out one's earthly tasks without undue attachment, since the ultimate fate of the world and its inhabitants lies beyond human control (3.19, trans. de Bary, 1958, 282). 'A person whose mind is deluded by the ego thinks: "I am the doer [of those actions]"', but in reality we can never fully determine the effects of our behaviour (3.27, trans. de Bary, 1958, 283). The appropriate response is not to refrain from action entirely, but to avoid attributing undue significance to the acts themselves.

The secular counterpart to these spiritual themes can be found in the contemporary emphasis on mindfulness as a component of psychological well-being. Mindfulness, in this sense, 'is characterised by dispassionate, nonevaluative and sustained moment-to-moment awareness of perceptible mental states and processes'. Structured and systematic practice of mindfulness has been found to offer a range of health benefits related to emotional processing, stress management, self-awareness and impulse control (Grossman et al, 2004, 36).

The mindful person, then, is aware of her state of being at each moment, rather than seeking satisfaction or control. This kind of outlook, if applied to law, might at first seem to involve abandoning the wider pursuit of order and justice. However, it is better viewed as reconstituting law's relationship to these goals. Law, on this view, is not an instrument to be used in service of other ends. Rather, a person acts lawfully when she adopts an open, loving and compassionate attitude in her relationships with others.

It is only by letting go of our illusions of control that we can create the kind of law that genuinely embodies peace, justice and harmony. In other words, we cannot pursue the ends of law directly, but only indirectly through non-attachment. What does this mean, then, for the practice of governance? This vision of law offered here may appear to be the opposite of governance, since governing something suggests a form of deliberate ordering. Is it possible to imagine an alternative form of governance: governance as letting go?

The start of this reimagining, it seems to me, is to stop thinking of governance in terms of control. Governance, on this view, is not about forcing people to do things; there are other ways to lead than by threats or sanctions. It is possible to govern by example, uniting people by humility, compassion and tolerance. This kind of governance begins with self-awareness and then focuses on building harmonious relationships within communities, making use of endogenous forms of social order based on local traditions and norms (Crowe, 2014a). Radical change must start on a small scale: first oneself, then one's community, then the world.

5. The law of war and peace

This book is about law's relation to global order and disorder. It is, then, a book about both law and history. Global law occurs against the backdrop of world politics and international relations. This is a complex topic, but certain themes recur. None is more fundamental than the oscillation between law and chaos. And this movement recurs in global law and governance. The United Nations, for example, which prompted the modern growth in human rights norms, was created as a result of war and premised on the pursuit of peace (*Charter of the United Nations,* 1945, art. 1(1)).

Martti Koskenniemi has written about the fundamental tension in international law between normativity and concreteness: norms are only regarded as legitimate if they simultaneously aspire to higher ideals and reflect the political interests of their subjects (Koskenniemi, 1990). I have likewise written with particular reference to international humanitarian and human rights law about the tension between coherence and acceptance: norms must both cohere with underlying principles and be acceptable to international actors (Crowe, 2014b). These tensions can be attributed in part to the history and politics of international relations: in particular the need to balance the aspirations of the world community against the principle of state sovereignty.

Human history, as Tolstoy realised, is fundamentally the history of war and peace (Tolstoy, 2008; 1951, ch. 6). And international law, for the same reason, is the law of war and peace. This means not only that it must deal with both wartime and peacetime scenarios (see Crowe & Weston-Scheuber, 2013, chs. 1–2), but that it embodies the perpetual oscillation of international relations between order and disorder. It reacts to disorder, as we have seen, by layering law upon law. However, the lesson of history is that bureaucratic law is prone to be unsettled by social restlessness and striving.

Recent political developments in the United Kingdom and elsewhere in Europe – representing social restiveness with the governance of the European Union – embody this basic tension, as do aspects of the current political climate in the United States and Australia. People chafe under the law when its yoke seems too heavy. We must let go of the law in order to fulfil it. This means relinquishing our illusion of control over other members of the world community – a particularly difficult task for that community's more powerful members.

There is a future for the law of peace, but what that future looks like is something we have not yet begun to imagine. Indeed, this is part of the point: it is not something we *can* imagine, so we should stop trying to imagine it. Instead, we should let go of our illusions of control and seek to *be* the law by cultivating non-attachment to wealth, security and a particular vision of the future. 'Therefore do not be anxious about tomorrow, for tomorrow will be anxious for itself' (Matthew 6:34 ESV). Retaliation is futile, not only because it fuels the cycle of war and violence, but because it destroys the inner peace that is necessary to bring a new law into being.

References

Bendiner, E. (1975). *A time for angels: The tragicomic history of the League of Nations.* New York: Knopf.

Charter of the United Nations, 24 October 1945, 1 UNTS XVI.

Crowe, J. & Weston-Scheuber, K. (2013). *Principles of international humanitarian law.* United Kingdom: Edward Elgar.

Crowe, J. (2008). Levinasian ethics and animal rights. *Windsor Yearbook of Access to Justice 26*, 313.

Crowe, J. (2014a). Radicalising Hayekian constitutionalism. *University of Queensland Law Journal, 33*, 379.

Crowe, J. (2014b). Coherence and acceptance in international law: Can humanitarianism and human rights be reconciled? *Adelaide Law Review, 35*, 251.

Crowe, J. (2015). The limits of legal pluralism. *Griffith Law Review, 24*, 314.

Crowe, J. (2016). Human, all too human: Human fallibility and the separation of powers. In Ananian-Welsh, R. and Crowe, J. (Eds.), *Judicial independence in Australia: Contemporary challenges, future directions.* Sydney: Federation Press.

De Bary, W. T. (Ed.) (1958). *Sources of Indian tradition.* New York: Columbia University Press.

Detmold, M. (1991). Australian law: Federal movement. *Sydney Law Review, 13*, 31.
Douzinas, C. (2000). *The end of human rights.* United Kingdom: Hart Publishing.
Gardner, J. (2006). Law's aim in *Law's Empire.* In Hershovitz, S. (Ed.), *Exploring Law's Empire: The jurisprudence of Ronald Dworkin* (pp. 207–24). London: Oxford University Press.
Grossman, P. et al. (2004). Mindfulness-based stress reduction and health benefits: A meta-analysis. *Journal of Psychosomatic Research, 57*, 35.
Grünbaum, A. (1963). *Philosophical problems of space and time.* New York: Knopf.
Koskenniemi, M. (1990). The politics of international law. *European Journal of International Law, 1*, 4.
Le Doeuff, M. (1989). *The philosophical imaginary.* London: Continuum.
Lyotard, J.-F. (1984). *The postmodern condition.* Minnesota: University of Minnesota Press.
MacIntyre, A. (1999). *Dependent rational animals.* Chicago: Open Court.
MacIntyre, A. (2007). *After virtue.* Indiana: University of Notre Dame Press.
Manderson, D. (2006). *Proximity, Levinas and the soul of law.* Montreal: McGill-Queen's University Press.
Olivelle, P. (Trans. and Ed.) (1988). *The early Upaniṣads: Annotated text and translation.* New York: Oxford University Press.
Rahula, W. (1974). *What the Buddha taught.* New York: Grove Press.
Raz, J. (1979). *The authority of law.* London: Oxford University Press.
Reichenbach, H. (1958). *The philosophy of space and time.* New York: Dover.
Smart, J. (1969). Causal theories of time. *The Monist, 53*(3), 385.
Steiner, H., Alston, P. & Goodman, R. (2008). *International human rights in context.* London: Oxford University Press.
Tolstoy, L. (1951). *The kingdom of God is within you.* United States: Watchmaker Publishing.
Tolstoy, L. (2008). *War and peace.* New York: Vintage.
Walshe, M. (Trans.) (1987). *Thus have I heard: The long discourses of the Buddha.* London: Wisdom.

4 How Anarchy Can Order the World

Susan Bird

Capitalism is a system designed to protect property rights. It relies on individual interests in land and goods. These rights are backed up by the legal system with its machinery of law and order. Anarchy is often defined in modern vernacular as the opposite of law and order. However, it has also been said that: 'Anarchy is one of the most abused and misunderstood words in common usage' (Masters, 1974). This chapter will discuss anarchy as an alternative political system and assert that a Stateless society is not necessarily a lawless one. Indeed, my research has shown that local communities can successfully regulate themselves. In this chapter, I will discuss three examples of grassroots anarchist movements that are setting the scene for the future. These include the Occupy movement, Green Governance and urban scavenging. These very different but connected activities draw on the concept of the 'commons' and assert that global harmony relies on the successful sharing of common resources, a process that often begins at a local level. In contrast to the well-known 'tragedy of the commons' thesis espoused by Garrett Hardin, writers such as Elinor Ostrom argue for a different form of regulation that flows from the 'bottom up'. This regulation embraces local knowledges in finding ways to share global resources for the benefit of all.

The world is facing some of its greatest challenges to date: climate change; pollution of the oceans; and displacement of people due to conflict and lack of opportunity. Global meetings such as climate change summits have done very little to address these issues in any real way (Weston & Bollier, 2014). Global governance is in the hands of an amorphous group of wealthy individuals using the breakdown of democracy and national sovereignty to feather their nests. The Panama Papers, the files of one law firm in one tax haven, demonstrate the ease with which national tax laws are avoided and evaded. Despite the warm rhetoric around 'free trade', with its images of peasants being lifted out of poverty, the bulk of world trade is in the areas of illegal drugs, war toys (often in breach of sanctions), hardcore and snuff pornography including the sex trade in bodies, and people smuggling (Stockholm International Peace Research Institute [SIPRI], 2013). The best-selling book *The Wolf of Wall Street* (Belfort, 2007) is a portrayal of the lifestyle that this form of neo-liberal capitalism allows. I argue that this decadence is not only accepted but facilitated by capitalism, which permits corporations to avoid the regulation of the State. Ironically, this global environment, where corporate bodies can exist free from State governance, could be defined as a form of anarchy. Here, the corporate 'human' is set loose from any kind of regulation and can migrate to any country to escape its responsibility to others. Those on the right would argue that the 'invisible hand' will regulate the corporation; that there is no need for State intervention. The mainstream left, while speaking tough, seem to do little to change laws that support corporate corruption and has moved to pro-capitalist, so-called centrist policies courting wealthy sponsors and donors. The pragmatic sellout of redistributive philosophy by left wing politicians has led to the near annihilation of the welfare State and associated social goods, such as free education and universal health care. Tariq Ali brilliantly displays the result of this adoption of neo-liberalism in his book: *The Extreme Centre: A Warning* (Ali, 2015).

However, there is growing public disenchantment about the lack of political alternatives given the 'extreme centre' politics espoused by the major parties in Western democracies such as the UK, US and Australia (Ali, 2015). This embitterment has seen a rise in ultra-right wing groups and those that respond to diminishing resources with a determination that they will not be the ones to miss out, exemplified by the success for example of the recent 'Brexit' poll, and re-election of parties such as 'One Nation' in Australia. There has also been a backlash from the left, and those believing that if we are going to survive the crises facing the world we need to find a new political system – one that responds more directly to the needs of the planet. These grassroots movements are breathing new life into the moribund left through a form of collectivism sometimes described as post-anarchism (Adams, 2016).

These movements reject traditional democracy as a solution to the world's problems and believe that a world without centralised government would not only work but thrive. The Occupy movement is one of these. This loosely organised movement sprang out of a disenchantment with world politics and inequality, in particular following the Global Financial Crisis. There have also been movements that seek to reinstall the commons as a form of organisation for managing shared resources (Weston & Bollier, 2014). Those in the 'Commons Strategies Group', for example, argue for a reconsideration of rights discourse that takes into account environmental concerns. They argue for new ways of governing resources based on an ethic of sharing rather than one of greed.

In this chapter, I will explore three unique responses to the current world order: the Occupy movement; efforts to create a 'commons'; and urban scavenging. These examples will demonstrate how anarchist practice, rather than resulting in chaos and disorder, has the potential to create a more peaceful society that responds more closely to the needs of its human and non-human citizens.

1. What is anarchy?

Anarchy as a political philosophy continues to be misinterpreted, although there are anarchist writings from pre-1800. Anthony Masters writes, 'Anarchy is one of the most abused and misunderstood words in common usage' (Masters, 1974). In *About Anarchism,* Nicholas Walter explains that this misunderstanding is in part due to the fact that the words "anarchy", as well as its Greek root, *anarkhia*, are both defined as meaning absence of government *and* chaos and confusion (2002, p. 27). Walter explains 'people who are not anarchists take [lack of government and chaos] to come to the same thing . . . [However] anarchists . . . believe not only that absence of governance will not mean chaos and confusion, but that a society without government will actually be better than the society we live in now' (2002, p. 27).

Anarchism defies easy definition. Apart from its numerous streams, its theoretical stance is not to prescribe any political system over others. Pëtr Kropotkin, one of the 'founding fathers' of anarchism, defined anarchism as:

> The name given to a principle or theory of life and conduct under which society is conceived without government – harmony in such a society being obtained not by

> submission to law, or by obedience to any authority, but by free agreements concluded between the various groups, territorial and professional, freely constituted for the sake of production and consumption, and also for the satisfaction of the infinite variety of needs and aspirations of a civilised being (Kropotkin in Masters, 1974, p. xviii).

In *Anarchism: Nomos XIX*, Clark writes that:

> In order for a political theory to be called "anarchism" in a complete sense, it must contain: (1) a view of an ideal, noncoercive, nonauthoritarian society; (2) a criticism of existing society and its institutions based on this antiauthoritarian ideal; (3) a view of human nature that justifies hope for significant progress toward the ideal; and (4) a strategy for change, involving immediate institution of noncoercive, nonauthoritarian, and decentralist alternatives (Clark in Pennock & Chapman, 1978, p. 12).

Although, as Clark writes, anarchism involves strategies for change, these cannot be set out in any clearly defined terms. This is not because the theory is underdeveloped but because 'the anarchist does not want to bind anyone to one vision of the ideal, since the acceptance of pluralism implies that various groups will create numerous variations on the general goal' (Clark in Pennock & Chapman, 1978, pp. 13–14). Nonetheless, it is possible to recognise two distinct streams: libertarian and communitarian.

The libertarian stream is based on a 'contractual' theory of self-interested individuals who, in the absence of the State, would deal directly with one another and be bound by their agreements with one another. This theory is an extension to the extreme of neo-liberalism where the State shrinks to non-existence and people are assumed to be on an equal footing in their dealings.

The communitarian streams of anarchism are closer to socialism. Many communitarian theories of anarchy see society existing as numerous, localised, smaller communities within which rules and laws are determined (Gaus & Chapman, 1978). Within the community, members decide how to govern themselves. People are able to engage in the production of all things that are needed, such as shelter or food. Within this kind of society, individuals are not alienated from what they make. Many communitarian anarchists see the liberation of humanity as originating with community (Gaus & Chapman, 1978; Walter, 2002; Ferrell, 2001, among others). Roberto Unger, although he does not label himself as an anarchist, theorises that society is organised by 'human nature', which is discovered through 'anarchist democracy'. Organic groups or communities develop where people know each other in many different capacities. He sees this as a way of breaking down the divisions between the public and private selves that will 'destroy domination' (Unger in Gaus & Chapman, 1978).

In contemporary thinking on the use of city space, anarchism has become a recurring theme for theorist Jeff Ferrell. His book, *Tearing Down the Street: Adventures in Urban Anarchy,* is critical of the postmodern city experience (Ferrell, 2001). Ferrell opens the book by asserting that 'Something's gone wrong' (Ferrell, 2001, p. 1). What has gone wrong, for Ferrell, is the loss of sense of community within the city, which has arisen through a fear of difference. Ferrell's writing gets to the heart of how postmodernity has turned its back on what makes us human – being able to exist in an open, accepting, self-regulating community.

The nature of communitarian anarchism is rule from the bottom up. Those choosing to live together agree on the rules that will govern them. Although certain rules may be evaded by anarchists operating within a State, the groups are not rule-free but have their own systems for regulating behaviour. These systems are envisaged by anarchists in their utopian vision for a more cooperative, harmonious world. We can see movements such as Occupy as sowing the seeds of anarchism and as a living example of how anarchist communities could grow into a reality.

An anarchist society is one that combines freedom and equality. Rather than being opposing forces, anarchists believe freedom and equality can, and should, exist together. This is where anarchism differs from both socialism and libertarianism, where one values equality over freedom, and the other, freedom over equality. Natasha Walter connects this philosophical stance to current anti-capitalist protest movements:

> [T]his insight, that freedom and equality are indivisible, is the characteristic insight of the current movement against global inequality, whose members use anti-authoritarian methods, working without hierarchies or leaders . . . and whose demands are both for a more equitable economic system and for greater freedom for every member of society (Walter, 2002, p. 10).

I will now explore one of these movements – Occupy Wall Street – and one of its many echoes, Occupy Melbourne.

2. Occupy movement

One grassroots movement that could be described as anarchist is the Occupy movement. The movement grew out of disenchantment by large sections of the left with the embrace of neo-liberal, capital-friendly policies by governments claiming to represent 'workers' and other disadvantaged groups. The action began as 'Occupy Wall Street' on September 17, 2011 (Schneider, 2013). Adbusters called for protest via their website and a poster that read: 'What is our one demand?' Adbusters is a Canadian anti-consumerist group that describes itself as 'a global network of activists writers artists designers hackers tricksters poets philosophers and punks' (Adbusters Magazine, n.d.). The organisers wanted to protest corporate influence on democracy, in particular the influence of political donations. The provision of financial relief to banks by taxpayers in the wake of the Global Financial Crisis provided a moment of clarity. The wealthy could use subprime mortgages, hedge funds and so on to transfer wealth from the poor to the executive class.

While it came as a response to the Global Financial Crisis, Occupy's aims and goals were deliberately broader. The philosophy of Occupy was not to speak for others but create a space where all could be heard, in a true public sphere. As Rebecca Solnit writes in *Thank you Anarchy: Notes from the Occupy Appocalypse,* 'the definition of "we" as the 99 per cent was so much more inclusive than almost anything before' (Solnit in Schneider, 2013, p. xi). Further, Occupy did not prescribe specific methods. There were no identified leaders, and each branch had its own general assembly where people could join in on a consensus-style decision-making process. This style of organisation is undeniably built on an anarchist philosophy. The overarching message of the movement was simply that something had gone wrong with the democratic process, and that something must be done to fix it. How could democracy allow the richest one percent to have so much power and influence, leading to such huge inequality between people, and the ruination of the planet?

Some members of the Occupy movement – for example, David Graeber, Nathan Schneider and Michael Kazin – do not hesitate to align the movement with anarchy. In 'Occupy

Wall Street's Anarchist Roots' (2001) Graeber writes that it was the movement's anarchist underpinnings that drew criticism from the press. Journalists suggested that the lack of leaders and consensus-style decision-making processes would lead the movement to fail. But what might success and failure be for an anarchist? Anarchy as a philosophy does not contend that it has leaders who will take over from current world powers and instate their own laws. It is about autonomy within groups, and people taking responsibility for their own leadership. As Graeber points out, the Occupy movement was very successful in raising awareness and has led to greater insistence from the general population that something needs to be done to quell the excesses of capitalism.

My own experience with the Occupy movement was fleeting, as the Melbourne authorities were quick to respond and close the encampment down. On October 15, 2011, I headed for Melbourne's city square and found a village within the city. Tents were tied with rainbow ribbons, and the fountain became a stream where people dipped and frolicked. The city square on the corner of Collins and Swanston streets in Melbourne is the traditional heart of protest and activism – close to the centre of town and marching distance to parliament house. In the 1990s, it was subdivided, half of this public space sold to a hotel chain for profit. This tent village formed by Occupy spoke of a simpler life, one where people took care of each other, and lived in harmony. Here, people were daring to take direct action and live as if the city was theirs and not the multinational corporations'. As Graeber writes, direct action is 'a matter of acting as if the existing structure of power does not even exist. Direct action is, ultimately, the defiant insistence on acting as if one is already free' (Graeber, 2011).

This defiance of the law continued as Occupy Melbourne remained in the city square in the belief that it was a space of the people, even when told by police to leave. This brings into focus another anarchist principle – that the mechanisms of the State, including police, have as their primary purpose the protection of private interests and the maintenance of inequality (Walter, 2002). In this way, the market/State becomes a unified opponent of the anarchist. The State supports capitalism and corporate greed by providing legal mechanisms that allow inequality to grow. As Natasha Walter writes:

> The essential function of the state is to maintain the existing inequality. This last statement may give those people in the current resistance movement who put all their faith in the state pause for thought. What are governments for? Can they be pushed to bring about equality and freedom or will they protect equality and freedom only so far as those rights do not conflict with wealth and power, and no further? (Walter, 2002, pp. 11–12).

It is not surprising that Occupy Melbourne became increasingly sceptical of the State. This culminated when the peaceful encampment was ultimately smashed by State violence when the police forcibly evicted Occupy from the square less than one week after the occupation started.

3. Green governance and the commons

The concept of the commons is having a resurgence in both academic and activist circles. Revived in 1968 by economist Garrett Hardin (1968), it was argued that common property leads to overuse and depletion of resources as self-interested individuals will always attempt to maximise their profits, no matter what the result. Hardin argued that the commons was possible in earlier times, because the planet was less populated, and it could therefore handle less efficient land use. In modern times, unless population was drastically curbed, Hardin argued the commons must be managed by individuals or the State, or disaster would surely follow (Hardin, 1968).

While not directly aligned with the anarchist movement, Green Governance and other environmental movements that reject Hardin's thesis have clear links to an anarchist philosophy. The most obvious of these is within their approach to property and its governance. Anarchists are against private ownership and the use of land as an asset rather than a resource. In 1840, Pierre-Joseph Proudhon, an early French anarchist writer, wrote that '[p]roperty is theft' (Proudhon, 1970): 'The proprietor, the robber, the hero, the sovereign . . . all these titles are synonymous – Property is the right to use and abuse'. Proudhon explained that private property works against equality as it is based on exclusion (Proudhon, 1970). This philosophy is a central tenet of anarchism and is shared with other anarchist thinkers, who believe the concept of private property is linked to authority. Charlotte Wilson, another anarchist writer, explains that:

> Property is the domination of an individual, or a coalition of individuals, over things; it is not the claim of any person or persons to the use of things -this is usufruct, a very different matter. Property means the monopoly of wealth, the right to prevent others using it, whether the owner needs it or not . . . If any individual shuts off a portion of it (which he is not using, and does not need for his own use) from his fellows, he is defrauding the whole community (2013, p. 17).

Elinor Ostrom (1990), author of *Governing the Commons: The Evolution of Institutions for Collective Action*, conducted research into communities living on and making use of communal ecosystems, such as rivers. She found that indigenous ways of sharing natural resources were often more effective than technological ones imposed from above. To preserve resources for future generations, a strong State or private ownership/governance was not necessarily the best way forward.

Part of Elinor Ostrom's rejection of Hardin's thesis was her belief that local cultures were closer to the resources that give them life and better able to manage them. She states that 'many solutions exist to cope with many different problems' (Ostrom, 1990). Her ethnographic work explains that the tragedy of the commons thesis is flawed because it does not recognise the unique nature of resources and the localised issues that are important in their management. Ostrom argues:

> Instead of presuming that the individuals sharing a commons are inevitably caught in a trap from which they cannot escape, I argue that the capacity of individuals to extricate themselves from various types of dilemma situations varies from situation to situation (Ostrom, 1990, p. 14).

Ostrom (2000) develops this theory in 'Collective Action and the Evolution of Social Norms'. Here, Ostrom argues that rather than all individuals being 'rational egoists' interested in their own good, most groups contain many different types of individuals who behave differently when given choices in collective action situations. This has been confirmed in lab experiments that do not support Hardin's thesis that all individuals will always act in their own self-interest. To preserve precious and delicate ecologies around the world, Ostrom argues that we need to tap into local and place-based knowledges. The knowledge of indigenous peoples in caring for the land has often been developed over tens to hundreds of thousands of years.

In their book *Green Governance: Ecological Survival, Human Rights and the Law of the Commons,* Burns Weston and David Bollier (2014) continue the work of Elinor Ostrom, also arguing for collective, local management of the environment. They also argue that the theory of the self-interested nature of humanity may be a myth:

> A growing body of scientific evidence suggests that social trust and cooperation may be an evolutionary force "hard-wired" into the human species. If true, many 18th and 19th Century notions of human beings as autonomous, selfish, rational individuals, upon which entire political and economic philosophies and institutional structures are built, deserve to be re-visited and re-thought. The idea of *homo economicus*, which modern-day economists and political theorists presume to be a universal norm, may in fact have very little basis in fact or history (Weston & Bollier, 2014, p. 82).

They discuss the failure of current world leaders to do anything that seriously addresses issues such as climate change and assert the need for a new way forward. For example, they suggest that, '[t]he State will not of its own provide the necessary leadership to save the planet' (Weston & Bollier, 2014, p. 20). In contrast, the commons offers a system of governance that stands outside of State and market. As Weston and Bollier contend:

> A *commons* . . . eschews individual property rights and State control. It relies instead on common property arrangements that tend to be self-organized and enforced in complicated, idiosyncratic social ways . . . the "unofficial" norms, institutions, and procedures that a peer community devises to manage community resources on its own. . . . In this way, the Commons operates in a quasi-sovereign manner, largely escaping the centralized mandates of the State and the structures of Market exchange while mobilizing decentralized participation "on the ground" 2014, p. 78).

In alignment with Occupy, Weston and Bollier write that part of the State's failure is caused by the power that the Market has over governments. The Market here refers to the economic philosophy and system in which the forces of supply and demand regulate the distribution of goods and wealth in societies. The Market, with its primary aim of maximising profits, exploits the commons as predicted by Hardin's thesis. Yet financial crises, global warming and the mishandling of resources that are governed across State boundaries have caused increasing numbers of people to question the ability of the Market to 'self-correct'.

4. Urban Gleaning and the informal waste commons

This chapter will now turn to a local solution to a global problem – that of waste. Urban Gleaning is an illustration of a local community that has developed around a kind of commons in suburban Melbourne. It highlights how the ethics of anarchy and the commons are coming together and proving to be a better waste management strategy than conventional ones.

In suburban Melbourne, and other Australian cities, there is a small strip of common land that runs adjacent to every street. This space is called the 'nature strip' and it challenges the public/private dichotomy by appearing to be both. Hard garbage collection occurs in many Melbourne suburbs about twice a year, which allows residents to deposit a set amount of cubic meters of waste onto the nature strip for pick up by private companies contracted by the council. The ownership of the items left on the nature strip is often ambiguous, due to the uncertain proprietary rights attached to the strip. Ownership and care of the strip or road verge tends to vary from council to council and is generally based on 'custom' rather than law (eMelbourne, 2016).

Urban Gleaning originates in the ancient practice of gleaning. Gleaning has a long history and is thought to have begun thousands of years ago. Early documentation of gleaning can be found in the Old Testament and Koran (Leviticus 19:9–10; Quran 6:141). Further, gleaning was an important right for the poor in feudal Britain who relied on it to feed their families (King, 1992, p. 1). It was also important during the eighteenth century, when work was poorly paid and increasingly difficult to come by (King, 1992, p. 1). Access to land for gleaning represented recognition of rights connected to communal ownership. Communal, customary rights, however, are at odds with the principles of capitalism and were therefore gradually overruled as feudalism gave way to 'modernity'. As Margaret Radin points out, within a capitalist framework, '[e]verything must be ownable or saleable' (Radin in Buck, 2006, p. 19). In late eighteenth century Britain, laws of the commons and enclosure were being fought in the English courts (for example, see *Steel v Houghton* (1788) 126 ER 32 126). As King writes, 'During the eighteenth and early nineteenth centuries, the laboring poor in many parts of England not only endured irregular employment and inadequate wages, but also suffered a series of attacks on their customary rights' (King, 1992, p. 2). These attacks on the peasants' rights came from both the farmers, who leased land from wealthy land owners, and from the land owners themselves, who were eager to enclose the land and enjoy exclusive rights to it. Many of the farmers employed the peasants as labourers, and it was therefore difficult for them to mount any challenge when their rights were eroded (King, 1992, p. 2). As Buck asserts in *The Making of Australian Property Law*:

> the law of property was being redrafted in England via the enclosure movement of the late eighteenth century . . . pre-capitalist (or more to the point – anti-capitalist) concepts of property and agrarian practice were being effectively negated and replaced by law in favour of a profit oriented conception of property as a tradeable commodity. (Buck, 2006, pp. 23–24).

As the commons has succumbed to enclosure, the original practice of gleaning continues in some countries, such as France (Varda, 2000). The use of the nature strip as a commons in Australia is a modern-day twist on this traditional practice where the gleaners resist overconsumption through repurposing.

The act of collecting discarded items from the nature strip subverts messages about the ways that we should acquire and dispose of items, and about how we view property. The activities create a playful, festive space where hierarchies are eroded and the usual exchange of goods for money is replaced with localised trade and sharing. The urban gleaners do not have a leader or any closely organised methodology. They have created online communities on social media, where people can discuss what they have seen, and offer to share items they no longer need. Like the commons in Medieval Britain, where peasants hunted and grazed animals, the nature strip is a modern-day example of the sharing of land and resource. As Ruth Lane asserts:

> Melbourne's hard rubbish collections form a kind of informal waste commons where discarded goods and materials are relinquished by their owners into the public space

> of the kerb-side for a brief period of time. The kerb-side or 'nature strip', where the transition in ownership takes place, is a critical locus for the categorisation of private property . . . It forms a boundary between public space formally managed by local government authorities and the private space of the domestic residence, although this boundary can be challenged through informal activities of residents (Lane, 2011, p. 398).

In *Empire of Scrounge,* Jeff Ferrell (2005) explores how scavenging connects people who are not usually connected. Scavenging creates communities, as seen in blogs and Facebook pages. People communicate online about when the next collection will take place and where. The community also exists offline. Wandering the streets, people meet their neighbours and learn more about them through the items they reject.

These communities involve both people who previously knew each other and those that were complete strangers before their encounters on the street. A system of rules has developed amongst the community that governs behaviour. These rules are at odds with, and ignore, the legal governance of hard waste, as dictated by the local councils. Items collected are usually shared with family, friends and other scavengers. The standard of behaviour of gleaners appears to hold a greater ethic of sharing, where those involved with a motive of profit may be looked down upon. Ruth Lane writes:

> The sense of mutual obligation around giving and receiving [amongst scavengers] clearly contributed to perpetuation of these practices. From this perspective the waste commons provided by hard rubbish was linked with practices of giving and receiving gifts, and the idea of communal benefits, rather than the acquisition of private property for personal gain (Lane, 2011, p. 401).

Widely accepted rules of scavenging include leaving enough for others, not making a mess and not damaging other people's property (Rush, 2006; Lane, 2011; Bird, Unpublished thesis, 2015).

Although research has shown that scavenging results in significant decreases in the amount of waste going to landfill (Lane, 2011, p. 395), legal responses to it are ambiguous. Attitudes to hard rubbish scrounging vary between local councils, where in some cases fines can be issued for removing discarded items from the nature strip. For example, in Frankston, a seaside suburb in outer Melbourne, the council has announced that it will be issuing fines to scavengers: 'Unauthorised removal of hard waste from the nature strip is theft. Frankston City Council may issue on-the-spot fines of $200 or prosecute offenders. Please report scavenging offences by phoning Council . . . ' (Frankston City Council, n.d.). As Lane observes, these attempts to reduce scavenging through regulation are not often successful, due to the ambiguity in ownership of the nature strip and items left on them: 'These measures inevitably fail because of the inability to secure exclusive property rights to materials on the kerb-side in any practical way' (Lane, 2011, p. 404).

In short, the gleaners reject the law of the State, developing a community-based response to the issue of waste. This direct action approach has proven to be more successful than council-mandated methods in the reduction of waste at a practical level (Lane, 2011). Further, the practice of gleaning has shown that it can operate successfully without State input, demonstrating that rule from the bottom up is often more effective in managing resources (Ostrom, 1990).

5. Conclusion

Francis Fukuyama (1992) declared the end of history with the fall of communism, arguing the achievement of Western, liberal democracy was the high point and the 'final form of human government'. Anarchists, however, 'have never stopped believing in an alternative' (Walter, 2002, p. 27).

In this chapter, I have explored three movements that share an overarching anarchist philosophy. These communities arise out of the dynamic spirit of people seeking an ethical life, sharing resources beyond the state/market. As Weston and Bollier assert, 'the once-impregnable edifice of the State/Market is now seen, correctly, as vulnerable' (Weston & Bollier, 2014, p. 20). Anarchist philosophies are raising awareness of these vulnerabilities and providing inspiration to those seeking an alternative to extreme centre politics.

The Occupy movement openly embraces anarchism as its organisational basis. Those who support the commons as a form of green governance share an anarchist stance on property and further envisage governance as operating outside of market and State. The urban gleaners who share resources to reduce waste do so in a less overt, but still clear way. They operate as if they are, as Graeber (2011) explains it, 'already free'. These movements exemplify how, in practice, anarchy does not lead to chaos and confusion, but to new forms of collective governance that operate from the bottom up. They do not present a utopia, or a dream of a distant future, but examples of real communities that already exist. In this sense, we do not have to wonder whether anarchy could work, because we can see that it already does. Anarchy does not propose replacing the current system of rules with a new authority but allowing individuals to take greater responsibility for their lives. Anarchism can take many forms, and, as Mohammed Banyeh writes in *Anarchy as Order,* 'spaces of anarchism live within existing systems . . . A space of anarchy is not the whole of society and certainly not a state' (Banyeh, 2009, p. 218). It would run against an anarchist philosophy for it to be so. In anarchy, it is up to each group of self-organising individuals to determine its own rules. The shared philosophy is only the belief that without a centralised, top-down authority, people will find order in freedom, equality and peace.

References

Adams, P. (presenter). (2016). Anarchy rules! *Late Night Live*. Radio National, Australia.

Adbusters Magazine (n.d.). Retrieved from: www.adbusters.org/.

Ali, T. (2015). *The extreme centre: A warning*. London: Verso.

Banyeh, M. (2009). *Anarchy as order: The history and future of civic humanity*. Lanham: Rowman and Littlefield.

Belfort, J. (2007). *The wolf of Wall Street*. New York: Bantam Books.

Bird, S. (2015). *Melbourne's wildscapes: A critical ethnography*. PhD thesis.

Buck, A. R. (2006). *The making of Australian property law*. Leichhardt: The Federation Press.

eMelbourne (2016). The encyclopaedia of Melbourne online. Retrieved from: http://www.emelbourne.net.au/.

Ferrell, J. (2001). *Tearing down the street: Adventures in urban anarchy*. New York: Palgrave.

Ferrell, J. (2005). *Empire of scrounge: Inside the urban underground of dumpster diving, trash picking, and street scavenging*. New York: New York University Press.

Frankston City Council (n.d.). Retrieved from: http://www.frankston.vic.gov.au/Environment_and_Waste/Waste_and_Recycling/Hard_Waste_Collection.

Fukuyama, F. (1992). *The end of history and the last man*. New York: Free Press.

Gaus G. and Chapman, J. (1978) 'Anarchism and political philosophy: An introduction' in Pennock, R. and Chapman, J. (eds) *Anarchism Nomos XIX*. New York: New York University Press.

Graeber, D. (2011). Occupy Wall Street's anarchist roots. *Al Jazeera*. Retrieved from: http://www.aljazeera.com/.
Hardin, G. (1968). The tragedy of the commons. *Science, 162*, 1243–1248.
King, P. (1992). Legal change, customary rights and social conflict in the late eighteenth century: the origins of the great gleaning case of 1788. *Law and History Review*, *10*(1), 1–31.
Lane, R. (2011). The waste commons in an emerging resource recovery waste regime: contesting property and value in Melbourne's hard rubbish collections. *Geographical Research*, *49*, 395–407.
Mansfield, B. (Ed). (2008). *Privatization: Property and the remaking of nature-society relations*. Malden MA: Blackwell.
Masters, A. (1974). *Bakunin: The father of narchism*. Boston: EP Dutton.
Ostrom, E. (1990). *Governing the commons: The evolution of institutions for collective action*. Cambridge: Cambridge University Press.
Ostrom, E. (2000). Collective action and the evolution of social norms. *The Journal of Economic Perspectives, 14*(3), 137–158.
Pennock, R. & Chapman, J. (Eds.) (1978). *Anarchism: Nomos XIX*. New York: New York University Press.
Proudhon, P. (1970) *What is property? Or, an inquiry into the principle of right and government* (trans Benj Tucker) New York: Dover.
Rush, E. (2006). *Skip dipping in Australia* (web paper). Canberra: Australia Institute. Retrieved from: http://www.tai.org.au/documents/downloads/WP85.pdf.
Schneider, N. (2013). *Thank you anarchy: Notes from the occupy apocalypse*. Berkley: University of California Press.
Stockholm International Peace Research Institute (2013). *SIPRI yearbook 2013*. Oxford and New York: Oxford University Press.
University of California (2009). Gleaning and religion. Retrieved from: http://humweb.ucsc.edu/gleaningstories/html/charity.html.
Varda, A. (director) (2000). *The gleaners and I* (Motion Picture). France: Ciné Tamaris.
Walter, N. (2002). *About anarchism* (2nd Edition). New York: Free Press.
Weston, B. & Bollier, D. (2014). *Green governance: Ecological survival, human rights, and the law of the commons*. Cambridge: Cambridge University Press.
Wilson, C. (2013). *Three essays on anarchism*. Hastings: Christie Books.

Case

Steel v Houghton (1788) 126 ER 32.

5 The Rise of China and Global Disorder – Can 'the Centre' Hold in the 21st Century?

Malcolm Davis

This chapter examines the rise of China. Specifically, it consider aspects of China's behaviour that may challenge the existing rules-based international order. The chapter argues that China is determined to reshape existing international architecture in political, economic and security domains in a manner that gives it more influence and allows it to achieve the China Dream of a rejuvenated 'middle kingdom'. This chapter examines in detail the issues related to China's activities in the South China Sea and considers the linkage between the South China Sea and China's broader 'grand strategy' for achieving the China Dream. It argues that Chinese actions in the South China Sea will mean that this dispute becomes the focal point for growing strategic competition between a rising China and the United States, in what commentators refer to as the Thucydides Trap. Yeats's poem 'The Second Coming', written in 1919 after the First World War and with its themes of instability, imminent change and dystopic foreboding of chaos, strongly resonates with these current world events.

Turning and turning in the widening gyre
The falcon cannot hear the falconer;
Things fall apart; the centre cannot hold;
Mere anarchy is loosed upon the world,
The blood-dimmed tide is loosed, and everywhere
The ceremony of innocence is drowned;
The best lack all conviction, while the worst
Are full of passionate intensity.

Surely some revelation is at hand;
Surely the Second Coming is at hand.
The Second Coming! Hardly are those words out
When a vast image out of Spiritus Mundi
Troubles my sight: somewhere in sands of the desert
A shape with lion body and the head of a man,
A gaze blank and pitiless as the sun,
Is moving its slow thighs, while all about it
Reel shadows of the indignant desert birds.
The darkness drops again; but now I know
That twenty centuries of stony sleep
Were vexed to nightmare by a rocking cradle,
And what rough beast, its hour come round at last,
Slouches towards Bethlehem to be born?

William Butler Yeats, 1919

Might is not right (cf. Redbeard, 1890). This is the organising principle that underpins the contemporary international order and its established structures of governance, legal norms, and international economic, political and security architectures – nominally referred to as the 'rules based international order'. Reinforcing a broad multilateral interest in preserving 'international order' – in which nation-states work together cooperatively to resolve disputes peacefully and respect the basic tenets of international legal tradition and principle – has been the aim of international affairs certainly since the end of the Second World War in 1945 and was key to the peaceful conclusion of the Cold War in 1991. Now, twenty-five years after the end of the Cold War, it is clear that the rules-based international order is under challenge like never before. The question of the future of the international order and the risk of growing disorder raises the vision promoted by the famous poem by Irish poet Yeats, 'The Second Coming', written in the aftermath of the First World War. In the poem, Yeats laments growing insecurity and instability across the world. Is the collapse of order that Yeats forebodes in the aftermath of 'the war to end all wars' once again relevant to the 21st Century international system?

The 'centre' in Yeats's poem is akin to the established rules-based international order that has emerged since the end of the Second World War, in the form of political, legal, economic and security structures and norms of international behaviour against the idea that 'might makes right'. Despite hopes for a peaceful and cooperative post-Cold War international order to emerge in the early 1990s, the reality of international behaviour suggests that idealistic aspirations were never realised. The notion of an 'end of history', as suggested by Francis Fukuyama (1992), has been proven to be false. Fukuyama suggests liberal-democratic traditions assume global dominance and thereby end ideological struggle between nations, enabling a form of 'democratic peace theory' to prevent recourse to war by states (see, Philips, 2008). The dreams of a new and more peaceful world, however, seem at risk. For example:

- an authoritarian Russia has re-emerged to challenge the West in Europe;
- a rising authoritarian China challenges the security interests of the United States and its allies in Asia;
- the 'Arab Spring' generates a counter-democratic dynamic that has seen pro-democracy movements stifled across the Middle East; and
- the rise of extremist forces such as Islamic State are a violent threat to democracy.

Further, a growing malaise in Western liberal-democratic traditions is enabling the political fringe to successfully challenge moderate voices. In short, 'mere anarchy' is being loosed upon the world; 'things are falling apart'; and the ideal of spreading democratisation leading to global stability seems more distant than ever. As noted at a recent Chatham House conference:

> The danger to the current order comes not from a single deathblow from a rival system, but from its gradual weakening in the face of widespread dissatisfaction among those it needs to serve. If the system is to survive, its weaknesses must be recognized and resolved, and it must adapt better and faster to the changing international situation (Royal Institute of International Affairs, 2015).

The particular challenge posed to the current world order by China is complex. In some ways, China is fully accepting of the established rules-based order and successfully operates within it to its benefit. China undertakes extensive roles within the United Nations. It supports the interests of international order through peacekeeping and through support for counter-piracy measures in the Gulf of Aden (Erickson & Strange, 2015). Further, China also supports international efforts towards arms control and non-proliferation and plays a valuable role in contributing to multilateral solutions to issues preventing the spread of nuclear weapons. For example, China participated in the P5+1 process leading to the Joint Comprehensive Plan of Action (JCPOA) to preclude Iran moving rapidly to acquisition of nuclear weapons (Scott, 2015).

In other ways, however, China is working to reshape aspects of the global rules-based order to best suit China's interests, and in some cases, it is acting to potentially erode and remove some components of world order. For example, as will be discussed further below, China is seeking to challenge the US defence and security role in Asia via the 'hub and spoke' arrangements and replace these with a Chinese-led order. In some cases, it is simply choosing to ignore established international norms and rules, or act directly against them, as shown by its actions and posture in the South China Sea (Stewart, 2016; see also International Institute for Strategic Studies, 2016).

While violation of international law by a superpower is not a novel occurrence (consider the international conduct of the United States, for example), the ramifications are of greater significance in the case of China. This is because China's continuing rise across all aspects of state power – in diplomacy, political influence, economic and industrial strength, and its rapidly growing military power – makes it the most important actor that is seeking to challenge the rules-based international order. China is completely different from the Soviet Union during the Cold War in that its economic and industrial strength makes it well placed to sustain competition with the United States much more effectively into the decades ahead, even with a slowing economy and significant internal challenges. At the same time that China's rise continues, there is a perception of US strategic decline. The so-called 'rise of the rest' – rapidly developing states in Asia, Africa and Latin America – is further challenging the traditional Euro-Atlantic core and generating a global power shift to Asia in a manner that heralds an ending to the Vasco de Gama era of Western dominance (Bell, 2007).

Importantly, it was 'the rest', led by China, that rode out the 2008–2010 Global Financial Crisis (GFC) with the least impact and have sustained rapid growth rates, even as US and European economies stagnated and then grew anaemically following the conclusion of the crisis (Zakaria, 2011). These developments represent potentially the beginning of a new era in international affairs, as Asia becomes the global centre of politics, economics and finance and international commerce and as China challenges the United States for military predominance. Andrew Erickson (2016), in relation to the size and capability of the People's Liberation Army Navy (PLAN), has observed that:

> China's shipbuilding industry is poised to make the PLAN the second largest navy in the world by 2020, and – if current trends continue – a combat fleet that in overall order of battle (i.e., hardware-specific terms) is quantitatively and even perhaps qualitatively on a par with that of the US Navy by 2030.

China's growing military power, in particular, the growth of its naval power, and the reality that China's economy overtook the US economy in purchasing power parity (PPP) terms in late 2014 (Bird, 2014) are two important indicators that this power shift is well underway. Naval power and economic strength represent two key pillars of US global power and prestige, and both are under challenge. The third – political influence – rests on the other two being strong.

As global power shifts from the old world to the new, it is natural for developing states to seek more power and influence within the established international order, or, alternatively, to challenge the existing structures to either reshape them or replace them. Neither is it unnatural for the established powers to resist such change that would see their political and strategic influence diminish. This tension between rising powers and established powers – and specifically, between a rising China and an established United States – is often referred to in the context of a 'Thucydides Trap'. A Thucydides Trap refers to a rising Athens challenging Sparta for dominance which ultimately lead to the Peloponnesian War between 431 BC and 411 BC (Allison, 2015).

Allison (2015) highlights that in twelve of the sixteen cases over the past 500 years of rising powers challenging an existing power, the result was war. The question of whether China and the United States can manage their relationship and avoid war emerging from a 21st Century Thucydides Trap is arguably the most important question in international affairs today. Allison notes that 'it required huge, painful adjustments in attitudes and actions on the part not just of the challenger but also the challenged' (Allison, 2015). The rise of China also may influence international understanding of a broader question, which is whether modernisation and development must lead to democratisation? If China can demonstrate that it can successfully rise, without democratisation occurring, then the post-war rules-based international order will perhaps be fatally weakened. Other states may choose to adopt a China model of development – a 'Beijing consensus' – over a Western 'Washington consensus' to achieve wealth, prosperity and power (Liu, 2015, p. 14).

1. China's efforts towards a new Asian 'community of common destiny' and the significance of 'One Belt One Road' as part of China's grand strategy

To understand where, and in what context, China's rise is challenging the established rules-based international order, the fundamental question is: what does China want? What are China's national interests that drive its grand strategy and guide its foreign and defence policy? If there is an overall vision of China's future goals, it is with Xi Jinping's promotion of the 'China Dream'. The China Dream envisages the rejuvenation of China into a 'rich country with a strong army' and its return to its rightful place as a Great Power within Asia with global influence.

Achieving the China Dream would also align with China's centenary goals. The 2021 goal, for 100 years of the existence of the Chinese Communist Party (CCP), is to see China's GDP double and China achieve the goal of a 'moderately prosperous society'. The 2049 goal, for 100 years of the existence of the People's Republic of China, will be achieved when 'China will have developed into a modernised socialist country that is rich, strong, democratic, civilised and harmonious.' ('Xinhua Insight', 2016; see also Lam, 2013).

China's objectives include ensuring the legitimacy of the CCP and its right to a monopoly on political power, and 'this will come under question if it cannot maintain economic growth at a pace that stays ahead of public discontent' (Roy, 2013, p. 19). Also important to China is defending national sovereignty and territorial integrity, and ultimately securing China's status as a great power that allows it to reacquire regional pre-eminence and safeguard its interests abroad (US Department of Defense, 2016).

To achieve these goals, it is essential for China to build 'Comprehensive National Power' which Pillsbury (2005, p. 203) defines as:

> an evaluation of current and future strength [that] requires the inclusion of a variety of factors, such as territory, natural resources, military force, economic power, social conditions, domestic government, foreign policy and international influence.

The significance of Comprehensive National Power is that it indicates that China seeks to avoid relying on just one dimension of power. In this way, China seeks to avoid repeating the mistake of the Soviet Union, which relied almost exclusively on military power. China instead seeks to develop a broad-based sustainable foundation for national and international power and influence.

These broad sets of national objectives – the China Dream, building Comprehensive National Power and achieving the Centenary goals – guide China's grand strategy in Asia and beyond. That influences the development of military strategy and thus the modernisation and operational posture of the People's Liberation Army (PLA) (Allen, Blasko, & Corbett, 2016).[1] It is important to understand that success in realising the China Dream is crucial to maintaining CCP legitimacy and continued perpetuation of one-party rule. If the CCP legitimacy is 'the end', then 'the means' to achieve that end lies in achieving the China Dream through Chinese Grand Strategy (referred to in China as 'national strategy').

The language of the China Dream seems to suggest anything but a peaceful rise towards a harmonious world. In my view, it instead promotes the idea of China challenging US strategic primacy across Asia, and globally, through promotion of new international political, economic and security architectures and organisations.

Liu (2015) sums up his perspective of the China Dream and argues that China seeks to challenge the United States to become 'the champion among nations' which he defines as:

> the nation that, after the formation of the modern world order, within the global framework and within the competitive framework among nations, is the strongest, most prosperous nation . . . that sets the tone for their era and wields enormous influence all over the globe (p. 23).

Liu (2015, p. 29) identifies three types of champion nations:

- colonisers that practice imperialism;
- hegemons that do not seek to expand territory but do seek to control regions or the world to their benefit, giving the United States as an example;
- and guiding nations, that employ soft power through cooperative and interdependent development, and the spreading of cultural tradition and heritage – which he argues is the model China will follow.

Liu (2015, p. 31) further suggests that champion nations 'design the world. This design includes crafting the international power layout, establishing new codes of behaviour for nation-states, new international institutions, a new world order and new international systems'.

1 China's armed forces include the ground forces (PLA Army or PLAA); the PLA Navy (PLAN); the PLA Air Force (PLAAF); the PLA Rocket Forces (PLARF); and the PLA Strategic Support Force (PLASSF) as well as People's Armed Police, Militias and Reserve units.

This more assertive posture seems to be what China is pursuing under Xi Jinping, with China using both soft power and hard power to establish its relationship with its neighbours.

To this end, China is promoting political, economic and security structures that would challenge the dominance of existing regional arrangements established and led by the United States. Most significant is the Asian Infrastructure Investment Bank (AIIB) and the 'One Belt One Road' initiative. 'One Belt One Road' (commonly abbreviated to 'OBOR' or 'Silk Road Initiative') includes the 21st Century Maritime Silk Road announced in October 2013 and the land-based 'Silk Road Economic Belt'.

The Maritime Silk Road is an essential element of a China–ASEAN 'Community of Common Destiny' that would promote 'peace, development, cooperation and mutual benefit, and meets the common interests of the people of Asia' ('High Time', 2013). The concept emerged at a Chinese government conference on diplomatic work with neighbouring countries, held in Beijing from 24–25 October 2013.

In turn, this laid the basis for Xi's notion of an 'Asia-Pacific Dream' prominent during the recent 2014 APEC CEO Summit in Beijing on 9 November 2014. Both concepts eschew what it refers to as 'Cold War mentality' and 'zero-sum game' mindsets in favour of all-round security, cooperation and common security. The language refers to the US alliance system that China perceives to be designed to contain China. This has become apparent in China's calls for new Chinese-led Asian security governance models with 'Asian Features' and its proclamation at the 2014 and 2016 Conference on Interaction and Confidence Building Measures in Asia (CICA) that the US rebalancing strategy (or pivot) to Asia was a failure. Xi reiterated this approach at the recent 2016 Conference on Interaction and Confidence Building Measures (CICA), stating:

> we should persist with or promote the Asian way that has been formed over a long period and is based on mutual respect, consensus building, and mutual concern. With this as foundation, we should take gradual steps in building a new regional security cooperation structure that complements Asia's unique traits (quoted in Prasad, 2015; see also Aneja, 2016 and Zhongsheng, 2016).

Chinese efforts to promote an Asian security governance model that challenges existing US-led structures is part of a process of restoring China to what it perceives to be its rightful place in Asia. Thomas Mahnken (2011) suggests three developments in this process that appear to be underway, noting:

> First, one would expect the Chinese to engage in behaviour designed to increase foreign perceptions of China as a regional and perhaps global leader . . . China's naval expansion [can be seen] in the same light as a concrete expression of China's international ambitions . . . second, one would expect the Chinese to be particularly sensitive to events they perceive as affronts to their dignity as individuals and as nations . . . third, one would expect the Chinese to react strongly to activity by powerful states on their periphery whether these states are actually encroaching or no (pp. 11–13).

China is determined to overturn the legacy of the century of humiliation, and 'make China rich and powerful and to regain the nation's former status as a "great power" that controls its own fate' (Lampton, 2008. p. 25). Henry Kissinger (2012) explains that the:

> 'return' of China, rather than a 'rise' is important to understand as the best way to characterize China's role in Asia, arguing that "China does not see itself as a rising, but

> a returning power. It does not view the prospect of a strong China exercising influence in economic, cultural, political, and military affairs as an unnatural challenge to world order – but rather as a return to a normal state of affairs (p. 546).

If Kissinger is correct, China may not perceive any risk in promoting its own perception of what a future China-centric regional order should be at the expense of the existing US-led regional order. The promotion of a China-led Asia based around the Community of Common Destiny seems to suggest this is exactly what Beijing has in mind. Erickson (2013) suggests that China's return to Great Power status would inevitably see a Chinese sphere of strategic influence emerge over much of the East Asia region. In his view, China seeks:

> to address historical grievances and rise again as a great power that commands neighbours deference, Beijing seeks to carve out from the global commons the Yellow, East and South China Seas and the airspace above them as a zone of exceptionalism within which existing global legal, security and resource management norms are subordinated to its national interests (Erickson, 2013).

Such a development would be seen as a clear and direct challenge to the established international order that could only be achieved through the displacement of the United States in Asia as the dominant power. Australian defence academic Dupont (2014) argues that such a challenge would represent a growing risk of strategic competition between China and the United States over which is the dominant power in Asia, and thus which version of the international order emerges. Specifically, Dupont (2014) has suggested as follows:

> China's re-emergence poses strategic challenges of a complexity and order of magnitude not previously experienced by the US-led international order . . . China's view of what the new Asian order should look like is clearly at variance with that of the US. Beijing makes no secret of its desire to use its newly acquired power to change the rules of the game and replace the US as the pre-eminent state in Asia. Whether China's ambitions extend to being the dominant global power will depend on how successfully it can compete with the US in Asia and to what extent the balance of economic and military power shifts in its favour in coming decades.

Former Australian Prime Minister and Foreign Minister Kevin Rudd has also weighed in on the question of China's ambitions and the implications for Asia emerging from them. Rudd (2013) suggests that 'if China begins to replace the American fulcrum, the legitimate question from us all is what sort of alternative regional and global order would China seek to construct in its place'.

Rudd's observation is critical. It is unknowable what a 'Pax Sinica' across Asia would mean in the absence of a 'Pax Americana'. This has implications for both regional security and the future of a rules-based international order. This is because the rules would be re-written by China, Russia and others. As was the case in 1945, the interests of the powers that write the rules would be reflected in the outcomes. The transition from one order to another could be violent, messy and prone to war – for it seems doubtful that the United States would willingly cede its influence. An understanding of what a Pax Sinica could look like may be determined by its actions, and perhaps most relevant therefore are China's actions in the South China Sea.

2. China and the South China Sea

A key aspect of the rules-based international order is the importance of international commerce and access to global commons including the sea, space and cyberspace. In particular, the importance of freedom of navigation on the high seas and international airspace and adherence to rules established under the United Nations Convention on the Law of the Sea (UNCLOS) are seen as central to maintaining stability and security. In this regard, China's actions in the South China Sea are significant. China has used 'grey area phenomena' – non-military assets such as fishing fleets and maritime security agency vessels – to harass and coerce littoral states over disputed territorial claims and more recently has begun large-scale land reclamation of disputed territories, with devastating environmental consequences. China is doing this to promote its internationally disputed claim to the self-declared 'nine-dash line' around the entirety of the South China Sea. These actions speak directly to concerns over what is a very clear challenge to the established rules-based order through overt territorial expansion. Evans (2016) argues in relation to China's actions that 'whatever else is going on in the South China Sea, it is not respect for a rules-based global order'.

China's approach to the South China Sea dispute is problematic because it has not clearly defined the scope of its maritime claims. China's self-declared 'nine-dash line' encompasses approximately two million square kilometres of maritime space, including waters, islands and resources. China claims it has 'indisputable sovereignty over the islands in the South China Sea and the adjacent waters and enjoys sovereign rights and jurisdiction over the relevant waters as well as the seabed and subsoil thereof' (US Department of Defense, 2016, p. 8; see also US Department of State, 2014). In effect, China's declared claim within its nine-dash line covers virtually the entirety of the South China Sea, and the language used by Chinese officials does not make it clear whether China is only claiming islands and adjoining waters or the entirety of the South China Sea within the nine-dash line (Gady, 2015; see also Evans, 2013).

The Chinese approach to managing territorial disputes in the South China Sea only reinforces a perception that China is not content to rise within the existing rules-based international order. Instead, it seeks to challenge this order through using military and quasi-military force to change the status quo over time. This is done using carefully calibrated actions that are designed to remain below the threshold that would trigger a military response, in a strategy often referred to in the West as 'salami slicing' (Haddick, 2014, pp. 78–80).

In a major analysis from the Lowy Institute, Townshend and Medcalf (2016) argue that China is seeking to advance its strategic objective of establishing a 'new status quo' in the East and South China Seas, which reshapes Asia's maritime order but in a manner that tactically reduces the risk of military clashes: They suggest (pp. 11–12):

> Beijing is continuing to advance its expansive strategic interests in more passive assertive ways. This has involved island building and militarisation of those islands, the creation of new spheres of military authority, the establishment of an air defence identification zone [in the East China Sea], and the expansion of 'grey-zone' military and coastguard activities. Over the past two years, these tactically non-confrontational but strategically assertive measures have assumed a central in Beijing's efforts to reshape Asia's maritime order.

In particular, land reclamation through island building on top of disputed territories controlled by China – and the subsequent militarisation of these new islands through construction of ports, airbases and the deployment of military forces – is now at the forefront of China's 'passive assertive' approach to asserting its control of the South China Sea. Although other claimant states – Vietnam, Malaysia, the Philippines and Taiwan – have expanded held territories in the Spratly chain within the South China Sea – it is China that has undertaken the greatest amount of land reclamation in the shortest period and is now equipping its new territory with facilities and features to support air and naval forces. This is in spite of a pledge by President Xi Jinping that China would not be engaging in militarisation of the South China Sea disputed territories (Watkins, 2015; Jennings, 2016).

The next key test of China's intentions regarding the South China Sea – and its intentions regarding acceptance or otherwise of the rules-based global order – will be its response to the handing down of the ruling of the UN Permanent Court of Arbitration (PCA) in the Hague in the case of *The Republic of Philippines v The People's Republic of China*. This case was lodged by the Philippines government on 22 January 2013 under Annex VII of UNCLOS 'with respect to the dispute with China over the maritime jurisdiction of the Philippines in the West Philippine Sea [South China Sea]'.

The decision was handed down in mid-2016. As expected, it went against China and in favour of the Philippines, upholding the legality and primacy of UNCLOS in determining the parties' maritime rights and asserting established procedures under Part XV of UNCLOS in this regard. This could seriously undermine China's influence over South China Sea stakeholders; domestically, it could challenge the credibility of its political leadership (Batongbacal, 2015). The finding in favour of the Philippines opens a Pandora's box for other claimants to take China to the PCA on its South China Sea claim, using the proven legal approach established by the current case – it creates a procedural roadmap that Vietnam, Malaysia and others may progress down in the future and weakens China's 'indisputable sovereignty' claim overall (Hayton, 2014, pp. 113–14).

China is trapped in this outcome. It could have chosen to abide by the ruling, claiming that it would act upon its obligations under UNCLOS and deflecting concerns over its strategic intentions in terms of challenging the rules-based order. However, it has rejected the ruling – unsurprisingly so, given that the Chinese Communist Party (CCP) could hardly reverse years of megaphone diplomacy that has proclaimed 'indisputable sovereignty over the islands in the South China Sea and the adjacent waters and sovereign rights and jurisdiction over the relevant waters as well as the seabed and subsoil thereof' (*Permanent Mission of the People's Republic of China*, 2009). Otherwise, this would be a huge loss of face for China and a massive blow to the credibility of the CCP in the eyes of the Chinese people. This is because of the strong nationalist message underpinning China's claim to the nine-dash line that encompasses the South China Sea. Furthermore, to cede its claim on the South China Sea would directly undermine China's ability to pursue development of, and ultimately sustain, a '21st Century Maritime Silk Road' as part of a 'One Belt One Road' initiative. This, in turn, underpins Xi Jinping's 'China Dream' of a rejuvenated China that has a rich economy and a strong army, and which is well placed to achieve centennial goals in 2021 and 2049. These milestones are based around centenary goals.

The South China Sea is vital to China, not only because of its huge resource wealth in terms of oil, natural gas, minerals and fisheries, but also because of its vital geostrategic location (see e.g., Davis, 2016). As Kaplan (2014, pp. 9–10) states:

> The South China Sea functions as the throat of the Western Pacific and Indian oceans – the mass of connective economic tissue where global sea routes coalesce. Here is the

> heart of Eurasia's navigable rimland, punctuated by the Malacca, Sunda, Lombok and Makassar straits. More than half of the world's annual merchant fleet tonnage passes through these choke points, and a third of all maritime traffic worldwide. The oil transported through the Malacca Strait from the Indian Ocean, en-route to East Asia through the South China Sea, is triple that amount that passes through the Suez Canal and fifteen times the amount that transits the Panama Canal. Roughly two thirds of South Korea's energy supplies, nearly 60 percent of Japan's and Taiwan's energy supplies, and 80 percent of China's crude oil imports come through the South China Sea. Whereas in the Persian Gulf only energy is transported, in the South China Sea you have energy, finished goods and unfinished goods.

The geostrategic importance of the South China Sea, as highlighted by Kaplan (2014), is accentuated because the 21st Century Maritime Silk Road *starts and finishes* in the waters in which China is reclaiming land and militarising these features. Along the 21st Century Maritime Silk Road, Chinese investment in developing states' economies obviously is a 'win-win' for these states, in particular because Chinese investment is on an unconditional basis in terms of that state's willingness, or otherwise, to engage in political reform. But it is also a 'win-win' for China in that by investing in the economies of developing states – and seeking to promote interdependent development – the recipient's economic well-being and future is ever-more tied to China's continued rise.

China will also gain access to new markets for trade and providers for critical resources. Capital and resource inflow along the 21st Century Maritime Silk Road helps to sustain the accumulation of comprehensive national power that is the basis of the China Dream. By extension, the continuing political legitimacy of the Chinese Communist Party in the eyes of the Chinese people is secured. Although Chinese government rhetoric emphasises the 'outward' aspects of 'win-win' with regard to the 21st Century Maritime Silk Road (and the 'Silk Road Economic Belt' that runs through Eurasia into Europe overland), the unstated inward 'win-win' benefits highlight the fact that all roads lead to Beijing. In short, the 21st Century Maritime Silk Road begins and ends in the South China Sea, and specifically, key ports along China's eastern seaboard.

Accepting a legal constraint on its ability to use the South China Sea as it sees fit as a result of accepting the PCA ruling would, therefore, weaken the potential for China to shape the security and foreign policies of recipient states along the 21st Century Maritime Silk Road. It would weaken its ability to shape new security structures that focus on what President Xi Jinping stated in 2014 should be an 'Asia for Asians' approach that would ultimately replace the US-led 'hub and spokes' security arrangements in Asia (Jakobson, 2016).

By refusing to recognise the finding of the PCA on the South China Sea, China has sent a strong signal that it is not prepared to accept international legal outcomes ('China warns ASEAN', 2016). The adverse result has been an 'embarrassing public rebuke,' and 'any attempt to enforce the ruling [would be interpreted to be a threat] to Chinese territorial integrity, a core national interest, and will likely face intense domestic pressure to reassert their claims [in the South China Sea]' (Klipper, 2016).

China's options might include declaring an Air Defence Identification Zone (ADIZ) as it has done in the East China Sea (Ministry of Foreign Affairs of the People's Republic of China, 2015); further militarising disputed territory including existing reclaimed islands; or potentially militarising the Scarborough Shoal, near the Philippines ('China reiterates non-acceptance', 2015; Ide & Dasgupta, 2016).

Further, the building of large air bases with long runways on Mischief Reef and Fiery Cross already allow China to forward deploy PLA Air Force (PLAAF) combat aircraft to these reclaimed territories, and the militarisation of Scarborough Shoal, 225 kilometres from Manila, would be a strong signal of 'push-back' from Beijing and would also strengthen China's efforts to undertake dissuasion against the Philippines pressing for further measures through legal means. It would strengthen China's ability to control the Babuyan Channel between the Philippines and Taiwan and enhance its ability to undertake 'Offshore Active Defence', which is the PLA's formal military strategy for naval and air operations within the First and Second Island Chains. This is becoming even more relevant given the growing importance of the South China Sea as a potential deep-water bastion for PLA Navy (PLAN) Type 094 *Jin* class ballistic missile submarines (SSBNs), which form the 'secure second strike' capability of China's small strategic nuclear forces. Militarising existing reclaimed territories, and building new bases on Scarborough Shoal, contributes to the option of declaring an ADIZ that would also reinforce China's declaration of 'indisputable sovereignty'. This is because it raises the stakes in a crisis to a level that China's neighbours in the South China Sea would not be prepared to match in counter-responses, and yet still remains below a threshold that would generate a US military response. It contributes towards the steady salami-slicing strategy mentioned earlier that is challenging the established status quo – and weakening the existing rules-based international order. Townshend and Medcalf (2016, p. 13) sum up the military importance of Chinese moves to militarise the disputed islands:

> These strategic outposts will permit Beijing to enhance it power projection capabilities and establish anti-access zones right across the South China Sea. China will be able to extend the range and endurance of military and coastguard patrols; forward deploy air force, naval and coastguard assets; and conduct aerial patrols over disputed waters, possibly in support of a future ADIZ. A combination of ground-based radars, air defences, anti-ship missiles, and forward-based fighters would facilitate the development of 'mini denial zones' extending southwards from Hainan Island. Furthermore, there is speculation these outposts could assist China to lay a network of hydrophone arrays to detect US and other submarines, helping Beijing to establish a sanctuary [i.e. a Bastion] for its nuclear-armed submarines.

Therefore, the stakes are very high in the South China Sea. Allowing China to 'salami slice' the status quo and establish *de facto* if not *de jure* control over the islands, maritime spaces and resources within its self-declared nine-dash line not only weakens the established rules-based order and reinforces a message that 'might does make right' – which other states will take on board – but also poses real and significant military risks for the United States, Japan and its other allies in the Asia-Pacific, including Australia (Davis, 2015).

3. Conclusion

Considering and exploring the future security and strategic outlook is complex and always uncertain, and no one can accurately predict the future. China's rise, which commenced shortly after the end of the Maoist period with Deng's four modernisations in the late 1980s, continues to astound the world in its sheer pace and scope. China has emerged from a backward, insular state to be a global power in every sense and looks set to challenge the United States for eventual global leadership, certainly in economic terms, and potentially in political and security terms as well.

As China continues to rise, its actions on the international stage and, in particular, in the Asia-Pacific region, will shape perceptions of its intent. There is a disconnect between Chinese rhetoric of peaceful rise and 'win-win' cooperation on the one hand, and its actions in the South China Sea, for example. China is very clearly no longer 'biding its time and hiding its strength' but is strongly asserting its power and interests in a manner that is undermining regional security and causing growing apprehension on the part of China's neighbours.

China's unwillingness to abide by international norms of behaviour and recognise the rights of other states under UNCLOS, and most recently, its construction of artificial islands on disputed territories, does not bode well for confidence that China will rise peacefully within the established rules-based international order. Further, the refusal to accept the Permanent Court of Arbitration ruling on the South China Sea dispute seems likely to be the focal point for this emerging strategic competition that drives the Thucydides Trap.

More broadly, China seems to be establishing new structures in political, economic and security dimensions that would seek to challenge the role and rationale of existing architecture. In so doing, China directly challenges US influence in Asia. As noted earlier by Liu (2015, p. 14), China seeks to be a Champion state but would prefer to be a 'guiding nation' that reshapes the international order through soft power, political influence and economic dependence. Clearly, China will use hard power when necessary to defend its interests, but it would prefer to 'win without fighting', and follow the advice of Sun Tzu.

So what of the 'centre' – and can it hold? This chapter has focused on only one (albeit very significant) challenge to the rules-based international order. Yeats's poem, written in 1919, was written in a post-war world that was coming to terms with the horrors of the Great War. The key issue in 2016, as the rules-based international order faces not just a rising China, but also a resurgent Russia, and rapidly spiralling violence and instability across the Middle East, is whether the current rules-based order is able to bring a sense of equilibrium and stability or whether it, too, will see mere anarchy loosed upon the world.

The United States, the European Union and key US allies in Asia, such as Japan, Australia and South Korea, have difficult choices to make in how they manage a rising China or a resurgent Russia. In Asia, it is China's rise and its regional posture and behaviour that is the overwhelming question that must be addressed. It seems unlikely that the United States and its allies will simply cede strategic space to a rising China, and Allison's (2015) idea of the Thucydides Trap raises the prospect of the potential for competition to turn into conflict if both sides are unwilling to come to a settlement. Is then the prospect of things falling apart, and a blood-dimmed tide loosed upon the 21st Century, in much the same way that occurred in the last century? The nature of international affairs is inherently realist, though not exclusively so. The United States will not willingly cede strategic space – in political, economic or military spheres – to a rising China. Nor is a rising China likely to surrender its China Dream. Liu Mingfu notes that 'In the 21st Century China and the United States will square off and fight to become a champion among nations'. As unappealing as that vision is, Liu (2015) is probably correct, and Yeats's nightmare will be revisited yet again.

References

Allen, K., Blasko, D., & Corbett, J. (2016, February 4). The PLA's new organisational structure: What is known, unknown and speculation (Part 1). *China Brief*, *16*(3). Retrieved from http://www.jamestown.org/uploads/media/Updated_The_PLA_s_New_Organizational_Structure_-_What_is_Known__Unknown_and_Speculation_Parts_1_and_2.pdf.

Allison, G. (2015, September 24). The Thucydides Trap: Are the U.S. and China headed for war? *The Atlantic*. Retrieved from http://www.theatlantic.com/international/archive/2015/09/united-states-china-war-thucydides-trap/406756/.
Aneja, A. (2016, May 3). Beijing unveils doctrine to counter US Pivot. *The Hindu*. Retrieved from http://www.thehindu.com/news/international/china-unveils-new-security-doctrine-to-counter-us-pivot-to-asia/article8547554.ece.
Batongbacal, J. (2015). *Implications of the Philippines v China award on jurisdiction* (online: Asia-Maritime Transparency Initiative). Retrieved from http://amti.csis.org/implications-of-the-philippines-v-china-award-on-jurisdiction/.
Bell, C. (2007). *The end of the Vasco da Gama era – The next landscape of world politics* (Lowly Institute Paper No. 21). Sydney: Lowy Institute for International Policy.
Bird, M. (2014, October 9). China overtook the US as the world's largest economy. *Business Insider Australia*. Retrieved from http://www.businessinsider.com.au/china-overtakes-us-as-worlds-largest-economy-2014-10.
China's initiatives on building Silk Road Economic Belt and 21st Century Maritime Silk Road. (2014). *Xinhua*. Retrieved from http://www.xinhuanet.com/english/special/silkroad/.
China reiterates non-acceptance of South China Sea arbitration. (2015, December 1). *Xinhua*. Retrieved from http://news.xinhuanet.com/english/2015-12/01/c_134874385.htm.
China warns ASEAN against statement on S. China Sea arbitration (2016, May 3). *Kyodo News*. Retrieved from http://news.abs-cbn.com/global-filipino/world/05/03/16/china-warns-asean-against-statement-on-s-china-sea-arbitration.
Davis, M. (2015, November 11). China's militarisation of the South China Sea and Australian defence policy. *The Strategist*. Retrieved from http://www.aspistrategist.org.au/chinas-militarisation-of-the-south-china-sea-and-australian-defence-policy.
Davis, M. (2016, March 21). Seeing the dragon on our doorstep (Part 1). *The Strategist*. Retrieved from http://www.aspistrategist.org.au/seeing-the-dragon-on-our-doorstep-part-1/.
Dupont, A. (2014, November 29). On the brink of a new cold world. *The Australian*. Retrieved from http://www.lowyinstitute.org/publications/brink-new-cold-world.
Erickson, A. S. (2013, December 11). China's naval modernization: Implications and recommendations. *U.S. Asia-Pacific Strategic Considerations Related to PLA Naval Forces: Hearing before the House Armed Services Committee Seapower and Projection Forces Subcommittee*. Washington.
Erickson, A. S. (2016, May 19). Steaming ahead – Course uncertain: China's military shipbuilding industry. *The National Interest*. Retrieved from http://www.andrewerickson.com/2016/05/steaming-ahead-course-uncertain-chinas-military-shipbuilding-industry/.
Erickson, A. S., & Strange, A. M. (2015) *Six Years at sea . . . and counting: Gulf of Aden anti-Piracy and China's maritime commons presence*. Washington DC: The Jamestown Foundation.
Evans, G. (2013, October 2). The South China Sea and Australia's regional security environment. *The Strategist*. Retrieved from http://www.aspistrategist.org.au/the-south-china-sea-and-australias-regional-security-environment/.
Evans, G. (2016, April 2016). Playing by the rules in Asia. *The Strategist*. Retrieved from http://www.aspistrategist.org.au/playing-by-the-rules-in-asia/.
Fukuyama, F. (1992). *The end of history and the last man*. New York, US: Avon Books Inc.
Gady, F. S. (2015, September 16). Chinese admiral: South China Sea 'belongs to China'. *The Diplomat*. Retrieved from http://thediplomat.com/2015/09/chinese-admiral-south-china-sea-belongs-to-china/.
Haddick, R. (2014). *Fire on the water – China, America and the future of the Pacific*. Annapolis, US: Naval Institute Press.
Hayton, B. (2014). *The South China Sea – The struggle for power in Asia*. New Haven, US: Yale University Press.
High time to build new maritime Silk Road (2013, October 4). *Xinhua*. Retrieved from http://news.xinhuanet.com/english/indepth/2013-10/04/c_132771084.htm

Ide, W., & Dasgupta, S. (2016, May 6). Beijing warns critics over South China Sea dispute. *Voice of America*. Retrieved from http://www.voanews.com/content/beijing-warns-critics-over-south-china-sea-dispute/3318147.html.

International Institute for Strategic Studies. (2016). Chapter Four: The militarisation of the South China Sea. *Asia-Pacific Regional Security Assessment 2016: Key developments and trends*. London: IISS.

Jakobson, L. (2016). Reflections from China on Xi Jinping's 'Asia for Asians'. *Asian Politics and Policy, 8*(1), 219–23.

Jennings, P. (2016). Heading for confrontation: China's Paracel play. *The Strategist*. Retrieved from http://www.aspistrategist.org.au/heading-for-confrontation-chinas-paracel-play/.

Kaplan, R. (2014). *Asia's cauldron – The South China Sea and the end of a stable Pacific*. New York: Random House.

Kissinger, H. (2012). *On China*. New York, New York: Penguin Books.

Klipper, R. (2016). Why China might seek to occupy Scarborough Shoal. *The Diplomat*. Retrieved from http://thediplomat.com/2016/03/why-china-might-seek-to-occupy-scarborough-shoal/.

Lam, W. (2013). Fierce debate erupts over the meaning of the 'China Dream'. *China Brief, 13*(9), 3–6.

Lampton, D. (2008). *The three faces of Chinese power: Might, money and minds*. Berkeley: University of California Press.

Liu, M. (2015). *The China dream – Great power thinking and strategic posture in the post-American era*. New York: CN Times.

Mahnken, T. (2011). *Secrecy and strategem: Understanding chinese strategic sulture*. Sydney: Lowy Institute.

Ministry of Foreign Affairs of the People's Republic of China (2015, May 7). [Press conference]. Retrieved from http://www.fmprc.gov.cn/mfa_eng/xwfw_665399/s2510_665401/2511_665403/t1261660.shtml.

Permanent Mission of the People's Republic of China. Notes Verbales CML/17/2009 and CML/18/2009 (7 May 2009) Retrieved from http://www.un.org/Depts/los/clcs_new/submissions_files/mysvnm33_09/chn_2009re_mys_vnm_e.pdf and http://www.un.org/Depts/los/clcs_new/submissions_files/vnm37_09/chn_2009re_vnm.pdf.

Philips, M. (2008, September 19). The end of the end of history. *Newsweek*. Retrieved from http://www.newsweek.com/fukuyama-end-end-history-88537.

Pillsbury, M. (2005). *China debates the future security environment*. Honolulu: University Press of the Pacific.

Prasad, N. (2015, December 4). Understanding China's foreign policy perspective. *East Asia Forum*. Retrieved from http://www.eastasiaforum.org/2015/12/04/understanding-chinas-foreign-policy-perspective-2/.

Redbeard, R. (1890). *Might is right*. United States: Auditorium Press.

Roy, D. (2013). *Return of the dragon – Rising China and regional security*. New York: Columbia University Press.

Royal Institute of International Affairs (2015). *Challenges to the rules-based international order*. Background paper, London Conference 2015. Retrieved from https://www.chathamhouse.org/london-conference-2015/background-papers/challenges-to-rules-based-international-order.

Rudd, K. (2013, December 16). *China's impact on regional and global order*. Alastair Buchan Memorial Lecture, Arundel House, London. Retrieved from https://www.iiss.org/en/events/events/archive/2013-5126/december-c771/rudd-buchan-083c.

Scott, E. (2015). A nuclear deal with Chinese characteristics: China's role in the P5+ talks with Iran. *China Brief, 15*(14). Retrieved from http://www.jamestown.org/chinabrief/.

Stewart, C. (2016, June 4). Rising Threat in the Spratlys. *The Weekend Australian*, p. 20.

The Republic of Philippines v The People's Republic of China (Award) (Permanent Court of Arbitration, 22 January 2013) Retrieved from http://www.pcacases.com/web/view/7.

Townshend, A., & Medcalf, R. (2016). *Shifting Waters: China's new passive assertiveness in Asian maritime security*. Sydney: Lowy Institute.
US Department of Defense (2015, August 21). *Asia-Pacific maritime security strategy: Achieving national security objectives in a changing environment*. Retrieved from http://www.defense.gov/Portals/1/Documents/pubs/NDAA%20A-P_Maritime_SecuritY_Strategy-08142015-1300-FINALFORMAT.PDF.
US Department of Defense (2016). *Annual report to Congress: Military and security developments involving the People's Republic of China*. Retrieved from http://www.defense.gov/Portals/1/Documents/pubs/2016%20China%20Military%20Power%20Report.pdf.
US Department of State (2014, December 5). *China: Maritime claims in the South China Sea* (Limits in the Seas No. 143). Retrieved from http://www.state.gov/e/oes/ocns/opa/c16065.htm.
Watkins, D. (2015, October 27). What has China been building in the South China Sea. *New York Times*. Retrieved from http://www.nytimes.com/interactive/2015/07/30/world/asia/what-china-has-been-building-in-the-south-china-sea.html?_r=1.
Xinhua Insight: CPC's new governance theories steer China on fast track to "two centenary goals" (2016). *Xinhua*. Retrieved from http://news.xinhuanet.com/english/2016-05/04/c_135334465.htm.
Zakaria, F. (2011). *The Post-American world and the rise of the rest*. London: Penguin.
Zhongsheng. (2016, April 28). CICA holds the key to security issues. *People's Daily Online*. Retrieved from http://en.people.cn/n3/2016/0428/c98649-9050891.html.

Part II

Case Studies

Citizens

6 Nationality and Extraterritoriality

A Disordered Paradigm?

Danielle Ireland-Piper

The principles of extraterritorial jurisdiction under international law allow States to assert legal authority over their citizens abroad on the basis of nationality. Conceptions of nationality, however, have become blurred. Individuals are more mobile than ever before. They can live and work in different parts of the world. They may have a connection to more than one State. Similarly, serious crimes, such as acts of terrorism, need know no national boundaries, and armies can attract foreign recruits. Some States, such as Australia and the United Kingdom, have responded to their citizens serving as foreign recruits by legislating to allow for the revocation of citizenship. This has produced a burgeoning literature on citizenship-stripping in an age of heightened security risks. However, none of the analysis has considered the questions from the perspective of the principles of extraterritorial jurisdiction and the power of the State over its nationals when abroad. This chapter reconsiders the legitimacy of States relying on assertions of extraterritorial jurisdiction to deprive citizenship. The chapter argues that it is an abuse of rights. If a State can assert its rights over citizens abroad, then a State is violating its responsibilities for its nationals under international law by removing those citizens from its realm of responsibility.

"Take care . . . how your present decrees may affect posterity" (Julius Caesar, objecting to illegal execution of captured conspirators, 63 B.C.)

The principles of extraterritorial criminal jurisdiction allow States to assert authority over conduct occurring extraterritorially on the basis of nationality. Conceptions of nationality, however, have become blurred. Individuals are more mobile than ever before. They can live and work in different parts of the world. They may even have a connection to more than one State. Serious crimes, such as acts of terrorism, need know no national boundaries, and armies can attract foreign recruits. Some States, such as Australia and the United Kingdom, have reacted to this by enacting legislation that allows for the revocation of citizenship when particular crimes are committed extraterritorially. Such legislation has existed in various forms for some time, but recent amendments have extended its reach. This has produced a burgeoning literature on citizenship-stripping in an age of heightened security risks. None of the analysis to date, however, has considered the issue from the perspective of the principles of extraterritorial jurisdiction and the power of the State over its nationals when abroad. This chapter re-examines whether States can deprive citizenship by relying on principles of extraterritoriality. It argues that, in some circumstances, depriving citizenship as a reaction to the commission of criminal offences is an abuse of rights. If a State can assert its rights over its citizens abroad, then a State is acting inconsistently with its responsibilities for its nationals under international law by removing those citizens from its realm of responsibility when outside the State.

The link between notions of citizenship and nationality, on the one hand, and exercises of extraterritorial criminal jurisdiction, on the other, is the central concern of this chapter. To interrogate this link, this chapter will proceed as follows. First, it will introduce the 'nationality' principle of jurisdiction under international law and the relationship between extraterritoriality and the abuse of rights doctrine. Second, it will identify and explain the position of citizenship under international law, particularly as it relates to revocation of citizenship. Third, it will critically analyse the legitimacy of domestic legislation purporting to strip citizens of their citizenship. Specifically, the chapter will ask: if a State has the authority to exercise extraterritoriality over the conduct of its nationals, does it have a responsibility to exercise that authority in particular circumstances, such as when the national perpetrates a serious crime overseas? If so, does the State unlawfully abdicate this responsibility by revoking citizenship?

1. The 'nationality' principle of jurisdiction: an overview

At the emergence of the sovereign nation State, jurisdiction was generally understood by reference to geographical borders (Ireland-Piper, 2013; Ireland-Piper, 2017). Assertions by States of jurisdiction over crimes occurring outside their territory, such as piracy or treason, occurred as an exception to the rule (Ireland-Piper, 2013). This is particularly the case in common-law jurisdictions.[1] The late twentieth and early twenty-first centuries, however, have seen an increase in transnational organised crime (see, for example, Williams and Savona, 1996; Rollins, 2010; Ireland-Piper, 2013). States became interested in criminal activity occurring in other parts of the world, either because of the unwillingness or inability of the other State to prosecute serious crime, or because it served some sort of domestic or foreign political agenda. In response, the international community developed treaties that either called for, or permitted, extraterritorial application of certain types of domestic criminal offences.

Under customary international law, States generally derive authority to exercise jurisdiction from three main principles: territoriality, universality and nationality (Ryngaert, 2008; Triggs, 2006, 345; Zerk, 2010; Chehtman, 2010). The territoriality principle may be invoked where conduct either takes place within a nation's borders (subjective territoriality) or the effects of the conduct are felt within the borders (objective territoriality) (Ryngaert, 2008; Triggs, 2006, p. 345; Zerk, 2010; Chehtman, 2010). The universality principle is reserved for conduct constituting an international crime, such as piracy, genocide and crimes against humanity (Chehtman, 2010, p. 67). Of particular relevance to this chapter, the nationality principle can provide a basis for jurisdiction where a State's citizen is either a victim (passive nationality) or a perpetrator (active nationality). The existence and use of the passive nationality principle is particularly controversial. As a ground of criminal jurisdiction, some have described it as the 'most contested in contemporary international

1 Assertions of extraterritoriality in the common-law world tend to be *ad-hoc*. By contrast, criminal codes in European jurisdictions such as Switzerland, France, Spain and Belgium often have a generic extraterritorial reach over nationals.

law' (Chehtman, 2010, p. 67). For this reason, the focus in this chapter is on the active nationality principle.[2]

Civil-law jurisdictions rely on the active nationality principle to a 'far greater extent' (Akehurst, 1972–1973, p. 152) than common-law countries. For example, countries such as India, the United States, Canada and Australia tend to assert nationality jurisdiction on an *ad-hoc* basis and for specific offences, such as money laundering, terrorist acts, child sexual offences, migrant smuggling, and offences relating to national security. This means that not all criminal offences in those jurisdictions will have extraterritorial effect, and they are generally presumed not to unless otherwise specified. By contrast, European countries such as France and Switzerland have a broader range of offences with extraterritorial reach (eg, Penal Code (France), 1810, arts 113–6, 113–7). Either way, it is an accepted legal principle that a State is entitled to regulate the extraterritorial conduct, including the extraterritorial criminal conduct, of its nationals.

The question that follows is whether a State has a *responsibility* to regulate the extraterritorial criminal conduct of its nationals, particularly when such conduct may constitute a serious international or transnational crime? If so, is revocation of citizenship an abdication of that responsibility? Given that all rights at international law come with corresponding responsibilities and an exercise of a right at international law in a manner inconsistent with those responsibilities may be an 'abuse of rights' (Ireland-Piper, 2013; Ireland-Piper, 2017), this chapter submits that the answer to both questions, at least in the specific context of serious transnational crime, is yes.

To explain this submission, the chapter now revisits the principles of citizenship under international law in the specific context of citizenship revocation.

2. Citizenship under international law: revocation

Citizenship matters. As Kim Rubenstein has observed, citizenship is a 'legal, political and social construct that has domestic and international consequences' (Rubenstein, 2007, p. 88). This then begs the question – how are questions of nationality to be understood as a question of law and policy? Nationality is not a fixed concept. As Manley Hudson and Richard Flournoy observe, the term nationality has

> no positive, immutable meaning. On the contrary its meaning and import have changed with the changing character of States . . . it may acquire a new meaning in the future as the result of further changes in the character of human society, and developments in international organisation. Nationality always connotes, however, membership of some kind in the society of a state or nation (The American Society of International Law, 1929, p. 21).

Mutability aside, the concept of nationality is, in many ways, an 'indispensible legal concept' (Sloane, 2009, p. 1), because, as Robert Sloane (2009, p. 1) observes, it serves to mediate the 'derivative rights and obligations of individuals relative to States in diverse areas,

2 For the sake of completeness, international law also recognises a 'protective principle' which permits a State to assert jurisdiction over foreign conduct which threatens national security (Triggs, 2006, 356-7; Zerk, 2010, 19; Krizek, 1988) and the more controversial 'effects principle' which supports jurisdictional claims over extraterritorial conduct if the effects are felt within a territory (Parrish, 2008, 1470).

including diplomatic protection, war, state responsibility, jurisdiction, and extradition'. International law is generally understood by the academic community as being neutral toward a *grant* of nationality, provided the granting State does not breach certain international obligations, such as those under the *1961 Convention on the Reduction of Statelessness* ('*1961 Convention*'). For that reason, this chapter seeks to revisit the principles of citizenship and nationality under international law through the lens of revocation.

This chapter uses the terms 'nationality' and 'citizenship' interchangeably. Technically, they differ, in the sense that 'nationality' is more often used in the context of international law sense, and citizenship in domestic law. As Helene Lambert, however, observes, 'no real difference exists in public international law between 'nationality' and 'citizenship'' (Lambert, 2014, p. 3). Similarly, Kim Rubenstein, although acknowledging a technical legal difference, points out that 'they are generalisable concepts' (Rubenstein, 2007, p. 89).

Article 1 of the 1930 Hague *Convention on Certain Questions Relating to the Conflict of Nationality Laws* (League of Nations, 1930) provides:

> It is for each State to determine under its own law who are its nationals. This law shall be recognised by other States in so far as it is consistent with international conventions, international custom and the principles of law generally recognised with regard to nationality.

As Sloane observes, 'while nationality serves vital roles in international law . . . by far the most significant legal consequences of nationality remain internal' (Sloane, 2009, p. 2). Nonetheless, international law is not devoid of content on nationality and citizenship. In asserting a grant of nationality as against another state, for example, international law requires that a 'genuine connection' exist (*Nottebohm Case,* 1955), and, as I have argued previously, such a grant should not constitute an abuse of rights (Ireland-Piper, 2013; see also Sloane, 2009). Nationality has been loosely defined by the ICJ in the *Nottebohm Case* as a legal bond that has, as its basis, 'a social fact of attachment, a genuine connection of existence, interests and sentiments' (*Nottebohm Case,* 1955, p. 23). Further, international law recognises a 'right to nationality', prohibits its arbitrary deprivation, and limits the circumstances under which citizenship may be revoked, particularly where such revocation results in statelessness.

2.1 Human Rights Declarations and Conventions

A number of international and regional instruments make specific reference to citizenship or nationality:

- the *Universal Declaration of Human Rights* ('*UDHR*'),
- the *International Covenant on Civil and Political Rights* ('*ICCPR*'),
- the *Convention on the Rights of Persons with Disabilities,*
- the *International Convention for the Protection of All Persons from Enforced Disappearance,*
- the *International Convention on the Protection of the Rights of All Migrant Workers and Members of Their Families,*
- the *Convention on the Rights of the Child,*
- the *Convention on the Elimination of All Forms of Discrimination Against Women,*
- the *International Convention on the Elimination of All Forms of Racial Discrimination,*

- the *Convention on the Nationality of Married Women*,
- the *African Charter on the Rights and Welfare of the Child*,
- the *Protocol to the African Charter on Human and Peoples' Rights on the Rights of Women in Africa*,
- the *Covenant on the Rights of the Child in Islam*,
- the *American Convention on Human Rights*,
- the *American Declaration of the Rights and Duties of Man*,
- the *Arab Charter on Human Rights*,
- the *Convention on Human Rights and Fundamental Freedoms of the Commonwealth of Independent States*, and
- the *Resolution of the Asian African Legal Consultative Organization on Legal Identity and Statelessness.*

Most relevant to the issue of revocation of citizenship, however, is art 15 of the *UDHR*; arts 2 and 26 of the *ICCPR*; and the two conventions on statelessness – the *1954 Convention Relating to the Status of Stateless Persons* ('*1954 Convention*') and the *1961 Convention.*

Specifically, art 15 of the *UDHR* provides that 'everyone has the right to a nationality' and that 'no one shall be arbitrarily deprived of his nationality nor denied the right to change his nationality'. The Human Rights Council ('UNHRC') has confirmed that this establishes the right to nationality as a fundamental human right (UNHRC, 2008; UNHRC, 2009; UNHRC, 2010; UNHRC, 2012). Article 15 also prohibits 'arbitrary deprivation' of nationality (Ki-Moon, 2013, p. 8). A UNHRC report to the General Assembly (UNHRC, 2012, p. 61) considered the constituent elements of arbitrariness under customary international law. The UNHRC observed that arbitrariness is not the same as 'against the law', because legislation in itself can be arbitrary. Instead, arbitrariness 'must be interpreted more broadly to include elements of inappropriateness, injustice, lack of predictability and due process of law' (UNHRC, 2012, p. 61). It includes the requirement that a particular form of deprivation of liberty is taken in accordance with the applicable law and procedure and that it is proportional to the aim sought, reasonable and necessary (UNHRC, 2012, p. 61).

In a report on 'Human Rights and Arbitrary Deprivation of Nationality', the UNHRC has also stated that to comply with international law, any deprivation of nationality must meet certain conditions. The deprivation of citizenship should be: (a) for a legitimate purpose; (b) the least intrusive instrument to achieve the desired result, and (c) proportional to the interest to be protected (UNHRC, 2009). Importantly, international law strictly limits the circumstances in which loss or deprivation of nationality leading to statelessness serves a legitimate purpose (UNHRC, 2009). This is because where 'loss or deprivation of nationality leads to statelessness, the impact on the individual is particularly severe' (UNHRC, 2009, p. 4).

A law depriving nationality should also not distinguish on the basis of factors such as 'race, colour, sex, language, religion, political or other opinion, national or social origin, property, birth or other status'. This is due to art 2(1) of the *ICCPR*:

> Each State Party to the present Covenant undertakes to respect and to ensure to all individuals within its territory and subject to its jurisdiction the rights recognized in the present Covenant, without distinction of any kind, such as race, colour, sex, language, religion, political or other opinion, national or social origin, property, birth or other status.

Further, art 26 of the *ICCPR* provides:

> All persons are equal before the law and are entitled without any discrimination to the equal protection of the law. In this respect, the law shall prohibit any discrimination and guarantee to all persons equal and effective protection against discrimination on any ground such as race, colour, sex, language, religion, political or other opinion, national or social origin, property, birth or other status.

This is relevant because if a revocation of citizenship can only apply to dual nationals, for example, then those laws discriminate on the basis of national origin and do not provide equal treatment before the law, in contravention of arts 2 and 26, respectively. Further, art 12(4) of the *ICCPR* provides that 'no one shall be arbitrarily deprived of the right to enter his own country'. The general commentary on this article observes that 'the right has various facets' (UNHRC, 1999, p. 19) and includes 'the right to return after having left one's own country' (UNHRC, 1999, p. 19). Further, the use of the words 'his own country' is not the same as the concept 'country of his nationality' (Human Rights Committee, *Stewart v Canada,* 1993). Rather, the words are:

> not limited to nationality in a formal sense, that is, nationality acquired at birth or by conferral; it embraces, at the very least, an individual who, because of his or her special ties to or claims in relation to a given country, cannot be considered to be a mere alien. This would be the case, for example, of nationals of a country who have there been stripped of their nationality in violation of international law, and of individuals whose country of nationality has been incorporated in or transferred to another national entity, whose nationality is being denied them (UNHRC, 1999, p. 20).

For example, in *Nystrom v Australia* (Human Rights Committee, 2011, 7.5), the UNHRC found that the term 'his own country' referred to Australia, even though Mr Nystrom was a Swedish national. This was because 'the strong ties connecting him to Australia, the presence of his family in Australia, the language he speaks, the duration of his stay in the country and the lack of any other ties' mattered more than his Swedish nationality (Human Rights Committee, *Nystrom, Nystrom and Turner v Australia*, 2011, 7.5).

In essence, 'there are few, if any, circumstances in which deprivation of the right to enter one's own country could be reasonable' (UNHRC, 1999, p. 21). As noted above, this is particularly the case where such deprivation results in statelessness. The statelessness conventions are now considered.

2.2 *The Statelessness Conventions*

Article 1(1) of the *1954 Convention* defines a Stateless person as a 'person who is not considered as a national by any State under the operation of its law' (*Convention Relating to the Status of Stateless Persons*, 1954). According to the International Law Commission, this definition has customary international law status (ILC, 2006, pp. 48–9). The link between statelessness and deprivation of nationality is obvious: without a nationality, a person is stateless. It follows, then, that the provisions of the two Statelessness Conventions are generally concerned with the obligation of States to avoid a person becoming stateless. For example, one of the more relevant provisions for current purposes is art 8(1) of the *1961 Convention* (*Convention on the Reduction of Statelessness*, 1961) which provides that 'a

Contracting State shall not deprive a person of his nationality if such deprivation would render him stateless'. Sixty-three States, including Australia, are party to the *1961 Convention*.

Article 8 of the *1961 Convention*, however, does allow deprivation of nationality even if it leads to statelessness in certain circumstances. Briefly, these circumstances, according to art 8, are limited to where the person has:

- voluntarily acquired another nationality;
- committed fraud or misrepresentation in obtaining the nationality;
- performed services to a foreign government or military in contravention of an express prohibition;
- been absent for seven years or more under very strict conditions; or
- engaged in conduct 'prejudicial to the vital interest of the State'.

As art 8(4) sets out, each of these exceptions is subject to the 'right to a fair hearing by a court of other independent body'. Importantly, deprivation of nationality can only be justified where the 'fraud or misrepresentation was perpetrated for the purpose of acquiring nationality and was material to its acquisition' (UNHRC, 2009, p. 10). Further, as noted in a 2013 report of the Secretary General:

> [W]ith any decision to deprive a person of a nationality, States have a duty to carefully consider the proportionality of this act, especially where statelessness results. The nature or gravity of the fraud or misrepresentation must be weighed against the consequences of denationalization. In this context, considerations such as the person's links with the State, including the length of time that has elapsed between acquisition of nationality and discovery of fraud also need to be taken into account (UNHRC, 2009, p. 10).

A person who engages in 'acts seriously prejudicial to the vital interests of the State' 'may be deemed to have breached the duty of loyalty which stems from nationality' (UNHRC, 2009, p. 12). Therefore, States may provide for the deprivation of nationality, 'be it as a form of punishment or as a response to the apparently broken bond of allegiance' (UNHRC, 2009, p. 12). While article 7(3) of the *European Convention on Nationality* prohibits deprivation of nationality on this ground if it leads to statelessness, the *1961 Convention* permits States to retain the power to do so, but only where their domestic law 'already provided for this at the moment of accession and a declaration was made to that effect' (UNHRC, 2009, p. 12). Notably, the *1961 Convention* does not allow States to deprive a person of nationality on the basis of the commission of an ordinary criminal offence. In any event, to do so may breach prohibitions on double punishment.

The words 'Services to a foreign government or military', as grounds to deprive citizenship, should be construed narrowly, according to the same 2013 report of the Secretary General. The report observes:

> A number of countries provide for a "warning" to first be issued to the individual concerned, and deprivation of nationality is pursued only if the person ignores an explicit request to cease rendering services to a foreign State. This is a welcome safeguard, for it ensures that the State's action is predictable, gives the individual the opportunity to amend his or her behaviour in order to avoid this severe legal consequence and is also in keeping with the 1961 Convention (UNHRC, 2013, p. 15).

Effectively, the circumstances under which the stateless conventions permit a deprivation of nationality must be narrowly construed – even more so if deprivation would result in statelessness. In all such circumstances, the basic principles of proportionality and due process apply, and arbitrariness is prohibited.

In summary, then, there are at least seven key principles of nationality under international law:

1 The 'right to nationality' is a recognised human right.
2 The right of a person to return to their 'own country' is not limited to formal citizenship.
3 Nationality can be a legitimate basis for the exercise of extraterritorial jurisdiction by nation states, provided it is not an abuse of rights.
4 A *grant* of nationality is generally left to the discretion of individual nation states, provided there is a 'genuine connection', and it is not an abuse of rights.
5 A *deprivation* of nationality is prohibited if:

   a if is arbitrary; and/or
   b it discriminates on the basis of race, colour, sex, language, religion, political or other opinion, national or social origin, property, birth or other status.

6 A *deprivation* of nationality must also be:

   a for a legitimate purpose;
   b the least intrusive instrument to achieve the desired result; and
   c proportional to the interest to be protected.

7 A *deprivation* of nationality is unlikely to be for a legitimate purpose if it leads to statelessness, except in the very narrow circumstances provided for in the Statelessness conventions.

In context of these principles, I now explore examples of laws revoking citizenship, including the relationship between these laws and the nationality principle of jurisdiction.

3. Revocation of citizenship and extraterritorial responsibility

Citizenship-stripping laws are a response to one of the greatest threats to humanity in the twenty-first century: the violent extremism of organised non-state actors, such as the group commonly referred to as Islamic State, Daesh, 'IS' or 'ISIS'. Consider the following grim tale:

> In a procession were a long line of at least 17 foreign fighters, many of them white-skinned Europeans, each guiding with his left hand a prisoner identified as a Syrian soldier. Only one wore a mask, the British fighter known as 'Jihadi John,' who had executed James Foley and other American and European hostages. After the jihadists had hacked through the necks of their victims, the camera played over the faces of the executioners, ensuring that they were clearly visible and sparking a rush to identify them. Media reports identified the perpetrators as French, German, British, Danish, and Australian citizens, although some of these claims were tentative (Stern & Berger, 2015).

Stern and Berger suggest that ISIS propaganda is 'disproportionately slanted toward foreign fighters, both in its content and its target audience' (Stern & Berger, 2015). The radicalisation of Australian and other Western nationals has brought the conflict to doorsteps far and wide. Reportedly, about 70 per cent of IS suicide operations in Syria were conducted by foreign nationals, and foreign nationals were also those most likely to carry out excessively brutal operations, such as beheadings, torture and suicide missions (Liddy & Gourlay, 2015). At the time of writing, the International Centre for the Study of Radicalisation estimated over 20,000 foreign nationals have travelled to Iraq and Syria to fight (Neumann, 2015). Of those, approximately 4,000 have been from western European nations, with the majority from France, the United Kingdom and Germany (Neumann, 2015). Further, estimates are that between 100 and 250 foreign fighters have departed from Australia to take part in the Syrian conflict (Neumann, 2015). This presents liberal democracies with a complex problem: how to counter terrorism without undermining the very rights and liberties – such as citizenship and its associated rights – that should characterise modern progressive societies.

Australia's response was the *Australian Citizenship Amendment (Allegiance to Australia) Act 2015* (Cth) ('ACAA'). The ACAA amended the *Australian Citizenship Act 2007* (Cth) ('ACA') to allow for revocation of citizenship by the Minister for Immigration on the basis of various kinds of conduct, including acts of terrorism and serving in foreign armed forces. As Senator Colbeck observed in his speech to Parliament:

> We face a heightened and complex security environment. Regrettably, some of the most pressing threats to the security of the nation and the safety of the Australian community come from citizens engaged in terrorism. It is now appropriate to modernise provisions concerning loss of citizenship to respond to current terrorist threats. The world has changed so our laws should change accordingly (Commonwealth, *Parliamentary Debates,* Senate, 30 November 2015, 9355) (Richard Colbeck, Senator).

And while the Immigration Minister claimed that the intention behind the laws is 'the protection of the community and the upholding of its values, rather than punishing people' (Commonwealth, *Parliamentary Debates,* House, 24 June 2015, 7369 (Peter Dutton, MP), the same speech also included the following statement:

> Australian citizenship is something to be treasured. It is a common bond which unites us all, whether we were born here or chose to make Australia our home. Australian citizenship involves a commitment to this country, its people and its democratic rights and privileges. Australian citizenship should not be taken lightly (Commonwealth, *Parliamentary Debates,* House, 24 June 2015, 7369) (Peter Dutton, MP).

The core claim here appears to be that citizenship, once acquired, is a privilege rather than a right and that not all persons 'deserve' to become citizens. Under Australian citizenship laws, revocation only applies to dual nationals and therefore, in theory, avoids breaching international law on statelessness. In practice, however, the laws still have the potential to cause *de facto* statelessness, given that the mere holding of a passport, as noted in *Nystrom* (Human Rights Committee, *Nystrom, Nystrom and Turner v Australia*, 2011, 7.5), does not always equate to true membership of a society.

At the time of writing, the Act's provisions also extend to persons who acquired their Australian citizenship by birth and allow for the Minister to revoke the citizenship of a child of a person who has committed the offending conduct. Any person who has their Australian citizenship revoked is excluded from ever becoming an Australian citizen again, other than through the Minister exercising their power to exempt such a person. However, for certain types of conduct, mostly relating to terrorist activities, there can be no resumption of citizenship. Incidentally, given that a person can cease to be an Australian citizen at the time of a conviction for a particular crime, the revocation of citizenship may function as a double punishment, because it operates in addition to any other punitive measures provided for in the *Criminal Code* (Cth) and *Crimes Act 1914.* Double punishment is prohibited by the *ICCPR* to which Australia is party.

Unsurprisingly, the legislation has not been without its critics. For example, Peter Hughes referred to the potential social costs and the potential devaluation of Australian citizenship:

> Australia is a country of immigration and Australian citizenship has, since its inception in 1949, played an important role in integrating newcomers into society. Easy deprivation of Australian citizenship on loose criteria, without due process, would seriously devalue it. Why bother to become an Australian citizen if it can be taken away on suspicion? Some communities would definitely feel targeted by such legislation and their sense of alienation would be increased rather than diminished (Hughes, 2015).

The relevant provisions in this legislation also apply extraterritorially, which are understandable in the context of foreign nationals fighting in Syria and other jurisdictions. But, in turn, this raises questions about the 'order' – the coherence and certainty – in the conceptual relationship between nationality and extraterritoriality. This chapter has already established that extraterritoriality allows States authority to regulate conduct over their citizens overseas. But with authority comes responsibility. Does stripping citizenship abdicate this responsibility? This leads to a paradox – after all, how can the *exercise* of an authority over nationality simultaneously *abandon* its exercise? This is jurisdictional disorder.

The Australian case illustrates this. Australia is a State wanting to exercise extraterritorial *authority* without extraterritorial *accountability*. Many provisions of the *Criminal Code* apply extraterritorially, because the Commonwealth seeks to regulate extraterritorial conduct (*Criminal Code Act 1995* (Cth) divs 91, 101–3, 131–2, 135–6, 141, 144, 268, 274). For example, the Australian Parliament recently inserted section 35P into the *Australian Security Intelligence Organisation Act 1979* (Cth), which applies to conduct both within Australia and overseas, regardless of the nationality of the accused, and makes it an offence to disclose information that relates to a special intelligence operation. In effect, the provisions can apply to anyone anywhere in the world, including academics and journalists. At the time of writing, doctors and social workers seeking to report concerns about the welfare of asylum seekers in offshore detention centres may be subject to criminal penalties that apply to extraterritorial conduct (*Australian Border Force Act 2015* (Cth) ss. 7, 42).

On the other hand, however, Australia has legislated to abdicate its extraterritorial responsibilities, including by refusing to take appropriate responsibility for the conduct of their nationals in other countries by simply revoking their nationality and setting them loose on other parts of the world, possibly in less stable regions that may be poorly equipped to respond to the need to prosecute such persons. Other examples of Australia abdicating its extraterritorial responsibilities include the use of offshore detention centres for 'extraterritorial processing of refugee applications and the excision of certain territories as so called "international zones"' (de Boer, 2015, p. 119) 'to evade jurisdiction and *ipso facto* legal obligations' (de Boer, 2015, p. 119). As Tom de Boer observes: '[P]roblematically, extraterritorialization and privatization do not just restrict the protection of refugees within the international refugee law regime, they actually serve to evade the regime as a whole, including the judicial scrutiny of the courts' (de Boer, 2015, p. 119).

Thomas Gammeltoft-Hansen makes a similar point when he suggests that offshore processing and the use of private security companies 'are used as a pretext for effectively circumventing basic human rights obligations, either because they are not applicable extraterritorially or when private actors carry out controls, or because these rights are simply not realised' (Gammeltoft-Hansen, 2011, p. 3). Such abdication of extraterritorial responsibility, whether by revocation of nationality or by other means, is the legal equivalent of having one's cake and eating it too. Not only does this undermine the rule of law, it is also counter-productive because isolating people can make them more vulnerable to radicalisation. Further, whatever conduct made a person unworthy of a particular citizenship would 'presumably make him or her equally unworthy of citizenship elsewhere' (Tully, 2015, p. 10). Other States could deprive an individual of nationality so as to avoid their obligation to accept them upon expulsion, thereby leaving an individual stateless within a particular State (Tully, 2015, p. 10).

Australia is not the only country to implement or consider implementing such legislation. The United Kingdom has also implemented laws permitting revocation of citizenship. The United Kingdom ratified the *1961 Statelessness Convention* in 1966, opting to make a reservation under art 8(3) that it retained the power to make individuals stateless if they acted in a manner that was 'seriously prejudicial to the vital interests of Her Britannic Majesty' (*Convention on the Reduction of Statelessness*, 1975). The original *British Nationality Act 1948* (UK) reflected this 1966 reservation (*British Nationality Act 1948*, s 20). This Act was subsequently replaced by the *British Nationality Act 1981* (UK) ('*BNA*'). The provision reflecting the reservation was substantially re-enacted in s 40 of the revised *BNA*. In 2002, however, s 4 of the *Nationality, Immigration and Asylum Act 2002* (UK) inserted a new s 40(4) into the *BNA*. This amendment removed the provision reflecting the 1966 reservation. This meant that, under its own legislation, the United Kingdom was not able to revoke citizenship if to do so would result in statelessness.

The *BNA* has been judicially considered. For example, in *Al-Jedda v Home Secretary*, the Home Office made an attempt to deprive a naturalised British national of his citizenship (*Al-Jedda v Home Secretary*, 2014, 270). Al-Jedda was previously a citizen of Iraq by birth but, upon acquiring his British citizenship, he lost his Iraqi nationality due to the operation of Iraqi law. The Home Office argued that it was reasonably satisfied that, if an application was made, Al-Jedda's Iraqi nationality would be restored – therefore, an order made under s 40(2) *BNA* would not render him stateless and would not be in contravention of s 40(4) *BNA*. On appeal, the Supreme Court rejected this argument and quoted the United Nations High Commissioner for Refugees that 'an individual's nationality is to be assessed as at the time of determination of eligibility . . . it is neither a historic nor a predictive exercise'. Therefore, the Court held that it was unlawful to withdraw citizenship on grounds of national security if it would leave the individual stateless, even though there might be a possibility of the individual reacquiring a nationality he had automatically lost.

In response to the *Al-Jedda* decision, ss 40(4A) and 40B were inserted into the *BNA* in 2014. However, the United Kingdom's derogation under art 8(3) of the *1961 Convention* may not extend to new laws that would have the consequence of rendering persons stateless. This is because the derogation ceased to have effect once s 40(4) was added to the *BNA* and the laws under which the declaration was given were repealed without being immediately re-enacted (Open Society Justice Initiative, 2014). Put another way, by enacting legislation that prohibited revocation of citizenship resulting in statelessness after its reservation to the *1961 Convention*, the United Kingdom may have waived its right to render a person stateless under art 8(3) of the Convention.

Subsequently, the decision in *Pham v Secretary of State for the Home Department* was handed down. Pham was a national of Vietnam by birth. Vietnamese law was ambiguous as to the status of individuals who had dual citizenship. The Home Office sought to revoke Pham's citizenship under s 40(2) of the *BNA*, and the Secretary of State was of the opinion that the order would not make Pham stateless, contrary to s 40(4). After the s 40(2) order, however, the Vietnamese government refused to confirm Pham's citizenship. On appeal, the Supreme Court held that the meaning of 'under the operation of its law' in art 1(1) of the *1954 Convention* should be interpreted widely, looking not only at not the text of the relevant legislation but also state practice (*Pham v Secretary of State for the Home Department*, 2015, 1602). In this instance, the Vietnamese legislation 'was deliberately ambiguous on the issue of dual nationality, so as to allow the executive to make whatever decisions it wished' (*Pham v Secretary of State for the Home Department*, 2015, 1605). The government had not made any decision or adopted any practice in relation to Pham such as to deprive him of his Vietnamese citizenship as at the date of the s 40(2) order. Pham had Vietnamese nationality when the Secretary of State made her decision: he had not automatically lost it upon acquiring British nationality, and the Vietnamese government had taken no action to deprive him of it. The possibility that the Vietnamese government could subsequently refuse to confirm his citizenship was not enough.

In a global legal context, this raises broader questions as to '*de facto*' statelessness and the manner in which extraterritorial jurisdiction is exercised. The chapter argues that because States have the legal right to exercise extraterritorial jurisdiction over its nationals, they may also have the legal responsibility to do so for crimes that threaten world security, as those who fight with terrorist organisations certainly do. Therefore, revoking the nationality of a national, such as legislated for by Australia and the United Kingdom, is an abdication of that responsibility.

3.1 Question of Efficacy

There is a broader policy question here about efficacy. Aside from whether retention of citizenship, obtained either by birthright of naturalisation, is to be understood as a right or as a privilege to be revoked, there are other questions as to whether revocation of a person's citizenship is actually an effective tool in fighting terrorism and other transnational crimes.

It is not always clear from general media statements made by governments advocating for the revocation of citizenship whether the objective of the proposed legislative reform is deterrence, punishment or both. The better question, however, is whether revoking a person's citizenship is actually an effective tool in fighting terrorism and other transnational crimes. This is considered from three angles: first, the achievement of military objectives; second, the 'mechanics of substitution'; and third, the likelihood of individual deterrence.

3.1.1 Military objectives

One motivation for revoking citizenship is to enhance military operations through expanded intelligence sharing. For example, forces are restricted from sharing intelligence on their own citizens (Brennan, 2015). The revocation of citizenship of persons fighting with ISIS may allow such forces to share and act on intelligence more freely. Rodger Shanahan describes the situation as follows:

> As part of those military operations, individuals of sufficient importance are placed on a High Value Target List (HVTL), and when actionable intelligence becomes available they may be targeted. Australia faces difficulties, however, because of constraints that prohibit the passage of information on Australian citizens to third parties. Given we are in a coalition, any Australian on a HVTL is therefore protected to a degree by their citizenship. It is reasonable to expect that if he has another citizenship available to him, then his Australian citizenship should be stripped so that Australia can provide intelligence on him to the coalition, thus allowing that individual to be targeted (Shanahan, 2015).

Richard Barret, a former counter-terrorism chief at MI5 and MI6, however, argues that citizens returning from Iraq and Syria are the best placed to dissuade others from going to fight. In the context of British legislation, he is reported to have argued as follows:

> These are the people who can expose the true nature of the Islamic State and its leadership. Their stories of brutality and the motives behind it will be far more credible and persuasive than the rhetoric of men in suits. These repentant fighters need a way out, and although the law must take its course, they need to know there is a place for them back at home if they are committed to a non-violent future (Townsend, 2014).

Hughes also makes a similar observation in the Australian context:

> The Australian Government is right to be concerned about the activities of violent jihadists and to consider its options. But it would be wise to consider carefully the collateral damage from any changes to citizenship law before deciding to use revocation as a tool. Prosecution, conviction and incarceration of those who have broken Australian law are likely to be much more effective weapons (Hughes, 2015).

Similar, Elliot Brennan suggests that, 'stripping citizenship may be stripping nations of the best assets available to them in counterterrorism' (Brennan, 2015).

3.1.2 The Mechanics of Substitution

Another efficacy problem is what criminologists refer to as the 'mechanics of substitution'. In his 2005 discussion, Patrick Keenan argues 'substitution' can occur where effective regulation of criminal activity in one venue leads to those engaged in such activity merely substituting one venue for another (Keenan, 2006, p. 514). Keenan argues increased accessibility to cheap international travel and wealth disparities between the developing and developed world has facilitated the displacement or substitution of transnational crime to destinations less willing or able to prosecute (Keenan, 2006, p. 514). This means that law enforcement successes in some countries can morph into 'social disasters' for others (Keenan, 2006, p. 514).

By way of analogy, if a person who fights with ISIS or other 'terrorist' groups no longer deserves to retain one of their dual nationalities, the same argument could be just as easily be made for a person who engages in child sexual offences overseas; they no longer 'deserve' to be a citizen, and laws revoking citizenship might act as a deterrent to persons considering such conduct. But is refusing such a person a right to return to their country of nationality actually effective in reducing instances of child sexual abuse? This is unlikely. In the context of child sex tourism, this is because the economic divide between developed nations such as Australia and poorer destination countries such as Thailand and Cambodia is obvious. Therefore, countries like Australia face a moral-political pressure to regulate the behavior of their citizens overseas for the simple reason that other countries cannot or will not do so.

The same argument can be made in the context of 'foreign fighters' or those involved in transnational crimes, such as terrorism. If States decline to take responsibility for the actions of their nationals by simply revoking their citizenship, the conduct of that person does not 'magically' cease. Even though other countries may still have the legal authority to exercise jurisdiction on a ground other than nationality, the burden of responding is simply shifted rather than resolved – and potentially to countries less willing or able to do so. In short, revoking citizenship may simply free up individuals to pursue extremist causes and political violence elsewhere (Hughes, 2015).

3.1.3 The likelihood of individual deterrence

Although the prospect of losing citizenship may act as a possible deterrent to some potential offenders, this is not so for a particular category of Western foreign fighters, young males whose decision to fight overseas may not necessarily be rational and well-thought-out. Research by the International Centre for the Study of Radicalisation has examined tens of thousands of statements by foreign fighters (Liddy and Gourlay, 2015). The research shows that while there is no homogenous profile of the Western foreign fighter, there are a number of common narratives. For example,

> it is very clear that for a certain demographic of Western foreign fighter – let's say young males – the notion of adventure is important . . . The idea of brotherhood, going there, fighting for a good cause, becoming a hero, hanging out with the bros . . . The appeal to Western Muslims was very simple. It was: "no-one is helping us, America is not helping us, the West is turning a blind eye because only Muslims are being killed, we need you, we understand you're studying, you're working, you have a family, but at this point in time if being Muslim means anything to you, you have to step up and come here and help out and defend your brothers and sisters" (Liddy & Gourlay, 2015).

Since the emergence of ISIS, two further dominant themes have emerged among foreign recruits: 'a fascination with the establishment of a caliphate, and the notion of the West being at war with Islam' (Liddy & Gourlay, 2015). In the view of the International Centre for the Study of Radicalisation, this message has appealed to a more extremist group than the first wave of foreign fighters and to those who might lack 'a strong sense of meaning in their own lives in the West' (Liddy & Gourlay, 2015).

For this more extreme or marginalised demographic, the revocation of citizenship may not necessarily function as a deterrent. Instead, States could do more by way of counter-radicalisation.

For example, Hussain Nadim (2015) has suggested a number of approaches to prevent and counter radicalisation. Most important, in Nadim's view, is 'exposure to government'. Writing in the Australian context, he writes that:

> The majority of Australian Muslims come from Pakistan, Afghanistan and the Middle East, where a government job is considered the most legitimate job – a symbol of respect and acceptance in society. The British Empire in India offered government positions to locals in order to pacify any revolt against the Empire, and it worked. Given the negligible presence of Australian Muslims in government and law enforcement, something as small as specialised fellowships or internships for Australian Muslims to spend a summer or winter break inside government will have an overwhelming and permanent impact on young Australian Muslims (Nadim, 2015).

In a similar vein, Brennan suggests that enabling individuals with moderate views to 'become role models in the public space is one of the best ways to counter extremist narrative' (Brennan, 2015).

3.2 Devaluing Citizenship

More generally, even aside from questions of efficacy, if the governments of nations are too ready to revoke citizenship, there is a risk of devaluing that citizenship. This, in turn, weakens social cohesion. Thus:

- Dual citizens may develop a fear of investing time and energy into being a productive and devoted citizen if revoking citizenship is an ever-present possibility. In turn, this may serve to undermine the loyalty a person may feel to their nation(s) of citizenship, rather than to cement it.
- Some communities may feel targeted and 'their sense of alienation would be increased rather than diminished' (Hughes, 2015; Brennan, 2015). This can have adverse effects on a person's 'social capital' and they will become further disconnected from the narrative of the broader community. Social capital means 'the forces that shape the quality and quantity of social interactions and social institutions' (McKenzie, Whitley, and Weich, 2002, p. 280) and the 'glue that holds societies together' (McKenzie, Whitley, and Weich, 2002, p. 280). As Putnam (1996, p. 7) writes, social capital refers to the features of 'social life – networks, norms, and trust – that enable participants to act together more effectively to pursue shared objectives'. Low 'social capital' has been linked with adverse consequences for health and well-being (see, for example, Dale and Newman, 2008), which, in turn, could also make a person more vulnerable to radicalisation.
- This potential alienation of individuals, combined with legal distinctions made between those with dual and single citizenships, is unhelpful in migrant and multicultural societies. It could serve to create divides between and within communities. In turn, such divides can lead to disharmony and dysfunctional communities.

These social costs similarly reduce the likelihood of citizenship-stripping deterring individuals from committing specific crimes overseas.

4. Conclusion

International law is generally understood as being neutral in relation to the grant of citizenship by a State. The issues central to this chapter, however, concern not the *grant* of citizenship, but its *revocation* for crimes committed extraterritorially. On this, international law is not silent. Analysis undertaken in the early parts of this chapter suggests that there are at least seven key principles of citizenship under international law that relate to the revocation of citizenship. In summary, these are as follows:

1 The 'right to nationality' is a recognised human right.
2 The right of a person to return to their 'own country' is not limited to formal citizenship.
3 Nationality can be a legitimate basis for the exercise of extraterritorial jurisdiction by nation states, provided it is not an abuse of rights.
4 A *grant* of nationality is generally left to the discretion of individual nation states, provided there is a 'genuine connection', and it is not an abuse of rights.
5 A *deprivation* of nationality is prohibited if:

    a if is arbitrary; and/or
    b it discriminates on the basis of race, colour, sex, language, religion, political or other opinion, national or social origin, property, birth or other status.

6 A *deprivation* of nationality must also be:

    a for a legitimate purpose;
    b the least intrusive instrument to achieve the desired result; and
    c proportional to the interest to be protected.

7 A *deprivation* of nationality is unlikely to be for a legitimate purpose if it leads to statelessness, except in the very narrow circumstances provided for in the Statelessness conventions.

Therefore, the circumstances under which international law permits revocation of citizenship are few. And even where international law permits revocation, this needs to be taken in context of the relationship between nationality and extraterritoriality. Under the nationality principle of jurisdiction, States have a right to regulate the conduct of their citizens. Rights, however, rarely come unburdened by responsibilities. By stripping the citizenship of those who commit serious crimes overseas, States may fail to fulfil an international responsibility. Revocation of citizenship simply rids the State of its undesirable citizens, leaving the problems in the hands of others.

In essence, revocation of citizenship as a response to the commission of serious crimes is legally questionable, and it offends good policy. It may constitute an abdication of a State's responsibilities at law, and, in any event, it may not necessarily be effective in fighting transnational crime. And so a jurisdictional connection may shatter into disarray: an abdication of responsibility, the potential devaluation of citizenship and the loosening of the anchor between a State and citizen.

References

African Charter on the Rights and Welfare of the Child, opened for signature 11 July 1990, OAU Doc CAB/LEG/24.9/49 (entered into force 29 November 1999). Retrieved from http://pages.au.int/acerwc/documents/african-charter-rights-and-welfare-child-acrwc.

Akehurst, M. (1972–1973). Jurisdiction in international law. *British Yearbook of International Law, 46*, 145–257.
Al-Jedda v Home Secretary [2014] AC 253.
American Convention on Human Rights, opened for signature 22 November 1969, 1144 UNTS 123 (entered into force 18 July 1978). Retrieved from http://www.oas.org/dil/treaties_B-32_American_Convention_on_Human_Rights.htm.
American Declaration of the Rights and Duties of Man, Res. XXX, Final Act, Ninth International Conference of American States, OAS Off Rec OEA.Ser.L.V/II.82 doc.6 rev.1 (22 May 1948). Retrieved from https://www.cidh.oas.org/Basicos/English/Basic2.American%20Declaration.htm.
The American Society of International Law (1929). Draft Conventions and Comments on Nationality, Responsibility of States for Injuries to Aliens and Territorial Waters. *Supplement to the American Journal of International Law, 23*(2).
Arab Charter on Human Rights, opened for signature 22 May 2004, 12 *International Human Rights Report* 893 (entered into force 15 March 2008). Retrieved from https://www1.umn.edu/humanrts/instree/loas2005.html.
Australian Border Force Act 2015 (Cth).
Boer, T. de (2015). Closing legal black holes: The role of extraterritorial jurisdiction in refugee rights protection. *Journal of Refugee Studies, 28*, 118–34.
Brennan, E. (2015). *In terror fight, Australia debates revoking citizenship* (online: The Diplomat). Retrieved from http://thediplomat.com/2015/06/in-terror-fight-australia-debates-revoking-citizenship.
British Nationality Act 1948 (UK).
Chehtman, A. (2010). *The philosophical foundations of extraterritorial punishment.* Oxford: Oxford University Press.
Commonwealth, *Parliamentary debates,* House, Australian Citizenship Amendment (Allegiance to Australia) Bill 2015, Second Reading Speech, 24 June 2015, 7369 (Peter Dutton MP).
Commonwealth, *Parliamentary debates,* Senate, Australian Citizenship Amendment (Allegiance to Australia) Bill 2015, Second Reading Speech, 30 November 2015, 9355 (Senator Richard Colbeck).
Code Pénal [Penal Code] (France) 1810.
Convention on the Elimination of All Forms of Discrimination Against Women, opened for signature 18 December 1979, 1249 UNTS 14 (entered into force 3 September 1981). Retrieved from http://www.ohchr.org/Documents/ProfessionalInterest/cedaw.pdf.
Convention on the Nationality of Married Women, opened for signature 20 February 1957, 309 UNTS 66 (entered into force 11 August 1958). Retrieved from https://treaties.un.org/doc/Treaties/1958/08/19580811%2001-34%20AM/Ch_XVI_2p.pdf.
Convention on the Rights of Persons with Disabilities, opened for signature 30 March 2007, UN Doc A/RES/61/106 (entered into force 3 May 2008). Retrieved from http://www.un.org/disabilities/convention/conventionfull.shtml.
Convention on the Rights of the Child, opened for signature 20 November 1989, 1577 UNTS 3 (entered into force 2 September 1990). Retrieved from http://www.ohchr.org/en/professionalinterest/pages/crc.aspx.
Convention Relating to the Status of Stateless Persons, opened for signature 28 September 1954, 360 UNTS 117 (entered into force 6 June 1990). Retrieved from http://www.unhcr.org/3bbb25729.html.
Convention on the Reduction of Statelessness, opened for signature 30 August 1961, 989 UNTS 175 (entered into force 13 December 1975). Retrieved from http://www.unhcr.org/3bbb286d8.html.
Criminal Code Act 1995 (Cth).
Dale, A. & Newman, L. (2008). *Social capital: a necessary and sufficient condition for sustainable community development.* Oxford: Oxford University Press and Community Development Journal.

European Convention on Nationality, opened for signature 6 November 1997, ETS No 166 (entered into force 1 March 2000). Retrieved from https://rm.coe.int/CoERMPublicCommonSearchServices/DisplayDCTMContent?documentId=090000168007f2c8.

Gammeltoft-Hansen, T. (2011). *Access to asylum: International refugee law and the globalisation of migration control.* London: Cambridge University Press.

Hughes, P. (2015). *Revoking citizenship: A weak weapon in the fight against terrorism* (online: The Lowy Interpreter). Retrieved from http://www.lowyinterpreter.org/post/2015/02/17/Revoking-citizenship-weak-weapon-in-fight-against-terrorism.aspx.

(UNHRC) *Human Rights and Arbitrary Deprivation of Nationality*, HRC Res 7/10, UN Doc A/HRC/7/78 (27 March 2008).

(UNHRC) *Human Rights and Arbitrary Deprivation of Nationality*, HRC Res 10/13, UN Doc A/HRC/10/29 (26 March 2009).

(UNHRC) *Human Rights and Arbitrary Deprivation of Nationality*, HRC Res 13/2, UN Doc A/HRC/Res/13/2 (24 March 2010).

(UNHRC) *Human Rights and Arbitrary Deprivation of Nationality*, HRC Res 20/5, UN Doc A/HRC/Res/20/5 (16 July 2012).

Human Rights Committee, *General Comment No 27: Article 12 (Freedom of Movement)*, 67th sess, UN Doc CCPR/C/21/Rev.1/Add.9 (2 November 1999).

Human Rights Committee, *Views: Communication No 538/1993*, 58th sess, UN Doc CCPR/C/58/D/538/1993 (16 December 1993) ('*Stewart v. Canada*').

Human Rights Committee, *Views: Communication No 1557/2007*, 102nd sess, UN Doc CCPR/C/102/D/1557/2007 (18 July 2011) [7.5] ('*Nystrom, Nystrom and Turner v. Australia*').

Independent States, *Convention on Human Rights and Fundamental Freedoms of the Commonwealth of Independent States*, opened for signature 26 May 1995, 17 HRLJ 159 (entered into force 11 August 1998). Retrieved from http://www.cartercenter.org/resources/pdfs/peace/democracy/des/commonwealth_inedpendent_states_convention_human_rights_fund.pdf.

International Convention for the Protection of All Persons from Enforced Disappearance, opened for signature 6 February 2007, UN Doc A/61/488 (entered into force 23 December 2010). Retrieved from http://www.ohchr.org/EN/HRBodies/CED/Pages/ConventionCED.aspx.

International Convention on the Elimination of All Forms of Racial Discrimination, opened for signature 21 December 1965, 60 UNTS 212 (entered into force 4 January 1969). Retrieved from http://www.ohchr.org/EN/ProfessionalInterest/Pages/CERD.aspx.

International Convention on the Protection of the Rights of All Migrant Workers and Members of Their Families, opened for signature 18 December 1990, 2220 UNTS 3 (entered into force 1 July 2003). Retrieved from http://www2.ohchr.org/english/bodies/cmw/cmw.htm.

International Covenant on Civil and Political Rights, opened for signature 16 December 1966, 999 UNTS 171 (entered into force 23 March 1976). Retrieved from http://www.ohchr.org/en/professionalinterest/pages/ccpr.aspx.

International Law Commission. (2006). *Draft Articles on Diplomatic Protection with Commentaries.* Retrieved from http://legal.un.org/ilc/texts/instruments/english/commentaries/9_8_2006.pdf.

Ireland-Piper, D. (2013). Prosecutions of extraterritorial criminal conduct and the abuse of rights doctrine. *Utrecht Law Review, 9*(4), 68–89.

Ireland-Piper, D. (2017). *Accountability in Extraterritoriality: A Comparative and International Law Perspective.* London: Edward Elgar, 2017.

Karassev v Finland (European Court of Human Rights, Chamber, Application No 31414/96, 12 January 1999).

Keenan, P. (2006). The new deterrence: Crime and policy in the age of globalisation. *Iowa Law Review, 91*(2), 505–60.

Ki-Moon, Secretary-General B., *Human Rights and Arbitrary Deprivation of Nationality*, 25th sess, UN Doc A/HRC/25/28 (19 December 2013).

Krizek, M. (1988). The protective principle of extraterritorial jurisdiction: A brief history and an application of the principle to espionage as an illustration of current United States practice. *Boston University International Law Journal, 6*(2), 337–60.
Lambert, H. (2014). *Refugee status, arbitrary deprivation of nationality, and statelessness within the context of Article 1A(2) of the Convention and its 1967 Protocol relating to the status of refugees.* Legal and Protection Policy Research Series, Geneva, Switzerland: UNHCR. Retrieved from http://www.unhcr.org/5433f0f09.pdf.
League of Nations, *Convention on Certain Questions Relating to the Conflict of Nationality Law*, opened for signature 13 April 1930, 179 LNTS 89 (entered into force 1 July 1937). Retrieved from http://www.refworld.org/docid/3ae6b3b00.html.
Legal identity and statelessness, Asian African Legal Consultative Organization, 45th sess, Res/45/SP.1 (8 April 2006).
Liddy, M. & Gourlay, C. (2015). *Explained: Where do foreign fighters in Iraq and Syria come from?* (online news: ABC News). Retrieved from www.abc.net.au/news/2015-02-06/map-foreign-fighters-iraq-syria/6052544.
Mckenzie, K. Whitley, R. & Weich, S. (2002). Social capital and mental health, *British Journal of Psychiatry, 181*(4), 280–3.
Nadim, H. (2015). *The right way to stop Muslim radicalisation* (online: The Lowy Interpreter). Retrieved from http://www.lowyinterpreter.org/post/2015/06/03/right-way-to-stop-Muslim-radicalisation.aspx.
Neumann, P. (2015). *Foreign fighter total in Syria/Iraq now exceeds 20,000; surpasses Afghanistan conflict in the 1980s.* (online: International Centre for the Study of Radicalisation, Kings College London). Retrieved from icsr.info/2015/01/foreign-fighter-total-syriairaq-now-exceeds-20000-surpasses-afghanistan-conflict-1980s/.
Nottebohm Case (Liechtenstein v Guatemala) (Second Phase) [1955] ICJ Rep 4.
Open Society Justice Initiative. (2014). *Opinion on clause 60 Of UK Immigration Bill & Article 8 of United Nations Convention on Reducing Statelessness.* Retrieved from www.opensocietyfoundations.org/sites/default/files/briefing-clause60-03112014.pdf.
Organization of the Islamic Conference, *Covenant on the Rights of the Child in Islam*, opened for signature June 2005, OIC/9-IGGE/HRI/2004/Rep.Final (entered into force June 2005). Retrieved from http://www.refworld.org/docid/44eaf0e4a.html.
Parrish, A. (2008). The effects test: Extraterritoriality's fifth business. *Vanderbilt Law Review, 61*(5), 1455–1505.
Pham v Secretary of State for the Home Department [2015] 1 WLR 1591.
Protocol to the African Charter on Human and Peoples' Rights on the Rights of Women in Africa, opened for signature 13 September 2000 / 11 July 2003, AU Doc CAB/LEG/66.6 (entered into force 25 November 2005). Retrieved from http://www.achpr.org/files/instruments/women-protocol/achpr_instr_proto_women_eng.pdf.
Putnam, R. (1996). The strange disappearance of civic America. *The American Prospect, 7*(24), 3–15.
Rollins, J. (2010). *International terrorism and transnational crime: Security threats, U.S. policy, and considerations for Congress.* United States: Diane Publishing.
Rottmann v Freistaat Bayern (C-135/08) [2010] ECR I-1449.
Rubenstein, K. (2007). Citizenship in an age of globalisation: The cosmopolitan citizen? *Law in Context, 25*, 88–111.
Ryngaert, C. (2008). *Jurisdiction in international law.* London: Oxford University Press.
Shanahan, R. (2015). *Dual-citizen Jihadis do not deserve protection* (online: The Lowy Interpreter). Retrieved from www.lowyinterpreter.org/post/2015/06/01/Dual-citizen-jihadis-do-not-deserve-protection.aspx.
Sloane, R. (2009). Breaking the genuine link: The contemporary international legal regulation of nationality. *Harvard International Law Journal, 50*, 1-60.

Stern, J. & Berger, J. (2015). *ISIS and the foreign-fighter phenomenon* (online newspaper: The Atlantic). Retrieved from http://www.theatlantic.com/international/archive/2015/03/isis-and-the-foreign-fighter-problem/387166/.

Townsend, M. (2014). *Tracy McVeigh and Andrew Anthony, 'Isis fighters must be allowed back into UK, says ex-MI6 chief'* (online newspaper: The Guardian). Retrieved from http://www.theguardian.com/world/2014/sep/06/richard-barrett-mi6-isis-counter-terrorism.

Triggs, G. (2006). *International law: Contemporary principles and practices* (2nd ed.). Sydney: LexisNexis Butterworths.

Tully, S. (2015). Citizen deleted. *Australian Year Book of International Law, 33*, 131-162.

Universal Declaration of Human Rights, GA Res 217A (III), UN GAOR, 3rd sess, 183rd plen mtg, UN Doc A/810 (10 December 1948). Retrieved from http://www.un.org/en/universal-declaration-human-rights/.

Williams, P. & Savona, E. U. (1996). *The United Nations and transnational organized crime.* Oxford: Frank Cass & Co.

Working Group on Arbitrary Detention. (2012). *Report of the Working Group on Arbitrary Detention*, UN HRC, 22 sess, Agenda Item 3, UN Doc A/HRC/22/44.

Zerk, J. (2010). *Extraterritorial jurisdiction: Lessons for the business and human rights sphere from six regulatory areas* (Working Paper No 59, Harvard Corporate Social Responsibility Initiative). Harvard University, Cambridge, USA.

7 Stateless Rohingyas in Bangladesh and Refugee Status

Global Order and Disorder under International Law

Sanzhuan Guo and Madhav Gautam

International law seeks to provide a legal "order" for statelessness. The existence of statelessness, however, reflects a "disorder" of the law in practice. The plight of stateless Rohingyas in Bangladesh is one such case. This chapter explores the complex history of Rohingyas in Myanmar and Bangladesh so as to understand their current plight. Despite all persons having a right to nationality under international law, the Rohingyas have been – and continue to be – denied nationality under the domestic laws of both Myanmar and Bangladesh. In that context, this chapter seeks to answer two questions: first, do stateless Rohingyas qualify as 'refugees' under the *1951 Convention relating to the Status of Refugees* and its *1967 Protocol*? And second, if so, is Bangladesh then subject to the obligation of non-refoulement?

Statelessness is evidence of disorder in the global legal community. This is because the nation-state remains the key actor in the human rights protection system. Without the benefit of nationality, stateless persons are denied access to human rights protections. This means that stateless people are among the most vulnerable people in the world.

International law seeks to address the problem of statelessness – at least on paper. It distinguishes statelessness from refugee status by constructing separate legal frameworks for each: the *1954 Convention Relating to the Status of Stateless Persons* and the *1961 Convention on the Reduction of Statelessness* on one hand, and the *1951 Convention relating to the Status of Refugees* and the *1967 Protocol relating to the Status of Refugees* on the other. Further, the *Universal Declaration of Human Rights* recognises the right to nationality. Thus, international law, in theory, assembles a legal "order" intended to ensure the protection of stateless people across the globe. However, in practice, this chapter argues that justice for stateless peoples is still in a state of disorder. An assessment of the plight of the Rohingya people in Bangladesh is used to illustrate this point.

The Rohingya people are a Muslim group from the state of Rakhine, Myanmar. They were rendered stateless by Myanmar's *Citizenship Law (1982)* which declared that most Rohingyas were "non-nationals" or "foreign residents" in Myanmar. Relentlessly persecuted, many fled to Bangladesh due to its geographical (Uliah, 2011, p. 140) and cultural proximity (Palmer, 2011). According to a 2015 *Report of the United Nations High Commissioner for Refugees* (UNHCR), the UNHCR 'provides support to more than 32,000 registered Rohingya refugees in two official camps (Nayapara and Kutupalong) in the district of Cox's Bazar' in Bangladesh (UNHCR, 2015, p. 2). In addition, there are about 200,000 to 500,000 unregistered Rohingya Muslims residing in unofficial Bangladeshi camps or villages where there is no legal protection from arrest or abuse and little to no humanitarian assistance (UNHCR, 2015, p. 2; Reynolds, 2015).

This chapter first examines the history of Rohingyas in Myanmar and Bangladesh. Second, it then analyses citizenship laws in both of these countries, particularly as such laws relate to the Rohingya people. This is done so as to ascertain their current predicament. The human rights challenges faced by registered Rohingya refugees in Bangladesh are then considered so as to understand the refugee registration process in Bangladesh and the complexity of the issue. This then leads to an assessment as to whether arbitrary deprivation of nationality constitutes persecution for the purpose of a determination of refugee status in the context of unregistered Rohingyas in Bangladesh. Ultimately, the chapter concludes by exploring solutions to the "disorder" faced by stateless Rohingyas in Bangladesh.[1]

1. Historical context

To contextualise the issues, the chapter begins with a historical survey of the Rohingya people in Myanmar and Bangladesh. Colonisation – with its territorial carve-ups – provides the broader narrative within which this history unfolds.

1.1 Who are the Rohingyas?

Rohingya Muslims are a minority group in the state of Rakhine (formerly Arakan) in Myanmar.[2] Buddhists make up the majority. Rohingya Muslims mainly reside in two townships in Rakhine: 90% in Maungdaw and 80% in Buthidaung (Kipgen, 2014, 236–7; Anand, 1978). Rohingya Muslims were originally Arabic traders who came to the area in the eighth century and settled at Wesali near the Mrohaung Kingdom in Arakan (Human Rights Watch, 2000, p. 5). Gradually they moved into Arakan. Buddhist kings ruled Mrohaung, but Muslim officials often played important roles in court (Human Rights Watch, 2000, p. 5; Abrar, 2003, p. 88).

1.2 How did the Rohingya people settle in Bangladesh?

Myanmar shares a border with Bangladesh. According to the Human Rights Watch report in May 2000, 'thousands of Rohingya fled to what is now Bangladesh in four main periods: the late 1700s and early 1800s, the 1940s, 1978 and, most recently, in 1991 and 1992' (Human Rights Watch, 2000, p. 5). This pattern of exodus occurred because Myanmar never accepted Rohingyas as part of society but as immigrants from Bengal. This attitude persisted before, during and after the colonisation and decolonisation of Myanmar.

The first exodus was triggered by the conquest and incorporation of the Arakan region into the central Burma kingdom. Many Rohingyas fled to East Bengal (now Bangladesh). Significantly, these refugees from Arakan were the original residents of the region between Teknaf and Cox's Bazar in Bangal (Abrar, 2003, p. 8). Between 1784 and 1824, some dissatisfied Rohingyas rebelled against the Burman King, although the King managed to push them back to Bengal (Human Rights Watch, 2000, pp. 5–6).

1 The chapter states the law as of 18 June 2016. At the time of writing, Bangladesh's proposed *Citizenship Law 2016* had not yet become law nor been made available to the public.

2 Today, Myanmar has seven provinces (or divisions) (Sagaing, Taninthayi, Bago, Magway, Mandalay, Yangon and Ayeyarwady) primarily composed of the Burman majority group, and seven states (Kachin, Kayan, Kayin, Chin, Mon, Rakhine and Shan) composed of minority ethnic groups (UN Doc CRC/C/70/Add.21, [3]) (Figure 1).

The second period coincided with the end of the British colonial rule in the region and during World War II. In 1824, Burma (now Myanmar) was colonised by the British Empire and incorporated into British India as a province until 1937. Bangladesh was also part of British India until 1947. As Myanmar and Bangladesh were two provinces of British India, moving from one to another state was not unusual.[3] When the British government separated Myanmar from India, a large number of Rohingyas returned to Arakan (Abrar, 2003, pp. 88–9). In 1942, when the Japanese invaded Myanmar, about 22,000 Rohingyas fled to Bengal due to the war (Human Rights Watch, 2000, 6). To fight against the Japanese, the British government promised the Rohingya Muslims a Muslim National Area. Britain never delivered on this promise (Human Rights Watch, 2000, 5; Abrar, 2003, p. 89).

The third wave occurred after General Ne Win and the Socialist Programme Party (BSPP) assumed rule over Myanmar in 1962. They began to dissolve Rohingya social and political organisations (Human Rights Watch, 2000, p. 7). In 1978, the Ne Win government conducted Operation Dragon King to register citizens and scrutinise foreigners prior to the national census. It was reported that the Myanmar army forcibly evicted Rohingyas during the operation (Smith, 1991, p. 241; Human Rights Watch, 2000, 7). The operation led to about 200,000 Rohingyas fleeing to Bangladesh (Human Rights Report, 2000, p. 7).[4] With the assistance of the UN and after the negotiation between Bangladesh and Myanmar, the Myanmar government finally accepted the return of Rohingyas (Human Rights Watch, 2000, p. 5). However, only half of them went back to Myanmar (Blaustein, 1992).

The fourth period coincided with the State Law and Order Restoration Council (SLORC) military government in 1991 and 1992. About 250,000 Rohingya people fled Myanmar from forced labour, rape and religious persecution (Kipgen, 2014, p. 237; Ragland, 1994; Human Rights Report, 2000, p. 8). Under the auspices of the UN and NGOs, the Bangladeshi government set up 19 camps to shelter Rohingya refugees in the area of Cox's Bazar (Human Rights Watch, 2000, p. 8). Immediately after the crisis, Bangladesh, under the auspices of the UN, negotiated with the Myanmar government for the repatriation of the Rohingya people. However, the repatriation was criticised as involuntary (Abrar, 2003, pp. 91–2).

More recently, during June and October 2012, there was communal violence in Northern Rakhine of Myanmar between ethnic Rakhine Buddhists and Rohingya Muslims, which was triggered by the alleged rape and murder of a 27-year-old Buddhist woman by three Muslim men (Human Rights Watch, 2013, pp. 21–2; Yale Law School, 2015, pp. 18–29). It led to 140,000 people, the majority of them Rohingyas, being displaced. The Bangladeshi government closed its borders and started to push back Rohingyas fleeing persecution. It marked the first time Bangladesh refused to accommodate Rohingyas from Myanmar (Huda, 2013). The Bangladeshi government decided not to welcome the Rohingya refugees in the territory of Bangladesh because of national security concerns and the significant socio-economic burden. Authorities claimed that 'Rohingya refugees have been staying in Bangladesh for more than 20 years without contributing any economic and social benefit to the host country' (Huda, 2013).

3 The current boundary between Myanmar and Bangladesh can be traced back to the line between two provinces in British India in 1937.

4 In 1971, when Bangladesh seceded from Pakistan, the border between Myanmar and Pakistan became the border between Myanmar and Bangladesh.

Further, in June 2012, Bangladeshi security forces turned back 16 boats carrying more than 660 Rohingya people, most of them women and children, as they tried to enter from neighbouring Myanmar crossing the Naf River (AFP, 2012). In the first seven months of 2013, an estimated 4,200 Rohingyas who attempted to seek safety in Bangladesh were pushed back (APRRN Annual Report 2013, 12). In 2014, Bangladesh continued to repatriate Rohingyas back to Myanmar. The consequences of this were that Rohingya asylum seekers had to choose to flee to other countries rather than Bangladesh. In 2015, with more Rohingyas fleeing to Malaysia, Indonesia and Thailand, and even Australia, Rohinyga issues became truly a global concern.

This brief history demonstrates the movements – and the misery – of the stateless Rohingya people. Statehood – or, more precisely, the lack thereof – in Myanmar and Bangladesh is 'the root source of the problem' (Roberts and Bennett, 2015). On the one hand, Myanmar regards Rohingyas, legally and socially, as 'others'. Even the word 'Rohingya' is controversial. Rohingya people themselves use the term to self-identify as a minority group in Myanmar; however, their fellow citizens reject this designation because they view Rohingya people as Bengali. They think that Rohingya people are illegal Bengali immigrants who should return to Bangladesh. Even Aung San Suu Kyi, the 1991 Nobel Peace Prize Laureate, has consistently maintained her silence on the Rohingya issue (Kristof, 2016). When 200,000 Rohingyas left Myanmar for Bangladesh in 1978, for example, the Myanmar government denied that they were their nationals:

> the 'refugees' are in fact illegal immigrants or fugitives from law. The so-called refugees, it is contended, are Bangladesh nationals, who had illegally settled along the border inside Burma. According to the official Burma News Agency (NAB) the 'Bengalis' had fled because they lacked proper entry registration papers and also because of instigation by 'unscrupulous persons'. They wanted to escape the scrutinisation drive, code-named 'Nagamani', launched in the region commencing on March 17 to classify the status of residents – bona fide citizens and foreigners; and they preferred to flee rather face detection and prosecution (Anand, 1978, p. 1100, cit in Kipgen, 2014, p. 236).

Bangladesh condemned the Myanmar government for using excessive force to drive away the Rohingyas into Bangladeshi territory (Kipgen, 2014, p. 236), but regard the Rohingyas as illegal migrant labourers.

2. Do Rohingyas have a right to nationality under international law?

This history of marginalisation and political exclusion means that the Rohingya people are *de jure* stateless.[5] This is because neither Myanmar nor Bangladesh recognises their nationality

5 International law distinguishes between *de jure* and *de facto* statelessness. *De jure* statelessness is where a person is not considered to be a national of any state. *De facto* statelessness refers to situations where a person may technically have a nationality but is unable to enjoy its benefits (Shearer and Opeskin, 2012, 102). Although the concept of *de facto* statelessness is important in practice, international instruments addressing the issue of statelessness are generally limited to *de jure* statelessness because of the imprecise nature of *de facto* statelessness (for example, the *1954 Convention Relating to the Status of Stateless Persons*, Article 1).

nor grants them citizenship.[6] The question that arises is: whether the Rohingya people are entitled to nationality or citizenship and, if so, with whom: Myanmar or Bangladesh? To answer this question, the preliminary issue is whether international law recognises a general right to nationality.

Although the *International Covenant on Civil and Political Rights* (ICCPR) and the *International Covenant on Economic, Social and Cultural Rights* (ICSECR) do not include a general right to nationality, various other international instruments – including the *Universal Declaration of Human Rights* (UDHR, Article 15), the *American Convention on Human Rights* (ACHR, Article 20), the *European Convention on Nationality* (Article 4), the *Arab Charter on Human Rights* (Article 29) and the *ASEAN Human Rights Declaration* (para 18) – do. Specifically, these instruments recognise that: (1) Everyone has the right to a nationality. (2) No one shall be arbitrarily deprived of his or her nationality. (3) No one shall be denied the right to change his or her nationality.

Article 2 of the UDHR entitles everyone to their "rights and freedoms", including their right to nationality, 'without distinction of any kind, such as race, colour, sex, language, religion, political or other opinion, national or social origin, property, birth or other status'. Article 5 of the *European Convention on Nationality* also expressly prohibits discrimination on the ground of 'sex, religion, race, colour or *national* or ethnic origin'.

Further, Article 24(3) of the ICCPR provides that 'every child has the right to acquire a nationality'. Article 7 of the *Convention on the Rights of the Child* (CRC) provides that any child has a right to be 'registered immediately after birth and shall have the right to a name [and] the right to acquire a nationality'. And Article 9 of the *Convention on the Elimination of All Forms of Discrimination against Women* (CEDAW) states that men and women should have equal rights to acquire, change or retain their nationality.

However, as Bialosky observes:

> given the unbinding nature of the UDHR, and, because of either their limited ratification or their focus on specific aspects of nationality [referring to 1954 and 1961 statelessness conventions], no international instrument has been able to enshrine a universal right to a nationality protected on a global scale (Bialosky, 2015, p. 159).

Despite this, we argue, as others have, that there is, at the very least, an implied right to nationality in international law, if for no other reason than because the UDHR has been widely regarded as customary international law (Ziemele and Schram, 1999, pp. 321–3). More importantly, by reading together all regional mechanisms – including Inter-America, Europe, Arab, ASEAN and Africa – as well as the specific provisions of ICCPR, the CRC and the CEDAW regarding nationality, 'nationality has increasingly been viewed as a fundamental right that states must protect' (Bialosky, 2015, p. 189).

6 Nationality and citizenship, although linked concepts, are legally distinct: nationality is the subject of international law; citizenship, domestic law (Rubenstein and Adler, 2000, 521; Weis, 1979, 4–5). To be sure, citizenship is subject to *some* scrutiny by international law (von Glahb, 1992, 204-8; see, eg, *Lichtenstein v Guatemala*, 1955, 23); however, largely, citizenship rights derive from domestic laws. Thus, it is well accepted that each State has 'a sovereign right to decide what aliens to admit, to whom to grant citizenship, and under what conditions' (von Glahb, 1992, 208).

3. Do Rohingyas have a right to citizenship under domestic laws?

3.1 Myanmar's 1982 Citizenship Law

If Rohingyas have a right to a nationality under international law, is Myanmar then obliged to grant them nationality?

Under Myanmar's *1982 Citizenship Law*, there are three different types of citizenship: *full citizenship*, *associate citizenship* and *naturalised citizenship*. The Central Body, composed of Minister Chairman Ministry of Home Affairs, Minister Member Ministry of Defence and Minister Member Ministry of Foreign Affairs (Article 67), decides if a person is a full citizen, an associate citizen or a naturalised citizen (Article 68).

Article 3 of the *1982 Citizenship Law* affords *full citizenship* to:

> Nationals such as the Kachin, Kayah, Karen, Chin, Burman, Mon, Rakhine or Shan and ethnic groups as have settled in any of the territories included within the State as their permanent home from a period anterior to 1185 B.E., 1823 A.D. are [Myanmar] citizens.

However, the Council of State retains final authority to decide whether any ethnic group is a national or not (Article 4). Even though Article 3 could be interpreted to include Rohingyas because they have resided in Myanmar since the eighth century, the Myanmar government applies a different historical reading. According to Myanmar's State Report to the UN regarding Children's Rights, Myanmar has 135 ethnic races (UN Doc CRC/C/70/Add.21, [3]).[7] This list does not include the Rohingyas[8] because they arrived after 1823 (Tang, 2005, p. 156). The UN General Assembly passed the resolution on 29 December 2014 to 'call upon the Government . . . . to allow . . . equal access to full citizenship for the Rohingya minority' (UN General Assembly, UN Doc A/RES/69/248).

Because Rohingyas have no access to full citizenship, the next question becomes whether they are able to obtain *associate citizenship* or *naturalised citizenship* and, if so, whether these are sufficient to safeguard Rohingyas' membership in Myanmar.

Associate citizenship is not clearly defined under the *1982 Citizenship Law*. One interpretation is that it refers to those who arrived in Myanmar after 1832 and applied for citizenship under the *1948 Union Citizenship Act* (Article 23 of the *1982 Citizenship Law*). *Naturalised citizenship* refers to those who 'entered and resided in the State prior to 4 January, 1948, . . . may, if they have not yet applied under the Union Citizenship Act, 1948, apply for naturalised citizenship to the Central Body, furnishing conclusive evidence' (Article 42 of the *1982 Citizenship Law*).

As Benjamin Zawacki, the Senior Legal Advisor for Southeast Asia at the International Commission of Jurists, observes, associate citizenship under the *1982 Citizenship Law* 'requires an awareness of the law that few Rohingya posses[s] and a level of proof that even fewer are able to provide' (2013, pp. 18–9). Because few Rohingyas have applied for

7 Although the previous parliamentary government (1948–1962) listed 144 ethnic groups in Myanmar including Rohingyas, the Ne Win government shortlists only 135 groups (see Global Voice, *Bangladesh: Citizenship Rights for Myanmar's Rohingya*? (online) https://globalvoices.org/2012/08/07/bangladesh-citizenship-rights-for-myanmars-rohingya/).

8 Rohingyas are not the only ethnic group excluded from full citizenship.

citizenship under the *1948 Union Citizenship Act*, the only choice left to them is to apply for naturalised citizenship. Although there is no apparent legal limitation preventing Rohingyas from doing so, the practical obstacle lies in furnishing 'conclusive evidence' to prove that they have resided in Burma before 4 January 1948. This is almost impossible for Rohingyas to obtain (Stewart, 2013, pp. 440–1). Further, the Central Body can deny citizenship even if all criteria have been met.

Although full citizens enjoy rights under state laws, the Council of State reserves the power to curtail the rights of associate and naturalised citizens (Tang, 2005, pp. 156–7; Article 30(c) and Article 53(c) of the *1982 Citizenship Law*). In addition, according to Articles 16 and 34 of the *1982 Citizenship Law*, any citizen or associate citizen leaving the country permanently ceases to be a citizen or associate citizen, respectively. Whether a citizen or associate citizen has left the country permanently or not will be decided by the Myanmar government, and individuals who have left without government approval are deemed to have left the country permanently and, therefore, lose their citizenship (Paxton, 2012, p. 630). For those Rohingya people with associate or naturalised citizenship, a difficult choice confronts them when they need to decide whether or not to flee the country.[9]

In our analysis, Myanmar's 1982 *Citizenship Law* arbitrarily denies citizenship to Rohingyas in violation of their right to nationality as expressed in the UDHR (Stewart, 2013, p. 441).

3.2 Bangladesh Citizenship Law

If, as Myanmar law, policy and practice dictate, Rohingyas are foreign residents in Myanmar and illegal immigrants from Bangladesh, the next issue arises as to why Rohingyas cannot receive citizenship from Bangladesh.

Bangladeshi citizenship law derives from the *1951 Pakistan Citizenship Act* which remains valid in Bangladesh even following its independence in 1971 (hereinafter referred to as *Bangladesh 1951 Citizenship Act*) (Kelley, 2010). This is supplemented by the *Bangladesh Citizenship (Temporary Provisions) Order 1972* (P.O. No. 149 of 1972, hereinafter referred to as '*1972 Presidential Order*'), a Presidential Order passed to temporarily govern the citizenship of Bangladesh.

However, in February 2016, the Bangladeshi Cabinet approved a new citizenship bill, which is intended to consolidate the existing *1951 Citizenship Act* and the *1972 Presidential Order* (Dhaka Tribune, 2016). As a well-known Bangladeshi scholar has commented, this new citizenship law 'falls short of being a good law' and the government should take 'a fresh look at the text before placing it before the National Parliament' as some provisions are 'not only contrary to the Constitution, international treaties that Bangladesh has ratified, and the principle of natural justice, they are also discriminatory, unreasonable and non-enforceable' (Abrar, 2016a). In addition, as Abrar (2016a) criticises, the draft *2016 Citizenship Law* has not been made available in the public domain. From the available information so far, the new citizenship law does not seem to change the basic structure of the *1951 Citizenship Act* and the *1972 Presidential Order*, except for provisions on dual citizenship and restrictions on citizenship by birth when the child's parents are not Bangladeshi citizens (Rahman, 2014; Abrar, 2016b).

9 However, this is not discriminatory against Rohingya people because the rule applies to all ethnic groups.

As Latifur Rahman said in the *Professor Golam* case (*Bangladesh v. Professor Golam Azam and Others* (1994) 23 CLC (AD)), '[t]he provisions of the Act and the Order are to be read together to get a complete picture of the law of citizenship in Bangladesh' (quoted in Paulsen, 2006, p. 58). Thus, first, similar to deemed Pakistani citizens under s 3 of the 1951 Citizenship Act, Article 2 of the *1972 Citizenship Presidential Order* recognises 'deemed Bangladeshi citizens' as follows:

> Notwithstanding anything contained in any other law, on the commencement of this Order, every person shall be deemed to be a citizen of Bangladesh –
>
> (i) who or whose father or grandfather was born in the territories now comprised in Bangladesh and who was a permanent resident of such territories on the 25th day of March, 1971, and continues to be so resident; or
> (ii) who was a permanent resident of the territories now comprised in Bangladesh on the 25th day of March, 1971, and continues to be so resident and is not otherwise disqualified for being citizen by any other law for the time being in force . . ."

Thus, unless a Rohingya person was a permanent resident in Bangladesh on 25 March 1971, he or she would not fit into this definition of deemed citizenship. Because Rohingyas are generally regarded as coming from Bangladesh to Myanmar in 1948 when Myanmar gained its independence, they would not meet the requirement of permanent residency of Bangladesh in 1971 when Bangladesh became independent.

In addition, Bangladesh recognises both citizenship by birth and by descent. Section 4 of the *1951 Bangladesh Citizenship Act* provides citizenship by birth on the basis of *jus soli*. This means anyone who is born in Bangladesh after the commencement of the Act becomes a citizen of Bangladesh. For example, the Bangladesh High Court has ruled in several cases that Urdu-speaking people, 'who had been either permanently resident in Pakistan since independence (and therefore citizens per the Citizenship Order) or born there (and therefore citizens per the Citizenship Act), can get *jus soli* citizenship' (Kelley, 2010, 360–6). There are two exceptions to s 4: diplomatic/consulate immunity and enemy alien, neither of which applies to the Rohingyas. Therefore, according to s 4 of the *1951 Citizenship Act*, those Rohingyas born in Bangladesh after 1951 should automatically receive the citizenship of Bangladesh. As many Rohingya refugees have lived in Bangladesh for decades, this section could have saved their children from statelessness. As the UNHCR has reported, refugee children currently represent 59% of the camp population, more than half of them born in Bangladesh (UNHCR Policy Development and Evaluation Service, 2011, p. 3). However, the new *Citizenship Law 2016* may change this section (Rahman, 2014), which will require further evaluation when the law becomes available.

Notably, s 5 of the *1951 Bangladesh Citizenship Act* grants citizenship by descent on the basis of *jus sanguinis*. This means that if one Rohingya gets Bangladeshi citizenship, his/her descendants will also become Bangladeshi.

Unlike Myanmar's *1982 Citizenship Law*, Bangladesh's citizenship laws did not attract much criticism regarding the legal status of Rohingya stateless people. This is probably because Bangladesh's *1951 Citizenship Act* and *1972 Citizenship Presidential Order* did not discriminate against Rohingyas, but rely on more objective criteria. However, in 2014, to respond to the flow in Rohingyas to Bangladesh, the Bangladeshi government imposed a ban on marriage between Bangladeshis and Rohingyas to stop Rohingyas from getting permanent residency in Bangladesh (Dhaka Tribune, 2014). The ban was heavily criticised inside and outside Bangladesh as it violates the basic human right to marriage (Abrar, 2015a; Union of Catholic Asian News, 2014). In the draft *2016 Citizenship Law*, s 11(d) limits the citizenship by marriage to those who are not 'illegal immigrants in Bangladesh' (cited in Abrar, 2016b). This means that Rohingyas would no longer be able to obtain the citizenship of Bangladesh by marriage after the draft *2016 Citizenship Law* becomes effective.

4. Do Rohingyas have protections as refugees?

4.1 Registered Rohingya refugees in Bangladesh

As discussed earlier, only about 10% of stateless Rohingyas in Bangladesh – about 30,000 people – have been registered with the UNHCR as refugees. Two issues arise here: first, how does Bangladesh determine refugee status; and, second, what are the human rights protections afforded to those Rohingya refugees who have successfully obtained refugee status? Registration as a refugee with UNHCR/Bangladesh is important because it creates rights and benefits. However, refugee status may not be sufficient to guarantee basic human rights to stateless Rohingyas in Bangladesh.

There are two different types of registered Rohingya refugees in Bangladesh. One is the group which has been registered with both Bangladesh and the UNHCR. The other is the group registered only with the UNHCR, but not the government of Bangladesh (UNHCR Policy Development and Evaluation Service, 2011). About 20% of the registered Rohingya refugees are not on the government's list (UNHCR Policy Development and Evaluation Service, 2011).

Bangladesh has signed neither the *1951 UN Convention relating to the Status of Refugees* nor its *1967 Protocol*. In 1993, the UNHCR signed a *Memorandum of Understanding* with the government of Bangladesh, which continues to be the only legal basis of the UNHCR's operations in the country, focusing on repatriation and the provision of care and maintenance assistance to refugees who were required to remain in camps (UNHCR Policy Development and Evaluation Service, 2011).

By way of background, the UNHCR operations in Bangladesh are coordinated with the Refugee, Relief and Repatriation Commissioner (RRRC) which is located in the Ministry of Food and Disaster Management (MFDM) (UNHCR Policy Development and Evaluation Service, 2011). The UNHCR pays the salary of the camp authority. The UNHCR attends to the documentation of refugees, such as birth certificates, especially of the children of refugees, while the camp authority can permit or refuse marriage. In essence, although Bangladesh has dealt with the Rohingya refugee issues for many years, there has been no national legal framework or action plan put in place in Bangladesh (Refugee and Migratory Movements Research Unit, 2014).

The government of Bangladesh, however, did issue a 'Strategy Paper on Addressing the Issue of Myanmar Refugees and Undocumented Myanmar Nationals in Bangladesh: A Summary Presentation' on 9 September 2013 (Ministry of Foreign Affairs, Government of the People's Republic of Bangladesh, 2014). However, as Professor Abrar, an eminent Bangladeshi scholar, observes, there was 'no consultation with civil society or stakeholders other than various ministries and departments of the government' (Abrar, 2014). According to the 2013 Strategy Paper, 'the Refugee Relief and Repatriation Commissioner will continue to coordinate the issues concerning the 30,000 or so refugees living in the two registered camps' (Ministry of Foreign Affairs, Government of the People's Republic of Bangladesh, 2014).

This strategic paper shows that Bangladesh is continuing its previous practice and focuses on management of Rohingya issues (especially voluntary repatriation to Myanmar) in a reactionary sense, rather than establishing a national legal framework to determine whether the stateless Rohingyas in Bangladesh are entitled to refugee status.

Further, even if a Rohingya person is registered as a refugee, the lack of legal frameworks and refugee policy in Bangladesh on refugee issues means that a person still faces serious challenges. For example, the UNHCR supported the repatriation of 238,000 refugees from Bangladesh to Myanmar from 1992 to 2003 (Abrar, 2003, pp. 91–2). The idea was that the Rohingyas would be better off in Myanmar rather than 'languishing in camps' in Bangladesh (Abrar, 2003, p. 93). This is because there were significant issues regarding Rohingya refugees in Bangladesh, including food and nutrition, health and health care, housing and water, among others (Abrar, 2003, pp. 95–6).

This is problematic because, having ratified both the ICCPR and the ICESCR, Bangladesh does have an obligation under international law to respect and protect the Rohingyas. As indicated by the General Comment No 15, and confirmed in the General Comment No 31,

> the enjoyment of Covenant rights is not limited to citizens of States Parties but must also be available to all individuals, regardless of nationality or statelessness, such as asylum seekers, refugees, migrant workers and other persons, who may find themselves in the territory or subject to the jurisdiction of the State Party' (Human Rights Committee's General Comment No 31, [10]).

To name a few, the following sample list demonstrates the human rights concerns faced by registered Rohingya refugees (UNHCR, 2007):

(i) **Right to Food (Article 11 of ICESCR):** Registered refugees are 'not entitled to receive the food and other assistance' (UNHCR Policy Development and Evaluation Service, 2011, [16]).

(ii) **Right to Education (Articles 13 and 14 of ICESCR):** Even for Rohingyas who have refugee status in Bangladesh, the Bangladeshi government does not permit them to pursue education (Abrar, 2003, 91).

(iii) **Right to Work (Articles 6 and 7 of ICESCR):** Even registered refugees are not legally permitted to work or go outside the camps. According to a report of Refugee International, an international NGO focusing on refugee issues, refugees receive no food assistance and have no work permits, so they take what work is available or beg to survive (Refugee International, 2012). They risk exploitation by employers and arrest by government officers coupled with long periods of detention, which can become indefinite because Myanmar will not accept their return.

(iv) **Freedom of Movement (Article 12 of ICCPR):** Registered Rohingya refugees also face relocation to remote areas. In 2015, the Head of the Government's Rohingya Refugee Cell and the Ministry of Disaster Management and Relief confirmed plans to relocate Rohingyas to a remote island (Abrar, 2015b).

(v) **Right to Marry (Article 23(2) of ICCPR):** In 2015, the Bangladeshi government initiated a policy banning marriage between Bangladeshi nationals and Rohingyas (Abrar, 2015b).

Of course, it must be acknowledged that Bangladesh is not a wealthy country. It is ranked amongst the poorest countries in the world (UN, List of Least Developed Countries (as of

May 2016)). It faces many multi-faceted problems of its own, including frequent natural disasters and food shortages and more recently, has been subjected to terror attacks. Ideally, wealthier and more developed countries would assist in the resettlement of registered refugees. Nonetheless, the point is that Bangladesh does owe legal obligations to the Rohingyas, which it is not currently meeting.

4.2 *Undocumented Stateless Rohingyas in Bangladesh*

After 1992, the Bangladeshi government officially stopped accepting Rohingya people fleeing from Myanmar. In reality, however, many Rohingyas still fled to Bangladesh. Consequently, those who entered Bangladesh after May 1992 have been deemed illegal migrants by the Bangladeshi government (Abrar, 2003, p. 97). Abrar (2003, p. 97) called for a national law on refugees to solve the problem.

In its 2013 Strategy Paper, the government of Bangladesh officially recognised the existence of about 300,000 to 500,000 undocumented stateless Rohingyas in Bangladesh. According to the 2013 Strategy Paper, there should be a three-stage coordination mechanism at the national level, comprising:

(i) A National Coordination Committee under the leadership of the Foreign Minister;
(ii) A National Taskforce under the Chair of the Foreign Secretary; and
(iii) Local Taskforces at District/Upazilla levels under the Chair of Deputy Commissioners/ Upazilla Nirbahi Officers (UNOs).

As mentioned at the outset, stateless people and refugees are two different legal categories and so, technically, fall under two separate international treaties. Specifically, stateless persons are the subject of the *1954 Convention Relating to the Status of Stateless Persons,* Article 1 of which provides the *de jure* definition of statelessness. Further, the *1961 Convention on the Reduction of Statelessness* sets out rules for conferral and non-withdrawal of citizenship to prevent and/or avoid statelessness (Articles 1–10). Persons who are refugees, however, are the subject of the *1951 Convention relating to the Status of Refugees* and the *1967 Protocol relating to the Status of Refugees.* Nonetheless, these two regimes are both managed by the UN High Commissioner for Refugees (UNHCR).

This raises two questions in the context of stateless Rohingyas in Bangladesh:

(i) Do stateless Rohingyas qualify as 'refugees' under the *1951 Convention relating to the Status of Refugees* and its *1967 Protocol*?
(ii) If so, is Bangladesh then subject to the obligation of non-refoulement?

These questions are now considered.

4.2.1 *Do stateless Rohingyas qualify as 'refugees' under the 1951 Convention relating to the Status of Refugees and its 1967 Protocol?*

The *1951 Convention relating to the Status of Refugees* and its *1967 Protocol* provide that a person is to be considered a refugee if he/she has a 'well-founded fear of being persecuted for reasons of race, religion, nationality, membership of a particular social group, or political opinion' (Article 1, the *1951 Convention*).

The question in relation to unregistered Rohingyas in Bangladesh is whether the refusal of the Bangladeshi government to allow a determination process for 'new arrivals' of Rohingya peoples constitutes persecution, so as to satisfy this criteria. This is because unregistered Rohingyas in Bangladesh are particularly vulnerable. According to the Refugee International report on Bangladesh (n.d.),

> These unregistered refugees live a hand-to-mouth existence – only marginally worse off than the host population. Humanitarian needs continue to grow for Rohingya refugees. In one unofficial camp, malnutrition rates are twice the emergency threshold. The lack of assistance for both unregistered refugees and host communities have increased tensions over scarce resources such as water and firewood, leading to physical and sexual violence against refugees, particularly women and girls. There is little security for undocumented refugees and no access to the police or justice system.

There is also a further question as to whether Myanmar's denying citizenship to the Rohingya constitutes arbitrary deprivation of nationality, and whether, in turn, that constitutes persecution under the *1951 Convention relating to the Status of Refugees*. Lambert has examined this issue based on the state practice of various countries, including the US, UK, New Zealand, Australia, Germany, Spain and Belgium, and concluded that the approach to recognising deprivation of nationality as 'persecution' should be accepted (Lambert, 2015, pp. 32–7). In essence, this is not only because arbitrary deprivation of nationality may lead to serious practical consequences or severe discrimination (such as institutionalised, widespread or systematic discrimination), but it is a 'severe and serious violation of human rights', which is the right to have rights (Lambert, 2015, pp. 32–7).

4.2.2 Is Bangladesh then subject to the obligation of non-refoulement?

Bangladesh is not a party to the *1951 Convention relating to the Status of Refugees* nor its *1967 Protocol* (see UN Treaty Collection official website https://treaties.un.org). In addition, it is not a party to the *1954 Convention Relating to the Status of Stateless Persons* and *1961 Convention on the Reduction of Statelessness*. However, this does not mean that Bangladesh is free to deal with Rohingyas as it chooses. This is because the non-refoulement principle under the *1951 Refugee Convention* (amended by the *1967 Protocol*) may have become customary international law. For example, on 31 January 1994, the UNHCR explained in its *Response to the Questions Posed to UNHCR by the Federal Constitutional Court of the Federal Republic of Germany in Cases 2 BvR 1938/93, 2 BvR 1953/93, 2 BvR 1954/93* that the principle of non-refoulement constitutes a rule of international customary law (UNHCR, *The Principle of Non-Refoulement as a Norm of Customary International Law*).

Further, as Bangladesh has ratified various international human rights treaties, including the *Convention against Torture and Other Cruel, Inhuman or Degrading Treatment or Punishment* (CAT) and the ICCPR (UN Treaties Ratification Status for Bangladesh), it is bound by the non-refoulement obligations under those treaties. Specifically, Article 3 of the CAT clearly provides that: 'no state party shall expel, return or extradite a person where there are substantial grounds for believing that he would be in danger of being subjected to torture'. Further, The UN Human Rights Committee's General Comment No 31 (2004, p. 12) recognised that the member states of the ICCPR have:

> an obligation not to extradite, deport, expel or otherwise remove a person from their territory, where there are substantial grounds for believing that there is a real risk of irreparable harm, such as that contemplated by articles 6 and 7 of the Covenant, either in the country to which removal is to be effected or in any country to which the person may subsequently be removed.

Given the history of the treatment of the Rohingyas by Mynamar, if stateless Rohingya people are pushed back by Bangladesh to Myanmar, there is a strong likelihood they would face an immediate threat to life and freedom and a danger of irreparable harm. The manner of refoulement, by push-backs into dangerous waters, including in unsafe vessels, is also dangerous in and of itself.

Although Bangladesh may have the obligation of non-refoulement from the perspective of international law, this does not mean that Bangladesh is obliged to do so as a matter of domestic law. Bangladesh, like Australia, for example, adopts a 'dualist' approach to international law (Karim and Theunissen, 2011, p. 101). In essence, this means international treaties do not have legal force at the domestic level in the absence of domestic legislation to that effect. The status of customary international law, however, is slightly different. It is generally accepted that customary international law is part of Bangladeshi law if it is not contrary to domestic law (Karim and Theunissen, 2011, p. 106). However, if there is any conflict between domestic law and international law, the court is obliged to respect domestic law (Karim and Theunissen, 2011, p. 109). Nonetheless, the point is that despite efforts made under international law to bring order to the issue of statelessness, the approach taken by Bangladesh – and the lack of concern shown by other wealthier countries – has contributed to further disorder.

5. Conclusion

In this chapter we have set out the history of the Rohingya peoples and their relationship with both Bangladesh and Myanmar. We have done this so as to illustrate the legal 'black-hole' that the Rohingyas find themselves in. This is in spite of efforts made in international treaties to bring 'order' to the issue of statelessness and determination of refugee status. Ultimately, we have concluded that the treatment of Rohingya peoples by both Myanmar and Bangladesh may found a basis of persecution for the purposes of the *1951 Convention relating to the Status of Refugees*. If this is the case, then obligations of non-refoulment do arise as a matter of customary international law.

This chapter demonstrates that the right to nationality in international law does not grant Rohingyas citizenship of either Myanmar or Bangladesh in practice. The existence in customary international law of the non-refoulement principle is unlikely to improve the Rohingya people's plight. Without teeth and a stronger implementation mechanism, the order offered by international law is closer to disorder in reality. More importantly, if nation-states and sovereignty remain key threads to the fabric of international law, the disorder of statelessness will endure, especially if nation-states remain unwilling to cooperate. The only way out of this impasse is designing and implementing a creative notion of 'global citizenship' – for example, under which the UNHRC could grant stateless Rohingyas some sort of citizenship/passport without attaching it to any nation-state. This should be the next stage in the research agenda on statelessness in the global order/disorder.

References

Abrar, C. R. (2003). Still waiting for a better morrow: A decade of Burmese refugees in Bangladesh. In P.R. Chari, J. Mallika and S. Chandran (Eds.), *Missing boundaries: Refugees, migrants, stateless and internally displaced persons in South Asia* (pp. 87–98). New Delhi: Manohar.

Abrar, C.R. (2013). Multilevel approaches to human security and conflict management: The Rohingya case, NTS Policy Brief No. PO13-03. Singapore: RSIS Centre for Non-Traditional Security (NTS) Studies.

Abrar, C. R. (2014, June 21). Government strategy paper on Rohingyas. *The Daily Star*. Retrieved from: http://www.thedailystar.net/government-strategy-paper-on-rohingyas-29526.

Abrar, C. R., (2015a, March 8). Marriage ban on Rohingyas. *The Daily Star*. Retrieved from: http://www.thedailystar.net/marriage-ban-on-rohingyas-33343.

Abrar, C. R. (2015b, July 13). Why relocating Rohingyas is not the answer. *The Daily Star* (13 July 2015). Retrieved from: http://www.thedailystar.net/op-ed/why-relocating-rohingyas-not-the-answer-111529.

Abrar, C. R. (2016a, June 4). The curious contents of the Citizenship Law. *The Daily Star*. Retrieved from: http://www.thedailystar.net/op-ed/politics/the-curious-contents-the-citizenship-law-1233943.

Abrar, C. R. (2016b, June 10). Citizenship Law 2016: Need for thorough scrutiny, drastic revision. *New Age*. Retrieved from: http://newagebd.net/234574/citizenship-law-2016-need-thorough-scrutiny-drastic-revision/.

AFP (2012, June 13). Bangladeshi authorities turn away Rohingya refugees. Retrieved from: http://www.dvb.no/news/bangladeshi-authorities-turn-away-rohingya-refugees/22428.

Anand, J. P. (1978). Bangladesh: Refugees from Burma. *Economic and political weekly*, *13*, 27.

Asia Pacific Refugee Rights Network. (n.d.). Country fact sheet – Bangladesh. Retrieved from: http://www.aprrn.info/1/index.php/programmes/geographic-programmes/south-asia-working-group/189-country-profiles-bangladesh>.

Asia Pacific Refugee Rights Network. (2013). Annual report 2013. Retrieved from: http://www.aprrn.info/1/pdf/Annual%20Report%202013.pdf.

Bialosky, J. (2015). Regional protection of the right to nationality. *Cardozo Journal of International & Comparative Law*, *24*, 153–92.

Blaustein, S. (1992). Burma shave. *The New Republic*, *206*(19), 17.

Huda, M.S. (2013). The Rohingya refugee crisis of 2012: Asserting the need for constructive regional & international engagement. *South Asian Journal*, *7*. Retrieved from: http://southasiajournal.net/2013/03/the-rohingya-refugee-crisis-of-2012-asserting-the-need-for-constructive-regional-international-engagement/.

Human Aid (n.d.). Burma appeal. Retrieved from: http://www.human-aid.org/projects/burma/.

Human Rights Watch (2000). Burmese refugees in Bangladesh: Still no durable solution. Retrieved from: http://www.hrw.org/report/2000/05/01/burmese-refugees-bangladesh/still-no-durable-solution.

Karim, B. and Theunissen, T. (2011). Bangladesh. In D. Shelton (Ed.), *International law and domestic legal systems: Incorporation, transformation and persuasion* (pp. 98–115). Oxford: Oxford University Press.

Kelley, N. (2010). Ideas, interests, and institutions: Conceding citizenship in Bangladesh. *University of Toronto Law Journal*, *60*, 349–71.

Kipgen, N. (2014). Assessing Rohingya problem. *Journal of Asian and African Studies*, *49*(2), 234–47.

Kristof, N. (2016, January 30). Myanmar's Aung San Suu Kyi: The dark side of the hero. *The Age*. Retrieved from: http://www.theage.com.au/comment/myanmars-aung-san-suu-kyi-facing-ethnic-cleansing-coverup-20160127-gmf0wu.html.

Lambert, H. (2015). Comparative perspectives on arbitrary deprivation of nationality and refugee status. *International and Comparative Law Quarterly, 64*(1), 1–37.

Law Commission (2005). *Report on the proposed Law of Citizenship of Bangladesh*. Retrieved from: http://www.lawcommissionbangladesh.org/reports/67.pdf.

Ministry of Foreign Affairs, Government of the People's Republic of Bangladesh (2014). *Letter to the UN organizations and other international organizations with the attachment of 'Strategy Paper on Addressing the Issue of Myanmar Refugees and Undocumented Myanmar Nationals in Bangladesh: A Summary Presentation*. Retrieved from: https://assets.documentcloud.org/documents/1363897/un-hr-bangladesh.pdf.

Palmer, V. (2011). Analysing cultural proximity: Islamic relief worldwide and Rohingya refugees in Bangladesh. *Development in Practice, 21*(1), 96–108.

Paulsen, E. (2006). The citizenship status of the Urdu-speakers/Biharis in Bangladesh. *Refugee Survey Quarterly, 25*(3), 54–69.

Paxton, A. (2012). Finding a country to call home: A framework for evaluating legislation to reduce statelessness in Southeast Asia. *Pacific Rim Law & Policy Journal, 21*, 624–53.

Ragland, T. K. (1994). 'Burma's Rohingyas in crisis: Protection of "humanitarian" refugees under international law. *Boston College Third World Law Journal, 14*(2), 301–36.

Rahman, M. (2014, October 20). New citizenship law in the offing. *New Age* (20 October 2014). Retrieved from: http://newagebd.net/59222/new-citizenship-law-in-the-offing/.

Refugee and Migratory Movements Research Unit (2014). *Addressing the plight of the Rohingyas summary* (Policy Brief No 9).

Refugee International (2012). Rohingyas in Bangladesh, maintaining the status quo, squandering a rare opportunity, *Refugee International Report*.

Refugee International (2016). Bangladesh. Retrieved from: https://www.refintl.org/where-we-work/asia/bangladesh (unavailable now, but available at http://archive.is/7kr3m).

Reynolds, S. (2015). Things get worse: Rohingya in Bangladesh. Retrieved from: http://www.refugeesinternational.org/blog/2015/8/16/things-get-worse-rohingya-in-bangladesh.

Roberts, G. and Bennett, J. (2015, May 21). Tony Abbott rules out resettling Rohingyas in Australia, Indonesia says it is obliged to. *ABC News*. Retrieved from: http://www.abc.net.au/news/2015-05-21/rohingyas-migrants-indonesia-says-australia-obliged-resettle/6486590.

Rubenstein, K. and Adler, D. (2000). International citizenship: The future of nationality in a globalized world. *Indiana Journal of Global Legal Studies, 7*, 519–48.

Shearer, I. and Opeskin, B. (2012). Nationality and statelessness. In B. Opskin, R. Perruchoud and J. Redpath-Cross (Eds.), *Foundations of international migration law* (pp. 93–122). Cambridge: Cambridge University Press.

Stewart, M. (2013). Development in the international field: 'Rotting of the flower': Persecution of the Rohingya threatens Myanmar's democratic transition and further imperils the right to a nationality. *Georgetown Immigration Law Journal, 27*(3), 437–443.

Tang, L.L. (2005). *Statelessness, human rights and gender: Irregular migrant workers from Burma in Thailand*. Leiden: Nijhoff.

Uliah, A.A. (2011). Rohingya refugees to Bangladesh: Historical exclusions and contemporary marginalization. *Journal of Immigrant & Refugee Studies, 9*, 139–61.

Union of Catholic Asian News (2014). Rohingya banned from marrying Bangladesh nationals. Retrieved from: http://www.ucanews.com/news/rohingya-banned-from-marrying-bangladesh-nationals/71388.

United Nations (2016). *List of least developed countries (as of May 2016)*. Retrieved from: http://www.un.org/en/development/desa/policy/cdp/cdp_ldcs_countryfacts.shtml.

United Nations High Commissioner for Refugees (2015). Bangladesh fact sheet. Retrieved from: http://www.unhcr.org/50001ae09.html.

UNHCR (1994). The principle of non-refoulement as a norm of customary international law. Response to the questions posed to UNHCR by the Federal Constitutional Court of the Federal Republic of Germany in Cases 2 BvR 1938/93, 2 BvR 1953/93, 2 BvR 1954/93. Retrieved from: http://www.refworld.org/docid/437b6db64.html.

UNHCR (2007). Bangladesh: Analysis of gaps in the protection of Rohingya refugees. Retrieved from: http://www.unhcr.org/46fa1af32.pdf.

UNHCR Policy Development and Evaluation Service (2011). States of denial: A review of UNHCR's response to the protracted situation of stateless Rohingya refugees in Bangladesh. Retrieved from: http://www.unhcr.org/4ee754c19.pdf.

Von Glahb, G. (1992). *Law among nations: An introduction to public international law*. New York: MacMillan Publishing Company.

Yale Law School (2015). *Persecution of the Rohingya Muslims: Is genocide occurring in Myanmar's Rankine State? A legal analysis*. Retrieved from: http://www.fortifyrights.org/downloads/Yale_Persecution_of_the_Rohingya_October_2015.pdf.

Zawacki, B. (2013). Defining Myanmar's 'Rohingya problem'. *Human Rights Brief, 20*, 18–25.

Ziemele, I. and Schram, G.G. (1999). Article 15. In G. Alfredsson and A. Eide (Eds.), *The Universal Declaration of Human Rights: A common standards of achievement* (pp. 297–323). The Hague: Martinus Nijhoff.

Case

Lichtenstein v Guatemala (Second Phase), Judgment of International Court of Justice on 6 April 1955.

Conventions and Legislations

1948 Union Citizenship Act (Myanmar)

1951 Bangladesh Citizenship Act

1951 Pakistan Citizenship Act

1982 Citizenship Law (Myanmar)

American Convention on Human Rights, opened for signature 22 November 1969, 1144 UNTS 123 (entered into force 18 July 1978)

Arab Charter on Human Rights, adopted in Cairo on 15 September 1995 by the League of Arab States

ASEAN Human Rights Declaration, adopted in Phnom Penh, Cambodia on 18 November 2012 by the ASEAN Member States

Bangladesh Citizenship (Temporary Provisions) Order 1972 (P.O. No. 149 of 1972)

Constitution of the People's Republic of Bangladesh 1972

Convention against Torture and Other Cruel, Inhuman or Degrading Treatment or Punishment, opened for signature 10 December 1984, 1465 UNTS 112 (entered into force 26 June 1987)

Convention on the Elimination of All Forms of Discrimination against Women, opened for signature 18 December 1979, 1249 UNTS 13 (entered into force 3 September 1981)

Convention on the Reduction of Statelessness, opened for signature 30 August 1961, 989 UNTS 175 (entered into force 13 December 1975)

Convention on the Rights of the Child, opened for signature 20 November 1989, 1577 UNTS 3 (entered into force 2 September 1990)

Convention relating to the Status of Refugees, opened for signature 25 July 1951, 189 UNTS 137 (entered into force 22 April 1954)

Convention relating to the Status of Stateless Persons, opened for signature 28 September 1954, 360 UNTS 117 (entered into force 6 June 1960)

European Convention on Nationality, opened for signature 6 November 1997, ETS No 166 (entered into force 1 March 2000)
Human Rights Committee, *General Comment No 31: Nature of the General Legal Obligation on States Parties to the Covenant*, UN Doc. CCPR/C/21/Rev.1/Add.13 (2004)
International Covenant on Civil and Political Rights, opened for signature 19 December 1966, 999 UNTS 171 (entered into force 23 March 1976)
International Covenant on Economic, Social and Cultural Rights, opened for signature 16 December 1966, 993 UNTS 3 (entered into force 3 January 1976)
Protocol relating to the Status of Refugees, opened for signature 31 January 1967, 606 UNTS 267 (entered into force 4 October 1967)
Universal Declaration of Human Rights, adopted by the UN General Assembly on 10 December 1948
UN General Assembly, *Question of the Establishment, in accordance with the* Convention on the Reduction of Statelessness, *of a Body to which Persons Claiming the Benefit of the Convention may Apply* (resolution adopted on 10 December 1974), UN Doc A/RES/3274 (XXIX)
UN General Assembly, *Situation of Human Rights in Myanmar* (resolution adopted on 24 December 2014), UN Doc A/RES/69/248

Capitalism

8 Caring Capitalism?

The Case of Japanese Employment

Leon Wolff

Capitalism is the dominant model of economic governance in the world today. Among the varieties of capitalisms, Japan's is said to exemplify a benign, kinder form than the neo-liberal ideal – a capitalism with a human face, a capitalism that cares. To test this claim, this chapter explores the realm of work in Japan, especially Japan's institution of lifelong employment. Lifelong employment is a good case study for two linked reasons. First, by guaranteeing workers a job for life, it expresses a concern for employee welfare over the immediacy of profit-making. Second, by making employees an important stakeholder in corporate governance, it represents a Japanese alternative to the Western model of shareholder primacy. However, this chapter argues that Japanese capitalism does not have a beating heart. Instead, an analysis of the legal regulation of employment rights in Japan reveals a dark side to lifelong employment's promise of employment stability to Japanese workers.

For a time, Coates (2007, p. 179) writes, the Japanese economy was revered as a model of progressive capitalism. Central to this case was Japan's employment system (eg, Abe & Shimizutani, 2005, pp. 1–2; Shimoda, 2016, p. 754). In particular, lifelong employment – a corporate practice that elevates employee interests over shareholder returns – was said to exemplify the "human" side to Japanese-style capitalism (eg, Ozaki, 1991). The firm is a family, not a corporate entity (Dore, 2000, p.107; Inagami & Whittaker, 2005); employees are stakeholders, not human resources (Araki, 2005, pp. 26–27; Jacoby, 2005b); employment is a community of mutual interests, not a bifurcation of managers and operatives (Coates, 2000, p. 59; Dore 2000, p. 107; Wolff, 2008, pp. 56–57). Employers invested in their workers' career development. Employees repaid with their loyalty. Drawing on the productive power of the cooperative workplace ruled by relational ties of trust and goodwill (Lazonick, 1992, p. 144; Coates, 2000, pp. 127–128; Haley, 2005b; Wolff, 2008, p. 57), the Japanese economy boomed – at least between 1965 and 1990 when nominal GDP increased ten-fold (Rosenbluth & Thies, 2010, p. 72).

Then, in the 1990s, things changed. The asset bubble burst. Land prices collapsed. Secured loans became worthless. Banks folded or merged. Business investment sank. Companies filed for insolvency in record numbers. Unemployment spiked (Citrin and Wolfson, 2006; Cook and McKay, 2006; Tsutsui & Mazzotta, 2014, pp. 67–68). Japan went from "economic power house" to "basket case" (Rosenbluth & Thies, 2010, p. 73; see also Tsutsui & Mazzotta, 2014, pp. 67–73). Growth rates hovered at less than 1% in 1992 and 1993, pitching into negative territory in 1998 and 2001. Japan's share of world GDP shrunk from 9% in 1991 to 6% in 2010 (Tsutsui & Mazzotta, 2014, p. 67). Following the turn of the century, a return to 2–3% growth levels led some to pronounce that "Japan was back!" (Citrin and Wolfson, 2006). The good news, however, was short-lived. In 2008, the global financial crisis caused a crash on the Nikkei Index; in March 2011, the triple disaster of earthquake, tsunami and nuclear fallout crippled the Tohoku region; and, today, "Abenomics", the aggressive economic policies of Prime Minister Shinzo Abe following his landslide election in December 2012, have had little lasting effect (Tsutsui & Mazzotta, 2014, pp. 72–73).

As Japan's economic system "soured" (Katz, 1998), the world turned its admiring eyes away from its brand of capitalism. Following a period of praise for its economic success in the 1970s ("Japan-admiring") and then fear for its export-oriented trade performance in the 1980s that led to trade imbalances with major partners ("Japan-bashing"), a new phenomenon emerged in the 1990s: "Japan-passing" (Stockwin, 2003; Drysdale, 2004). Japan became largely forgotten as world leaders, policy-makers and academics rushed to engage with the emerging economic powerhouses of China and India. In the 1990s, Japan was not just lost; it was slipping into irrelevance.

Lifelong employment, unsurprisingly, underwent a scholarly re-appraisal. After all, lifelong employment is more than just an industrial relations system (eg, Boyer and Juillard, 2000); it is a symbol of Japan's (now failed) model of economic governance (Gilson & Roe, 1999, p. 509; Abe & Shimizutani, 2005, pp. 1–2; Shimoda, 2016, p. 754). Critics began dismissing lifetime employment as an anachronism (Ahmadjian and Robinson, 2001, p. 624; Boyer and Yamada, 2000a, p. 3). By locking in employees, they reasoned, it caused labour mobility inefficiencies; by preventing employers from re-structuring, it saddled firms with surplus labour in the face of heightened international competition, rising debts and weakening sales (Ahmadjian and Robinson, 2001, pp. 624–625). The ageing of the population, too, meant firms had a preponderance of their workers in the higher salary brackets (Mouer and Kawanishi, 2005, p. 258). Scholars also started to predict the "end of history" (Hansmann and Kraakman, 2001) for lifelong employment, forecasting it would eventually de-institutionalise as a distinctive feature of Japanese economic governance (eg, Ahmadjian and Robinson, 2001; McAlinn, 2007) and undergo "Americani[s]ation" (Kelemen and Sibbitt, 2002) into a more neo-liberal market design (cf Tsuruta, 2005; Wolff, 2008, 2010, 2016).

These criticisms, however, are incomplete. In targeting the merits of lifelong employment, they strike to its *mind* (the economic logic) and its *body* (institutional robustness). But what about its *heart*? The scholarship on the normative appeal of lifelong employment – as a kinder, more benign expression of capitalism – almost completely departed the literature on Japanese economic governance and regulation in the early 21st century (Coates, 2005, p. 179), coinciding, no doubt, with cumulating evidence of Japan's economic decline. This chapter seeks to resurrect it as a case study – not to comment on its *economic* virtues or *institutional* evolution in Japanese capitalism, but to explore its potential insights into the *emotional* core of capitalism itself. This chapter argues that an analysis of lifelong employment, including its design, empirics and legal regulation, can help us answer the larger question: can capitalism, as the dominant form of economic governance globally today, care?

This is not an easy argument to mount. For example, why *should* capitalism care – after all, it is an economic order aimed at accumulating wealth and lifting living standards, not a social welfare system. Part 1 addresses this concern. Although acknowledging the systemic and hegemonic dominance of capitalism as a model of global economic governance today, Part 1 refers to the literature on Varieties of Capitalism and Regulationist[1] Theory to demonstrate that capitalism is also a social and political system – and that it makes sense to scrutinise capitalism for its ability to serve the interests of human society.

Even so, *why consider* Japan – and, in particular, Japan's system of lifelong employment – as a case study into this inquiry? Part 2 responds that, although the Japanese economy no longer enjoys miracle status, it is still a major economy, and its trajectory of boom and bust is actually typical of all capitalist orders. Further, lifelong employment is a good case study for three reasons: first, according to the empirical evidence, it still survives as a distinct institution of the Japanese economy; second, according to some scholarly accounts, it demonstrates a human concern for employee welfare over shareholder return; and, third, it is not an isolated feature of Japanese capitalism but interlocks with other institutions (such as *keiretsu* corporate groups and main bank debt financing) to form a logically coherent economic system. In short, this chapter does *not* set up a straw man argument, and it does *not* fall into the trap of selection bias in its choice of case study. Lifelong employment exists; it exhibits traits relevant to the research question; and it complements other economic institutions in Japan's system of economic governance.

But does lifelong employment furnish evidence that capitalism can care? This is the subject of Part 3. Drawing on broader socio-legal explanations of Japanese law and governance, Part 3 posits three possibilities:

- The strong case is that capitalism *can* care because human values of care and compassion can infuse it;
- The weak case is that capitalism *might* care, but only if its economic institutions make friendly relations economically efficient (eg, Puchniak, 2008); and
- The negative case is that capitalism *cannot* care, because wealth-seeking behaviour comes with inevitable social costs.

Part 3 looks to how Japanese law regulates work to select among these three options. Although Japan has no direct law that guarantees lifelong employment (Araki, 2005, 2007), it does erect an indirect regulatory scheme, through a network of statutory provisions and judicial statements, assuring employees employment security (Foote, 1996; Yamakawa, 2001; Araki, 2005, 2007; Wolff, 2016). However, there is a trade-off – employers enjoy significant flexibility to deploy their workforce, not only within the firm but within the larger corporate group. This flexibility carries significant social and economic costs for Japanese workers. Capitalism, the chapter concludes, does not care – or, if it does, it does so with half a heart.

1. The capitalist "order"

Capitalism is the dominant model of economic governance today. According to Lippit (2005, pp. 2–3), capitalism entrenched itself as the preferred economic system by the 16th century. It achieved "maturity" – that is, it cohered with political and social systems – by the 19th century,

1 This chapter uses the term regulation*ist* theory to distinguish it from regulat*ory* theory. Regulat*ory* theory, common in legal scholarship, is a "focused attempt to alter the behaviour of others according to defined standards or purposes with the intention of producing a broadly defined outcome or outcomes . . . " (Black, 2002, p. 26); see further O'Leary in Chapter 14. Regulation*ist* theory, by contrast, is an economic theory that seeks to explain the political, social and economic contradictions and imbalances that underpin different regimes of accumulation (Boyer, 2001; 2005; Boyer & Juillard, 2000; Boyer & Yamada, 2000a; 2000b).

largely due to "British hegemony . . . , the social and economic implications of the Industrial Revolution, and . . . the global echoes of the French Revolution" (Levi-Faur, 2005, p. 15). "By the 1990s," with the collapse of the Soviet Union and the economic surge of China to the second-largest economy in the world, "it has become clear that [it] is the only game in town . . . worldwide" (Lippit, 2005, p. xv). It is likely to persist for centuries to come. It has no viable competitor (Lippit, 2005, p. 3; see also Boyer, 2005, p. 510).

Capitalism is a regime of accumulation (Levi-Faur, 2005, p. 15). It has only one goal and rationale – to generate prosperity (Lippit, 2005, p. 2). This has been the case ever since Adam Smith penned *An Inquiry into the Nature and Causes of the Wealth of Nations* in 1776. Individual effort, open markets and rational, self-interested behaviour not only bring individual material rewards; "it can [also] generate positive social and economic consequences for the entire community" (Lippit, 2005, p. 2). On this score, capitalism has been a singular success. It has lifted living standards across the globe and brought the pleasures of consumption to successive generations (Vrasti, 2011). Asia is the current beneficiary. Since the turn of the century, Asia's contribution to world economic growth has matched that of the United States and Europe combined, and, since 2006, has even exceeded it (International Monetary Fund, 2011; Neumann and Arora, 2011). In 2016, it still leads global economic growth (International Monetary Fund, 2016). "Billions of Asians," declares Mahbubani (2008, p. 3), "are marching to modernity."

Little wonder, then, that capitalism is entrenched as a hegemony (see also Lippit, 2005, pp. 2–3). As Bird (Chapter 4, this volume) observes, it is embraced by the Right, and it is increasingly accepted by the Left. It needs little justification to defend and "increasingly dangerous acrobatics" to criticise (Vrasti, 2011). An alternative economic logic is almost impossible to image, "akin to envisioning an alternative universe" (Lippit, 2005, p. 2).

Capitalism, however, is not a monolith. Although an economic model to generate wealth, its institutions, practices and norms configure themselves differently depending on time (eg, Levi-Faur, 2005) or space (eg, Coates, 2000; Hall & Soskice, 2001; Boyer, 2005; Clarke, 2016). This is the empirical finding of Variety of Scholars (VoC) scholars (Hall and Soskice, 2001; Hall, 2003; Crouch, 2005) and Regulationist Theorists (eg, Boyer & Juillard, 2000; Coates, 2000). Different classificatory schemes exist. The simplest is Hall and Soskice's (2001) which contrasts only two key types of capitalism: neo-liberal orders (exemplified by the United States) and coordinated market economies (epitomised by Germany). Slightly more diverse is Coates's (2000, pp. 9–10) which distinguishes three styles: market-led capitalism, where private firms make economic decisions based on market considerations of profitability (the US and the UK); State-led capitalisms, where State agencies and officials guide market decisions (Japan and South Korea); and negotiated or consensual capitalism, where social democratic or Christian democratic values give political primacy to worker's rights and social welfare (West Germany and Scandinavian countries). Boyer's (2005, pp. 529–533) is a four-part typology: market-led (the US and UK), meso-corporatist (Japan and South Korea), State-driven (European Union economies) and social-democratic (Scandinavia). And one of the more complex is Clarke's (2016) which identifies seven types: competitive capitalism, organised capitalism, state capitalism, regulated capitalism, welfare capitalism, planned capitalism and neo-liberal capitalism. Compared to these geographical carve-ups, Levi-Faur models global capitalism in historical moments (2005, pp. 15–16): laissez-faire capitalism (1800s–1930s);

welfare capitalism (1940s–1970s) and regulatory capitalism (1980s–) (for a critique, see Hay, 2000, pp. 509–515).

This variety opens up the study of capitalism beyond economists. The role of the State in economic institutional design attracts the interest of political scientists (eg, Amyx, 2006). Norms of economic organisations entice the attention of anthropologists (Dore, 1993, 2000). The regulation of entities, institutions and economic practices appeal to legal scholars (eg, Hansmann & Kraakman, 2001; cf Nottage & Wolff, 2004). And the social impacts of economic governance draw the scrutiny of sociologists (eg, Mouer & Kawanishi, 2005). Capitalism, in short, is more than a mode of economic governance. It represents diverse social and political systems or "market societies" (Wailes, Kitay & Lansbury, 2008, p. 20).

This has two implications:

- First, it is *possible* to compare the different versions of capitalism and search for an "exemplar" (cf Lippit, 2005, pp. 2–4).
- Second, it makes *sense* to approach this search, not only by considering each version's propensity to generate prosperity, but also in terms of its political, social and moral suitability for human society (cf Burkett & Hart-Landsberg, 1996, p. 630).

This justifies the question posed in this chapter: can capitalism care – or, more precisely, is there a "variety" of capitalism that can?

2. A Japanese exemplar?

2.1 *The case for lifelong employment*

Enter Japanese capitalism – and, in particular, the system of lifelong employment. Lifelong employment, as its name suggests, is a job for life. Graduates enter a firm – and stay until they reach retirement. Resignations and mid-career hires are rare. Firms offer employees in-house training and promotion; increase salaries in line with length of service; and provide health care and other welfare. Employees do not necessarily perform the same task for their entire careers; indeed, many employees take advantage of internal opportunities – either within the firm or in related entities – to extend their skill-sets (Haley, 2005b). However, job-hopping from firm to firm or from industry to industry is uncommon (Dore, 1993, p. 68). Lifetime tenure brings lifelong commitment. Employees strongly identify with their firms and are loyal to their employers; many even derive self-esteem and social prestige from their association with their firms (Ahmadjian and Robinson, 2001, pp. 623–624; Blanpain et al., 2007, pp. 526–527; McAlinn, 2007, pp. 403–407).

Lifelong employment, however, is more than an isolated employment practice (Coates, 2000, p. 127; Boyer & Yamada, 2000b, p. 14). It is a core feature of both Japanese corporate governance (Aoki, 1988; Gilson & Roe, 1999; Konzelmann, 2005, pp. 593–594; Abe & Shimizutani, 2007; Shimoda, 2016, p. 754) and its capitalist style (Boyer, 2001; Boyer & Yamada, 2000a; 2000b; Wolff, 2008). As such, an analysis of lifelong employment and its regulation should afford penetrating insights into all corners of the Japanese economy: from Japanese industrial relations to corporate governance to Japanese-style capitalism itself. It is an important piece of a larger economic jigsaw puzzle.

From a purely economic viewpoint, lifetime employment offers advantages to the J-firm. For example, the long-term attachments make it worthwhile for firms to invest in the technical training of their workforce in a planned and coordinated way. Early-career employees can be rotated throughout the different divisions within the firm or enterprise group to acquire a broad set of company-specific skills (Haley, 2005b). When companies decide to embark on new business strategies requiring new skills, they have the incentive to re-train their mid-career personnel (Lazonick, 1992, p. 144). Employees, too, are more likely to be industrious, to cooperate with their colleagues, and to limit wage demands to reasonable levels (Coates, 2000, pp. 127–128).

From a normative perspective, lifelong employment is admired for its "left-liberal" values: employees are respected, treated with dignity and are not alienated from management (Burkett & Hart-Landsberg, 1996, p. 65). It exemplifies Japan's gentler, more moral brand of capitalism: a "proletarian paradise" (Coates, 2000, p. 131), a "community firm" (Inagami and Whittaker, 2005) or "human capitalism" (Ozaki, 1991). Key to these assessments is that lifelong employment represents a "stakeholder model of corporate governance" (Araki, 2007; see also Jacoby, 2005b), privileging people over profit, unlike the Anglo-American shareholder primacy model:

> Traditionally, Japanese firms have been "organisation oriented" while American firms have been more "market oriented". This is reflected in the dominant features of corporate governance and work organisation, where . . . the Japanese system of *stakeholder*-oriented corporate governance and its view of labour as productive resource continues to stand in sharp contrast to the American *shareholder*-based system and view that labour is a factor of production with a *cost* to be minimised (Konzelmann, 2005, pp. 593–594).

The workplace is like a family (Dissanayake, 2012, p. 194). Dore, for example, draws on the imagery of the clan to differentiate the Japanese firm from its American cousin. The Japanese company, he writes, is a "transcendental entity"; managers are more "elders of an enterprise community" than "the agents of shareholder principals"; and employees have a "relationship with their firm comparable to a soldier's sense of regimental loyalty". This is a "long way" from the view of the firm as a nexus of contracts (Dore, 2000, p.107). Even those who describe Japanese corporate governance in more prosaic language see lifelong employment as evidence of "collective capitalism" rather than US-style "proprietary capitalism" (eg, Jacoby, 2005b; Lazonick, 1992).

2.2 *The case against lifelong employment*

Even so – who cares? *First*, why bother with the Japanese case at all? After all, since the 1990s, the Japanese economy has stagnated, limping lifelessly with low and even occasional negative growth rates (Katz, 1998). By contrast, China has emerged as an economic super-power (see, further, Davis, Chapter 5, this volume), eclipsing Japan as the second-largest economy in late 2010 (Monahan, 2011). By the 21st century, there was "sunset in the Land of the Rising Sun" (Black & Morrison, 2010). Academic interest in Japan began to wane (eg, Stockwin, 2003). World leaders turned away from Japan to focus more on China. Japan itself feared its growing global irrelevance (Mulgan, 2005, p. 104).

This objection can be swiftly dealt with. For one, despite its recent struggles, the Japanese economy – indeed, Japan itself – remains an important global figure (eg, Mulgan, 2005). As Rosenbluth and Thies (2008, p. 3) explain:

> Despite nearly two decades of economic stagnation, Japan remains a colossal power. Its economy is enormous and although it has been surpassed in absolute size by China's (with China's ten-times-as-large population), Japan is economically still more than a third larger than fifth-ranked Germany and twice as large as the United Kingdom or France. Although Japan officially has no army, navy, or air force, owing to its constitutional renunciation of war, the Japan Self Defence Forces (SDF) are in fact a formidable military by another name. By many other measures as well, Japan is an extremely influential player who actions have bearing for world peace, prosperity, and health.

For another, all economies go through cycles of boom and bust. Japan's is no exception. As Tsutsui & Mazzotta (2014, p. 73) rightly observe:

> If anything, the Japanese experience of bubble, bust, and stagnation just serves to confirm some fundamental truths that are as universal as they are commonsensical. Greed is part of human nature. Hindsight is 20/20. The optimal balance of free-market and public intervention is an elusive and ever-changing objective for regulators and market participants. Quick fixes seldom work. Drastic measures are often politically unappealing and yield unwelcome social disruption. And, sobering though it may be, not all stories – even ones that start as optimistically as that of Japan's postwar economy – have happy endings.

Second, why analyse lifelong employment, if, according to the evidence, it is a dying institution (eg, Ahmadjian & Robinson, 2001)? This objection has some anecdotal and empirical heft to it.

For example, McAlinn (2007, p. 408) reports an upward trend in job mobility in Japan in the early 21st century and an apparent decline of generic skills-training in favour of more focused specialities, such as in-house legal practice. Economic writers at the *Yomiuri Shimbun*, one of Japan's four major daily newspapers, predict the development of a stronger, more competitive external market for labour in Japan. The newspaper sees the emergence of the 'new' Japanese white-collar worker (*shinsha sarariiman*) who is more willing to test his or her worth on the open market and seek merit-based remuneration accordingly (Mouer & Kawanishi, 2005, pp. 258–259). These anecdotal and journalistic accounts have some support in survey data. A survey by Nikkei Research in February 2002, for example, indicated that over half of the 800 firms surveyed could no longer sustain permanent employment practices (Moriguchi and Ono, 2006, p. 167). Another of the 805 firms listed on Tokyo Stock Exchange and JASDAQ in November 2001 revealed that 82 firms had announced that they would retrench a total of 120,000 workers (Moriguchi & Ono, 2006, pp. 167, 172).

However, these conclusions sit uneasily with other empirical evidence. Abe and Shimizutani (2007, p. 347), for example, cite recent studies indicating a general increase in job tenure for full-time workers until the mid-1990s – and even until 2000. Further, a series of surveys on hiring practices among large Japanese corporations points to the continuance of lifelong employment practices. For example, a survey by the Japan Institute of Labour in 1999 found that 33.8% of respondents (690 companies out of 2,370 that employ 1,000 or more workers) intended to maintain lifelong employment, 44.8% would retain it in modified form, and only 17.1% would revisit the practice (Yamakawa, 2001, p. 630). A METI survey on the Corporate System and Employment in 2003 (cited in Jackson, 2007, p. 283) likewise revealed that most Japanese firms still commit to lifelong employment either in whole (85%) or in part (2%). Finally, a Ministry of Finance survey in 2002 (cited in Jackson, 2007, p. 283) reported that 79% of respondents maintain traditional lifelong employment and only 16% do not.

The better view of the evidence, therefore, is that lifelong employment is still intact, even though ongoing economic uncertainty is placing it under sustained institutional pressure (see further Wolff, 2008, 2009).

Third, and finally, why scrutinise lifelong employment given that it is just *one* dimension to Japanese capitalism? Might it not be an outlier institution when compared to Japanese banking practices, investment patterns, product markets or director–shareholder relationships? The best response to this concern is Aoki's (1988; 1994; 2007) influential theory of contingent corporate governance. In Aoki's view, lifelong employment exists in a complementary and co-dependent relationship with a constellation of other institutions of corporate governance – such as main-bank monitoring, insider-dominated boards, cross-shareholdings and a weak external market for corporate control – to form a cohesive, economically efficient system that promotes long-term productivity over short-term profiteering. In very brief terms, the institutions cohere as follows. Insider boards ensure that management and employees have shared views and interests. *Keiretsu* cross-shareholdings create a stable set of shareholders who then protect management from the threat of takeovers and free them to take a longer-term view of productive growth. The main bank, as part of the *keiretsu* corporate group, monitors management and takes action when the firm shows sign of decline or difficulty. Lastly, the promise of lifelong employment enables workers to commit long-term to the firm, as well as encourages them to work hard to avoid the threat of the main bank liquidating the business. Taken together, these "complementary" institutions not only create an alternative model of corporate governance to that of shareholder primacy; they also function, as rules of the game, to ensure its overall efficiency.

Therefore, lifelong employment *is* a legitimate case study into whether or not Japanese-style capitalism is a more humane version compared to other models, especially the Anglo-American neo-liberal model. First, Japan's is still a major economy globally, making its brand of capitalism worthy of scholarly investigation. Second, lifelong employment – painted in "romantic" terms (Wolff, 2008, p. 56) for its emphasis on welfare over profit – makes it an appropriate case study into the normative supremacy of Japanese capitalism. Third, since lifelong employment still endures as an institutionalised labour practice and co-exists logically with other corporate governance institutions, the case study is neither atypical nor specious.

3. How can capitalism care?

So how might lifelong employment represent a Japanese-style caring form of capitalism? There are three possibilities:

1 The *strong* case is that capitalism *can* care because human values of care and compassion can infuse it (eg, Dore, 1993, 2000).

2 The *weak* case is that capitalism *might* care, but only if its economic institutions make friendly relations economically efficient (eg, Puchniak, 2008).
3 The *negative* case is that capitalism *cannot* care, because wealth-seeking behaviour comes with inevitable social costs (eg, Burkett & Hart-Landsberg, 1996).

To test these possibilities, this part applies the socio-legal models of Japanese law that best "fit" these three cases: namely, the *cultural*, *institutional* and *political* theories of Japanese law (eg, see Port, 1994). It then explores the extent to which the law relating to lifelong employment furnishes support to any of these models.

3.1 Strong Case – Cultural Model

The strong case of a caring capitalism assumes that capitalism is an expression of a society's cultural values. Capitalisms, according to this view, vary across nation-states because they express the different cultural values of the people who operate within their systems of governance. So if a society is caring, so, too, should be its brand of capitalism. For this strong case to apply to Japanese capitalism, a cultural explanation of lifelong employment, as an economic expression of employee welfare, needs to be viable.

To be sure, a cultural explanation of lifelong employment *is* common in the literature (eg, Dore, 1993, 2000). The thrust of this model is that Japanese cultural preferences have informed the lifelong employment system. Strong group consciousness (eg, Kim & Lawson, 1979) among the Japanese underscores employee loyalty to the firm. The importance of extended family (*ie*) relationships enables employees to see the firm as a substitute family which, in turn, fosters cooperative, collegiate relationships. The vertical integration of social organisation guarantees diligence by employees and the paternal benevolence of employers (eg, Foote, 1996). The aversion to 'black-and-white' law ensures that the promise of job security does not require formalisation into a written contract. The preference for harmony over conflict ensures industrial peace and the humanistic practices of personnel managers (Coates, 2000, p. 127).

Legally, this cultural explanation is tempting. This is because there is no *direct* legal guarantee of lifelong employment in Japan. Lifelong employment, therefore, is a "practice", not a legal mandate (Araki, 2007). It is an "unwritten . . . guarantee" (Dore, 2000, p. 107), a "social norm" (Jackson, 2007, p. 282) or a "moral imperative" (Ahmadjian & Robinson, 2001, p. 624). For example, the Japanese Constitution states that citizens have a "right and duty" to work – yet, according to the Supreme Court (Judgment of 10 September 1958), the State is not required to give citizens any position they want or guarantee them a job for life. Corporate law makes little mention of the rights and interests of workers (Araki, 2007, p. 26), despite assumptions in the literature that employee welfare is the cornerstone of Japanese-style corporate governance (eg, Dore, 2000; Jacoby, 2005a, 2005b, 2005c). Employment contracts are silent on employment tenure (Miwa & Ramseyer, 2002). And Japanese labour statutes offer no assurance of permanent employment; on the contrary, article 20 of the Labour Standards Act (Law No. 49 of 1947) expressly entitles employers to dismiss employees "for any reason".

Despite this, however, the cultural model fails to convince. The key problem with the model lies in the significance given to the variable of culture. First, "culture" assumes a set of norms and behavioural practices that are universal and persistent (Coates, 2000, pp. 133–134). Yet lifelong employment applies to a core workforce of mostly male workers in large companies or major institutions, such as government ministries and agencies, schools and banks. Ono (2007, p. 33) estimates it applies to only one-fifth of the working population. It is hardly universal. Nor is it a long-standing convention, even in larger firms. Historical research shows that, despite some early roots in the 1920s, lifelong employment was first institutionalised in the 1950s and only became popular from the 1970s onwards (Sako, 2005, p. 527). In addition to attracting scarce labour into the private sector, the pledge of lifelong employment was a political compromise between labour and management to preserve industrial peace (Coates, 2000, p. 133). Second, if culture were the primary driver of industrial relations practices, then these practices should largely survive globalisation. Yet, according to some studies, foreign subsidiaries of Japanese multinationals are selective in the employment practices they export: they retain quality circles, long hours and enterprise unions, but they do not guarantee lifelong employment (Coates, 2000, p. 134).

Another problem with the cultural model is that Japanese law *does* regulate lifelong employment – albeit *indirectly*. This is through the judicial doctrine against unjust dismissals (Foote 1996; cf. Kettler & Tackney 1997). According to the Supreme Court of Japan, a dismissal lacking reasonable grounds is an "abuse of rights" that offends the "common sense of society" (Judgment of 25 April 1975, 29–4 *Minshu*, p. 456).[2] Although, to be sure, the doctrine against unjust dismissal does not uphold a "default" of permanent employment, it does negatively prevent employers from terminating employment arbitrarily and at will. And it is a powerful defence, too, because employees are not limited to a remedy for economic loss; they can also petition for injunctive relief to restore their employment. This demonstrates that lifelong employment operates in the shadow of the law (cf. West, 2006). It is misleading to characterise it as a mere cultural practice.

Therefore, a cultural model of lifelong employment is not compelling. By extension, a strong case of a caring Japanese capitalism cannot hold.

3.2 *Weak case – institutional model*

Even if capitalism does not *spontaneously* express benevolence, it may still *notionally* care. This is if its institutional design facilitates "friendly" economic transactions (Puchniak, 2008). This is the weak case of a caring capitalism –weak because capitalism's compassion is contingent on economic efficiency, not its innate nature and instinct. For this case to explain Japanese capitalism, an institutional explanation of the friendliness of lifelong employment needs to convince.

2 The courts strictly scrutinise the employee's reasons for dismissal. The high water-mark was reached in the widely-cited Supreme Court decision (Judgment of 31 January 1977, 268 *Rodo Hanrei*, p. 17) invalidating the dismissal of a presenter of an early morning news bulletin who had overslept twice in a fortnight, once missing the entire broadcast and another missing half of the program. The company argued that the employee was irresponsible and his actions had harmed the reputation of the station. However, the Court ruled that the dismissal was unduly harsh and unreasonable. This was because the radio station did not take steps – such as by offering a wake-up call service – to assist the announcer to arrive in time for his early morning shifts. Two years later, the Supreme Court (Judgment of 20 July 1979, 33–35 *Minshu*, p. 582) further invalidated as abusive the withdrawal of a provisional offer of employment to a university graduate who the personnel director later thought was too "gloomy" for the position.

Puchniak's (2008) theory of the "efficiency of friendliness" in Japanese economic governance is one such institutional account. Applying Aoki's (1988; 1994; 2007) model of complementary economic institutions, Puchniak (2008, p. 8) argues that lifelong employment – along with the main bank system, *keiretsu* groups and stable shareholdings, and a weak market for hostile takeovers – acts as a "self-reinforcing web of governance mechanisms that minimi[ses] agency costs and ensure[s] that capital [is] efficiently allocate throughout the economy". Put differently, employees, executives, main banks and stable shareholder are loyal to one another because it is in their mutual self-interests to do. Everyone benefits from stability that comes from mutual loyalty. Managers benefit because they can focus on long-term productivity rather than short-term profits, without fearing the loss of their jobs. Employees benefit because a stable firm is better for long-term employment than a fluctuating one. Banks benefit because they can be confident of regular repayments of their loans. *Keiretsu* shareholders benefit because they can get support from the wider corporate group.

> Japanese corporations could credibly make [the] promise [of lifetime employment] because main banks and stable shareholders largely protected companies from hostile takeovers and helped them restructured in times of financial crisis. In return, employees gave an implicit promise not to abandon the company, reinforced by a non-existent external labo[u]r market and a "top heavy" compensation system. The result of lifetime employment was that the survival of the company was intrinsically tied to the economic fortunes of executives and employees – the ultimate incentive for minimizing agency costs.

An institutional account of lifelong employment, however, has its drawbacks. The first problem is its assumption of the *a priori* existence of institutional forms. The theory does not explain how Japanese institutional forms came into existence, nor why they coalesced into a cohesive system in the way that they did. The second is the notion of the 'systemic complementarity' or the structural fit of institutional forms. As Aoki (2007, p. 441) puts it, the institutions of Japanese corporate governance existing in a mutually reinforcing, dynamic relationship, with a change or breakdown of one institution triggering cumulative shifts in the other forms towards a new equilibrium. The difficulty with this view is explaining how an institutional architecture that, for most of the post-war period, sustained high growth in the Japanese economy could suddenly lead to the prolonged economic slump in the 1990s and beyond. If there were a significant exogenous shock – such as the oil crises in the 1970s – then this might provide an answer, but arguably the collapse of the asset bubble was largely an endogenous and domestic event (Boyer & Juillard, 2000, pp. 121–122).

Therefore, the weak case of a caring capitalism, premised on the economic efficiency of friendliness, is not made out. This is because lifelong employment cannot be satisfactorily explained in institutional terms.

3.3 Negative case – political model

This leaves the negative case. The negative case is that capitalism cannot care because, politically and ideologically, compassion is irrelevant to its operation. For this to be the inexorable conclusion, a political explanation has to account for lifelong employment's features and traits.

A political model of lifelong employment has parallels with the institutional model but meets its limitations. The political model – relying on both economic history (Gilson & Roe, 1999; Sako, 2005, p. 527) and the economic school of regulationist theory (Boyer, 2001; 2005; Boyer & Juillard, 2000; Boyer & Yamada, 2000a; 2000b) – holds that lifelong employment was a political invention of the post-war period. As a political compromise forged between labour and management to preserve industrial peace and attract scarce labour away from government into the corporate sector, lifelong employment has underpinned Japan's wage-labour nexus and has sustained its ensuing regime of accumulation. Like the institutional model, it believes in the structural complementarity of institutional forms in the economy. According to regulation theory, it is the mode of regulation that defines the substantive design of institutions or practices. In the case of lifelong employment, for example, the mode of regulation is that of 'flexicurity' – a balance between security of tenure and flexibility of working conditions (Wilthagen & Tros, 2004). Flexicurity means that core workers in major firms can obtain permanent positions provided they accept: (i) lower-than-market wages in the early stages of their careers; (ii) rotations across different departments and branch offices at the discretion of personnel managers; and (iii) the possibility of early retirement or deployment to smaller, affiliated businesses on lower wages in the later stages of their professional careers.

This is exactly what Japanese law does. As a trade-off for the legal restrictions on employee dismissals, Japanese law affords employees with a number of tools to ensure flexible working practices. These tools roughly divide into two types: (i) those that empower management to command labour; and (ii) those that allow the outsourcing of work (Mouer and Kawanishi, 2005, p. 111). Recent legislative amendments have mostly operated to increase these powers.

First, Japanese corporate and competition law affords firms considerable freedom to structure their businesses into an enterprise group. The longstanding prohibition on holding companies since the end of the war was lifted by 1997 reforms to the Anti-Monopoly Law (No. 54 of 1947, amended by No. 87 of 1997). Subsequent reforms to the Commercial Code in 1999 and 2000, retained in the new Company Law (No. 86 of 2005), facilitated the creation of holding companies and corporate divisions by obviating the need for the individual consent of creditors. This reform has allowed firms to create more distinct business units through which they can rotate their personnel freely (Inagami and Whittaker, 2005, ch. 6).

Second, the Labour Standards Act authorises employers to unilaterally alter working conditions, including specifications about the type and place of work. This frees up Japanese companies to transfer redundant staff above their objections to other divisions or affiliated businesses. Although the Act provides that the employment contract must specify the conditions of work, including the location and required duties, it also allows employers to promulgate work rules that apply across the whole organisation (art. 89). Employers are expected to consult with worker representatives but are not required to obtain their consent. Employers typically reserve in their work rules a right to transfer staff, and the courts have generally not interfered with the exercise of this right.

Third, a range of judicial and legislative developments permits employers to weaken working conditions to protect their firms against souring business conditions. For example, the Supreme Court (Judgment of 25 December 1968, cited in Araki, 2007, p. 251) held that companies may make an unfavourable modification of their work rules, provided they are reasonable in the circumstances. In addition, although the Labour Standards Act states that contractual working conditions cannot be inferior to the work rules (art. 93), the judiciary has allowed the converse – namely, work rules that are inferior to contractual conditions. Further, 1998 amendments to the Labour Standards Act have introduced a discretionary work scheme for most white-collar workers. This defines working time by reference to the tasks completed rather than the hours worked. Since this separates overtime entitlements from actual hours worked, the Law allows companies to control their overtime budgets as well as foster increased competition among workers and intensified working practices (Mouer & Kawanishi, 2005, p. 111).

Fourth, Japanese law has increased the power of firms to casualise their workplaces. Under former law, the legal maximum limit for an employment contract was one year. However, the 2003 amendment to the Labour Standards Law has increased this upper limit to three years. This is attractive to managers for two reasons. One is that it allows them to 'lock-in' a casual workforce rather than rely on annual contract renewals. The other is that it provides an opportunity to make strategic, medium-term hires of professional staff or skilled technicians and thereby externalise some of the costs of training. Moreover, the Worker Dispatching Law (No. 88 of 1985) has been dramatically deregulated. Originally restricting legal dispatch of temporary workers to sixteen highly specialised occupation categories, the number of categories was lifted to twenty-six in 1996. In 1999, the in-principle prohibition on worker dispatch was removed and the supply of temporary labour became available for most occupational fields (Araki, 2007, p. 276; Mouer & Kawanishi, 2005, p. 115). In 2003, the prohibition on dispatching workers to production sites was removed altogether.

Some empirical studies show that employees are making use of these flexible powers over employees. For example, there is survey data that show larger firms intensifying flexible employment techniques in a bid to avoid excessive over-supply of labour. For example, firms are squeezing older workers out through early retirement schemes and deployment to smaller, affiliated firms. Japanese companies are also increasingly resorting to cuts or freezes in graduate entry programs, affecting younger workers (Jackson, 2007, p. 290).

Further, non-standard workers – part-time, casual or agency workers – are occupying a larger share of the labour market compared to permanent employees (Aoki, 2007, p. 432; Araki, 2007, p. 255). Between 1997 and 2001, the number of full-time employees waned by 1.71 million while the number of non-standard workers jumped by 2.06 million (Kwon, 2004, p. 338). In the fifteen years since 1990, the proportion of non-standard workers jumped from one-fifth to nearly one-third of the working population. In 1990, non-regular employees comprised 20.2% of the labour market; in 1994, 22.8%; in 1999, 27.5%; and in 2004, 31.5% (Yamakawa, 2001, p. 629; Araki, 2005, p. 36).

A crisis in Japanese industrial relations is now in train. Large-scale businesses, which introduced lifelong employment in the 1950s to lure skilled and committed workers, are beginning to lose their attraction as places to work (Kwon, 2004, pp. 336–337). The command that management can now exercise over labour is strengthening (Mouer & Kawanishi, 2005, p. 111). To make matters worse, the chasm between the elite core and the periphery is widening (Coates, 2000, p. 134).

4. Conclusion

When it was at the height of its economic prowess, Japanese capitalism was admired as an alternative model of progressive capitalism. As it has limped into the 21st century, the admiration has largely gone. This chapter has argued, however, that Japanese capitalism is still worth a second look. Can it better serve human society compared to more familiar

Anglo-American models? Lifelong employment, as a governance practice that seemingly privileges workers over profits, makes for a good case study to explore this question.

Through a process of elimination, however, this chapter ends on a sombre note. Japanese capitalism is neither a cultural expression of human kindness, nor institutionally locked to make human-centred relational transactions *de facto* efficient. Neither law nor theory makes these two possibilities credible.

Instead, Japanese capitalism is a political compromise. It was a political compromise when it was first conceived in the post-war period to ensure industrial peace and redress the problem of a shortage of workers. It remains a political compromise today. As the economy struggles, the tenured core of the workforce faces unrequested transfers and unilateral modifications to their working conditions. Older and younger workers are being squeezed out of the lifetime employment system. More Japanese are working in fragile positions, part-time, casually or as temps. Japanese capitalism, like any other, is a regime of accumulation albeit with its own defined set of strategic choices. In particular, there is nothing progressive about lifelong employment. It is rooted in inequality, and always was. If anything, the inequality is increasing. As Coates concludes (2005, p. 193):

> There is a general lesson in this for all of us: the danger of establishing too close a linkage between political projects to reform capitalism and the defence of existing models of capitalism, however relatively superior those models may appear to be. For capitalism is not a system given to stasis. What works in one period is unlikely to do so in the next; and even when it 'works', its distribution of costs and benefits is never socially equal. So when deciding which tiger to ride, it is worth remembering that the choice is only between tigers; and that if a safe ride is what you want, you would do well not to ride tigers at all. For a time, a certain section of the intellectual Left forgot that, and ended up – if not with egg on their face – then at least with sushi.

References

Abe, N. & Shimizutani, S. (2007). Employment policy and corporate governance – An empirical comparison of the stakeholder and the profit-maximization model. *Journal of Comparative Economics*, *35*, 346–368.

Ahmadjian, C. L. & Robinson, P. (2001). Safety in numbers: downsizing and the deinstitutionalization of permanent employment in Japan. *Administrative Science Quarterly*, *46*, 622–654.

Amyx, J. (2006). Japan's financial crisis: Institutional rigidity and reluctant change. Princeton and Oxford: Princeton University Press.

Aoki, M. (1988). *Information, incentives, and bargaining in the Japanese economy*, Cambridge: Cambridge University Press.

Aoki, M. (1994). Monitoring characteristics of the Main Bank system: An analytical and developmental view. In M. Aoki and H. Patrick (Eds), *The Japanese Main Rank system: Its relevance for developing and transforming economies* (pp. 109–142). Oxford: Clarendon Press.

Aoki, M. (2007). Conclusion: Whither Japan's corporate governance? In M. Aoki, G. Jackson and H. Miyajima (Eds). *Corporate governance in Japan: Institutional change and organizational diversity* (pp. 427–48). Oxford: Oxford University Press.

Araki, T. (2005). Corporate governance reforms, labor law developments, and the future of Japan's practice-dependent stakeholder model. *Japan Labor Review*, *2*(1), 26–57.

Araki, T. (2007). Changing employment practices, corporate governance, and the role of labor law in Japan. *Comparative Labor Law and Policy Journal*, *28*(2), 251–281.

Black, J. (2002). Critical reflections on regulation. *Australian Journal of Legal Philosophy*, *27*, 1–35.

Black, J.S. & Morrison, A.J. (2010). *Sunset in the land of the rising sun*. London & New York: Palgrave Macmillan.

Blanpain, R., Bisom-Rapp, S., Corbett, W.R., Josephs, H.K., Zimmer, M.J. (2007). *The global workplace: International and comparative employment law – Cases and materials*. New York: Cambridge University Press.

Boyer, R. (2005). How and why capitalisms differ. *Economy and Society*, *34*(4), 509–557.

Boyer, R. & Juillard, M. (2000). The wage labour nexus challenged: more the consequence than the cause of the crisis. In R. Boyer and T. Yamada (Eds.), *Japanese capitalism: A regulationist perspective* (pp. 119–137). London: Routledge.

Boyer, R. & Yamada. T. (2000a). Introduction: A puzzle for economic theories. In R. Boyer & T. Yamada (Eds.), *Japanese capitalism: A regulationist perspective* (pp. 3–16). London: Routledge.

Boyer, R. & Yamada. T. (2000b). Conclusion: An epochal change . . . but uncertain futures. In R. Boyer and T. Yamada (Eds.), *Japanese capitalism: A regulationist perspective* (pp. 192–214). London: Routledge.

Burkett, P. & Hart-Landsberg, M. (1996). The Use and abuse of Japan as a progressive model. In L. Panitch (Ed.), *The Socialist Register 1996* (pp. 62–92). London: Merlin Press.

Citrin, D. and Wolfson, A. (2006). Japan's back! After its lost decade, Japan's economy is set on a recovery path. *Finance and Development*, *3*(2), Retrieved from: http://www.imf.org/external/pubs/ft/fandd/2006/06/citrin.htm.

Clarke, B. (2016). *The evolution of economic systems: varieties of capitalism in the global economy*. NY: OUP

Coates, D. (2000). *Models of capitalism: Growth and stagnation in the modern era*, Cambridge: Polity Press.

Coates, D. (2005). The rise and fall of Japan as a model of progressive capitalism. In D. Bailey, D. Coffey and P. Tomlinson (Eds). *Crisis or recovery in Japan: State and industrial economy* (pp.179–96). Cheltemham: Edward Elgar.

Cook, M. & McKay, H. (2006). Japan: Ripe for reassessment. *Lowy Institute: Perspectives*, 1–35

Dissanayake, W. (2012). Asian television dramas and Asian theories of communication. *Journal of Multicultural Discourses*, *7*(2), 191–196.

Dore, R. (1993). What Makes the Japanese Different? In C. Crouch, and D. Marquand (Eds.) *Ethics and markets: Co-operation and competition within capitalist economies*. Oxford: Blackwell Publishers and the Political Quarterly Publishing Co. Ltd.

Dore, R. (2000). Will global capitalism be Anglo-Saxon capitalism? *New Left Review*, *6*, 101–119.

Drysdale, P. (2004). Reflections on the relationship with Japan. *Japanese Studies*, *24*(2), 159–168.

Foote, D. H., (1996). Judicial creation of norms in Japanese labor law: Activism in the service of stability? *UCLA Law Review*, *43*, 635–709.

Gilson, R. J. & Roe, M. J. (1999). Lifetime employment: Labor peace and the evolution of Japanese corporate governance. *Columbia Law Review*, *99*, 508–540.

Hall, P. A., & Soskice, D. (2001). *Varieties of capitalism: The institutional foundations of comparative advantage*. Oxford: Oxford University Press.

Haley, J. O. (1998). *Spirit of Japanese law*. Athens: University of Georgia Press.

Haley, J. O. (2002). Litigation in Japan: A New Look at Old Problems. *Williamette Journal of International Law and Dispute Resolution*, *10*, 121–142.

Hansmann, H. & Kraakman, R. (2001). The end of history for corporate law. *Georgetown Law Journal*, *89*, 439–68.

Hay, Colin (2000). Contemporary capitalism, globalization, regionalization and the persistence of national variation. *Review of International Studies*, *26(4)*, 509–531.

Inagami, T. and Whittaker. D.H. (2005). *The new community firm: Employment, governance and management reform in Japan*. Cambridge: Cambridge University Press.

International Monetary Fund (2011). *Regional Economic Outlook: Asia and the Pacific* (April 2011). Washington DC, International Monetary Fund.

International Monetary Fund (2016). *Regional Economic Outlook: Asia and the Pacific* (April 2016). Washington DC, International Monetary Fund.
International Monetary Fund. (2016). Asia still growth champion, but must watch its step. Retrieved from: http://www.imf.org/en/News/Articles/2016/10/06/AM16-NA100616AsiaStillGrowthChampion.
Jackson, G. (2007). Employment adjustment and distributional conflict. In M. Aoki, G. Jackson and H. Miyajima, (Eds.) *Corporate governance in Japan: Institutional change and organizational diversity* (pp. 282–309). Oxford and New York: Oxford University Press.
Jacoby, S. M. (2005a). Corporate governance and society. *Challenge*, *48*(4), 69–87.
Jacoby, S. M. (2005b). Business and society in Japan and the United States. *British Journal of Industrial Relations*, *43*(4), 617–634.
Jacoby, S. M. (2005c). *The embedded corporation: Corporate governance and employment relations in Japan and the United States*. Princeton, N.J.: Princeton University Press.
Katz, R. (1998). *Japan: The system that soured: The rise and fall of the Japanese economic miracle*. London and New York: Routledge.
Kettler, D. & Tackney, C. T. (1997). Light from a dead sun: the Japanese lifetime employment system and Weimar labor law. *Comparative Labor Law and Policy Journal*, *19*, 1–41.
Kim, C. & Lawson, C. M. (1979). The law of the subtle mind: the traditional Japanese conception of law. *International & Comparative Law Quarterly*, *28*(3), 491–513.
Konzelmann, S. J. (2005). Varieties of capitalism: production and market relations in the USA and Japan. *British Journal of Industrial Relations*, *43*(4), 593–603.
Kwon, H. (2004). Japanese employment relations in transition. *Economic and Industrial Democracy*, *25*(3), 325–345.
Lazonick, W. (1992). Business organization and competitive advantage: Capitalist transformations in the twentieth century. In G. Dosi, R. Giannette & P. A. Toninelli (Eds.), *Technology and enterprise in a historical perspective* (pp. 119–162). Oxford: Clarendon Press.
Levi-Faur, D. (2005). The global diffusion of regulatory capitalism. In D. Levi-Faur & J. Jordana (Eds.), *The rise of regulatory capitalism* (pp. 12–32), London: Sage.
Lippit, V.D. (2005). *Capitalism*. London and New York: Routledge.
Mahbubani, K. (2008). *The new Asian hemisphere: The irresistible shift of global power to the East*. New York: Public Affairs.
McAlinn, G.P. (2007). Employment and labor law. In G.P. McAlinn (Ed.), *Japanese business law* (pp. 403–452). The Hague: Kluwer Law International.
Miwa, Y. & Ramseyer, J. M. (2002). The myth of the main bank: Japan and comparative corporate governance. *Law & Social Inquiry*, *27*(2), 401–424.
Monahan, A. (2011, February 14). China overtakes Japan as world's no. 2 economy. *Wall Street Journal*. Retrieved from: http://www.wsj.com/articles/SB10001424052748703361904576142832741439402.
Moriguchi, C. & Ono, H. (2006). Japanese lifelong employment: a century's perspective. In M. Blomstrom and S. La Croix (Eds.), *Institutional Change in Japan* (pp. 152–176). Oxford and New York: Routledge.
Mouer, R. & Kawanishi, H. (2005). *A Sociology of Work in Japan*. Cambridge: Cambridge University Press.
Mulgan, A.G. (2005). Why Japan still matters. *Asia Pacific Review*, *12*(2), 104–121.
Neumann, F. & Arora, T. (2011, August 26). Can Asia save the world? *Macro Asian Economics*. Retrieved from http://www.research.hsbc.com.
Noda, Y. (1976). *Introduction to Japanese law* (A. H. Angelo, Trans.) Tokyo: University of Tokyo Press.
Nottage, L. & Wolff, L. (2005). Corporate governance and law reform in Japan: From the Lost Decade to the End of History? In R. Haak and M. Pudelko (Eds). *Japanese management: The search for a new balance between continuity and change* (pp. 133–). New York: Palgrave Macmillan.

Ono, H. (2007). Lifetime employment in Japan: concepts and measurements. *SSE/EFI Working Paper Series in Economics and Finance, 624*, 1–58.
Ozaki, R. (1991). *Human capitalism: The Japanese enterprise system as World Model.* Tokyo: Kodansha.
Port, K. (1994). The case for teaching Japanese law at American law schools. *Depaul Law Review, 43*, 643–671.
Puchniak, Dan W. (2008). The efficiency of friendliness: Japanese corporate governance succeeds again without hostile takeovers. *Berkeley Business Law Journal, 5*(2), 195–262.
Rosenbluth, F.M & Thies, M.F. (2010). *Japan transformed: Political change and economic restructuring.* Princeton and Oxford: Princeton University Press.
Sako, M. (2005). Does embeddedness imply limits to within-country diversity. *British Journal of Industrial Relations, 43*(4), 585–592.
Shimoda, S.A. (2016). Time to retire: Is lifetime employment in Japan still viable? *Fordham International Law Journal, 39*(3), 753–789.
Stockwin, J. A. A. (2002). Why Japan still matters. *Japan Forum, 15*(3), 345–360.
Tsuruta, M., (2005). Respecting differences in the Anglo-American, European, and Japanese models of capitalism. *The Japanese Economy, 33*(2), 18–25.
Tsutsui, W. M. & Mazzotta, S. (2014). The bubble economy and the Lost Decade: Learning from the Japanese economic experience. *Journal of Global Initiatives: Policy, Pedagogy, Perspective, 9*(1), 57–74.
Vrasti, W. (2011). "Caring" capitalism and the duplicity of critique. *Theory & Event, 14*(4).
Wailes, N., Kitay, J., & Lansbury, R.D. (2008). Varieties of capitalism: Corporate governance and employment systems in Australia. In Marshall, S., Mitchell, R., & Ramsay, I. (Eds.), *Varieties of capitalism, corporate governance and employees*, pp. 19–38. Melbourne: Melbourne University Press.
West, M. D. (2006). *Law in Everyday Japan: Sex, Sumo, Suicide, and Statutes.* Chicago and London: University of Chicago Press.
Wilthagen, T. & Tros, F. (2004). The concept of "flexicurity": A new approach to regulating employment and labour markets. *Transfer: European Review of Labour and Research, 2(4)*, 166–86.
Wolff, L. (2008). The death of lifelong employment in Japan? In L. Nottage, L. Wolff and K. Anderson (Eds.), *Corporate governance in the 21st century: Japan's gradual transformation* (pp. 53–80). Cheltenham: Edward Elgar.
Wolff, L. (2010). Lifelong employment, labor law and the lost decade: The end of a job for life in Japan? In P. Haghirian (Ed.), *Innovation and change in Japanese management* (pp. 77–99). London and New York: Palgrave Macmillan.
Wolff, L. (2016). Japanese employment law. In P. Haghirian (Ed.), *Routledge handbook of Japanese business and management* (pp. 150–158). London and New York: Routledge.
Yamakawa, R. (2001). Labor law reform in Japan: A response to recent socio-economic changes. *American Journal of Comparative Law*, 49, 627–651.

9 Monopolisation, Market Liberalisation and Madness

Order and Disorder in Water Supply Governance

Victoria Schnure Baumfield

This chapter considers governance issues in the context of a ubiquitous and necessary resource: water. In many countries, water was traditionally supplied to the public through monopolistic, often government-run, entities. Over the past quarter century, governments around the world have moved from government-owned and operated monopolistic water supply structures to corporatised or, in some cases, privatised regimes for the supply of water to households and businesses. Some jurisdictions have even introduced competition in water supply. The variety of ways that jurisdictions have tackled these issues, and the extent to which these reforms have, themselves, been subject to change, illustrate the increasing level of disorder that currently characterises the global water sector. What had been a staid, stable sector is now in a state of flux across jurisdictions. Such changes have raised questions as to the best ways to balance efficient management of water assets, particularly given the prevalence of natural monopoly characteristics in the industry; the desire for profitability; conservation and safety concerns; and the critical issue of affordability of this necessary good. Accordingly, this chapter first examines structural characteristics of the water supply industry. It next reviews how the Australian water supply regime has evolved over the past 20 years. It then examines how jurisdictions in the United Kingdom have approached the supply of water and considers the extent to which options tried there may offer lessons for Australia. The chapter concludes that models trialed in other countries may indeed offer useful solutions as the Australian water industry continues to evolve. At the same time, the chapter concludes that global disorder in this area, as a result of attempts to tailor solutions to local conditions, might be a positive outcome.

Water supply[1] management is a crucial global issue that is currently characterised by a divergence of approach, as well as widespread reform, across jurisdictions.[2] In recent decades, relative stability – order – has given way to disorder. In an age of cash-strapped governments facing budget shortfalls and deficits, relatively stable but inefficient government

1 For purposes of this chapter, the term 'water supply' encompasses both water and wastewater (sewerage) supply, which tend to be provided by the same entities (e.g., LECG Limited Asia Pacific, 2011, p. 7). The term 'water supply' will be used interchangeably with other terms such as the 'water sector'.

2 To illustrate the global scope of the issue, the following sources discuss efforts to implement water reform measures in representative jurisdictions: Australia (Baumfield, 2013); Australia, England, Wales, and Scotland (Hendry, 2015); Bolivia (Hailu, Osorio, & Tsukada, 2012); European Union jurisdictions, with a focus on Eastern Europe countries in particular (Hall & Lobina, 2007); Estonia (Vinnari & Hukka, 2007); Finland (Hukka & Vinnari, 2007; Vinnari, 2006); Grenoble, France (Lobina & Hall, 2007); France and England (Dore, Kushner, & Zumer, 2004); Peru (Alcazar, Xu, & Zuluaga, 2000); and the United States of America (Arnold, 2005, 2009; Beecher & Kalmbach, 2013; MacDonald, 2010).

supply in many jurisdictions has been transformed by efforts to apply commercial principles, including corporatisation and privatisation. Monopoly is being challenged by the promise of free market principles and the lure of competition, although the applicability of those principles in a sector affected by natural monopolistic factors is still being determined. Supervision by responsible government officials – politicians – is being replaced by increasing reliance on expert (theoretically) independent economic regulators. Low water bills enabled by government subsidies are being replaced by higher bills and transparent pricing as the focus across jurisdictions has begun shifting from supplying cheap water as a political function to supplying water at an efficient price. The shift in pricing is intended to enable water businesses to cover their costs, pay for necessary infrastructure investments and upgrades, and send a price signal to consumers to conserve water. It also has generated healthy profit margins in many jurisdictions – a development that has been the subject of less public debate than it perhaps should. At the same time, there are indications that 'water poverty' – difficulties paying one's water bill – has increased in some jurisdictions and fears that it will increase in others (Barraqué & Montginoul, 2015). And it seems that the rules keep changing.

Whether the changes described above are cause for celebration or despair depends on political judgments and policy preferences. To the average citizen, the changes no doubt seem random and chaotic. One can imagine a connection between the dismay that many members of the public have expressed at these destabilizing developments (e.g., Meek, 2014) and the rise of the populist movements that in 2016 have led to such disruptive events as the rise of Donald Trump as a presidential candidate in the United States and the shock vote to leave the European Union (Brexit) in the United Kingdom. At the political level, tension exists between the theoretical desire for economic efficiency supported by regulatory independence and the desire of politicians to appease vocal interest groups. Order has given way to disorder, and that disorder may have political consequences. It may also ultimately change water supply governance for the better.

The successful management of change in the water supply industry is of critical importance because, like other public utility industries, water supply is an essential service needed by the entire community, be it households requiring residential water supply, businesses and public facilities such as schools requiring a commercial supply, or farms requiring an agricultural supply for purposes such as irrigation. There are equity concerns arising from the need to ensure that water remains both available and affordable to all. Like other public utilities, water supply also requires the construction of extensive, expensive infrastructure networks including highly capital-intensive individual components such as dams or reservoirs, water treatment facilities, and pipe networks. In water-poor areas, it may even require the construction of other, more specialised facilities to guarantee water security such as desalination plants. Due to their expense, these investments are not easily duplicated, thus creating inherent monopolistic characteristics. They also must be paid for.

To understand the causes and consequences of the current disorder in the global water sector, this chapter investigates changes in global approaches to the supply of water, the political and economic rationales behind these trends, and the extent to which those approaches may solve the puzzle of how to provide safe, affordable water to all. It does so through a comparative study of four jurisdictions that have chosen different solutions to the puzzle: Australia; England; Wales; and Scotland, with Australia as the primary jurisdiction to which the others are compared. Space constraints prevent the inclusion of additional comparators, such as France and the United States, which provide yet further models on how water systems can be structured and governed.[3] Australia and the selected British jurisdictions make a convenient comparison because they all started out with similar water supply systems, yet, over a comparable time span, have followed different paths to water sector reform. The similarity of political and legal systems helps keep the focus on differences in their water sectors as opposed to extraneous complicating factors. The final shape of water supply is not yet certain in any of these countries, but enough progress has been made to allow for observations about the strengths and weaknesses of each alternative.

The remainder of this chapter, therefore, is structured as follows. Section 2 describes the context in which water supply governance must be considered, including the extent to which water supply is a natural monopoly and the consequences that might flow therefrom. Section 3 examines the evolution of water supply in Australia, including how it may evolve in the future. Section 4 performs a similar analysis for the selected British jurisdictions. Section 5 concludes by considering what Australia and the sector globally can learn from each jurisdiction's experience and how this disorder might eventually play out.

1. Context

1.1 Unique issues affecting water

Water supply presents unique governance challenges. Unlike other public utilities such as electrical power and telephony, water supply has critical safety requirements arising from the need to achieve minimum levels of water quality in order to protect human health.[4] The need to maintain a safe water supply acts as a constraint upon options for reform. For example, the introduction of water collected by third parties into the community water supply (including water collected by individual homeowners' water tanks or water collected by a hypothetical independent water producer) risks the contamination of the entire system and accordingly has been traditionally prohibited. The general prohibition on third-party participation in water supply systems distinguishes water supply from other public utilities such as electrical power and telephony, where in many jurisdictions around the world

3 For a good overview of the French franchise models, including *gérances*, *régies intéressées*, leases, and concessions, as well as full privatisations, see Huet & Saussier (2003). Useful discussions of the kaleidoscope of US options, including various forms of public ownership and regulated private water suppliers, including the increasing participation of multinational water companies in the US market, can be found in Arnold (2005), Arnold (2009), and Beecher & Kalmbach (2013).

4 Consider, for example, the water crisis that has been facing the American municipality of Flint, Michigan in 2015–16 as a result of elevated lead levels in the community water supply. Flint's water became contaminated with lead leaching from old pipes after the city switched from buying cleaner but more expensive water from the Detroit water system (which obtained fresh water from Lake Huron, one of the Great Lakes) to cheaper but dirtier water from the Flint River, which had previously been the site of toxic waste disposal by General Motors. The Flint River water, which was 19 times more corrosive than the water from Lake Huron, was not treated with anti-corrosives. As a result, it corroded the protective coating on old lead water pipes, resulting in the lead exposure. As of April 2016, even though Flint had reverted to purchasing water from the Detroit water system, damage to the pipes meant that many local residents still needed to use bottled rather than tap water even for bathing as well as drinking or cooking until the damaged pipes are replaced, a process that will not only require a multi-million dollar investment but will take many months (e.g., Bosman, 2016a; Bosman, 2016b; Ganim & Tran, 2016). A similar crisis is currently occurring in the Australian community of Oakey, Queensland, where it has recently come to light that the town water supply has been contaminated for years with toxic chemicals from a nearby military base (Deutrom, 2016).

capacity has been increased by the introduction of independent producers and providers into the market.

The conversation surrounding water supply is also subject to sustainability concerns arising from the growing demand for water by expanding populations in regions facing ancient or new struggles with water scarcity. The issue of water scarcity is especially relevant in arid, yet increasingly populated, regions such as the American Southwest (incorporating California, Nevada, Arizona, New Mexico, and Utah) (MacDonald, 2010) and much of Australia, where droughts are common. Furthermore, the relentless advance of global industrialisation places further strain on water demand.

1.2 Water supply as a natural monopoly

Many of the difficulties in developing an acceptable water supply regime arise because the significant investments required to develop and maintain a safe and modern water supply system tend to render it a natural monopoly. A natural monopoly can be defined as '[a] firm or industry whose average cost per unit of production falls sharply over the entire range of its output' so that, under the subadditivity principle, 'a single firm, a monopoly, can supply the industry output more efficiently than can multiple firms' (Samuelson & Nordhaus, 1992, p. 742). Posner has observed that:

> If the entire demand within a relevant market can be satisfied at lowest cost by one firm rather than by two or more, the market is a natural monopoly, whatever the actual number of firms in it. If such a market contains more than one firm, either the firms will quickly shake down to one through mergers or failures, or production will continue to consume more resources than necessary. In the first case competition is short-lived and in the second it produces inefficient results. Competition is thus not a viable regulatory mechanism under conditions of natural monopoly (1969, p. 548).

Natural monopolies can occur as a result of *economies of scale* or *economies of scope* (e.g., Decker, 2015, pp. 368–371). These are discussed in turn.

1.2.1 Economies of Scale

Economies of scale tend to exist where a large proportion of the cost of producing an asset arises from fixed costs, such as where expensive machinery or research and development is necessary to produce the asset (Decker, 2015, pp. 14–15). In those cases, it is more efficient for a supplier to produce a large quantity of the output than a smaller quantity because the proportionate share of the fixed cost attributable to each unit decreases as more units are produced, at least until the source of the economy of scale (e.g., the production equipment) is at capacity (e.g., Samuelson & Nordhaus, 1992, pp. 110–112, 165). Once full capacity has been reached, then it will be necessary to incur further fixed costs to increase production further, increasing the average cost per output. Furthermore, as production increases, complexities and costs arising from, for example, the need to deliver the product to geographically dispersed markets start to counterbalance the efficiency gains arising from the increased production (e.g., Samuelson & Nordhaus, 1992, p. 112; The Economist, 2008). So even for industries exhibiting economies of scale, at some point further production will lead to diseconomies of scale (e.g., Silberston, 1972).

Like other public utility industries such as electricity, gas, and telecommunications, water requires significant capital expenditure to produce or capture the resource and deliver it to homes, commercial businesses, and industrial users (Abbott & Cohen, 2009, p. 234).[5] Specific components of the above relevant to the water supply industry include the dams, reservoirs, pipe networks, and treatment facilities that comprise a functioning water supply system (Byatt, Ballance, & Reid, 2006, p. 372). The 1993 Hilmer Report on Australian national competition policy recognised that, in the case of monopolistic public utility industries, 'technological changes and other developments have shown that the area of genuine natural monopoly is relatively small and diminishing' (Commonwealth of Australia, 1993, p. 12). Nevertheless, understanding how to open water supply to competition has proven challenging, even in comparison to other public utility industries. Conversely, the desire to ensure that infrastructure costs can be recouped appears to explain why many jurisdictions still mandate statutory monopolies for water within set geographical areas.

Empirical research adds nuance to this picture. There is no consensus as to precisely how large water utilities should be in order to operate efficiently (Abbott & Cohen, 2009, p. 236; Carvalho, Marques, & Berg, 2012, pp. 41, 43; Decker, 2015, p. 370). Moreover, teasing out the extent of economies of scale (and scope, as discussed below) can be complicated by 'operating conditions, legal context, income levels, and other factors' (Carvalho et al., 2012, p. 41). Abbott & Cohen (2009, pp. 236–237) reviewed the literature and found that there is much complexity as to when and in what circumstances economies of scale will exist in the water sector. Citing 11 studies, they noted that '[t]he studies that looked at small water businesses generally found that economies of scale could be reaped if they became larger' (Abbott & Cohen, 2009, p. 236). Abbott & Cohen (2009, p. 236) noted, however, that 'at some level economies of scale were exhausted'. Some studies found that the existence of economies of scale varied by market segment, such as drinking water versus non-residential water supply or water distribution versus water production (Carvalho et al., 2012, p. 42).

To quantify the foregoing, a report commissioned by England and Wales' then water regulator, the Office of Water Services (Ofwat), covering the period 1992–93 to 2002–03, found that in England and Wales 'the cost-minimising scale for water supply undertakings is estimated to be around a population served of 650,000', while a Japanese study estimated the efficient scale in Japan as serving a population of around 760,000 (Byatt et al., 2006, pp. 374–375; Abbott & Cohen, 2009, p. 237). Carvalho et al. (2012, p. 43) cited a study finding that economies of scale existed up to a population of around one million in Italy. Other studies in various countries identified that diseconomies of scale commenced in some cases above 125,000 connections, although not in other cases (Abbott & Cohen, 2009, p. 237).

Limits on economies of scale might be attributed, among other factors, to the costs of expanding the pipe network out of a limited geographical area (especially into rural areas), the cost of expanding water treatment facilities to be able to handle increased demand, the cost of building additional dams and reservoirs, and the greater administrative burden of dealing with a larger and more complex customer base. Therefore, as Abbott and Cohen explain, '[i]n larger metropolitan areas, with bigger markets and a reliance on multiple sources of water, the coexistence of several vertically integrated entities is also common,

5 Consideration of agricultural water supply, which in Australia is governed by separate rules, is beyond the scope of this chapter.

with each operating as a separate local distribution network in separate parts of the city' (2009, p. 234).

The literature suggests that the extent of economies of scale in the water industry may vary by location. Carvalho et al. (2012, p. 42) and Abbott & Cohen (2009, p. 237) cited studies supporting the existence of limited economies of scale in England and Wales, Italy, France, Portugal, Japan, South Africa, Colombia, Moldova, and Vietnam, but not Brazil. In those jurisdictions, the evidence indicates that the largest water utilities will face diseconomies of scale. There is disagreement in the literature as to whether there were diseconomies for the largest water utilities in the United States, although most studies seem to support that conclusion (Abbott & Cohen, 2009, p. 237; Carvalho et al., 2012, p. 42). Moreover, Carvalho et al.'s (2012, p. 42) and Abbott & Cohen's (2009, p. 237) reviews of the literature indicated that water supply evidenced economies of scale in South Korea, Germany, Latin America, Peru, Spain, and Canada. But some of those studies related to small water supply businesses and do not necessarily contradict studies indicating that diseconomies will exist in the case of larger businesses. Carvalho et al. (2012, p. 43) therefore concluded that:

> It is generally agreed that small water utilities providing only one service or that are not vertically integrated have significant scale and scope economies that seldom are achieved due to relatively low levels of output (reflecting underlying demand within the service territory); large or vertically integrated utilities seem to have scale and scope diseconomies at the levels of output they produce.

Other research indicates that water suppliers become more efficient as a function of population density rather than simply scale (Foellmi & Meister, 2012; Carvalho et al., 2012, p. 43). Furthermore, water is difficult and expensive to transport long distances, and long-distance transfer degrades water quality (Department for Environment, 2011a; Foellmi & Meister, 2012, p. 25). Those technical factors further limit economies of scale. It seems that, overall, increased connections are efficient, up to a point, but water supply, at least for the moment, remains essentially local.

1.2.2 Economies of scope

Economies of scope exist where it is more efficient for one supplier to supply multiple products than for a set of different suppliers to supply one of the products each (e.g., Samuelson & Nordhaus, 1992, p. 340; Wetzstein, 2013, pp. 433–436). Economies of scope exist, for example, where two or more products can be produced using the same equipment or infrastructure. The concept also covers the use of common management, finance, and administrative resources (Abbott & Cohen, 2009, p. 237; Carvalho et al., 2012, p. 43). If one producer supplies both products, duplicate creation of the relevant infrastructure is avoided, lowering the average cost per unit of both products.

In the case of water, economies of scope may potentially arise from the joint production of different activities within the water supply chain (i.e., vertical integration) as well as from complementarities in the operation of water supply and sewerage (wastewater) activities (Abbott & Cohen, 2009, p. 237). And indeed, in many jurisdictions all of the above are (or, until recently, were) provided by single combined water supply entities. As with economies of scale, the literature on economies of scope in the water industry reveals mixed evidence as to whether such economies of scope exist in practice (Decker, 2015, pp. 370–371 and the authorities cited therein; Abbott & Cohen, 2009; Carvalho et al., 2012). As Decker explains:

> Some studies find support for scope economies in these circumstances (especially for small companies). Other studies find no such evidence, or suggest diseconomies of scope in combining different activities. . . . [T]he costs and benefits associated with vertical integration *vis-à-vis* separation can be finely balanced . . . On the one hand, separation of different activities can improve the information available to the regulator, and increase the potential for certain activities in the supply chain to be outsourced or operated under a concession arrangement [discussed later in this chapter]. On the other hand, vertical separation can result in a loss of certain efficiencies associated with shared cost (such as management, etc), reduce efficiencies and know-how associated with the joint operation of water distribution and wastewater facilities, and restrict the ability of the operator to internalise some of the externalities associated with undertaking the different activities in the supply chain (for example, to take account of the location of water treatment facilities when deciding where effluent should be released).

1.2.3 Vertical integration of the water supply chain

Water supply comprises a number of different discrete activities including water abstraction, treatment, storage, distribution, and retail (Decker, 2015, pp. 363–368; Hendry, 2015). Some of those activities, in particular responsibility for constructing and maintaining pipe networks, may be natural monopolies due to economies of scale or scope while others may be potentially contestable. This ability to reduce water supply into its component parts has been a key element in efforts to introduce competition into the water industry, even while acknowledging that certain steps in the process may remain the province of a sole monopolist supplier.

1.2.4 Consequences of natural monopoly

Economic theory warns of the possible negative consequences of a lack of competition: absent regulation, prices are likely to be higher than in a competitive market and quality lower (which in the case of water implicates safety), and innovation and investment in better or more efficient ways to source, treat, and deliver the product may be lacking. Higher prices might be driven not only by the ability of providers to take increased profits but by the monopolistic environment's removal of pressure to operate efficiently, driving up costs (Explanatory Notes, Queensland Competition Authority Bill, 1997, p. 2; Farrar & McCabe, 1995, pp. 31–33).[6] The lack of market pressure to operate efficiently will enable managers to shirk or act in their own interests at the organisation's expense (Alchian & Demsetz, 1972; Jensen & Meckling, 1976).

Further, there is evidence that where the business is government-owned, as are most of Australia's monopolist water providers (LECG Limited Asia Pacific, 2011, pp. 7–8), that fact alone may increase its inefficiency because: (a) government owners may not monitor as well as private shareholders due to rent-seeking, which blurs objectives away from the

6 In a competitive market, inefficient firms will lose sales to firms with lower costs. Not so in a market with one supplier, particularly when the product is a necessary good where refusing to buy is not an option.

presumptive sole ultimate focus in private companies of profitability, although when decisions become politically sensitive monitoring may increase; (b) there is no risk of takeover if the business is inefficiently run (i.e., no market for corporate control); and (c) poor managers face less risk of being replaced than in the private sector (Vickers & Yarrow, 1991, pp. 113–114; Vining & Boardman, 1992).[7] Abbott and Cohen (2009, pp. 238–239), however, list 24 studies comparing the efficiency of public and private firms and find that in the water sector, where 'the overwhelming majority of private owned companies are monopolies and not any more the subject of competitive pressures, and the incentives these can provide, than government owned ones', ownership status makes little difference. Shifting from standard government provision of utility services to corporatisation, however, did appear to improve efficiency. So did economic regulation of corporatised or privatised utilities (Abbott & Cohen, 2009, pp. 239–240).

For these reasons, there is broad agreement that the risks to consumers and society arising from the natural monopoly scenario, at least in the case of essential services, calls for government intervention (e.g., Easterbrook & Fischel, 1991, pp. 22–23; Vickers & Yarrow, 1991, p. 114; Whincop & Keyes, 1997, p. 68). There is less agreement, however, over what form that intervention should take. The standard response tends to be *ex ante* public utility regulation, in which economic regulators administer detailed rules as to such matters as pricing, levels of investment required to expand and maintain the network, services that may be offered, and who may offer the service (e.g., Decker, 2015, p. 48). Others, such as Posner, argue that limiting regulation to the *ex post* prosecution of monopolists who violate antitrust (competition) laws is preferable (1969, p. 549; see, generally, Decker, 2015, p. 49). Even Posner (1969, pp. 549–550), however, assumes the creation of government regulation in the form of generally applicable antitrust laws. Further, jurisdictions vary as to what extent these issues should be open to input from politicians as opposed to supposedly independent regulators.

These high-level debates as to the preferable nature and extent of government regulation to protect the public from the abuse of monopoly positions are to a certain extent reflected in the water supply governance systems adopted in various jurisdictions. For example, as discussed in section 4, in England and Wales, future years' pricing is contingent on regulatory approval from the independent economic regulator, Ofwat, through which approval must be justified based on a variety of factors such as relative efficiency and the need for investments in the maintenance and construction of infrastructure. In Queensland, Australia, in contrast, the economic regulator's role is limited to *post hoc* review of prices. Instead, politicians acting as the relevant water entities' owners or responsible ministers (keeping in mind that in some cases the owners of the business are local councils) are involved in forward planning processes and through that process in some cases may have veto power over proposed business activities (Baumfield, 2013, pp. 20–21, 39–40, 58–60).

1.3 Other issues affecting water supply governance

As an essential service, water supply, like other public utility industries, is typically subject (at least in developed countries) to universal service obligations (USOs) whereby the water

7 It must be noted, however, that Vining and Boardman's paper focused on government-owned businesses operating in competitive (i.e., non-monopolistic) markets. Aspects of the detailed economic regulations governing monopolistic utility providers may counterbalance some of the effects that Vining and Boardman observed.

supplier is required to sell to all within the supplier's geographical area of service who wish to purchase water (e.g., Hendry, 2015, pp. 85–87). USOs mean that those water suppliers must incur the expense of providing water service even to customers who live in remote or not-easily-accessible locations. For example, in Queensland, Australia, the *Water Supply (Safety and Reliability) Act* (2008) states:

> (1) The service provider must, to the greatest practicable extent, ensure that—
>
> (a) all premises in the service area are able to be connected directly and separately to the service provider's infrastructure for the area (s 164).

There are of course nuances to how the universal service principle is applied. In Queensland, for example, the USO does not cover customers where 'the service provider can not supply water from its infrastructure to the premises at a satisfactory pressure because of physical constraints' although even then '[t]he service provider must supply water to the premises if the owner installs enough water storage tanks and pumps to ensure that water can be supplied at a satisfactory pressure and flow' (*Water Supply (Safety and Reliability) Act* (2008), s 166).

USOs cover service not only to an entire geographic area, but also to customers regardless of income level or ability to pay. The cost of supplying water to customers on limited incomes or installing the infrastructure necessary to comply with applicable USOs will in some cases be uneconomic for the water supplier absent subsidies from the government. Accordingly, as water supply has become commercialised (see section 3), governments have become legally required to compensate water suppliers for the cost of performing uneconomic USOs, also known as community service obligations (CSOs) (Baumfield, 2013, p. 52).

Meanwhile, water's status as a necessary good means that there is justifiable political pressure on governments to keep water affordable for all (Barraqué & Montginoul, 2015, p. 8; Department for Environment, 2011a). That political pressure operates in tension with the need to pay for the expensive capital costs associated with water supply,[8] as well as the opportunities to charge excessive prices that arise as a result of the natural or statutory monopoly. The capital costs, meanwhile, imply the need for long time horizons to pay for them.

Many countries have traditionally viewed the need to provide universal and affordable access to water as fundamentally incompatible with the for-profit business model, under which commercial businesses are operated to maximise profits. As a result, many countries traditionally assigned responsibility for water supply to the government, just as governments traditionally took responsibility for kindred industries such as the postal service, public transportation, and, in many jurisdictions, telephone and electricity services. Over the past several decades, however, a more nuanced view has developed as the worldwide corporatisation and privatisation wave took hold in the late 1970s through 1990s. This point is developed in subsections 3 and 4 below.

8 For example, in Southeast Queensland, a decline in water consumption as the population has become more water efficient – at the government's urging – has led to unwanted revenue shortfalls.

2. The evolution of water supply in Australia: from government-*run* to government-*owned* . . . and beyond?

Under Australia's federal system of government, there is no single federal regime for the supply of water and sewerage services. Its six states and two major territories[9] have significant control over the structure and details of how water is supplied in their respective jurisdictions. Furthermore, different water regimes (which vary depending on the state or territory) govern: the 'urban water sector', which supplies water to the vast majority of Australia's population; rural water supply; and the supply of water for agricultural use.[10] As a relatively arid continent with recurring droughts,[11] water supply in recent years has become a matter of persistent public concern.

2.1 *The traditional system: the government supply of water*

Until the introduction of microeconomic reforms starting in the 1990s, the Australian jurisdictions favoured a traditional government ownership model where water supply was provided by the government itself as an essentially political function and was not treated as a separate business. In population-dense Southeast Queensland (SEQ), for example, home to Brisbane and the Gold Coast, Australia's third and sixth largest cities, respectively (Australian Bureau of Statistics, 2016), water services were supplied by local city or regional councils.[12] Because finances for the provision of water services were typically not kept separate from other governmental functions, there was a lack of information about the cost of providing services, as well as the cost of government subsidies. The funds to build and maintain necessary infrastructure and run the business came from the government, and water charges were paid not to the business itself but back to the government via government rates notices.

2.2 *The rise of commercialisation and corporatisation in Australian water supply*

Perspectives began to change in the late 1970s and 1980s with the rise of conservative governments espousing free market principles, in particular the election of Margaret Thatcher in the United Kingdom (UK). Reversing the nationalisation policies of previous Labour

9 Queensland, New South Wales, Victoria, Tasmania, South Australia, and Western Australia, along with the Northern Territory and Australian Capital Territory. Technically, there is a third mainland Australia territory, Jervis Bay Territory, but it is so tiny as to be insignificant for most purposes. Jervis Bay Territory's water supply is interesting, however, as its essential services are supplied by commercial suppliers, and the federal government is authorised to on-sell (presumably excess) water and electricity 'to any person outside the Territory' (Department of Infrastructure and Regional Development, 2016; *Jervis Bay Acceptance Act* (1915), s 4E). There are also a number of offshore territories (e.g., Christmas Island, the Cocos Islands). Their water supply is beyond the scope of this chapter.

10 For example, agricultural users may participate in interstate water trading, which is not available to retail water customers.

11 For detailed charts illustrating the relative distribution of rainfall from 2005–11 and a discussion of steps that Australian water suppliers have taken to augment supply in recent years, see Byrnes (2013).

12 For example, the Gold Coast City Council was the water and sewerage provider for the City of Gold Coast, Queensland, Australia.

governments, Thatcher oversaw the privatisation of state industries on the theory that private businesses would be more efficient and improve Britain's economy (Osborne, 2013).[13]

In Australia, in 1992, the Commonwealth government appointed a National Competition Policy Review Committee to assess whether Australia should adopt a national competition policy. In particular, the Policy Review Committee, chaired by Professor Fred Hilmer, sought to investigate what opportunities existed to strengthen competition in the Australian economy, thereby improving efficiency and, ultimately, living standards. In 1993, the Commonwealth government issued a major report setting forth the results of that inquiry (Commonwealth of Australia, 1993, the 'Hilmer Report').

Following the recommendations of the Hilmer Report, government began taking steps to increase the transparency and accountability of monopoly service providers, including monopolist water suppliers (Byrnes, 2013, p. 16; Hendry, 2015, p. 96). In particular, governments at both the state and federal levels began taking steps to effect:

- the separation of regulatory and commercial functions of public monopolies;
- the separation of natural monopoly and potentially competitive activities; and
- the separation of potentially competitive activities into a number of smaller, independent business units (Commonwealth of Australia, 1993, p. xxxi)

In 1995, the new National Competition Policy was adopted, and government policy moved squarely in favor of applying commercial principles to government businesses and privatising them where possible (Commonwealth of Australia, 1993). A 2015 Commonwealth review of the National Competition Policy noted that relevant commercial principles included separate accounting for, and funding of, non-commercial activities such as community service obligations, and separating regulatory functions from commercial activities (Commonwealth of Australia, 2015, p. 257). Indeed, some states, such as Queensland, had begun corporatising government-owned businesses and imposing commercial principles even before the Commonwealth-level reforms were implemented (Booth & Noon, 2013, p. 117).[14]

A key plank of the National Competition Policy was the imposition of competitive neutrality, which was intended to put Australian government-owned businesses (GOBs) on a level playing field with private competitors through the removal or neutralisation of characteristics that are thought to give GOBs an unfair advantage. Competitive neutrality includes not only the use of 'cost-reflective pricing' to eliminate governmental cross-subsidies that keep prices artificially low, but also charges and payments to compensate for the financial and other advantages that GOBs have compared to private businesses. Such payments that GOBs must make include 'tax equivalent payments' to state governments equivalent to the taxes they would have paid the Commonwealth government had they been private businesses (Australian Taxation Office, 2012) and financing fees to counterbalance the presumption of greater creditworthiness that GOBs may receive due to their connection to the

13 And indeed, although privatisation brought a new set of problems, there is evidence of large productivity gains after many British businesses were privatised (Vickers & Yarrow, 1991, pp. 117–118, 121).

14 Corporatisation involves 'creating a separate legal business entity to provide the relevant goods and services' (Commonwealth of Australia, 2015, p. 257). The Harper Report noted that '[s]uch an entity is characterised by: clear and non-conflicting objectives; managerial responsibility, authority and autonomy; independent and objective performance monitoring; and performance-based rewards and sanctions' (Commonwealth of Australia, 2015, p. 257).

government (Commonwealth of Australia, 2015). They also normally include the payment of a commercial rate of return on capital to the government owners (Crase, Pawsey, & Cooper, 2015, p. 18).

Under Australia's federal system, the implementation of these principles was left largely to individual state governments, but the state and federal governments regularly consulted and agreed on policy at Council of Australian Governments (COAG) meetings. In 1994, COAG agreed to a water reform framework that, among other things, required urban water retailers to commence consumption-based pricing on water bills where cost effective to do so and, generally speaking, to fully pass on the cost of water to consumers (Council of Australian Governments, 1994). In 1995, the Commonwealth, states and territories agreed to a program to implement the National Competition Policy and related reforms, including the 1994 water reform principles (*Agreement to Implement the National Competition Policy and Related Reforms*, 1995). Under this agreement, signatories would face the loss of significant Commonwealth government funding to the extent that they did not comply with the principles.

The move to full-cost pricing has typically been accomplished through the introduction of two-part tariffs 'comprising an access or connection component together with an additional component or components to reflect usage' (Council of Australian Governments, 1994). The access component, at least in principle, is supposed to reflect the customer's pro rata share of paying for the sunk cost of the infrastructure necessary to supply water to the community as well as the commercial rate of return to the government owner. The usage component is intended to send a price signal to the consumer to conserve water, although changes to consumption ultimately affect a relatively small portion of the user's total bill.

In 2004, COAG agreed to a National Water Initiative (NWI) (*Intergovernmental Agreement on a National Water Initiative*, 2004). In accordance with the NWI, a National Water Commission (NWC) was created, which was responsible for assessing governments' implementation of the COAG water reforms. The NWC periodically reported to COAG on the progress of water reform until it was abolished in 2014. Since 2014, the NWC's roles have been allocated to a number of different bodies including the Productivity Commission (National Water Commission, 2014).

Although water supply still has not been opened up to competition, another consequence of the application of the National Competition Policy to the Australian water sector has been the encouragement of structural reforms to monopolist GOBs to separate potentially contestable elements of their businesses from the natural monopoly aspects (Commonwealth of Australia, 2015, p. 191). The separation of the potentially contestable elements paves the way for the potential introduction of competition into water supply in the future.

2.3 Southeast Queensland's experience applying the water reforms

Queensland's experience reforming the supply of water to its main population centre, the southeast Queensland corner of the state, illustrates how that principle worked in practice.[15] The first part of the reforms took place in 2006, when the SEQ water supply system was restructured to eliminate vertical integration of the then council-owned water retailers and separate out various segments of the water supply chain. Under the 2006 reform, the

15 For a discussion of the reforms that were undertaken in Melbourne and Sydney, see Byrnes (2013, pp. 16–17).

state took over certain water assets that had previously been under the control of local city council owners. The assets that were newly allocated to the state government included dams and other 'bulk water' infrastructure necessary for the abstraction, treatment, and storage of water (Baumfield, 2013, p. 4). Under the original restructuring under the 2006 reforms, the various 'bulk water' assets were allocated into a number of separate corporatised businesses:

- Seqwater owned the dams, groundwater infrastructure, and water treatment plans and supplied water to the SEQ Water Grid Manager, which managed the newly-created 'SEQ Water Grid'.
- The SEQ Water Grid Manager operated the water grid, oversaw the flow of water through the grid, and sold water to the retail water suppliers.
- Linkwater took ownership of all the major pipelines in SEQ and, along with Seqwater, was responsible for the construction and maintenance of new infrastructure.
- WaterSecure was given management of the state's 'manufactured water' assets, including a new desalination plant and water recycling plant (Baumfield, 2013, p. 4).

The 2006 reforms did not reach the ultimate supplier of water at the retail level; those retailers remained the local councils for the time being. A second set of reforms enacted in 2009 required the approximately 14 local council-based water businesses in the SEQ region to consolidate into three regional, corporatised water businesses known as 'distributor-retailers' on 1 July 2010 (Baumfield, 2013, p. 5; *South-East Queensland Water (Distribution and Retail Restructuring) Act* (2009)). An economic regulator, the Queensland Competition Authority, monitors prices, but the final say over pricing rests with the state government (e.g., Crase et al., 2015, p. 28).

Not everything went according to plan. The regionalisation of water retail, while theoretically more efficient, created political havoc in certain of the affected areas, namely, the Gold Coast, where regionalisation brought with it 20% price increases. A protest group called 'Disconnex' – a play on the name of the new local water retailer, Allconnex – was formed and communicated with the public through a variety of means including the website goldcoastfightsallconnex.com.au. Unhappy residents, using the power of the internet to band together and organise themselves, held rallies and captured the attention of the media. Local newspapers and television stations ran an unrelenting stream of stories on the situation. As described in detail in Baumfield (2013, pp. 6–7) and the numerous sources cited therein, the outcry was so intense that the state government was forced to announce a one-time opportunity for councils to withdraw from the distributor-retailers they had been forced into. As a result, Allconnex, the distributor-retailer servicing the Gold Coast, was disbanded two years after its creation and water supply returned to the three local councils whose services had been transferred to that supplier (Baumfield, 2013).

At the same time, the creation of multiple new wholesale and infrastructure water businesses was criticised by some as inefficient and needlessly complex (e.g., McArdle, 2012). Accordingly, by late 2012 the various new wholesale and infrastructure entities created under the 2006 reforms had been re-integrated into a single supplier of water at the wholesale level, which retained the name Seqwater (*South-East Queensland Water (Distribution and Retail Restructuring) and Other Legislation Amendment Act* (2012)). The retail end of the supply chain retained the (new) status quo: the individual water retailers no longer have the facilities to manufacture or abstract their own water, although they are responsible for delivering it from Seqwater to the end customer. That even holds for the council non-corporatised water businesses that resumed after the dissolution of Allconnex. The Gold Coast City Council, for example, did not resume ownership of what had previously been its main water source, the Hinze Dam. So the current status quo in SEQ is that one monopolistic entity collects, treats, and distributes water at the wholesale level and then on-sells the finished product to a number of different retailers, each of which is a statutory monopolist in its geographical region, for final supply to residential and commercial customers.

2.4 Evaluation of Queensland's Reforms

The original division of functions in the water supply chain into separate business entities under the 2006 reforms facilitated the removal of cross-subsidies from different aspects of the water supply process and improved transparency, all of which would have facilitated the eventual introduction of competition to some if not all parts of the process. In that respect, Queensland's 2006 and 2009 reforms reflected the principles agreed to under the National Competition Policy and NWI. On the other hand, the later re-consolidation of the bulk water activities into the single corporatised entity Seqwater should theoretically increase efficiency through economies of scope and perhaps scale (see sections 1.2.1 and 1.2.2) as duplication of administrative and other functions is eliminated. At the same time, the consolidation of businesses associated with different parts of the supply chain will make it harder to maintain financial transparency as to the activities that had earlier been split into separate businesses. That is because particularised costings for the separate functions carried out by the consolidated business will no longer be available: the new Seqwater's publicly available annual reports present its financial reporting on a consolidated basis. Among other things, the lack of transparency may facilitate the continuation of cross-subsidies between more and less profitable parts of the water supply chain.

The tradeoffs that Queensland has made as it has refined the structure of the wholesale water industry and the related upstream activities would appear to reflect a policy preference for which there is no single correct answer concerning the separation and consolidation of activities. The current preference for consolidation of the upstream activities into the wholesale water supplier also reflects perhaps a tacit acknowledgement that there is limited feasibility for competition in any of the activities that lead to the supply of water in the 'bulk water' market, and therefore no need to maintain the separation of activities in order to facilitate the entrance of non-existent competitors.

On the retail level, the reforms left supply in the hands of monopolist suppliers, but the Queensland legislation, as written, seems to explicitly contemplate that at some point private suppliers might be allowed to enter the SEQ retail market (Baumfield, 2013, p. 5). In particular, s 22 of the *South-East Queensland Water (Distribution and Retail Restructuring) Act* (2009) (the '*Restructuring Act*') provides that participation agreements between the new regional SEQ distributor-retailers and their council owners may provide for both the transfer of participation rights (i.e., the owner's shares) and the creation of classes of participants. Moreover, s 29 of the *Restructuring Act* provides that the question of 'who may become a participant' (i.e., an owner of the distributor-retailer) is a 'restricted matter' that requires Ministerial approval, but that the responsible minister may approve 'a person' – i.e., *any* person – to become a participant. There is no explicit restriction on who such a person must be. In other words, there is no legal barrier to the private ownership of the distributor-retailers, merely a requirement that such private ownership be government-approved. That means that a mere change of government policy could be enough to set the privatisation of the distributor-retailers in motion, although any actual deals to sell participation rights would be subject to the terms of the participation agreement governing relations between the current owners of the applicable distributor-retailer and the distributor-retailer itself. Any such deal would also likely require the negotiation of a new participation agreement with the distributor-retailer and other participants.

The move to full-cost pricing for end customers, which helps implement competitive neutrality, will also enable the state to potentially remove the current statutory monopolies and open up retail water supply to competition of some sort in the future. For example, it is possible that at some point in the future the law will require the local suppliers, as has been done in the UK, to open up their pipe networks as essential facilities to competitors who would either input their own water into the system or purchase their own supplies of water from Seqwater for delivery to customers through the incumbent former monopolists' pipe networks.[16] That, of course, raises the sorts of issues that must always be considered when opening up network facilities to competitors, including the possibility of competitors picking off the profitable customers and leaving the incumbent supplier with the obligation to supply water under universal service obligations to less profitable customers while at the same time being responsible to maintain the pipe network (Crew & Parker, 2006, p. 18).[17]

The Queensland reforms' effect on major infrastructure investment is equally nuanced. The move to full-cost pricing itself is alleged to provide benefits, including:

> encouraging better use of existing infrastructure, which can delay the need for infrastructure investment. Where cost-reflective pricing is present, consumer demand will also provide a more accurate guide to infrastructure investment. This increases the likelihood that such investment is efficient and responds to actual changes in demand and consumer preferences. These factors lower the cost and increase the responsiveness across markets to the benefit of consumers. It also means governments can better target assistance to vulnerable consumers in those markets, reducing the burden on taxpayers (Commonwealth of Australia, 2015, p. 194).

Furthermore, during the long drought that severely affected Queensland during the first decade of the twenty-first century, in particular from approximately 2005 through 2010, the alleged lack of adequate infrastructure to ensure water security was blamed in part on the state's fragmented water supply regime, under which no one entity was responsible for ensuring adequate water infrastructure investment. Turning over control of bulk water infrastructure to the state enabled the state government to relatively rapidly arrange for the construction of significant new water infrastructure, including the Gold Coast Desalination Plant, a new water recycling plant, and major new water pipelines to move water around the region. All of this may have seemed reassuring at a time when the combined capacity level for SEQ's major dams had descended to near 15% of capacity, as prominently reported in

16 A detailed examination of essential facility issues is beyond the scope of this chapter. For a detailed discussion of the essential facility problem in the context of Australian natural monopolies, see Commonwealth of Australia (1993, pp. 240–268).

17 In fact, it was allegedly for this reason that Scotland did not open its household water market to competition when it enacted legislation in 2005 that legalised competition for commercial customers starting in 2008 (Sawkins, 2012). There is a large literature analysing issues arising in connection with common carriage and the opening up of essential network facilities to competitors (e.g., Baumol, 2001; Hern, 2001). For a detailed discussion, with ample reference to further sources, see Decker (2015).

the local news on a daily basis. On the other hand, after the drought broke, critics alleged that the state panicked and overinvested in white elephants[18] without adequate analysis of the options, leaving Queensland residents with a $9 billion debt that will require decades to repay. The Queensland Audit Office (QAO) criticised the process under which the relevant projects were built as hasty, inefficient, and approved without an adequate business case (Queensland Audit Office, 2013). This led the QAO to conclude: 'What however could and should have been done better, even in time of emergency, was to have a thorough and rigorous assessment of all costs and of the social, economic and environmental benefits; [sic] in all likely modes of operation' (Queensland Audit Office, 2013, pp. 1–2).

The Productivity Commission has similarly criticised decisions in Sydney, Perth, and elsewhere to build desalination plants at all, or at such high levels of capacity, as well as other high-cost infrastructure investments over lower-cost alternatives (Productivity Commission, 2011, p. xxiii).

2.5 *Future directions for Australian water supply*

In 2011, the Productivity Commission reviewed Australia's urban water sector and considered the best ways to increase efficiency. Its wide-ranging report suggested a number of possibilities, including:

- that the government should consider 'removing "policy bans" on supply augmentation from certain sources, such as rural-urban trade' and properly treated recycled water (2011, p. xxxii);
- structural changes such as aggregating smaller utilities to achieve economies of scale and disaggregating larger utilities in order to facilitate the introduction of yardstick competition (discussed in section 4) (2011, p. xli); and
- that the industry consider incorporating a role for a consumer representative group, as is done in the United Kingdom, United States, and Canada (discussed in section 4) (2011, p. xxxviii–xxxix).

In March 2015, the first comprehensive Commonwealth review of competition policy since the 1993 Hilmer Report was released. The 2015 Competition Policy Review Final Report, issued by the review panel chaired by Professor Ian Harper (the 'Harper Report'), reiterated support for the NWI and proposed that a new, national Access and Pricing Regulator be created and given responsibility for working with state and territory regulators to implement the NWI principles (Commonwealth of Australia, 2015, pp. 53, 204). That national regulator would be able to assume responsibilities now undertaken by the patchwork of individual state economic regulators. As such, it would move Australia in the direction of a truly national water supply regime such as is seen in England (see section 4). It would also facilitate the development of competition because, as in other areas of the law, the creation of an entity facilitating the development of uniform rules would make it easier for not only the private sector to enter but also for the existing government water businesses to potentially compete with each other in contestable areas of the water supply chain.

18 Although the desalination plant proved useful when it was able to supply adequate clean water for several days after Brisbane's water supply was contaminated during a major flood.

Whether such a national regulator will be created, however, is uncertain. In its November 2015 response to the Harper Report, the Australian Government expressed its support for the Harper Report's proposals for continued reform of the Australian water sector but expressed the need for additional discussions with the states and territories before committing to the creation of the proposed national Access and Pricing Regulator (Australian Government, 2015, pp. 18, 38). It is unclear how the states and territories will respond to any proposal to refer regulatory functions in this area to a national regulator. Nonetheless, the current existence of a national electricity regulator (the Australian Electricity Regulator, which the Harper Report proposed to fold into the proposed Access and Pricing Regulator) provides some precedent.

3. Comparative water reform: what can Australia learn from other jurisdictions?

Innovations in the UK jurisdictions offer possibilities on how the Australian water industry may evolve.

3.1 England and Wales: privatisation, moves toward competition, and attempts to shift the focus to consumers

3.1.1 England

Water supply in the UK has undergone an even more profound transformation than the Australian industry has experienced over the past quarter century. English and Welsh water reform started in the 1970s, when hundreds of small water, river, and sewerage authorities were consolidated into ten Regional Water Authorities (RWAs) (e.g., Bakker, 2003, p. 361). In the 1980s, those government water suppliers were pressured to move from a social to a commercial outlook and provide better service more efficiently. The most significant change came in November 1989, when the RWAs were privatised pursuant to the *Water Act* (UK) (1989, ss 4, pp. 83–89). Now, every water supplier in England is privately owned (in some cases by foreign firms) and operated on a for-profit basis (Bakker, 2003, p. 367; Byatt, 2013; Dore et al., 2004, pp. 42–44; Hendry, 2015, p. 80; Lobina & Hall, 2001; McGuinness & Thomas, 1997; Ogden & Glaister, 1996; Ogden, 1995; Parker, 1997; Van den Berg, 1997). For example, Macquarie Bank, the Australian infrastructure investor, has owned 26% of Thames Water, England's largest water company, since 2006, during which time Macquarie has paid out £1.875 billion in dividends to investors (Plimmer, 2016a).[19]

It is widely recognised in the literature that privatisation led to large increases in infrastructure investment and drinking water quality (e.g., Cave, 2009, p. 5; Department for Environment, 2011a; Dore et al., 2004, p. 45; Hendry, 2015, p. 88; Van den Berg, 1997), although certain sources attribute at least part of the increases in investment and drinking water quality to the need to comply with mandatory technical standards for drinking

19 Macquarie announced that it would sell its stake in Thames Water by the end of 2016, although it is unclear whether uncertainty caused by the Brexit vote will wreak havoc on those plans. Other major shareholders in Thames Water include the Abu Dhabi Investment Authority, the China Investment Corporation, and the BT pension fund.

water quality imposed by European Union directives (eg, Hendry, 2015, p. 88).[20] Hendry (2015) suggests that the need to source the financing necessary to make the investments required to comply with those directives was a driver for privatisation. However, in the years immediately post-privatisation, water prices also went up significantly, leading to an increase in 'water poverty', while companies made large profits (Bakker, 2003, p. 363; Lobina & Hall, 2001). This led to efforts to rein in excess profits and caused the government to ban companies from disconnecting customers for failure to pay (*Water Industry Act* (UK) (1999)). Those efforts have not been entirely successful, however. For example, in early 2016 members of parliament criticised England and Wales' water regulator, Ofwat, for allowing water companies to make excess profits of £1.2 billion over the previous five years (Plimmer, 2016b).

There are still regional monopolies, but under 'yardstick' or 'comparative' competition, the economic regulator for England and Wales, the Water Services Regulation Authority (still known by its old name, Ofwat), compares the monopolistic water suppliers to each other based on a common set of economic criteria. Firms are rewarded or penalised in how much they may charge customers depending on how they compare to their peers. One side-effect has been to limit merger activity in order to maintain a large enough pool of comparator competitors for yardstick competition to be useful (Cave, 2009, pp. 87–88; Hendry, 2015, p. 93). However, the *Water Act* (UK) (2014) loosened the merger rules where 'relevant consumer benefits' will outweigh the harm to comparative competition.

Furthermore, there have been attempts to introduce competition into water supply, including individual sales outside of a water supplier's service area and the introduction of common carriage (Hern, 2001). Under the 'inset appointment' regime, water suppliers may sell bulk water to non-household customers in other suppliers' service areas (Hern, 2001, p. 118). As of 2009, use of the inset appointment regime had been disappointing, in particular because of bureaucratic requirements and the very large amount of water required to be sold in order to use the scheme (50 megalitres per year)[21] (Cave, 2009, p. 98). The threshold was dropped to five megalitres per year in 2011 (Department for Environment, 2011b, p. 4), and will be eliminated as of 2017. Under the *Water Act* (2014), all non-household consumers (including business, charity, and public sector

20 The British vote to exit the European Union (widely referred to as 'Brexit') occurred the week before this chapter was finalised. It is unclear what effect any eventual exit from the European Union by the UK or some fraction of the nations that currently comprise the UK will have on those countries' water supply systems going forward. In principle, Brexit should have little direct relevance, as the architecture of the British jurisdictions' water supply systems is set by local law, not EU regulation. It is not clear, however, how Brexit may affect the willingness of investors to finance or invest in British water companies. In the past week, the Brexit vote has already drawn into doubt the financing of investment in the British electricity sector (Shankleman & Hirtenstein, 2016). There may be further ramifications should Scotland, for example, withdraw from the UK and remain in the EU, in particular to cross-border water supply arrangements between Scotland and England that in some cases already exist or are currently under development. Brexit is clearly one of the most disruptive events to occur on the European and indeed global economic, regulatory, and governmental stage for many years. Nobody at this early juncture can accurately predict the consequences of such a cataclysmically disruptive event with any certainty. It is clear, however, that there will be consequences, whether minor or significant, to almost all aspects of British life, including the economics surrounding water supply. Brexit, therefore, can be seen as the epitome of global disorder potentially hitting British water supply in ways yet to be determined.

21 One megalitre equals one million litres.

customers) will be eligible to switch suppliers as of 1 April 2017, similar to the system that has been in place in Scotland since 2008 (Ch 1).

The *Water Act* (2014) also created a scheme to allow for cross-border sales between England, Wales, and Scotland (ss 6–7). If Scotland withdraws from the UK as a consequence of the Brexit vote, it is unclear how Scotland will treat UK-level legislation that previously applied. While presumably Scotland would pass a reception statute providing for the continuing validity of applicable UK law unless and until it is replaced, it is conceivable that the cross-border sales scheme set forth in the *Water Act* (2014) would no longer be valid and that new arrangements would have to be negotiated. This is one example of how the disorder caused by Brexit could create disorder in England and Scotland's water supply regimes.

The development of common carriage, which allows upstream competition in the development of water assets and downstream competition in the retail supply to consumers, has also been disappointing despite being legalised in 2003 (Hendry, 2015, p. 81). The Department for Environment, Food and Rural Affairs (known as 'Defra') reported in 2011, however, that recent requests to build pipelines between neighbouring water systems may enable limited sales of water into neighbouring systems (Department for Environment, 2011a, p. 25). Moreover, Chapter 2 of the *Water Act* (2014) has significantly strengthened the rules allowing for common carriage by allowing competition in new areas such as the wholesale water market. Those provisions will not come into effect until after 2019.

Steps have also been taken to protect consumers. The *Water Industry Act* (1991) created a Consumer Council for Water (CCWater) with the legal authority and obligation to provide advice and information to public authorities representing the views of consumers, including disadvantaged ones (*Water Industry Act* (1991), ch III). Recent proposals have suggested that the CCWater be given a formal role in negotiating 'regional agreements with companies reflecting local priorities and willingness to pay' (Cave, 2009; Littlechild, 2008).

3.1.2 Wales

Wales presents an especially interesting model. After Welsh Water's privatisation, it was initially operated as a for-profit business as part of the multi-utility company, Hyder PLC, which also operated electricity and gas distribution businesses in Wales (Owen, 2013). After a tumultuous period that culminated in Welsh Water's sale to WPD, a US power utility, Welsh Water was converted into a not-for-profit company, Glas Cymru (retaining the English language name 'Welsh Water'), in May 2001, with the support of the Welsh Assembly (Bakker, 2003; Owen, 2013). Along with its conversion from a profit-seeking to a not-for-profit business, Glas Cymru publicly committed that it would be run as a Welsh company serving Welsh stakeholders, with an emphasis on operating efficiently and sustainably while providing increased service quality and lower prices to customers (Owen, 2013, p. 345). Glas Cymru states that its 'business model aims to reduce Welsh Water's asset financing cost, the water industry's single biggest cost' (Welsh Water, 2016). As a company limited by guarantee, Glas Cymru has no shareholders and is wholly financed by debt and retained financial earnings (Welsh Water, 2016). As there are no shareholders, Glas Cymru pays no dividends (Thomas, 2000). Company members are a cross section of the community who act in the best interests of the company's customers (Welsh Water, 2016). Due to Glas Cymru's low-risk profile, it was able to finance itself through investment-grade bonds on attractive terms (Thomas, 2001). The lower cost of financing allowed Welsh Water to both invest in its network and lower customers' water bills. Under Glas Cymru's constitution, it owns water assets but must contract with an outside service provider to operate the assets.

It does so under a competitive tendering process (Thomas, 2001, p. 106). This opens up the Welsh market to a form of competition known as competition for the market, or franchising. Franchising is also being used successfully in France, among other places (Huet & Saussier, 2003).

When it was first created, the relevant regulators indicated that Glas Cymru's structure is not generally suitable (Thomas, 2001). Professor Martin Cave's review of competition and innovation in the UK water markets, however, noted the benefits of Welsh Water's business model, including 'a relative improvement in the overall performance assessment, the limited increase in household bills compared to other water companies, high customer satisfaction in relative and absolute terms, and a growth in reserves (or "customer equity")', and that 'there could be potential benefits for other customers if it were to be adopted elsewhere' (2009).

The creation of Glas Cymru was not the first attempt to create a not-for-profit in England and Wales. In 2000, Kelda Group, the owner of Yorkshire Water, had proposed mutualising Yorkshire Water, i.e., selling it to its customers (Bakker, 2003). Ofwat rejected the proposal because that particular transaction did not appear to hold any benefits to consumers due to Yorkshire Water's poor balance sheet and the inflated price that Kelda was seeking for Yorkshire Water's assets, although in the right circumstances, Ofwat indicated, mutualisation or some other new ownership structure might be approved (Thomas, 2001).

3.2 Scotland: a greater role for consumers

Unlike England and Wales, Scotland chose to retain public ownership over water supply but consolidated regional suppliers into a single entity, Scottish Water. Reform began in 1975, with the consolidation of the industry from a large number of local government water and sewerage entities into 12 councils. In April 1996, there was further consolidation into three Public Water Authorities (PWAs). This reform introduced a new customer body, the Scottish Water and Sewerage Customers Council, which gave consumers a legally recognised role for the first time (Sawkins, 2012). Over the next decade, further reforms took place, including the creation of a new economic regulator, the Water Industry Commissioner (WIC), in 1999 and the consolidation of the three PWAs into a single, state-owned corporation, Scottish Water, in 2002.[22] Especially notable was the 1999 creation of the Scottish Parliament and accompanying devolution of legislative authority over Scotland-specific issues thereto. This development was significant for the Scottish water industry because it opened up legislative time that had previously been lacking at Westminster for a comprehensive review of Scottish water industry legislation (Hendry, 2006/2007, pp. 154–155).

In 2005, the Scottish Parliament passed legislation reforming the Scottish water industry (*Water Services, etc (Scotland) Act* (2005) (the '*Water Services Act*')). Under the *Water Services Act*, the WIC was replaced by a commission, the Water Industry Commission for Scotland (WICS), which remains Scottish Water's economic regulator as of 2016 (Sawkins & Reid, 2007; Scottish Water, 2016). For the first time, the final decision-making authority for price setting was vested in the economic regulator. Previously, the economic regulator merely had the power to advise the responsible ministers (Hendry, 2006/2007). The *Water Services Act* also introduced competition in the supply of water to non-household

22 For detailed descriptions of the evolution of the Scottish water industry, see Hawkins (2012) and Hendry (2006/2007).

customers starting in 2008. This required Scottish Water to spin off its non-domestic business into a separate business, Business Stream (Hendry, 2015).

In 2011, a new customer body was created, the Customer Forum (Forum), with a legal right and capacity to participate in the 2015–21 official price review process. In that capacity, the Forum was empowered to negotiate with Scottish Water over certain aspects of its spending program (Hendry, 2015, p. 95). Customer engagement through the Forum has apparently led to a 'considerably more customer-friendly' approach at Scottish Water and increased satisfaction on the part of Scottish Water's customers (Littlechild, 2014, p. 19). Moreover, Scottish Water's most recent regulatory pricing review, in which the Forum participated, is said to have had a collaborative tenor, rather than the adversarial tone that had characterised past reviews (Hendry, 2015, pp. 95–96). Therefore, the introduction of a consumer representative body into the regulatory process has been regarded as a success. Scottish Water's relative performance compared to other British water suppliers has increased dramatically, as well. The foregoing leads Hendry to conclude that '[i]t does seem that the Scottish model has succeeded in regulating the public sector to private sector efficiency, whilst still maintaining a public sector ethos that is not diverted by the needs of investors or shareholders' (2015).

4. Conclusion

Water supply governance in Australia, England, Wales and Scotland over the past quarter-century has been characterised by persistent change affecting all facets of the industry. The profiled jurisdictions have seen evolution in ownership, profit orientation, number of participants, attitudes toward competition, type of regulation, relationship to the government, and consideration for and relationship to the consumer. Lack of stability – disorder – has ruled the day both on a domestic level in each of the profiled jurisdictions, as laws and policies have been subject to numerous revisions over relatively short periods of time, and globally, as each of the profiled jurisdictions has pursued a different path to the ultimate goal of an efficient, safe and sustainable water sector.[23]

We see a multitude of government-owned businesses operating as monopolies (for the moment, at least) in Queensland; a multitude of profit-driven private sector companies, acting for the most part as monopolists but subject to the growing threat of competition, in England; a single not-for-profit company outsourcing operations to for-profit companies on a competitive basis in Wales; and a single government-owned business operating monopolistically (for the moment) in the residential sector but on a competitive basis in relation to commercial customers in Scotland. Each jurisdiction has engaged in serious consultation with experts as part of its reform process, yet each has come up with a very different solution. Moreover, while space limitations prevented the consideration of yet additional jurisdictions, the diversity of approaches seen here mirrors what is happening within the sector on a global basis. Clearly there is no one-size-fits-all answer.

Worldwide disorder in water supply governance is not necessarily a bad thing. Section 2 reported the lack of consistency in the empirical research as to the optimal structure of water supply regimes. There is mixed evidence as to the best size, scope, and ownership structure of these businesses. There also is some evidence that what is best will vary by

23 The recent Brexit vote may also illustrate how disordering geopolitical events outside the strict confines of the water industry may have chaotic ripple effects within the industry.

location, reflecting the influence of geography, political system, legal system, and even relative wealth of the population. Jurisdictions' attempts to create bespoke systems tailored to their circumstances seems like a rational response to differing conditions and public expectations. Perhaps these attempts to tailor the water sector to local conditions will lead to eventual calm, and order once more, once the growing pains still afflicting this period of extraordinary upheaval in the water industry subside.

Alternatively, perhaps the most important point is the great learning opportunity presented by the variety of options being tested across jurisdictions. We are all witness to an ad hoc experiment on a worldwide basis. In the United States, the phrase 'states as labs' is used to describe the positive effects of having different US states apply different policy proposals to attack a common problem. The idea is that competition among states in this manner might lead to the identification of a clear best answer, which can then be widely adopted. The variety of proposed solutions currently being offered to the challenges facing the water sector may similarly be an example of countries as labs. Perhaps this period of widespread experimentation will lead in the long run to greater order in the water supply industry if an optimal industry structure emerges.

Seizing on the 'countries as labs' concept, the final subsection reflects on issues raised by the profiled jurisdictions' reforms of their water industries. The comments are specifically directed to Australia but may also be applicable to other jurisdictions depending on how the relevant features of those jurisdictions' water sectors are structured.

4.1 *Lessons for Australia, and perhaps elsewhere*

Comparing more than two decades of water reform in Australia to developments in the UK, several issues merit comment.

Efficiency concerns. The Australian water reforms generally were intended to introduce price signals to encourage water to move from less efficient uses to more efficient uses (Crase et al., 2015, p. 36). But residential use, which can never be eliminated, is never going to be the most 'efficient' use of water. So at some point the relentless drive to adjust prices until water usage is at its most efficient will have to confront the political reality that the populace will not allow itself to be priced out of access to water.[24] In fact, that push back is already being seen. Moreover, efficiency improvements must be reflected in customers' water bills. Efficiency gains that solely lead to increased dividends to shareholders (government or otherwise) will not be politically tenable, as was seen in England in the 1990s.

The questionable propriety of charging a commercial rate of return in a non-competitive environment. The notion that water suppliers (even government-owned ones) should be earning a commercial rate of return has been generally accepted ever since the Hilmer Report. But requiring GOBs to earn a commercial rate of return was originally intended to level the playing field in competitive environments so that GOBs would not have an unfair advantage due to their lack of need to factor a profit margin into their pricing. Water supply in Australia, however, is still monopolistic. There are no competitors to be disadvantaged, even after more than two decades of water reform. In a non-competitive

24 Whether the best way to ensure access to water for all is through price caps, some other mechanism such as welfare payments for those who cannot afford their water bills, or a return to the old days of government subsidies (hidden or overt) is beyond the scope of this chapter. For a good discussion of the options for dealing with the increasing problem of 'water poor' people in developed economies, see Barraqué & Montginoul (2015).

environment, the question must be asked: why should governments providing a service (even through a corporatised entity) be charging *any* return above the amount necessary to cover their costs? Charging water customers more than the true cost of water in order to provide a commercial return to government in the form of a dividend amounts to a hidden, regressive tax. The better off are not hit substantially harder unless they are extravagant users of water, such as through the constant running of sprinklers or topping up of swimming pools. It is true that the government needs to fund itself, but the level of public understanding about the existence and extent of this form of taxation appears to be very low. There should be more public debate about the propriety of the government profiting from water sales rather than earning revenue through other sources. The same questions can be raised about the other trappings of competitive neutrality, such as tax equivalent payments.

The extent to which the water supply market is contestable. Although the water supply market is clearly being re-positioned to eventually allow in new entrants, such as possibly private companies, and although competition as a general principle is clearly beneficial for consumers, it is not yet clear about the extent to which competition in *any* form will be successful in the water supply market. England and Wales are only now in a position to have a significant move away from their monopolist water suppliers in the next few years, if the *Water Act* (2014) reforms are successful, close to 30 years after privatisation. Nevertheless, there is potentially room for a franchise model (competition for the market). Moreover, as monopolistic water systems are connected through pipelines into grids, as occurred in SEQ, it becomes possible for systems to engage in water trading, which could benefit consumers where one system produces water more efficiently than the other. Common carriage regimes might also be possible.

A role for consumers? Developments in England, Scotland, and Wales have emphasised an increased voice for consumers, rather than expecting the economic regulator to adequately represent consumer interests. Outcomes in those jurisdictions appear to have been positive. Regardless of the direction in which the industry evolves, Australian jurisdictions should similarly consider appointing an official seat at the table for consumer representatives.

References

Abbott, M., & Cohen, B. (2009). Productivity and efficiency in the water industry. *Utilities Policy, 17*, 233–244.

Agreement to Implement the National Competition Policy and Related Reforms, Signed on 11 April 1995. (1995).

Alcazar, L., Xu, L. C., & Zuluaga, A. M. (2000). Institutions, politics, and contracts: The attempt to privatize the water and sanitation utility of Lima, Peru. Washington, DC: World Bank.

Alchian, A. A., & Demsetz, H. (1972). Production, information costs, and economic organization. *The American Economic Review, 62*, 777–795.

Arnold, C. A. (2005). Privatization of public water services: The states' role in ensuring public pccountability. *Pepperdine Law Review, 32*, 561–604.

Arnold, C. A. (2009). Water privatization trends in the United States: human rights, national security, and public stewardship. *William & Mary Environmental Law and Policy Review, 33*, 785–849.

Australian Bureau of Statistics. (2016, 30 March). 3218.0 – Regional Population Growth, Australia, 2014–15. Retrieved from http://www.abs.gov.au/.

Australian Government, the Treasury. (2015). *Australian Government response to the competition policy review*. Canberra: The Australian Government.

Australian Taxation Office. (2012). *National tax equivalent regime manual.* Canberra: Australian Government.

Bakker, K. J. (2003). From public to private to . . . mutual? Restructuring water supply governance in England and Wales. *Geoforum, 34*, 359–374.

Barraqué, B., & Montginoul, M. (2015). How to integrate social objectives into water pricing. In A. Dinar, V. Pochat, & J. Albiac-Murillo (Eds.), *Water pricing experiences and innovations* (pp. 359–371). Cham: Springer International Publishing.

Baumfield, V. S. (2013). The Allconnex Water debacle: lessons in devising better governance mechanisms for government business enterprises. *Bond Law Review, 24*(2), 1–63.

Baumol, W. (2001). Economically defensible access pricing, competition, and preservation of socially desirable dross dubsidy. *Utilities Policy, 10*, 151–159.

Beecher, J. A., & Kalmbach, J. A. (2013). Structure, regulation, and pricing of water in the United States: a study of the Great Lakes region. *Utilities Policy, 24*, 32–47.

Booth, T., & Noon, A. (2013). Corporatisation in Australia: a Queensland perspective. In J. H. Farrar & D. G. Mayes (Eds.), *Globalisation, the global financial crisis and the state* (pp. 117–139). Cheltenham, UK: Edward Elgar.

Bosman, J. (2016a, 12 April). As lead levels dip, Flint residents are urged: run your water. *The New York Times.* Retrieved from http://www.nytimes.com/2016/04/13/us/as-lead-levels-dip-flint-residents-are-urged-run-your-water.html.

Bosman, J. (2016b, 11 February). Why it won't be easy or cheap to fix Flint's water crisis. *The New York Times.* Retrieved from http://www.nytimes.com/2016/02/12/us/why-it-wont-be-easy-or-cheap-to-fix-flints-water-crisis.html.

Byatt, I., Ballance, T., & Reid, S. (2006). Regulation of water and sewerage services. In M. Crew & D. Parker (Eds.), *International handbook on economic regulation* (pp. 370–393). Camberly: Edward Elgar.

Byatt, I. (2013). The regulation of water services in the UK. *Utilities Policy, 24*, 3–10.

Byrnes, J. (2013). A short institutional and regulatory history of the Australian urban water sector. *Utilities Policy, 24*, 11–19.

Carvalho, P., Marques, R. C., & Berg, S. (2012). A meta-regression analysis of benchmarking studies on water utilities market structure. *Utilities Policy, 21*, 40–49.

Cave, M. (2009). *Independent review of competition and innovation in water markets: Final report.* London: Defra.

Commonwealth of Australia. (1993). *National competition policy.* Canberra: Australian Government Publishing Service.

Commonwealth of Australia. (2015). *Competition policy review final report.* Canberra: Australian Government.

Council of Australian Governments. (25 February 1994). Communique: Attachment A Water Resource Policy. Retrieved from http://www.coag.gov.au/coag_meeting_outcomes/1994-02-25/docs/attachment_a.cfm.

Crase, L., Pawsey, N., & Cooper, B. (2015). Water pricing in Australia: unbundled politics, accounting, and water pricing. In A. Dinar, V. Pochat, & J. Albiac-Murillo (Eds.), *Water pricing experiences and innovations* (pp. 15–39). New York: Springer.

Crew, M. A., & Parker, D. (2006). Development in the theory and practice of regulatory economics. In M. Crew & D. Parker (Eds.), *International handbook on economic regulation* (pp. 1–33). Camberly: Edward Elgar.

Decker, C. (2015). *Modern Economic Regulation: An Introduction to Theory and Practice.* Cambridge: Cambridge University Press.

Department for Environment, F. a. R. A. (2011a). *Water for life.* London: HM Government.

Department for Environment, F. a. R. A. (2011b). *Water for life: Market reform proposals.* London: HM Government.

Department of Infrastructure and Regional Development. (2016). Jervis Bay Territory Governance and Administration. Retrieved from http://regional.gov.au/territories/jervis_bay/governanceadministration.aspx.

Deutrom, R. (2016, June 17). Oakey water contamination: Toowoomba Regional Council had relaxed attitude to warnings. *The Courier-Mail.* Retrieved from http://www.couriermail.com.au/news/queensland/oakey-water-contamination-toowoomba-regional-council-had-relaxed-attitude-to-warnings/news story/3986cfcb3394fc63b73218a752ff2908.

Dore, M. H. I., Kushner, J., & Zumer, K. (2004). Privatization of water in the UK and France – what can we learn? *Utilities Policy, 12*, 41–50.

Easterbrook, F. H., & Fischel, D. R. (1991). *The Economic Structure of Corporate Law.* Cambridge: Harvard University Press.

Economist, The (2008, October 20). Economies of scale and scope. Retrieved from http://www.economist.com/node/12446567.

Explanatory Notes, Queensland Competition Authority Bill (1997).

Farrar, J., & McCabe, B. (1995). Corporatisation, corporate governance and the deregulation of the public sector economy. *Public Law Review, 6*, 24–43.

Foellmi, R., & Meister, U. (2012). Enhancing the efficiency of water supply – product market competition versus trade. *Journal of Industry, Competition and Trade, 12*, 299–324.

Ganim, S., & Tran, L. (2016, 13 January). How tap water became toxic in Flint, Michigan. *Cnn.com.* Retrieved from http://edition.cnn.com/2016/01/11/health/toxic-tap-water-flint-michigan/.

Hailu, D., Osorio, R. G., & Tsukada, R. (2012). Privatization and renationalization: what went wrong in Bolivia's water sector. *World Development, 40*, 2564–2577.

Hall, D., & Lobina, E. (2007). International actors and multinational water company strategies in Europe, 1990–2003. *Utilities Policy, 15*, 64–77.

Hendry, S. (2006/2007). Water for sale? Market liberalisation and public sector regulation in Scottish water services. *Utilities Law Review, 16*(4), 153–162.

Hendry, S. (2015). *Frameworks for Water Law Reform.* Cambridge: Cambridge University Press.

Hern, R. (2001). Competition and access pricing in the UK water industry. *Utilities Policy, 10*, 117–127.

Huet, F., & Saussier, S. (2003). Contractual arrangements and the provision of public interest services: a transaction cost analysis. *European Business Organization Law Review, 4*, 403–428.

Hukka, J. J., & Vinnari, E. M. (2007). Public-public partnerships in the Finnish water services sector. *Utilities Policy, 15*, 86–92.

Intergovernmental Agreement on a National Water Initiative, signed 25 June 2004. (2004).

Jensen, M. C., & Meckling, W. H. (1976). Theory of the firm: managerial behavior, agency costs and ownership wtructure. *Journal of Financial Economics, 3*, 305–360.

Jervis Bay Acceptance Act (1915) (Cth).

LECG Limited Asia Pacific. (2011). *Competition in the Australian Urban Water Sector.* Canberra: National Water Commission.

Littlechild, S. (2008). *Constructive engagement and negotiated settlements – a prospect in the England and Wales water sector?* Retrieved from http://www.eprg.group.cam.ac.uk/constructive-engagement-and-negotiated-settlements-a-prospect-in-the-england-and-wales-water-sector/.

Littlechild, S. (2014). *The Customer Forum: customer engagement in the Scottish water sector.* Retrieved from http://www.eprg.group.cam.ac.uk/the-customer-forum-customer-engagement-in-the-scottish-water-sector/.

Lobina, E., & Hall, D. (2001). *UK Water privatisation – a briefing.* Retrieved from http://www.archives.gov.on.ca/en/e_records/walkerton/part2info/partieswithstanding/pdf/CUPE18UKwater.pdf.

Lobina, E., & Hall, D. (2007). Experience with private sector participation in Grenoble, France, and lessons on strengthening public water operations. *Utilities Policy, 15*, 93–109.

MacDonald, G. M. (2010). Water, climate change, and sustainability in the southwest. *Proceedings of the National Academy of Sciences, 107*(50), 21256–21262. doi: 10.1073/pnas.0909651107.

McArdle, M., Minister for Energy and Water Supply. (2012). SEQ's "Back to the Future" Bulk Water Model Back on Track [Press release]. Retrieved from http://statements.qld.gov.au/Statement/Id/79640.

McGuinness, T., & Thomas, D. (1997). The diversification strategies of the privatised water and sewerage companies in England and Wales: a resource based view. *Utilities Policy, 6*, 325–339.

Meek, J. (2014). *Private Island: Why Britain Now Belongs to Someone Else*. London: Verso.

National Water Commission. (2014). Closure in 2014. Retrieved from http://www.nwc.gov.au/organisation/closure-in-2014.

Ogden, S., & Glaister, K. W. (1996). The cautious monopolists – strategies of Britain's privatized water companies. *Long Range Planning, 29*, 663–674.

Ogden, S. G. (1995). Transforming frameworks of accountability: the case of water privatization. *Accounting, Organizations and Society, 20*(2/3), 193–218.

Osborne, A. (2013, 8 April). Margaret Thatcher: one policy that led to more than 50 companies being sold or privatised. *The Telegraph*. Retrieved from http://www.telegraph.co.uk/finance/comment/alistair-osborne/9980292/Margaret-Thatcher-one-policy-that-led-to-more-than-50-companies-being-sold-or-privatised.html.

Owen, D. L. (2013). Glas Cymru: lessons from nine years as a not-for-profit public-private partnership. *International Journal of Water Resources Development, 29*(3), 343–351.

Parker, D. (1997). Price cap regulation, profitability and returns to investors in the UK regulated industries. *Utilities Policy, 6*, 305–315.

Plimmer, G. (2016a, May 26). Macquarie to start sale of Thames Water stake. *Financial Times*. Retrieved from http://www.ft.com/cms/s/0/2db37112–2309–11e6–9d4d-c11776a5124d.html#axzz4CTjADKRi.

Plimmer, G. (2016b, January 13). Water watchdog taken to task over sector's excessive profits. *Financial Times*. Retrieved from http://www.ft.com/cms/s/0/41491202-b92f-11e5-b151–8e15c9a029fb.html#axzz4DOw3f7NR.

Posner, R. A. (1969). Natural monopoly and its regulation. *Stanford Law Review, 21*(3), 548–643.

Productivity Commission. (2011). *Australia's urban water sector, Report No 55, Final Inquiry Report*. Canberra: Australian Government.

Queensland Audit Office. (2013). *Maintenance of water infrastructure assets* (Report to Parliament 14: 2012–13).

Samuelson, P. A., & Nordhaus, W. D. (1992). *Economics* (14th ed.). New York: McGraw-Hill.

Sawkins, J. W., & Reid, S. (2007). The measurement and regulation of cross subsidy. The case of the Scottish water industry. *Utilities Policy, 15*, 36–48.

Sawkins, J. W. (2012). The introduction of competition into the Scottish water industry. *Utilities Policy, 20*, 22–30.

Scottish Water. (2016). How the water industry is run in Scotland. Retrieved from http://www.scottishwater.co.uk/business/about-us/governance/water-industry-in-scotland.

Shankleman, J., & Hirtenstein, A. (2016, June 28). Who will now invest £100 billion to keep Britain's lights on? Retrieved from http://www.bloomberg.com/news/articles/2016–06–28/next-brexit-test-finding-136-billion-to-keep-u-k-s-lights-on.

Silberston, A. (1972). Economies of scale in theory and practice. *The Economic Journal, 82*(325), 369–391. doi:10.2307/2229943.

South-East Queensland Water (Distribution and Retail Restructuring) Act (2009) (Qld).

South-East Queensland Water (Distribution and Retail Restructuring) and Other Legislation Amendment Act (2012) (Qld).

Thomas, D. (2000). Hyder: The rise and fall of a multi-utility. *Utilities Policy, 9*, 181–192.

Thomas, D. (2001). Welsh Water: role model or special case? *Utilities Policy, 10*, 99–114.

van den Berg, C. (1997). Water privatization and regulation in England and Wales. Washington, DC: The World Bank, Private Sector Development Department.

Vickers, J., & Yarrow, G. (1991). Economic perspectives on privatization. *The Journal of Economic Perspectives, 5*(2), 111–132.

Vining, A. R., & Boardman, A. E. (1992). Ownership versus competition: efficiency in public enterprise. *Public Choice, 73*, 205–239.

Vinnari, E. M. (2006). The economic regulation of publicly owned water utilities: the case of Finland. *Utilities Policy, 14*, 158–165.

Vinnari, E. M., & Hukka, J. J. (2007). Great expectations, tiny benefits – decision-making in the privatization of Tallinn Water. *Utilities Policy, 15*, 78–85.

Water Act 1989 (1989) (UK).

Water Industry Act (1991) (UK).

Water Industry Act (1999) (UK).

Water Services, etc (Scotland) Act (2005) (Scotland).

Water Supply (Safety and Reliability) Act (2008) (Qld).

Welsh Water. (2016). Company information – Glas Cymru. Retrieved from http://www.dwrcymru.com/en/company-information/glas-cymru.aspx.

Wetzstein, M. E. (2013). *Microeconomic theory: Concepts and connections* (2nd ed.). London and New York: Routledge.

Whincop, M. J., & Keyes, M. E. (1997). Corporation, contract, community: an analysis of governance in the privatisation of public enterprise and the publicisation of private corporate law. *Federal Law Review, 25*, 51–96.

10 Domestic Regulatory Architectures for the Protection of Financial Stability after the GFC

Global Order or Disorder?

Louise Parsons[1]

1. The global financial crisis, financial instability and financial regulation: disruptive disorder

The Global Financial Crisis (GFC) was a protracted and hard-hitting crisis that personified disorder. Its disruptive effects were widespread, its reach was geographically broad, and it fundamentally affected companies, industries, and the personal lives of large numbers of people all over the world. The crisis resulted in the loss of equity, share value, credit ratings and, on a more personal level, jobs, money, homes, and even families.

Following on the 'Great Moderation' of 1985 to 2007 (Knight, 2014, p. 3), an era of profound prosperity and stability, the GFC was catastrophic and disorderly. Purely in financial terms, the cost of the GFC has been estimated to be between USD 2 and 3 trillion (Australian Financial Review, 2014) with a USD 3.9 billion loss to banks (Australian Financial Review, 2014). Just in the United States (US) alone, the GFC is said to have cost each US citizen USD 20,000 in terms of standard of living (Australian Financial Review, 2014) and USD 180,000 for each US citizen if wellbeing and the effect on government finances are taken into account (Australian Financial Review, 2014). More than eight years on, the negative impact of the GFC is still being felt in some places in the world (Edey, 2014).

Another key feature of the GFC was its international reach, as evidenced by its viral spread. Financial and economic disorder spread from a particular segment of the US housing market – the subprime mortgage market – to financial institutions in general in the US and to institutions abroad. It led to the demise of a number of significant financial institutions and severe liquidity or solvency problems for others, requiring public bailouts. The crisis further spread to national economies all over the world, resulting in actual or near recessions in multiple countries. Never before have economic prosperity and financial stability in different countries been shown to be so interlinked, and seldom, if ever before, did financial disorder envelop the globe in such a manner.

The causes of the GFC are not limited to the greed of subprime mortgage lenders – many of the problems arose because of regulatory failure. In fact, regulatory gaps and lapses received a lot of attention in the analysis of the causes of and solutions to the GFC (see, eg, Jácome & Nier, n.d.; Masciandaro, Vega-Pansini & Quintyn, 2012).

1 The comments of the editors on this chapter are gratefully acknowledged.

During and after the GFC, international and domestic leaders turned to regulation as one of the keys to creating order and stability again and to preventing future instances of such profound instability (see, eg, Davis, 2011). This run to regulation reflected what many acknowledge to be the purpose of regulation – modification of behaviour, setting of standards, and the gathering of information (the latter presumably to guide further regulatory interventions) (Black, 2002). It was evident that behaviour had to change and new standards had to be set for conduct in the financial sector and that timeous and accurate information was key to preventing future instances of financial disorder and financial crises. Leaders and analysts concluded that regulation – or, more accurately, deregulation in the lead-up to the GFC itself – contributed to financial instability. The prevailing philosophy among regulators pre-GFC was that markets would self-correct because of the 'market' theory of economics and minimum regulation (see, eg, Davis, 2011). It was assumed that, as Alan Greenspan put it, the self-interest of a few would also protect larger society (Beattie & Politi, 2008). Therefore, regulation, or the lack of appropriate regulation, was considered to be one of the causes of the crisis and of the disorder in financial markets; it was also considered to be one of the key tools for overcoming the crisis and recreating order.

Important issues in the discussions about regulation after the GFC included the international commensurability of domestic regulatory frameworks, the need to provide for cooperation between countries in domestic regulation, and the global and interconnected nature of banking and finance. Influential international bodies, such as the Group of Twenty (G20) and the Financial Stability Board (FSB), called for some commensurability in the different regulatory regimes in domestic jurisdictions for the protection of financial stability. One of the key issues identified after the GFC was the need to have an appropriate domestic regulatory architecture or framework of regulators that would support domestic and international financial stability.

From a regulatory perspective, the GFC cannot be ignored. It is precisely the kind of event from which governments would be expected to protect their citizens in the future. The protection against financial crises such as the GFC is perhaps one of the key areas where it can be said that there is a positive duty on governments to regulate/legislate (see, eg, Davis, 2011, p. 7) to avoid such a "tectonic shock" (Knight, 2014, p. 1) hitting the global economy again.

This chapter investigates whether regulation aimed at alleviating the disorder of the GFC and preventing similar recurrences of financial instability is itself in disorder. For this purpose, the chapter analyses the changes to the regulatory architectures in the G20 countries. (For the purposes of this chapter, 'G20 countries' excludes the European Union, because it is not a single domestic jurisdiction and therefore not an ideal comparator, but does include Spain, because, although not an official member of the G20, it has always been invited to and has attended G20 meetings.) The chapter assesses the regulatory architectures of the G20 countries against six key benchmarks, endorsed by a number of influential international bodies and notable experts after the GFC (see further Part Three). These key benchmarks can be described as emerging best practice in the domestic regulatory architecture for financial stability.

In this chapter, 'regulatory architecture' refers to "the organization of the agencies that regulate a particular policy sphere" (Murphy, 2013 p. 10). The regulatory architecture, therefore, comprises the design or structure of the regulators and supervisors involved in domestic financial regulation. It includes their interaction as well as their institutional structures and organisational underpinnings. The sources of regulation can be categorised into different levels (see Figure 10.1):

- At the highest level is the law, typically the constitution, that vests parliament (or an equivalent law-making national body) with sovereign legislative and regulatory power.
- The next level is the legislation that creates and controls regulators and/or supervisors, especially formal state-appointed and government-mandated regulators and supervisors. An example is legislation establishing and mandating a central bank. Importantly, not all bodies or institutions operating at this level would necessarily be statutory bodies and the subject of formal legislation. For example, in Australia, the Council of Financial Regulators, which nevertheless plays an important role in the regulatory architecture, is a non-statutory (therefore non-state-mandated) body.
- The lowest level is legislation that directly affects the activities of regulated entities/institutions, such as banks (the 'regulatees'). Included at this level are regulations issued by regulators within their statutory mandates, such as prudential standards for capital ratios. Regulatees are not only required to comply with legislation and regulations directly but may also be required to give effect to directions, requests, and orders by regulators or supervisors.

The focus of this chapter will be the middle level of the regulatory architecture (Level 2 in Figure 10.1).

Figure 10.1 Levels of regulation in a domestic jurisdiction

2. Significant changes in post-GFC regulatory architectures of G20 countries after the GFC

A comparative review of the domestic regulatory architectures of the G20 countries before and after the GFC reveals very little substantive change. For example, at an institutional level, the financial regulators before and after the GFC are largely the same: few regulators have been abolished, and hardly any new ones created. This is somewhat counterintuitive. Given the wide-ranging losses and destructive effect of the GFC, it would be reasonable to expect that, at the highest level of domestic regulation (the legislation creating and regulating the regulators), it would not be 'business as usual' after the GFC. If anything, the institutional lessons of the GFC should not be quickly forgotten (Laker, 2010).

This highest level of the regulatory architecture – the very identity of the regulators, supervisors, and other regulatory bodies – is of the utmost importance. It fundamentally influences the regulation of financial stability through the identities and roles of the key actors. Although there was no express recommendation by any of the international financial institutions, such as the IMF or the FSB, that countries should change their regulators, abolish some, and create new regulators, the G20 did call on countries to strengthen their domestic frameworks "to cope both with domestic vulnerabilities and with the increased global interconnectedness of the financial system" (Financial Stability Board [FSB], 2011a, p. 5). The need to re-evaluate the very fundamentals of regulatory architectures post-GFC is also evident from, for example, the need for regulators to have clear mandates, an appropriately defined regulatory perimeter, well-defined methods of cooperation and information-sharing, and clear allocations of responsibilities (see, generally, International Monetary Fund [IMF], 2009, 2013).

However, after the GFC, the vast majority of G20 countries did not change their regulatory architecture at the highest level at all. However, all effected reforms at lower levels of regulation, such as capital requirements, liquidity ratios, and the regulation of credit rating agencies (see, generally, Buckley, 2014). In some countries, the roles of existing regulators were extended, new specialised committees were created within existing regulators, and new councils came into existence. For example, in the US, the *Dodd-Frank Wall Street Reform and Consumer Protection Act* (enacted 21 July 2010; *Dodd-Frank Act*) created two new agencies (and numerous regulatory offices) and merged the Office of Thrift Supervision with the Office of the Comptroller of the Currency (Murphy, 2013, p. 10). The *Dodd-Frank Act* further provided the Federal Reserve with oversight authority, and the Federal Deposit Insurance Corporation with resolution authority, over the largest financial firms. Consumer protection rulemaking was also consolidated into the new Consumer Financial Protection Bureau (Murphy, 2013). The United Kingdom also made significant changes, abolishing one of the key regulators, the Financial Services Authority. The *Financial Services Act 2012* established an independent Financial Policy Committee (FPC) and a new Prudential Regulation Authority (PRA) as a subsidiary of the Bank of England and created new responsibilities for the supervision of financial market infrastructure providers. The reforms came into force on 1 April 2013 (Bank of England, 2016b). South Africa is currently in the process of implementing similarly significant changes in its regulatory architecture. If the proposed legislation is passed, the existing Financial Services Board will be reconstituted as the Financial Sector Conduct Authority (FSCA). A new body, the Prudential Authority, will be created as an independent body, but the Prudential Authority will be located within the administrative framework of the South African Reserve Bank (SARB), and SARB will provide the resources for the Prudential Authority (Minister of Finance Republic of South Africa, 2013; see also Mason & Gray, 2016).

At the highest level of the regulatory architecture, however, changes in the G20 countries were minimal.

3. Six key characteristics of emerging best practice in domestic regulatory architectures after the GFC

The most influential international institutions (G20, FSB, and IMF) did not make a general recommendation that domestic regulators as institutions should be changed after the GFC. They did, however, make a number of recommendations for optimal regulatory structures and also identified characteristics of domestic regulatory architectures that can be seen to be best practice after the GFC.[2] An analysis of the extent to which the G20 countries exhibit these characteristics of best practice provides insight into whether the world's dominant and leading economies have taken on board the lessons of the GFC at the level of their overall regulatory architecture.

The six characteristics selected for this discussion are key to the preservation of financial stability and lie at the heart of the structures in the financial architecture. The first characteristic or benchmark is that the regulatory architecture should demonstrate a clear focus on financial stability. This clear focus is evidenced by the second, third, and fourth characteristics or benchmarks. These are that a single regulator, with a clear mandate, is responsible for financial stability and that the central bank plays a lead role in financial stability. The fifth is that the regulatory architecture demonstrates a clear focus on macroprudential policy. The last is that the State has adopted an optimum structure for prudential and market-conduct supervision by regulators. The 'twin peaks' model – under which one 'peak' (or regulator) is responsible for prudential regulation and the other for market conduct and consumer protection[3] – is widely accepted as the optimum (Schmulow, 2016).

The chapter turns to discuss each of these characteristics and, based on available empirical evidence, the extent to which each of the G20 countries exhibits these in their regulatory structures.

3.1 The regulatory architecture demonstrates a clear focus on financial stability at a high level

One of the key lessons of the GFC highlighted by the G20 was that there should be a much more pronounced focus on financial stability, with a broader responsibility for and oversight of financial stability both in domestic economies and internationally (G20, 2010). This recommendation echoed the views of the IMF expressed a year earlier (IMF, 2009). In fact, "achieving and preserving financial stability has now become a key policy objective in our societies" (Praet, 2011). Financial stability is "not only a national but an international public good" (Blankart & Fasten, 2009, p. 50).

It would therefore be reasonable to expect that the regulatory architecture and framework of domestic jurisdictions would reflect the importance of financial stability. After

2 See further 3.1 to 3.6 in this section for both a general account and critical evaluation of these best practice recommendations.

3 Australia is an exemplar of the Twin Peaks model: the Australian Prudential Regulation Authority (APRA) is responsible for prudential regulation of financial institutions, and the Australian Securities and Investments Commission (ASIC) is responsible for market conduct regulation of financial institutions (Trowbridge, 2009, p. 2).

all, the institutional underpinnings – that is, the structure, role, and administration of the government-mandated regulators – are critically important (see Nier, Osiński, Jácome & Madrid, 2011), revealing the extent to which financial stability is a key consideration for the State. Thus, each jurisdiction should clearly identify the leading regulatory authority primarily responsible for financial stability and, further, "vest [it] with a clear mandate and commensurate powers, so that it can be held accountable for achieving its objectives" (Jácome & Nier, n.d.).

The second, third, and fourth characteristics, discussed in Sections 3.2–3.4, are indicia of the extent to which each country has met this first standard, namely to focus clearly on financial stability at the highest regulatory level.

3.2 *At the highest level, a single regulator is responsible for financial stability*

One way to promote financial stability is to increase high-level oversight of the stability of the entire financial system by a single body, institution, or regulator. Such an 'umbrella' domestic regulator would oversee or coordinate oversight over a variety of sectors and would consider international threats to financial stability as well as international regulatory issues. It would also be able to identify uncoordinated responses and fragmentation in regulation. Ideally, a centralised national government-mandated regulator or body should be made unambiguously responsible for financial stability overall. Issues of financial stability would therefore best be dealt with in an over-arching manner by a regulatory institution at a sufficiently high level in the regulatory architecture. In particular, scholars suggest that, in the interest of identifying potential systemic risk, one institution should have access to all relevant data (see, eg, Nier et al., 2011). Further, that institution should have access to information from microprudential supervisors, macroprudential policy-makers, market and competition supervisors, fiscal decision-makers, and monetary policy, given that financial stability is affected by a range of policies other than macroprudential policies (IMF, 2013, p. 9).

These scholars also suggest that the regulator with the lead role in financial stability should be the one with greatest expertise to assess systemic risk (Nier et al., 2011). The scholarly consensus is that the central bank should perform this function (see, eg, Goodhart, 2009).

As Table 10.1 shows, all G20 countries have a central bank responsible for financial stability, whether alone or together with another regulator. This is not surprising. Over the past 20 to 25 years, most G20 central banks have commenced publishing a separate financial stability review, whether or not they had been officially mandated to pursue financial stability (see, generally, Čihák, 2006; Saudi Arabia is, however, a notable exception; see Saudi Arabian Monetary Agency, 2015). Moreover, because central banks generally act as the lender of last resort in the interest of protecting financial stability through the avoidance of failed institutions and systemic risk (in deserving cases), the pursuit of financial stability is at the heart of central banking.

3.3 *The central bank plays a central role in financial stability*

During the GFC and in its aftermath, many experts pointed to the need for the central bank to not only play a lead role in financial stability, but also to have a financial stability mandate (Bank for International Settlements [BIS], 2011, pp. 1, 12) and play an important role in

Table 10.1 Regulator responsible for financial stability in G20 countries

No	*Country*	*Which regulator is ultimately responsible for financial stability?*
1	Argentina	The Central Bank of Argentina
2	Australia	The central bank of Australia, the Reserve Bank of Australia, together with the Australian Prudential Regulatory Authority (APRA)
3	Brazil	Central Bank of Brazil
4	Canada	Bank of Canada
5	China	People's Bank of China
6	France	The French central bank, Banque de France
7	Germany	The central bank of Germany, Deutsche Bundesbank
8	India	The Central Bank of India
9	Indonesia	The central bank of Indonesia, the Bank of Indonesia
10	Italy	The central bank of Italy (Banca d'Italia)
11	Japan	The central bank of Japan, the Bank of Japan
12	South Korea	The central bank of Korea, the Bank of Korea and the Financial Supervisory Commission
13	Mexico	Central bank of Mexico (Banco de Mexico)
14	Russia	The central bank of Russia, the Bank of Russia
15	Saudi Arabia	Saudi Arabian Monetary Agency (which is both central bank and bank supervisor)
16	South Africa	South African central bank, the South African Reserve Bank
17	Turkey	Central Bank of the Republic of Turkey
18	United Kingdom	Central bank of the UK, the Bank of England, incorporating the Financial Policy Committee
19	United States	The Financial Stability Oversight Council, part of the Federal Reserve System (The Federal Reserve Board of Governors is the central bank)
20	Spain	Central bank of Spain (Banco de España)

Note. Extracted and summarised from Banco de México (n.d.), Bank Indonesia (n.d.), (n.d. a), Bank of Canada (n.d.), Bank of England (n.d.) (2016a), (2016b), Bank of Italy (n.d.), Bank of Korea (2014), (n.d.), Bank of Russia (n.d.), Banque de France (n.d.), Brown, (2010), Buckley (2014), Central Bank of Brazil (n.d.), Central Bank of India (n.d.), Central Bank of Spain (n.d.), Central Bank of the Republic of Turkey (n.d.), Central Banks Guide (n.d.), Deutsche Bundesbank (n.d.), Erskine, A. (2014), Federal Reserve Board of Governors (n.d.), Financial Stability Board (2010), (2010a), (2010b), (2010c), (2011a), (2011b), (2011c), (2011d), (2011e), (2011f), (2011g), (2012), (2012a), (2012b), (2012c), (2013), (2013a), (2013b), (2013c), (2013d), (2014), (2014a), (2014b), (2015), (2015a), (2015b), (2015c), Fischer, (2012), International Monetary Fund (2011), (2012), (2012a) (2013) (2013a), (2014), (2015), (2015a), (2015b), (2015c), (2015d), Minister of Finance Republic of South Africa, (2013), Murphy (2013), Nier, Osiński, Jácome, & Madrid, (2011), Pereira da Silva, Sales, & Gaglianone, (2012), Reserve Bank of Australia (n.d.), Reserve Bank of the Argentine Republic (n.d.), and South African Reserve Bank (n.d.), (n.d. a).

all financial stability arrangements (IMF, 2015). Before the GFC, central banks were primarily focused on determining monetary policy and combatting inflation.

There are a number of reasons why the central bank should play an important role in financial stability. First, central banks have expertise in risk assessment (IMF, 2015) and, as potential lenders of last resort, are "motivated to take timely action to reduce the buildup [*sic*] of risks" (Jácome & Nier, n.d.). In addition, if the central bank plays a strong role in financial stability matters, coordination with monetary policy, which "sets the overall conditions that affect the demand for and the supply of credit" (Jácome & Nier, n.d.), is possible.

3.4 *The responsible regulator has been provided with a clear statutory/legislated mandate for financial stability*

Although central banks may have an implied mandate for financial stability because of their roles as lenders of last resort, best practice is to give the responsible regulators clear mandates. In most G20 countries, the central bank has an express mandate for financial stability. Australia is a notable exception among Western economies. In Australia, the statutory mandate of the Reserve Bank of Australia (RBA) for financial stability is limited to its role as payment systems supervisor (*Reserve Bank of Australia Act* (1959)). The first official endorsement and confirmation of the RBA's financial stability mandate by the Australian government was in 2010 in the Statement on the Conduct of Monetary Policy (The Treasurer and the Governor of the Reserve Bank, 2010), a document issued jointly by the then treasurer and the governor of the RBA. Although the lack of a formal statutory mandate for overall financial stability for the RBA may not have detracted from the performance of the RBA as regulator, a mandate for the financial stability regulator is nevertheless important.

In their country peer reviews, the IMF and FSB do not assess whether States have created a statutory financial stability mandate or are moving to do so. Regardless, this is an important issue that jurisdictions lacking a statutory mandate should address. A clear mandate not only enables the regulator – and, therefore, is conducive to financial stability – it also ensures accountability. A regulatory authority without a formal mandate may run into a range of difficulties, including an inability to enforce its decisions, and uncertainty over whether or not the regulator has complied with its tasks and acted within its authority. Moreover, a clear statutory mandate reaffirms the commitment of the government to the role of the regulator in financial stability and constitutes a political statement embodied in legislation about the importance of financial stability. The need for clear mandates has been emphasised in the Basel Core Principles for banking supervisors (BCP1) and also in the International Association of Insurance Supervisors (IAIS) Core Principles. The FSB in 2010, however, not only reemphasised the need for clarity in mandates, but even suggested that these core principles should be expanded in terms of "what is meant by 'clear' when describing an authority's responsibilities and objectives". (FSB, 2010b, p. 3).

As Table 10.2 shows, 13 of the G20 countries have provided the central bank/regulator with an express mandate for financial stability. In others, the mandate is either *de facto* or implied; that is, it arises by virtue of conduct condoned or encouraged by government.

3.5 *The regulatory framework includes a focus on macroprudential regulation and supervision*

The intense focus on financial stability as an issue to be considered by financial regulators during and after the GFC was accompanied by an increased interest in and commitment to macroprudential policy and regulation. Macroprudential policy looks to larger systemic interests beyond an individual institution, its compliance with regulation, and its individual risks (Pereira da Silva, Sales, & Gaglianone, 2012, p. 4). Macroprudential

Table 10.2 Type of financial stability mandate in G20 countries

No	*Country*	*Is the mandate for financial stability express or implied?*
1	Argentina	Express
2	Australia	*De facto* or implicit. The express mandate is very limited in ambit and scope.
3	Brazil	Express
4	Canada	Express
5	China	Express
6	France	Express
7	Germany	Express
8	India	Not express, probably implied
9	Indonesia	Express
10	Italy	Express
11	Japan	Express
12	South Korea	No express mandate but the Bank of South Korea has a statutory obligation to publish a financial stability review.
13	Mexico	Not express
14	Russia	Express
15	Saudi Arabia	Implied
16	South Africa	Not express
17	Turkey	Appears to be implied
18	United Kingdom	Express
19	United States	Express
20	Spain	Express

Note. Extracted and summarised from Banco de México (n.d.), Bank Indonesia (n.d.), (n.d. a), Bank of Canada (n.d.), Bank of England (n.d.) (2016a), (2016b), Bank of Italy (n.d.), Bank of Korea (2014), (n.d.), Bank of Russia (n.d.), Banque de France (n.d.), Brown, (2010), Buckley (2014), Central Bank of Brazil (n.d.), Central Bank of India (n.d.), Central Bank of Spain (n.d.), Central Bank of the Republic of Turkey (n.d.), Central Banks Guide (n.d.), Deutsche Bundesbank (n.d.), Federal Reserve Board of Governors (n.d.), Financial Stability Board (2010), (2010a), (2010b), (2010c), (2011a), (2011b), (2011c), (2011d), (2011e), (2011f), (2011g), (2012), (2012a), (2012b), (2012c), (2013), (2013a), (2013b), (2013c), (2013d), (2014), (2014a), (2014b), (2015), (2015a), (2015b), (2015c), Fischer, (2012), International Monetary Fund (2011), (2012), (2012a) (2013) (2013a), (2014), (2015), (2015a), (2015b), (2015c), Michael, (2014), Minister of Finance Republic of South Africa, (2013), Murphy (2013), Pereira da Silva, Sales, & Gaglianone, (2012), Reserve Bank of Australia (n.d.), Reserve Bank of the Argentine Republic (n.d.), and South African Reserve Bank (n.d.), (n.d. a).

regulation, therefore, involves a "greater appreciation of a more system-wide view of finance in all its aspects and of the various policies that can reduce the risk of crises and lower any excessive procyclicality" (Claessens, 2014, p. 4). Macroprudential policies "use primarily prudential tools to limit systemic or system-wide financial risks" (Nier et al., 2011, p. 5).

The Basel Committee on Banking Supervision, in its influential Core Principles on Effective Banking Supervision, advocates such a system-wide approach. The Core Principles emphasise that "the prevailing macroeconomic environment, business trends, and the build-up and concentration of risk across the banking sector and, indeed, outside of it, inevitably impact the risk exposure of individual banks. Bank-specific supervision should therefore consider this macro perspective" (BIS, 2012, p. 6). As this 'broad financial system perspective' is deeply ingrained in many of the Core Principles, the Basel Committee on Banking Supervision has not included a specific stand-alone Core Principle on macroprudential issues (BIS, 2012, p. 6).

During the GFC, it became evident that ensuring compliance at the individual institution level did not guarantee that the financial system as a whole would be stable (Pereira da Silva, Sales, & Gaglianone, 2012, p. 4). The IMF concluded that pre-GFC there was insufficient focus on macroprudential matters (IMF, 2013, p. 6) and in 2009 recommended a macroprudential approach to regulation. This recommendation reflected the concern that the coverage of prudential regulation before the GFC had been too narrow (IMF, 2009, p. 8). The IMF pointed out that macroprudential policy was needed "to achieve the stability of the system as a whole" (2013, p. 5). The FSB similarly expressed the view that all supervisory authorities should have a well-developed macroprudential surveillance approach (2010b, p. 18) and that such an approach should be "designed to identify trends and developments that might negatively impact the risk profile of its firms" (2010b, p. 18).

For macroprudential policy and regulation to be effective, "a clear mandate for taking the lead in monitoring systemic risk should be assigned to the agency best placed to do so at the national level" (IMF, 2009, p. 9). The first requirement is to identify the appropriate regulator for macroprudential policy. The macroprudential mandate must be "assigned to *someone*, a body or a committee", because this will strengthen the "willingness to act" (IMF, 2013, p. 29). Macroprudential supervision should be the responsibility of a separate supervisor, distinct from the microprudential supervisor (Masciandaro et al., 2012). Further, a clear mandate for macroprudential policy is critical. The mandate needs to be clearly identified and "matched by sufficient powers, including [the power] to initiate the use of prudential tools to address systemic risk" (Nier et al., 2011, p. 4). If no clear mandate has been assigned, "collective action problems lead to underinvestment in systemic risk identification and mitigation across agencies and reduce accountability, since in the end *no one* is fully responsible for the crisis outcome" (IMF, 2013, p. 29).

The IMF also recommended that "[t]he central bank should play an important role in macroprudential policymaking" (2013, p. 29; see also Nier et al., 2011; Masciandaro et al., 2012), possibly even performing the role of macroprudential authority. Because of the specific roles of the central bank, it can "support effective coordination of macroprudential policy with monetary as well as microprudential policy" (Nier et al., 2011, p. 4). A strong role for the central bank would allow for the harnessing of "institutional incentives and expertise available at the central bank" (Nier et al., 2011, p. 16) and assure "coordination with other central bank functions, including monetary policy, provision of liquidity, and payment systems oversight" (Nier et al., 2011, p. 21). Furthermore, countries should have a strong and flexible lender of last resort (typically, the central bank) because it is possible that systemically important organisations may face liquidity problems (IMF, 2015). Unsurprisingly, the macroprudential regulator in those G20 countries with one is either the central bank or a committee comprising a number of regulators that includes the central bank.

Although all G20 countries vest the responsibility for financial stability in their central banks, they diverge markedly in how they assign macroprudential responsibility. For example, the IMF has identified three different regulatory models, each reflecting different levels of involvement in macroprudential policy by the central bank in the G20 (IMF, 2013, p. 30):

- **Model 1:** The macroprudential mandate is assigned to the central bank, with macroprudential decisions ultimately made by its Board (as in the Czech Republic).
- **Model 2:** The macroprudential mandate is assigned to a dedicated committee within the central bank structure (as in the United Kingdom (UK)).
- **Model 3:** The macroprudential mandate is assigned to a committee outside the central bank, with the central bank participating on the macroprudential committee (as in Australia, France, and the United States (US)).

An alternative approach is to classify the macroprudential regulator by institutional design. For example, in some countries, responsibility for macroprudential policy and supervision is vested in a single authority (either expressly or impliedly). This single authority can be an independent statutory body, an independent non-statutory body, or a statutory body that is not independent. In others, the macroprudential function is shared among multiple regulators and bodies, with a further point of differentiation being that the responsibility can be express or implied. In yet others, it is not allocated to any specific regulator or body at all.

Table 10.3 sets out the different macroprudential regulatory models adopted among the G20 countries, including the relevant institution or body responsible for macroprudential policy. As Table 10.3 shows, a significant number of countries have placed macroprudential matters in the hands of more loosely structured institutions, such as, for example, the Council of Financial Regulators in Australia, which is not a statutory body and has no independent powers. At first glance, this may be disconcerting; however, when taking into consideration that macroprudential matters include the work of different regulators and/or supervisors, this type of structure is likely to be more conducive to cooperation among different regulators. Difficulties, though, may arise if the authority responsible for macroprudential policy is not also suitably empowered to act on macroprudential policy. In such circumstances, a formal institutional structure and mandate will both enable the regulator to take certain steps and also protect it when it decides to act in accordance with its mandate. The regulatory structure underpinning macroprudential policy is still a developing area for many countries.

3.6 An appropriate regulatory structure for regulators for prudential and market conduct regulation and supervision – such as the twin peaks model – has been adopted

As both prudential and market conduct regulation contribute to financial stability, an optimal regulatory structure should equally support those twin regulatory goals. The structure of microprudential regulation is just as important as that of macroprudential regulation. Indeed, microprudential regulators are often represented on macroprudential committees, such as the Council of Financial Regulators in Australia.

There are strong indications that the preferred and most effective model for regulation is the twin peaks model with central bank involvement in macroprudential supervision (Kawai, 2011; see also Schmulow, 2016). It can be considered as best practice because it has "garnered the most interest, and gained widespread recognition" (Schmulow, 2015, p. 2). Therefore, "the precrisis paradigm, supporting a trend towards supervision unification and central bank specialization is being replaced by a twin-peak model in supervision (macromicro), with central bank involvement, at least in macro supervision" (Masciandaro et al., 2012).

Table 10.3 Regulatory authority responsible for macroprudential policy in G20 countries

Different models: Regulatory architecture of the institution(s) responsible for macroprudential policy and supervision		*Countries*
A single authority		
	Independent statutory body	**Germany** – Financial Stability Committee
		Argentina – Central Bank of Republic of Argentina has a financial stability mandate which is equated to a macroprudential policy mandate by Argentina and the FSB.
		Indonesia – Bank of Indonesia
		Canada – Financial Institutions Supervisory Committee
		France – Haut Conseil de stabilité financière (HCSF – High Council for Financial Stability), is acknowledged to be the macroprudential authority, installed in June 2014.
		Russia – Central Bank of Russia
	Not independent but statutory body	**UK** – Financial Policy Committee under the central bank
		US – Financial Stability Oversight Council
		Brazil – Financial Stability Committee under the Central Bank of Brazil
		China – the People's Bank of China and Joint Ministerial Conference on Financial Regulatory Coordination (led by the People's Bank of China)
		Saudi Arabia – Saudi Arabian Monetary Agency with a Financial Stability Committee
		Turkey – Financial Stability Committee, incorporating government (Treasury) and the central bank of Turkey
	Independent non-statutory body	Many countries have a financial stability council, or a body aimed at encouraging cooperation between regulators, such as the Australian Council of Financial Regulators, with the main responsibilities falling under the key or mandated regulators.
	Not independent and non-statutory body	**India** – Joint Ministerial Conference on Financial Regulatory Coordination – all the regulatory agencies are part of this committee, and it is chaired by a government representative, although some functions are executed by the Bank of India.

Different models: Regulatory architecture of the institution(s) responsible for macroprudential policy and supervision		*Countries*
A split authority for macroprudential policy and supervision		
	Multiple regulators share the responsibility for macroprudential policy and supervision expressly	**Japan** – Bank of Japan and Financial Services Authority. Council for Cooperation on Financing Stability perform a coordinating function.
	Multiple regulators share the responsibility for macroprudential policy and supervision not expressly but implicitly/de facto	**Australia** (APRA and RBA)
	Multiple regulators have an express responsibility for macroprudential policy and supervision	**Korea** (the Bank of Korea and the Financial Services Commission each have statutory powers for macroprudential and financial stability functions)
No specific authority responsible for macroprudential policy and supervision		
	No specific authority responsible for macroprudential policy and supervision	**Italy** – still under consideration. Banca d'Italia, IVASS, and Consob share a financial stability mandate which has to some extent equated with a macroprudential policy mandate.
		Spain – still under consideration. Central bank has financial stability mandate.

Note. Extracted and summarised from Banco de México (n.d.), Bank Indonesia (n.d.), (n.d. a), Bank of Canada (n.d.), Bank of England (n.d.) (2016a), (2016b), Bank of Italy (n.d.), Bank of Korea (2014), (n.d.), Bank of Russia (n.d.), Banque de France (n.d.), Brown, (2010), Buckley (2014), Central Bank of Brazil (n.d.), Central Bank of India (n.d.), Central Bank of Spain (n.d.), Central Bank of the Republic of Turkey (n.d.), Central Banks Guide (n.d.), Deutsche Bundesbank (n.d.), Federal Reserve Board of Governors (n.d.), Financial Stability Board (2010), (2010a), (2010b), (2010c), (2011a), (2011b), (2011c), (2011d), (2011e), (2011f), (2011g), (2012), (2012a), (2012b), (2012c), (2013), (2013a), (2013b), (2013c), (2013d), (2014), (2014a), (2014b), (2015), (2015a), (2015b), (2015c), Fischer, (2012), International Monetary Fund (2011), (2012), (2012a) (2013) (2013a), (2014), (2015), (2015a), (2015b), (2015c), (2015d), Michael, (2014), Minister of Finance Republic of South Africa, (2013), Murphy (2013), Nier, Osiński, Jácome, & Madrid, (2011), Pereira da Silva, Sales, & Gaglianone, (2012), Reserve Bank of Australia (n.d.), Reserve Bank of the Argentine Republic (n.d.), and South African Reserve Bank (n.d.), (n.d. a).

In the view of the FSB, the importance of group-wide, consolidated supervision is a top priority (FSB, 2010b, p. 16). This requirement is particularly significant in relation to the supervision of systemically important financial institutions (SIFIs). The twin peaks model is ideally suited to meeting this requirement, although the FSB also cautions that where a single organisation is supervised by multiple regulators (as the case would be in the twin peaks system), there should be sufficient consideration given to communication between those authorities (FSB, 2010b, p. 16). A similar view was expressed by the FSB in relation to SIFIs and moral hazard. The FSB submits that "[j]urisdictions should provide for a national supervisory framework that enables effective consolidated supervision by addressing ambiguities of responsibilities, impairments related to information gathering and assessment when multiple supervisors are overseeing the institution and its affiliates" (2010b, p. 7). The FSB also recommended that there should be system-wide oversight frameworks that would cover the so-called shadow-banking system (2011g, p. 6). The twin peaks model would also give effect to these key recommendations. In addition, the twin peaks model reflects one of the key principles of the Basel Committee's Core Principles on Banking Supervision. Principle 12 on consolidated supervision states that an "essential element of banking supervision is that the supervisor supervises the banking group on a consolidated basis, adequately monitoring and, as appropriate, applying prudential standards to all aspects of the business conducted by the banking group worldwide" (BIS, 2012, p. 11).

Further, the Australian model of regulation by objective, which is reflected in the twin peaks model of regulation, has been considered to be an example of the most effective structure of regulators and regulation (see Kawai & Prasad, 2011, p. 195; see also Godwin, 2015, p. 24). It has been argued that "Australia's twin peaks regulatory model helped it . . . to avoid many of the problems that arose in the GFC" (Michael, 2014, p. 4; see also Brown, 2010). With Australia having largely survived the GFC unscathed, its twin peaks model has inspired others to adopt it or look to doing so, such as the South African regulators in their proposed changes for the regulatory architecture in South Africa (see, eg, Minister of Finance Republic of South Africa, 2013).

The twin peaks model of regulation involves two regulators "whose objectives are, alternatively, systemic stability, and market conduct and consumer protection" (Schmulow, 2015a, p. 32). As the distinctions among traditional 'banking', 'insurance' or 'securities' business have largely disappeared (Taylor, 2009, p. 10), a twin peaks model of regulation offers distinct advantages from both a systemic protection perspective as well as from a consumer protection perspective (Taylor, 2009, pp. 10–11).

The regulatory architecture in the G20 countries for prudential and market conduct supervision, however, varies quite significantly. The twin peaks model is evident only in four countries: Australia, the United Kingdom, Spain, and South Africa. Most countries have adopted a so-called integrated model which, although not optimal from a microprudential supervisory perspective, may have some advantages in the area of macroprudential oversight. This model – exemplified by the previous UK model involving the Financial Services Authority – is one in which "a single financial regulator [is] responsible for both safety and soundness and business conduct considerations" (Schmulow, 2015, p. 155). The two other regulatory approaches are (a) the *institutional* (traditional or silos) approach where the form of the legal entity that is subject to regulation determines to which regulator it is assigned (Schmulow, 2015, p.152); and (b) the *functional* approach where the type of transactions or products determines the applicable regulator, resulting in firms dealing in different products being subject to different regulators (Schmulow, 2016, p. 154). Neither of these models offers the benefits of the twin peaks model and, if anything, exemplifies pre-GFC style regulatory approaches.

The twin peaks model on its own is no magic bullet. It is simply "a good start" (Schmulow, 2015, p. 48), creating what is, according to available evidence, the best and most optimal regulatory architecture (Schmulow, 2015). Its effectiveness is influenced by the culture and leadership of the two 'peaks' and the extent to which they are willing to deal with difficult questions and vested interests (Schmulow, 2015a). The effective implementation of a twin peaks model depends on two key considerations: (a) a clear delineation between the objectives of the regulators and the boundaries between them, the so-called 'regulatory perimeter' (Godwin, 2015, p. 24); and (b) the effective cooperation and coordination between the regulators (Godwin, 2015, p. 24).

Table 10.4 sets out those G20 countries that have adopted the twin peaks model of financial system regulation and those that have adopted alternative structures.

Table 10.4 Regulatory model adopted in G20 countries[1]

	Type of regulatory model	*G20 countries that have adopted that model*
1	Institutional, traditional or silos approach	China Mexico
2	Functional approach	Italy France Brazil India US
3	Integrated or unified approach	Argentina[2] Japan Canada Germany Indonesia (internal twin peaks) Russia Saudi Arabia Turkey South Korea
4	Twin Peaks	Australia South Africa – currently in the process of passing legislation in this regard Spain UK (current model) Other G20 countries have expressed an interest too, including the US and Italy.

[1]The information in Table 4 has been extracted and summarised from the following sources: Banco de Mexico (n.d.), Bank Indonesia (n.d.), (n.d. a), Bank of Canada (n.d.), Bank of England (n.d.) (2016a), (2016b), Bank of Italy (n.d.), Bank of Korea (2014), (n.d.), Bank of Russia (n.d.), Banque de France (n.d.), Brown, (2010), Buckley (2014), Central Bank of Brazil (n.d.), Central Bank of India (n.d.), Central Bank of Spain (n.d.), Central Bank of the Republic of Turkey (n.d.), Central Banks Guide (n.d.), Deutsche Bundesbank (n.d.), Erskine (2014), Federal Reserve Board of Governors (n.d.), Financial Stability Board (2010), (2010a), (2010b), (2010c), (2011a), (2011b), (2011c), (2011d), (2011e), (2011f), (2011g), (2012), (2012a), (2012b), (2012c), (2013), (2013a), (2013b), (2013c), (2013d), (2014), (2014a), (2014b), (2015), (2015a), (2015b), (2015c), Fischer, (2012), Godwin & Ramsay, Godwin (2015), International Monetary Fund (2011), (2012), (2012a) (2013) (2013a), (2014), (2015), (2015a), (2015b), (2015c), (2015d), Mason & Gray (2016), Michael (2014), Minister of Finance Republic of South Africa, (2013), Murphy (2013), Nier, Osinski, Jacome, Madrid (2011), Pereira da Silva, Sales, & Gaglianone, (2012), Reserve Bank of Australia (n.d.), Reserve Bank of the Argentine Republic (n.d.), Schmulow (2015), (2015a), (2016), South African Reserve Bank (n.d.), (n.d. a) and Taylor (2009).

4. Conclusion: order or disorder in post-GFC financial regulatory architecture?

Nearly a decade after the GFC, little has changed in the financial regulatory architecture in G20 countries. This might surprise given the emphasis that was placed on the importance of the appropriate regulatory architecture to prevent future instances of financial instability ('disorder').

Yet, equally, it is not surprising to observe both the slow pace of change in some countries and the divergence in regulatory structures. The unique characteristics of domestic jurisdictions fundamentally influence domestic regulatory frameworks, and there is not a 'one-size-fits-all' standard for domestic regulatory architectures. Historical, social, economic, and political differences between countries influence law-making and regulating. Not all the G20 countries, after all, belong to the Western tradition. Regulation, as with many other things, requires making difficult judgements when balancing benefits and costs (IMF, 2015). Developments in macroprudential regulation and regulatory structures, such as the 'twin peaks' model, are still relatively new and untested. There is limited historical evidence about the efficacy of twin peaks regulation. Furthermore, the research on macroprudential policy and the use of tools are still relatively undeveloped (see, eg, Claessens, 2014).

This variation in regulatory approaches and structures, however, by itself does not indicate 'disorder'. Nor does the lack of a clear legislative framework for structuring financial regulatory architectures in some G20 countries – and the absence of an express mandate for financial regulators to pursue regulatory objectives in others – point to regulatory 'disorder'. This is because the use of 'race to the top' strategies by the FSB, to encourage compliance by member countries, exemplifies how non-statutory and non-legal tools can effectively guide domestic practices (FSB, 2009). Indeed, much of the 'regulation' of sovereign nations by international financial institutions is done on the basis of peer reviews and, inevitably, peer pressure.

Yet law still matters in financial regulation, including in the domestic regulation of financial regulators. It is an important tool for creating order and preventing disorder. It plays a vital role, in the form of enabling legislation, to empower regulators to achieve their goals. The absence of express, clear, and legislated mandates in some countries is problematic. Prudential supervision and resolution regimes cannot be implemented without properly authorised regulators, both to empower them to enforce regulatory standards and to protect them from legal liability for taking regulatory actions (FSB, 2010b, p. 5). Indeed, the first three of the 29 principles of effective banking supervision of the Basel Committee Core Principles for Banking Supervision – arguably one of the most authoritative and widely accepted documents on regulation – emphasise the importance of the black letter law for banking supervision, a core component of financial stability (BIS, 2012). The G20 Global Plan for Recovery and Reform, April 2009, also stresses the importance of formal law and regulation (G20, 2009). The G20 leaders affirmed the need for "strengthen[ing] financial regulation to rebuild trust" (G20, 2009, p. 1) through formal law and regulatory frameworks (G20, 2009, p. 3). The IMF, too, stated that "[s]trong institutional and governance frameworks are essential for the effective conduct of macroprudential policy. They can benefit from an appropriate strength of powers and clear accountability" (2013, p. 1).

A key lesson from the GFC is the need for strong domestic regulatory architectures that exhibit best practice standards in regulation. G20 countries have made significant progress to this end. Even in emerging fields of regulation, such as macroprudential supervision, there is evidence of reforms geared towards building stronger regulatory regimes based on best practice standards.

References

Australian Embassy Spain. (2014). *Australia's hosting year for the G20 (Elcano, 9 April 2014) Elcano G20 Speech*. Retrieved from http://spain.embassy.gov.au/madr/ElcanoG20speech.html.

Australian Financial Review. (2014, January 22). So how much did the GFC cost? *Australian Financial Review*. Retrieved from http://www.afr.com/news/policy/foreign-affairs/so-how-much-did-the-gfc-cost-20140121-iy7vy.

Australian Government, The Treasury. (2009). *Australia and the international financial institutions 2008–2009 annual report*. Retrieved from http://www.treasury.gov.au/PublicationsAndMedia/Publications/2011/Australia-and-the-IFIs/Australia-and-the-IFIs/Section-1-Responding-to-the-global-economic-crisis.

Bailey, A. (2011, January 10). *The outlook for financial regulation in the UK*. Speech delivered on a regional visit to Edinburgh. Retrieved from http://www.bankofengland.co.uk/archive/Documents/historicpubs/speeches/2011/speech469.pdf.

Banco de México. (n.d.). Financial system. Retrieved from http://www.banxico.org.mx/dyn/sistema-financiero/indexEn.html.

Bank for International Settlements. (2011, May). *Central bank governance and financial stability* (a report by a Study Group chaired by Stefan Ingves). Retrieved from http://www.bis.org/publ/othp14.pdf.

Bank for International Settlements, Basel Committee on Banking Supervision. (2012, September). Core principles for effective banking supervision. Retrieved from http://www.bis.org/publ/bcbs230.htm.

Bank Indonesia. (n.d.). Welcome to Bank Indonesia. Retrieved from http://www.bi.go.id/en/Default.aspx.

Bank Indonesia. (n.d. a). Financial system stability. Retrieved from http://www.bi.go.id/en/perbankan/ssk/ikhtisar/definisi/Contents/Default.aspx.

Bank of Canada. (n.d.). Financial system. Retrieved from http://www.bankofcanada.ca/core-functions/financial-system/.

Bank of China. (n.d.). Bank of China overview. Retrieved from http://www.boc.cn/en/aboutboc/ab1/200809/t20080901_1601737.html.

Bank of England. (2016a). Financial policy committee. Retrieved from http://www.bankofengland.co.uk/financialstability/Pages/fpc/default.aspx.

Bank of England. (2016b). History. Retrieved from http://www.bankofengland.co.uk/about/Pages/history/default.aspx#3.

Bank of England. (n.d.). Financial stability. Retrieved from http://www.bankofengland.co.uk/financialstability/Pages/default.aspx.

Bank of Italy. (n.d.). Our role. Retrieved from https://www.bancaditalia.it/compiti/index.html.

Bank of Japan. (n.d.). Outline of financial system stability. Retrieved from http://www.bok.or.kr/broadcast.action?menuNaviId=640.

Bank of Korea. (n.d.). Financial Stability. Retrieved from http://www.bok.or.kr/broadcast.action?menuNaviId=640.

Bank of Korea. (2014, October). Financial stability report. Retrieved from http://www.centerforfinancialstability.org/fsr/kor_fsr_201410.pdf.
Bank of Russia. (n.d.). Bank of Russia today. Retrieved from http://www.cbr.ru/Eng/today/.
Banque de France. (n.d.). Oversight tasks. Retrieved from https://www.banque-france.fr/en/financial-stability/payment-systems-and-market-infrastructure/oversight-tasks.html.
Beattie, A. & Politi, J. (2008, October 24). 'I made a mistake,' admits Greenspan, *Financial Times*. Retrieved from https://www.ft.com/content/aee9e3a2-a11f-11dd-82fd-000077b07658.
Black, J. (2002). Critical reflection on regulation. Retrieved from https://core.ac.uk/download/files/67/219186.pdf.
Blankart, C. B. & Fasten, E. R. (2009). Financial crisis resolution – The state as a lender of last resort? *Economic Affairs*, *29*(3), 47–52.
Brown, E. (2010). A comparison of the handling of the financial crisis in the United States, the United Kingdom and Australia, *Villanova Law Review*, *55*(3), 509–575.
Buckley, R. P. (2014). The G20's performance in global financial regulation, *UNSW Law Journal*, *37*(1), 63–93.
Central Bank of Brazil. (n.d.). About us. Retrieved from http://www.bcb.gov.br/en/#!/home.
Central Bank of India. (n.d.). About us: Profile. Retrieved from https://www.centralbankofindia.co.in/English/profile.aspx.
Central Bank of Russia. (n.d.). Bank of Russia today. Retrieved from https://www.cbr.ru/Eng/today/.
Central Bank of Spain. (n.d.). Financial stability. Retrieved from http://www.bde.es/bde/en/areas/estabilidad/.
Central Bank of the Republic of Turkey. (n.d.). Financial stability. Retrieved from http://www.tcmb.gov.tr/wps/wcm/connect/TCMB+EN/TCMB+EN/Main+Menu/MONETARY+POLICY/FINANCIAL+STABILITY/.
Central Banks Guide. (n.d.). China. Retrieved from http://www.centralbanksguide.com/peoples+bank+of+china/.
Chartered Insurance Institute. (2013, April). *The UK's new financial services regulatory landscape* (Policy Briefing April 2013). Retrieved from http://www.cii.co.uk/media/4372607/regulatory_landscape_update_april_2013_vfonline.pdf.
Čihák, M. (2006). *How do central banks write on financial stability? (WP/06/163)*. IMF working paper. Retrieved from http://www.imf.org/external/pubs/ft/wp/2006/wp06163.pdf.
Claessens, S. (2014). *An overview of macroprudential policy tools (WP/14/214)*. IMF working paper. Retrieved from https://www.imf.org/external/pubs/ft/wp/2014/wp14214.pdf.
Davis, K. (2011). Regulatory reform post the global financial crisis: An overview. Retrieved from http://www.apec.org.au/docs/11_CON_GFC/Regulatory%20Reform%20Post%20GFC-%20Overview%20Paper.pdf.
Deutsche Bundesbank. (n.d.). Tasks. Retrieved from https://www.bundesbank.de/Navigation/EN/Tasks/Financial_and_monetary_system/financial_and_monetary_system.html.
Edey, M. (2014, March 16). *Reflections on the financial crisis*. Speech delivered at the CFO Summit, Gold Coast. Retrieved from http://www.rba.gov.au/speeches/2014/sp-ag-160314.html.
Erskine, A. (2014). Funding Australia's future: Regulating the Australian financial system. *Australian Centre for Financial Studies*. Retrieved from https://fundingaustraliasfuture.com.
Federal Reserve Board of Governors. (n.d.). *The Economists – Financial Stability*. Retrieved from https://www.federalreserve.gov/econresdata/fsprstaff.htm.
Financial Stability Board. (2010, September 23). *Country review of Mexico: peer review report*. Retrieved from http://www.fsb.org/wp-content/uploads/r_100927.pdf.

Financial Stability Board. (2010a). *FSB framework for strengthening adherence to international standards.* Retrieved from: http://www.fsb.org/wp-content/uploads/r_100109a.pdf.
Financial Stability Board. (2010b). *Intensity and effectiveness of SIFI supervision: Recommendations for enhanced supervision.* Retrieved from https://www.imf.org/external/np/mcm/financialstability/papers/sifisup.pdf.
Financial Stability Board. (2010c). *Reducing the moral hazard posed by systemically important financial institutions: FSB recommendations and time lines.* Retrieved from http://www.fsb.org/wp-content/uploads/r_101111a.pdf?page_moved=1.
Financial Stability Board. (2011a, January 27). *Peer Review of Italy: Review report.* Retrieved from http://www.fsb.org/wp-content/uploads/r_110207b.pdf.
Financial Stability Board. (2011b, January 27). *Peer review of Spain: Review report.* Retrieved from http://www.fsb.org/wp-content/uploads/r_110207a.pdf.
Financial Stability Board. (2011c, September 21). *Peer review of Australia: Review report.* Retrieved from http://www.fsb.org/wp-content/uploads/r_110926b.pdf.
Financial Stability Board. (2011d, September 21). *Peer review of Australia: Review report.* Retrieved from http://www.fsb.org/wp-content/uploads/r_110926b.pdf.
Financial Stability Board. (2011e, January 27). *Peer review of Italy: Review report.* Retrieved from http://www.fsb.org/wp-content/uploads/r_110207b.pdf.
Financial Stability Board. (2011f, January 27). *Peer review of Spain: Review report.* Retrieved from http://www.fsb.org/wp-content/uploads/r_110207a.pdf.
Financial Stability Board. (2011g, October 27) *Shadow banking: Strengthening oversight and regulation – Recommendations of the Financial Stability Board.* Retrieved from http://www.fsb.org/wp-content/uploads/r_111027a.pdf?page_moved=1.
Financial Stability Board. (2012, November 18). *Consultative document – strengthening oversight and regulation of shadow banking: An integrated overview of policy recommendations.* Retrieved from http://www.fsb.org/wp-content/uploads/r_121118.pdf?page_moved=1.
Financial Stability Board. (2012a, January 30). *Peer review of Canada: Review report.* Retrieved from http://www.fsb.org/wp-content/uploads/r_120130.pdf.
Financial Stability Board. (2012b, February 5). *Peer review of South Africa: Review report.* Retrieved from http://www.fsb.org/wp-content/uploads/r_130205.pdf.
Financial Stability Board. (2012c, January 25). *Peer review of Switzerland: Review report.* Retrieved from http://www.fsb.org/wp-content/uploads/r_250112.pdf.
Financial Stability Board. (2013, September 5). *Overview of progress in the implementation of the G20 recommendations for strengthening financial stability: Report of the Financial Stability Board to G20 leaders.* Retrieved from http://www.fsb.org/wp-content/uploads/Overview-of-Progress-in-the-Implementation-of-the-G20-Recommendations-for-Strengthening-Financial-Stability.pdf.
Financial Stability Board. (2013a, February 5). *Peer review of South Africa: Review report.* Retrieved from http://www.fsb.org/wp-content/uploads/r_130205.pdf.
Financial Stability Board. (2013b, September 10). *Peer review of the United Kingdom: Review report.* Retrieved from http://www.fsb.org/wp-content/uploads/r_130910.pdf.
Financial Stability Board. (2013c, September 10). *Peer review of the United Kingdom: Review report.* Retrieved from http://www.fsb.org/wp-content/uploads/r_130910.pdf.
Financial Stability Board. (2013d, August 27). *Peer review of the United States: Review report.* Retrieved from http://www.fsb.org/wp-content/uploads/r_130827.pdf.
Financial Stability Board. (2014, April 9). *Peer review of Germany: Review report.* Retrieved from http://www.fsb.org/wp-content/uploads/r_140409.pdf.
Financial Stability Board. (2014a, February 28). *Peer review of Indonesia: Review report.* Retrieved from http://www.fsb.org/wp-content/uploads/r_140228.pdf.

Financial Stability Board. (2014b, November 11). *Peer review of the Netherlands: Review report.* Retrieved from http://www.fsb.org/wp-content/uploads/Netherlands-peer-review-report.pdf.
Financial Stability Board. (2015, November 5). *Peer review of Saudi Arabia: Review report.* Retrieved from http://www.fsb.org/wp-content/uploads/Saudi-Arabia-peer-review-report.pdf.
Financial Stability Board. (2015a, February 2). *Peer review of Russia: Review report.* Retrieved from http://www.fsb.org/wp-content/uploads/Russia-peer-review-report-final.pdf.
Financial Stability Board. (2015b, August 13). *Peer review of China: Review report.* Retrieved from http://www.fsb.org/wp-content/uploads/China-peer-review-report.pdf.
Financial Stability Board. (2015c, November 19). *Peer review of Turkey: Review report.* Retrieved from http://www.fsb.org/wp-content/uploads/Turkey-peer-review-report-19Nov15.pdf.
Financial Stability Board. (2016). *About the FSB.* Retrieved from http://www.fsb.org/about/.
Financial Stability Board. (2016a). *FSB members, Financial Stability Board.* Retrieved from http://www.fsb.org/about/fsb-members/.
Fischer, P. (2012, March 12). *Policy making at the Bank of England: The Financial Policy Committee.* Speech given at the University of Warwick, London Alumni Group, London. Retrieved from http://www.bankofengland.co.uk/archive/Documents/historicpubs/speeches/2012/speech550.pdf.
G20. (2009). G20 global plan for recovery and reform, April 2009. Retrieved from http://www.cfr.org/financial-crises/g20-global-plan-recovery-reform-april-2009/p19017.
G20. (2010, November 12). *G20 Seoul summit leaders' declaration.* Retrieved from http://www.g20.org/English/Documents/PastPresidency/201512/P020151225621107614573.pdf.
G20. (2013, September). *5th anniversary vision statement.* Retrieved from http://www.oecd.org/g20/summits/saint-petersburg/G20-5-Anniversary-Vision-Statement.pdf.
G20 2016 China. (2015). About G20. Retrieved from http://g20.org/English/aboutg20/AboutG20/201511/t20151127_1609.html.
Gadinis, S. (2012). The Financial Stability Board: The new politics of international financial regulation. *Texas International Law Journal*, 48(2), 157–176.
Godwin, A. (2015). Surveying the twin peaks of Australia's financial system. In S. McCracken and S. Griffiths (Eds.), *Making banking and finance Law: A snapshot*, (pp. 11–25). Sydney, Ross Parsons Centre of Commercial, Corporate and Taxation Law Publication Series.
Goodhart, C.A.E., & Tsomocos, D.P. (2007, May) *Analysis of financial stability (No. 173).* LSE Financial Markets Group Special Paper. Retrieved from http://www.lse.ac.uk/fmg/documents/specialPapers/2007/sp173.pdf.
Goodhart, C. A. E. (2009). The regulatory response to the financial crisis. Cheltenham UK: Edward Elgar.
International Monetary Fund. (2009). *Lessons of the financial crisis for future regulation of financial institutions and markets and for liquidity management.* Retrieved from https://www.imf.org/external/np/pp/eng/2009/020409.pdf.
International Monetary Fund. (2011). *IMF Country Report on China (No. 11/321).* Retrieved from https://www.imf.org/external/pubs/ft/scr/2011/cr11321.pdf.
International Monetary Fund. (2012). *IMF country report on Brazil (No. 12/206).* Retrieved from https://www.imf.org/external/pubs/ft/scr/2012/cr12206.pdf.
International Monetary Fund. (2012a). *IMF country report on Japan (No. 12/210).* Retrieved from https://www.imf.org/external/pubs/ft/scr/2012/cr12210.pdf.
International Monetary Fund. (2013). *Key aspects of macroprudential policy.* Retrieved from https://www.imf.org/external/np/pp/eng/2013/061013b.pdf.
International Monetary Fund. (2013a). *IMF country report on India (No. 13/8).* Retrieved from https://www.imf.org/external/pubs/ft/scr/2013/cr1308.pdf.

International Monetary Fund. (2014). *IMF country report on Korea (No. 14/126)*. Retrieved from https://www.imf.org/external/pubs/ft/scr/2014/cr14126.pdf.

International Monetary Fund. (2014). *IMF country report on Turkey (No. 14/329)*. Retrieved from http://www.imf.org/external/pubs/ft/scr/2014/cr14329.pdf.

International Monetary Fund. (2015). *Global financial stability report April 2015: Navigating monetary policy challenges and managing risks*. Retrieved from http://www.imf.org/External/Pubs/FT/GFSR/2015/01/index.htm.

International Monetary Fund. (2015a). *IMF country report on Korea (No. 15/5)*. Retrieved from https://www.imf.org/external/pubs/ft/scr/2015/cr1505.pdf.

International Monetary Fund. (2015b). *IMF country report on the United States (No. 15/170)*. Retrieved from http://www.imf.org/external/pubs/ft/scr/2015/cr15170.pdf

International Monetary Fund. (2015c). *IMF country report on Saudi Arabia (No. 15/286)*. Retrieved from https://www.imf.org/external/pubs/ft/scr/2015/cr15286.pdf.

International Monetary Fund. (2015d). *Understanding economics back to basics*. Retrieved from http://www.imf.org/external/pubs/ft/fandd/basics/macropru.htm

Jácome, L. I. & Nier, E. W. (n.d). *Macroprudential policy: Protecting the whole. IMF finance and development*. Retrieved from http://www.imf.org/external/pubs/ft/fandd/basics/macropru.htm.

Kawai, M. & Pomerleano, M. (n.d.). Financial stability regulator. *VOX CEPR's Policy Portal*. Retrieved from http://www.voxeu.org/debates/commentaries/financial-stability-regulator-masahiro-kawai-and-michael-pomerleano.

Kawai, M. & Prasad, E. S. (2011). Who should regulate systemic stability risk? In Kawai, M., & Pomerlano, M. (Eds.), *Financial market regulation and reforms in emerging markets* (pp. 171–202). Tokyo and Washington DC: Asian Development Bank Institute and Brookings Institution Press.

Knight, M.D. (2014). *Reforming the global architecture of financial regulation: The G20, the IMF and the FSB (No. 42)*. Centre for International Governance Innovation Papers. Retrieved from https://www.cigionline.org/sites/default/files/no42.pdf.

Laker, J. (2009, November 26). *APRA: The global financial crisis and beyond*. Speech delivered at the Australian British Chamber of Commerce, Melbourne. Retrieved from http://www.apra.gov.au/Speeches/Documents/26Nov09-JL-ABCC-Melb.pdf.

Laker, J. (2010, December 8). *Supervisory lessons from the global financial crisis*, Speech delivered at the AB+F leaders lecture lunch, Sydney. Retrieved from http://www.apra.gov.au/Speeches/Documents/09-ABF-8-December-2010.pdf.

Masciandaro, D., Vega-Pansini, R. & Quintyn, M. (2012). *The economic crisis: a story of supervisory failure and ideas for the way forward*. Retrieved from https://www.suerf.org/docx/s_936824c0191953647ec609b4f49bc964_3325_suerf.pdf#page=23.

Mason S. & Gray, J. (2016). *Financial regulation in South Africa – New developments*. Retrieved fromhttp://www.kwm.com/en/au/knowledge/insights/red-tape-financial-regulatory-reforms-developments-south-africa-20160614.

Michael, B. (2014). The 'twin peaks' regulatory model: The future of financial regulation? *Banking Today*, Mar-April 2014, 2-7. Retrieved from http://www.law.hku.hk/aiifl/wp-content/uploads/2014/09/Twin-Peaks.pdf.

Minister of Finance Republic of South Africa. (2013). *Implementing a twin peaks model of financial regulation in South Africa*. Retrieved from https://www.fsb.co.za/Departments/twinpeaks/Documents/Twin%20Peaks%2001%20Feb%202013%20Final.pdf.

Murphy, E. (2013). Changes to the Bank of England. *Bank of England Quarterly Bulletin*, 1. Retrieved from http://www.bankofengland.co.uk/publications/Documents/quarterlybulletin/2013/qb130102.pdf.

Nier, E.W., Osiński, J., Jácome, L.I., & Madrid, P. (2011, November 1). *Institutional Models for Macroprudential Policy (SDN/11/18)*. IMF Staff Discussion Note. Retrieved from https://www.imf.org/external/pubs/ft/sdn/2011/sdn1118.pdf.

OECD. (n.d.). *Pittsburgh, United States 2009.* Retrieved from https://www.oecd.org/g20/summits/pittsburgh/.

OECD. (2015). *OECD and the G20, Pittsburgh United States 2009.* Retrieved from http://www.oecd.org/g20/meetings/pittsburgh/.

Pereira da Silva, L. A., Sales, A. S., & Gaglianone, W.P. (2012). *Financial stability in Brazil (No. 289).* Working Paper Series. Retrieved from http://www.bcb.gov.br/pec/wps/ingl/wps289.pdf.

Praet, P. (2011, November 10). *The (changing) role of central banks in financial stability policies.* Speech delivered at the 14th Annual Internal Banking Conference, Federal Reserve Bank of Chicago and European Central Bank, Chicago. Retrieved from https://www.ecb.europa.eu/press/key/date/2011/html/sp111110.en.html.

Reserve Bank of the Argentine Republic. (n.d.). *Charter of the Central Bank of the Argentine Republic.* Retrieved from http://www.bcra.gov.ar/Pdfs/Institucional/CartaOrganica2012_i.pdf.

Reserve Bank of Australia Act (1959) (Cth) (Austl)

Reserve Bank of Australia. (n.d.). Financial stability. Retrieved from http://www.rba.gov.au/fin-stability/.

Reynolds, L. (2015, February 13). The Greek Economic Crisis, The Social Impacts of Austerity. Debunking the Myths. *Global Research, Centre for Research on Globalisation.* Retrieved from http://www.globalresearch.ca/the-greek-economic-crisis-the-social-impacts-of-austerity-debunking-the-myths/5431010.

Rimmer, S. H. (2014, November 3). Explainer: Who gets invited to the G20 summit, and why. *The Conversation.* Retrieved from https://theconversation.com/explainer-who-gets-invited-to-the-g20-summit-and-why-33308.

Saudi Arabian Monetary Agency. (2015). *Financial stability report.* Retrieved from http://www.sama.gov.sa/en-US/News/Pages/News07052015.aspx.

Schmulow, A. D. (2015). *Approaches to financial system regulation: An international comparative survey (No. 053/2015).* Centre for International Finance and Regulation working paper. Retrieved from http://www.cifr.edu.au/assets/document/WP053-2015%20Godwin%20E018%20Approaches%20to%20Financial%20System%20Regul.pdf.

Schmulow, A.D. (2015a). The four methods of financial system regulation: An international comparative survey. *Journal of Banking and Finance Law and Practice, 26,* 151–172.

Schmulow, A.D. (2016). Financial regulation: Is Australia's 'twin peaks' model a successful export? *The Interpreter.* Retrieved from http://www.lowyinterpreter.org/post/2016/03/01/Financial-regulation-Is-Australias-twin-peaks-model-a-successful-export.aspx; and http://journals.cambridge.org/action/displayAbstract?fromPage=online&aid=1207372&fileId=S1566752907002376.

South African Reserve Bank. (n.d.). *Rationale for a financial stability focus.* Retrieved from http://www.resbank.co.za/Financial%20Stability/Pages/Rationale-for-a-financial-stability-focus.aspx.

South African Reserve Bank. (n.d. a). *Financial stability.* Retrieved from https://www.resbank.co.za/Financial%20Stability/Pages/FinancialStability-Home.aspx.

Taylor, M. W. (2009, September). 'Twin Peaks' revisited a second chance for regulatory reform. *Centre for the Study of Financial Innovation, 89,* 1–30. Retrieved from http://static1.squarespace.com/static/54d620fce4b049bf4cd5be9b/t/55241044e4b03769e017208a/1428426820095/Twin+Peaks+Revisited.pdf

Trowbridge, J. (2009, September 22). *The regulatory environment – A brief tour.* Presented at the National Insurance Brokers Association (NIBA) Conference Sydney. Retrieved from http://www.apra.gov.au/Speeches/Documents/NIBA-Sep-2009.pdf.

Treasurer and the Governor of the Reserve Bank. (2010, September 30) *Statement on the Conduct of Monetary Policy.* Retrieved from http://www.rba.gov.au/monetary-policy/framework/stmt-conduct-mp-5-30092010.html.

Tucker, P. & Dombret, A. (2012, May 20). Blueprint for resolving regulation. *Financial Times*. Retrieved from http://www.bankofengland.co.uk/archive/Documents/historicpubs/speeches/2012/speech580.pdf.

Turner Review. (2009, March). A regulatory response to the global banking crisis. *Financial Services Authority*. Retrieved from http://www.fsa.gov.uk/pubs/other/turner_review.pdf.

Conflict

11 Governing the Oceans and Dispute Resolution

An Evolving Legal Order?

Douglas Guilfoyle

The UN Convention on the Law of the Sea 1982 (UNCLOS) established a legal order for the oceans. Recently it has been suggested that creative litigation by small States against great powers risks undermining that very order through pushing dispute settlement bodies to adopt novel and unanticipated interpretations of the Convention. That is, the argument goes, the very Convention itself is put in jeopardy if international judges or arbitrators interpret it in such a way that great powers consider themselves bound to a bargain they did not make. Such a result could undermine respect for international dispute settlement or adherence to UNCLOS. The argument is mistaken. The choice is not between an immutably fixed order and a freefall into disorderly judge-made law. Any legal order involving authoritative dispute settlement anticipates evolution through interpretation: order can be dynamic and adaptive. Further, a close examination of patterns of small State litigation under UNCLOS may tell us much about international law's idealist project to impose order on a disordered realist world.

The UN Convention on the Law of the Sea 1982 (UNCLOS) was hailed as providing a comprehensive legal order for the oceans. UNCLOS was an astonishing achievement. Following nine years of complex negotiations it codified much pre-existing law, settled previously intractable questions such as the width of the territorial sea, gave shape to the emerging concept of the Exclusive Economic Zone (EEZ), and set out a wide range of resource-management and environmental duties and powers. The Convention, having been negotiated by consensus and as a package deal, was said to be integral: every provision was carefully balanced against every other. The carefully crafted compromise was designed to give everyone enough reason to support it: both small States and great powers alike.

Nonetheless, this new order contained within it the seeds of disorder. With new rights and powers allocated to coastal and navigating States came the risks that the coherence so recently achieved could be fragmented by unilateral or self-serving interpretations. For some States, therefore, a compulsory dispute settlement system capable of promoting consistent interpretation of UNCLOS was vital to maintaining its integrity. Other States, particularly smaller and developing States, saw a threat in such a system: the possibility of expensive litigation and international judicial review in respect of any EEZ resource-management decision that was unpopular with distant-water fishing States. The result was a dispute settlement system which was, in principle, comprehensive but was balanced with a series of both opt-outs and compulsory inclusions and limitations. The resulting system seemed narrow, complex, and likely to be used infrequently.

In recent years, however, we've seen something which looks remarkable. Three smaller States have brought UNCLOS dispute settlement proceedings against great powers, permanent members of the Security Council. These three cases are: the dispute between Mauritius and the United Kingdom concerning the Chagos archipelago Marine Protected Area (*Chagos MPA*, 2015); the *Arctic Sunrise* case between the Netherlands and Russia (*the Arctic Sunrise Case*, 2013 & 2015); and the dispute concerning the South China Sea brought by the Philippines against China (*Philippines v China*, 2015). While it is much too early to declare a renaissance in law of the sea dispute settlement it is legitimate to ask: what might account for this seeming surge in small State litigation? One possible answer is that UNCLOS dispute settlement may provide an attractive forum for litigants. UNCLOS has the two distinct advantages of being an exceptionally widely ratified treaty binding 166 States and having a compulsory dispute settlement system (albeit subject to exceptions). Compulsory dispute settlement is rare in international law, the WTO system being the other notable exception. These features make it an attractive treaty under which to commence proceedings as, at a minimum, the other side is legally required to show up and is bound by the results whether they do or do not. There is thus a long acknowledged risk of litigation by 'salami slicing': bringing the elements of a broader dispute that one can before a tribunal with compulsory jurisdiction (Boyle, 1997, p. 54). That temptation is likely stronger when it is apparent the other side will not agree to consensual arbitration. While this might seem like forum shopping, international courts and tribunals have long acknowledged that complex international disputes may be multifaceted. That is, jurisdiction (where available) should not be declined simply because a dispute has other legal or political aspects going beyond the questions that a particular tribunal can address (e.g. *Philippines v China*, para. 152). Roughly speaking: resolving half a dispute is better than resolving none of it.

However, does such litigation carry risks? When small States litigate against great powers can they win? If they do, may there be undesirable systematic consequences? The conventional wisdom is that dispute settlement procedures under UNCLOS were deliberately crafted to be restrictive (Klein, 2005, pp. 352–362) and that any efforts to expand them through creative litigation risks backfiring (Ku, 2014). That is, so the argument goes, if great powers see themselves as being held to a bargain they did not make under UNCLOS they may simply ignore adverse rulings or even withdraw from the whole treaty. Such a result could significantly undermine the UNCLOS order and the law of the sea as a system. Similarly, it is sometimes suggested that in international relations only arbitration – in the sense of arbitration consented to *ad hoc* in respect of each dispute – brings results that parties will respect (Ku, 2014). This casts compulsory dispute settlement, as envisaged under UNCLOS, as somewhere between misguided and an invitation to 'lawfare' (Ku, 2014). On either analysis, we might expect smaller States to be reluctant to make novel uses of the UNCLOS dispute settlement system, and we would expect the system to come under significant strain if it were used *de facto* to pressure great powers on sensitive issues.

This chapter will examine such hypotheses in light of the three recent UNCLOS arbitration proceedings noted above: the case brought by the Netherlands against Russia regarding Greenpeace activists aboard the *MV Arctic Sunrise*; the case brought by Mauritius against the United Kingdom concerning the Chagos Archipelago; and the case brought by the Philippines against China regarding the South China Sea dispute. In so doing, this chapter contributes to the overarching themes of this book by examining the creative tension between order and disorder in the law of the sea. UNCLOS as a legal order cannot be upheld through a static, historically fixed process of interpretation. A legal order including judicial dispute settlement is inherently dynamic and adaptive. Law is obviously capable of at least incremental change through interpretation in response to unanticipated developments or social change. A rigidly static order is more likely to lapse into chaos. The conclusion here will be that the UNCLOS system may well be adaptive enough to provide effective legal recourse for smaller states against great powers and can do so without damaging the integrity of the Convention as a legal order.

1. The structure of dispute settlement under Part XV of UNCLOS

1.1 Introduction and overview

The complex system of compulsory dispute settlement which applies under UNCLOS is found in Part XV of the Convention. Part XV can only be understood in the context of the negotiations leading to UNCLOS. Notoriously, those negotiations were very long (nine years) and complex (resulting in a Convention running to over 300 articles and five annexes). Two principles guided the process: consensus decision-making and the 'package deal', meaning the Convention was to be a take-it-or-leave-it integral whole with no reservations permitted (Boyle and Chinkin, 2007, pp. 144–148; Tanaka, 2015, pp. 27–28). This process allowed complex compromises and trade-offs in the drafting, not only issue by issue but between disparate parts of the Convention. That is, one State might abandon an objection concerning the scope of innocent passage in the territorial sea in order to secure the benefit of another provision (for example, on fisheries).

The usual wisdom, therefore, is that the Convention must be interpreted cautiously (Boyle, 2005, p. 569), as unpicking any part would be tantamount to renegotiating the whole – thus binding the parties to obligations they did not intend (*Mauritius v UK*, transcript, vol. 1, p. 44). Indeed, much is written about what the parties 'intended' in drafting UNCLOS, but evidence of such intent is hard to come by. First, while there are enormous official and semi-official records of the preparatory documents, they are fundamentally incomplete: much of the work was done in working groups of which limited, partial, or no records were kept (Tanaka, 2015, p. 28). Second, because of the very large number of States involved and the diversity of their interests, reviewing the recorded debates on any question may be of little assistance in determining what the parties collectively intended (e.g. *Chagos MPA*, 2015, para. 215). As Allott has noted, these treaty negotiations functioned not unlike a domestic parliamentary procedure: the observable text which resulted was the result of a 'hidden hand' reconciling various competing interests, and to the extent it reflects an intention it can only be that of 'the legislator' (Allott, 1983, pp. 5 and 9–10). Legislative intent is, of course, a presumption or *post hoc* rationalisation which in its concrete application may tell us more about the lawyer invoking it than the (fictitious) corporate mind that produced the legislation.

The negotiation of Part XV of UNCLOS, however, was subject to a number of competing pressures. Many States regarded compulsory third-party dispute settlement as vital to maintaining the integrity of the package deal (Boyle, 1997, p. 38). Given the Convention was negotiated as one grand bargain, any system that allowed States to adopt unilateral and self-serving interpretations risked undermining the integrity of compromises reached on specific issues and the Convention as a whole. A compulsory dispute settlement system was seen as providing a useful brake on the possibility of fragmented and diverse interpretations of the Convention's provisions. That is, judicial dispute settlement was considered by some as vital to maintaining the integrity of the Convention as a legal order.

Nonetheless, this view was not universally held. A number of States espousing strong views of sovereignty regarded any form of compulsory dispute settlement as inimical to sovereign discretion. More narrowly, many developing states were concerned about the impact of compulsory dispute settlement on fisheries access. That is, having just secured extended resource jurisdiction over fisheries through the creation of the exclusive economic zone (EEZ) concept they feared that compulsory dispute settlement could make them vulnerable to expensive litigation or international judicial review of any fisheries management decisions taken contrary to the interests of distant-water fishing states (e.g. Official Records, Vol V, p. 36.). For their part, major naval powers obviously wanted exceptions dealing with military activities. The extent to which there should be any provision in Part XV for the compulsory settlement of maritime delimitation or boundary disputes was also highly contentious. Finally, there was not even agreement on where such disputes should be heard: before the ICJ (an option favoured by some major powers such as the UK); before a new specialised tribunal with a bench more broadly representative of the diversity of States in the post-colonial era (an option favoured by many of the Group of 77); or by an *ad hoc* arbitration panel (favoured by any state wishing to maintain a higher degree of control over proceedings). The relevant drafting committee had to craft extensive compromises to come up with a system acceptable to the great diversity of interests that had to be reconciled.

The major elements of the UNCLOS dispute settlement system as it now exists in Part XV are fivefold. First, there is a general principle that parties are free to settle their disputes by any peaceful and mutually agreed means; and there is a minimum requirement for an exchange of views regarding a dispute before proceeding to compulsory measures (articles 279 and 283). Second, in articles 286(1) and 288(1) a general principle is enunciated that all disputes concerning the interpretation and application of the convention may in principle be subject to compulsory dispute settlement under Part XV. Third, that broad proposition is qualified by a series of automatic limitations found in article 297. Fourth, the potential scope of the dispute settlement system is further narrowed by a series of optional exceptions in article 298. A general observation should be made here: the exceptions to jurisdiction in articles 297 and 298 often contain exceptions themselves. Thus, as a general rule, all disputes under UNCLOS fall within Part XV *unless* excluded under articles 297 and 298 *unless* brought back within jurisdiction by a further exception. (Everything is in, until it's out, unless it is brought in again.) Fifth, the parties have a choice of procedure available and may declare their preferred forum in advance, but where the parties express different preferences (or none) the default forum is an 'Annexe VII' arbitration tribunal. This default rule explains why all three cases under consideration here came before arbitration tribunals. However, in arbitration cases where urgent provisional measures are sought and a panel has not yet been constituted the International Tribunal for the Law of the Sea has jurisdiction to act on an interim basis (Article 290; Guilfoyle and Miles, 2014). Before turning to the particular disputes at hand, however, further consideration is given below to the exclusions to jurisdiction under Part XV.

1.2 *The automatic exclusions*

Article 297 has an odd structure. Its heading indicates it is concerned with 'limitations' to the dispute settlement system, and article 297(1) opens with the words: 'Disputes concerning the interpretation or application of this Convention with regard to the exercise by a coastal State of its sovereign rights or jurisdiction provided for in this Convention shall be subject to . . . [compulsory] procedures . . . in the following cases'.

At first, this looks a broad exception potentially excluding any 'sovereign rights or jurisdiction' disputes unless listed as an exception. It is more usually interpreted, including in *Chagos MPA* (para. 308), as *jurisdiction affirming* – there is jurisdiction over such disputes (unless excluded), and article 297(1) lists categories of disputes which can never be excluded (Klein, 2005, pp. 141–142). These are disputes concerning either freedom of navigation or 'specified international rules and standards for the protection and preservation of the marine environment'.

Article 297(2) and (3) contain substantive limitations. They *expressly* exclude from compulsory dispute settlement disputes over marine scientific research (an EEZ or continental shelf activity) and fisheries regulation (within the EEZ) but provide for a system of compulsory but non-binding conciliation in such cases.

1.3 *The optional exclusions*

Under article 298 a State party may declare it does not accept the application of Part XV to certain types of dispute. Article 298(1)(a)(i) is the most important in the present context. This is because it exempts maritime boundary disputes from the scope of Part XV, subjecting them instead to a special non-binding conciliation procedure. However, that conciliation procedure is said to exclude 'any dispute that necessarily involves the concurrent consideration of any unsettled dispute concerning sovereignty or other rights over continental or insular land territory'. This gives rise to a series of complex interpretative problems that turn around an *a contrario* question: does the placing of this 'sovereignty exclusion' in an *optional* exception mean that otherwise sovereignty disputes (at least where incidental to a boundary dispute) fall within Part XV? The received wisdom is that it was never intended that disputes as to sovereignty over coastline or maritime features such as island would fall within the Convention's dispute resolution system. However, if this was the intention of the drafters it was poorly expressed in the final text. At best, the usual wisdom is supported by the argument that the proposition was too obvious to warrant being expressly stated (*Chagos MPA*, 2015, paras. 215–217).

Article 298(1)(b) allows the optional exclusion of: military activities and EEZ law enforcement activities in respect of MSR or fisheries management (but *not* as regards freedom of navigation and environmental protection which always remain 'in' under Article 297(1)). Article 298(1)(c) concerns disputes in respect of which the Security Council is acting.

1.4 *The risks of the system as established*

The risks of this convoluted system premised on broad jurisdiction but with numerous carve outs are easily understood. The first two, as observed by Boyle (1997), are 'salami slicing' and careful framing of one's cause of action (see the discussion of *Philippines v China*). These two concerns are really different sides of the one coin. They describe the risk that a State will carve out what parts it can of a larger dispute to bring it within the Convention framework, slicing the issues down to size. As noted, there is a potential incentive for States to do just that. Very often the core difficulty in international litigation is finding a competent forum to hear a case. The starting point of Part XV is an assertion that there is always, as among Convention parties, a forum competent to hear *any* law of the sea dispute. In a sense, the Convention provides very easy access to compulsory procedures, even if it then imposes a series of further (often substantial) hurdles. As a matter of practicality though, these will be dealt with as jurisdictional challenges in litigation and will not prevent, for example, an arbitral tribunal being established.

2. The disputes at hand

2.1 Introduction

This section briefly outlines the three cases at hand in order to frame later discussion as to what these decisions may tell us about law of the sea dispute resolution generally. The focus will be upon questions of jurisdiction and applicable law. These include: the extent to which obligations arising under other agreements can be considered within a Part XV dispute; the role of human rights in law of the sea disputes; and whether a Part XV tribunal has any jurisdiction to decide questions of sovereignty. In essence, the questions are the same in each case: what falls 'outside' the scope of Part XV jurisdiction and to what extent can questions of law nominally on the 'outside' be brought 'in' where they are closely connected to the dispute at hand? I commence with a discussion of the *Mauritius v UK* arbitration as it has, generally, been the least commented upon. It is also notable for the fact that the UK participated in proceedings. Notoriously, in the two remaining cases (*Arctic Sunrise* and the South China Sea dispute) the respondent States, Russia and China, chose not to appear before the constituted arbitral tribunals.

The *Chagos MPA* case concerned the declaration by the UK of a marine protected area (MPA) around the Chagos archipelago – including a complete 'no take' ban on fishing throughout the archipelago's EEZ. It is no secret that the status of the Chagos archipelago (which includes Diego Garcia) has been a point of contention in relations between Mauritius in the United Kingdom since Mauritian independence in 1968. Prior to Mauritian independence the Chagos islands had been administered as part of the Mauritian colony; they were nonetheless excised from Mauritian territory (and depopulated) pre-independence in contemplation of a US airbase being created there. A crucial document in this context is the so-called 1965 'Lancaster House Undertakings' in which the UK promised the pre-independence colonial government of Mauritius that it would return the archipelago to Mauritius when it was no longer needed for defence purposes. Mauritius challenged the MPA on four main grounds:

- first, that the UK 'was not the coastal State' entitled to declare an EEZ or related measures because Mauritius – not the UK – was sovereign over the islands. This argument was based on the illegal excision or removal of the islands from Mauritius immediately prior to Mauritian independence in 1965. It was a controversial argument to bring under the Convention and, perhaps unsurprisingly, did not succeed;
- second, due to the Lancaster House Undertakings reached between the UK and Mauritius prior to Mauritian independence (which Mauritius considered legally binding upon the UK) Mauritius had certain rights in the islands meaning it was, at least for certain purposes, 'a coastal State' in respect of the islands and therefore the UK was not *exclusively* 'the coastal State' entitled to control of its maritime zones;

- third, that given the rights in oil and mineral resources Mauritius had under the Lancaster House Undertakings, the UK was not entitled to frustrate a submission by Mauritius to the UN Commission on the Limits of the Continental Shelf in respect of the archipelago; and
- fourth, the UK's declaration of the MPA violated rights Mauritius had in the waters of the Chagos Archipelago under the Lancaster House Undertakings in at least three ways: it effectively purported to extinguish Mauritian fishing rights in the territorial sea; there had been a failure by the UK to consider Mauritian rights and interests in the EEZ in proclaiming the MPA; and there had been breach of a duty to seek to agree common standards of pollution control among potentially affected States.

The first three grounds were found to fall outside the Tribunal's jurisdiction. On the fourth ground the Tribunal found for Mauritius, declaring the UK's MPA illegal. The case had been presumed by some to be likely to fail in its entirety on one of two grounds. First, that this was 'really' a dispute about sovereignty over the islands and therefore was inherently beyond the jurisdiction of the Tribunal; and, second, to the extent it was a dispute about fisheries the sweeping automatic exclusions from jurisdiction under article 297 would prevent the case being heard (e.g. Klein, 2014, pp. 361–362).

The *Arctic Sunrise* case concerned Greenpeace protestors who scaled a Russian oil exploration platform in the Barents Sea in 2013. Russian authorities arrested not only the protestors aboard the oil platform but also the crew of their support vessel, the *Arctic Sunrise*, and the *Arctic Sunrise* itself. The flag State, the Netherlands, commenced arbitration proceedings against Russia and – following Russia's refusal to participate – sought urgent provisional measures from the International Tribunal for the Law of the Sea (ITLOS) pending the establishment of the Tribunal.

ITLOS heard the request for provisional measures and ordered that the protestors and crew of the *Arctic Sunrise* ('the Arctic 30') be released on payment of a bond, along with the vessel itself, and that the vessel and crew should be free to leave Russia. After some delay, Russia released the Greenpeace members under an amnesty and (much later) it released the *Arctic Sunrise*. Notably, however, almost all the Arctic 30 had been released on bail prior to the ITLOS hearing.

Before ITLOS, *Arctic Sunrise* was not an easy case jurisdictionally or substantively. While there have been in the past numerous ITLOS 'prompt release' cases concerning seized fishing vessels these occur under a special procedure under article 292 UNCLOS. The difficulty was that the Netherlands was seeking the release of the *Arctic Sunrise* and all of its crew as an interim measure of protection. This was a remarkable request – interim measures are not supposed to prejudice the final disposition of a dispute (Guilfoyle & Miles, 2014). The dispute was precisely over the extent of Russian law enforcement authority and whether it had been validly exercised. Ordering the release of vessel and crew might be thought to fatally compromise Russia's ability to enforce its own laws in the event the arbitration panel later ruled in its favour. The order was all the more remarkable given that the Arctic 30 had already been released on bail, and part of the Netherlands' argument concerned whether their human rights had been infringed through a deprivation of liberty. The Netherlands' strategy was to frame the case as a question of freedom of navigation (an issue that is always within Part XV jurisdiction under Article 297(1)) with human rights elements and *then* to seek the substantive relief it wanted (the release of the vessel and crew). This was a successful exercise in salami slicing in that it dodged entirely Russia's strongest argument: that it had some claim to criminal jurisdiction over at least those protestors who boarded its oil exploration platform.

These issues were all taken up on the merits hearing where an arbitral tribunal found in favour of the Netherlands. The essence of the decision turned on the law of 'hot pursuit' and a conclusion that the Russian coast guard had effectively broken off pursuit during a period when it ceased signalling that the *Arctic Sunrise* should prepare for boarding and elected to watch and wait, simply preventing the vessel from approaching the oil platform again. It also did not help the Russian case that they had returned the two protestors who made it onto the platform's structure to the *Arctic Sunrise*. In its reasoning, the Tribunal usefully clarified a number of technical points relating to hot pursuit but, more importantly, clarified the role human rights law could play in a Part XV dispute. The latter point is returned to below.

At the time of writing, there has been a lengthy 2015 award on jurisdiction in *Philippines v China*, and the final award had only recently been handed down in July 2016. This discussion will necessarily focus more on the earlier award but has been updated where possible. The *Philippines v China* arbitration concerned two essential legal claims:

- first, that China's claim to a vast area of 'historic waters' within the so-called 'nine-dash line' (which encloses most of the South China Sea) comes to within 50 nm of the Philippines coast and therefore interferes with Philippines' rights in its continental shelf and 200 nm EEZ; and
- second, that some of the maritime zones claimed by China are projected from features which are not islands capable of generating a 200 nm EEZ and which are merely rocks capable of generating only a 12 nm territorial sea or which are maritime features not entitled to any zones at all. (That is, maritime features generate different legal entitlements over surrounding waters according to their legal status. 'Islands' generate a full suite of zones, 'rocks' a territorial sea, and reefs or rocks which are only above water at low tide have little legal effect unless close to shore: article 121, UNCLOS.)

The Philippines – for good legal reasons – was not disputing in this case which State is sovereign over these maritime features or asking for the arbitral tribunal to delimit a common maritime boundary. It is pursuing, in part, a long-anticipated legal strategy of debating whether certain features are legally islands or not (Boyle, 1997, p. 44; Klein, 2005, p. 279). China's publicly voiced objections to the proceedings (absent its formal participation) were:

- the underlying dispute is really about sovereignty over the islands, and such a dispute does not fall within the Convention;
- the Philippines proceeding to arbitration conflicts with obligations to settle relevant disputes by negotiation under the South China Seas code of conduct (and such obligations take precedence over Part XV); and
- even if the subject matter of the dispute did fall within the Convention, it forms an intrinsic part of a delimitation dispute or otherwise concerns 'historic bays or titles' and therefore is excluded from jurisdiction on the basis of China's optional declaration under Article 298(1)(a)(i).

Of these jurisdictional arguments the one that had even the slightest prospect for success was the last. A conservative approach to jurisdiction under Part XV might support such a conclusion. Nonetheless, the arbitral tribunal's preliminary 2015 award on jurisdiction found against China on most points (though reserving some arguments to consider further with the merits). As regards the argument that this was essentially a (non-justiciable) delimitation dispute, the Tribunal ruled that there was nothing wrong with a State bringing only a part of a complex and multifaceted dispute to arbitration if there was a genuine legal issue to resolve (*Philippines v China*, 2015, para. 152). The Tribunal held that: first, there was a dispute as to the correct legal classification of the various maritime features and their zonal entitlements and that this was a legal dispute within the Convention; and second, that there was a dispute within the Convention as to whether China's asserted 'historic rights' actually exist and, if so, how they interact with its UNCLOS obligations. The Tribunal noted, in particular, that:

> A dispute concerning the interaction of the Convention with another instrument or body of law, including the question of whether rights arising under another body of law were or were not preserved by the Convention, is unequivocally a dispute concerning the interpretation and application of the Convention (para. 169).

This gives potentially wide scope to the concept of disputes concerning the interpretation or application of UNCLOS. Ultimately it will be for a tribunal, not the parties, to conclude what instruments or bodies of law do interact with UNCLOS and are relevant to the case at hand. Nonetheless, there is a clear preference here for a 'systemic approach' (so-called because it sees international law as one system of law) in which other rules of general international law and even other treaties can be used to interpret UNCLOS (Pauwelyn and Elsig, 2013, p. 457). Such an approach is not uncommon but nor is it inevitable, with some international dispute settlement bodies preferring to characterise their governing treaties as creating a 'self-contained' legal order (Pauwelyn and Elsig, 2013, p. 457). This finding also clearly permitted the Tribunal to adjudicate two critical issues: whether various maritime features were islands capable of generating 200 nm maritime zones and China's 'historic waters' claim. This result was far from certain and one not necessarily considered desirable.

On both these points Philippines scored major victories in the 2016 final Award. First, after extensive analysis, the Tribunal concluded that none of the contested features in the South China Seas were islands capable of generating large maritime zones under article 121 and thus there were no potential overlapping claims to delimit under UNCLOS (*Philippines v China*, 2016, paras. 473–626 & 693–694). Further, most features were not even rocks capable of generating a territorial sea and were mere 'low tide elevations' (LTEs). The significance of this was that the Tribunal found that LTEs (unlike rocks or islands) cannot be appropriated as sovereign territory, they thus 'belong' to the zone in which they are found (*Philippines v China*, paras. 1018 & 1030). As a result the Chinese base constructed on Mischief Reef (an LTE) is effectively an illegally built artificial island within the Philippines EEZ (*Philippines v China*, paras. 374–378, 632–633 & 647).

Second, the final award further found that the Chinese historic rights asserted in the South China Seas were *rights* of use rather than claims of exclusive historic *title* and thus the article 298(1)(a)(i) exclusion did not apply (*Philippines v China*, paras. 200–278). In essence, the word *title* in the exclusion was held to require a claim of complete sovereignty. In sovereign waters foreign vessels have only a right of innocent passage, whereas China had consistently asserted its claims within the nine-dash line were consistent with freedom of navigation and overflight by third States (*Philippines v China*, para. 212). The

Tribunal found this view fatal to a claim of title and concluded that even if China had traditionally enjoyed special historic rights (which the Tribunal found it did not) those historic rights could not be upheld if inconsistent with UNCLOS (which they were as regards resource exploitation, given that the claimed rights directly conflicted with Philippines' rights in its EEZ).

Overall, the *Philippines v China* arbitration shows the benefits of a clever litigation strategy. Rather than disputing which State was sovereign over the miscellany of maritime features in the South China Sea, the Philippines' case was instead that – correctly classified – these features do not generate extensive maritime zones. Rather than arguing about sovereignty or seeking a maritime delimitation (which would be excluded in any event by China's optional article 298(1)(a)(i) declaration), the Philippines was able to argue there are no overlapping maritime claims to delimit. In a startling blow to realpolitik the Tribunal found for Philippines almost right down the line. While considering in remarkable detail all publicly available evidence of the Chinese position and all Chinese public statements, it made no real concessions to Chinese claims unsupported by law.

2.2 'Creeping jurisdiction' and UNCLOS dispute settlement?

A theme in the discussion above has been: how broad is the jurisdiction of a Part XV tribunal? That is, if such a body can potentially have regard to – and determine – legal questions going beyond a narrow conception of what it means to interpret and apply the Convention, the attractiveness of UNCLOS dispute settlement mechanisms may be greatly increased. The point is best made by illustrating the *narrowest* possible view. The critical provision of UNCLOS is the 'applicable law' clause in article 293(1): 'A court or tribunal having jurisdiction under this section shall apply this Convention and other rules of international law not incompatible with this Convention'. The meaning of this provision was hotly contested in *Chagos MPA*. The UK took a narrow view (with some support in the case law) that Article 293(1) existed only, 'to dispel any doubt that, in interpreting and applying the provisions of the Convention, a Part XV court [or] tribunal may have recourse to such secondary rules as the law of treaties, State responsibility, [etc.]' (*Chagos MPA*, 2014, para. 185).

All article 293(1) 'allows in' on this view is other rules of international law relevant to interpreting or applying the Convention *itself*. The question of 'regime interaction' between the Convention and other bodies of law (e.g. can UNCLOS fisheries provisions be interpreted in light of environmental law principles?) would thus fall outside Part XV dispute resolution. In a real-world dispute, this could scarcely be satisfactory. However, proponents of the narrow view argue that any broader approach would allow Part XV dispute settlement bodies to become courts of general jurisdiction by the back door. If Article 293(1) can let in all of international law, then so long as there is some UNCLOS element a Part XV tribunal could determine questions of sovereignty, trade law, the law of armed conflict, etc.

Unsurprisingly, in each of the three disputes the Tribunals avoided taking either a minimalist or maximalist position on article 293(1). As noted above, the award on jurisdiction in *Philippines v China* considers questions of 'regime interaction' to clearly fall within Part XV, including the question of whether pre-existing bodies of law survive under UNCLOS. In context, this was simply dynamite. It meant China could have its 'historic waters' claim to the South China Seas ruled on by an authoritative legal body. In *Artic Sunrise*, ITLOS did not explain in its provisional measures decision the basis on which it could have recourse to human rights law (which it seemingly did). This led to some criticism (Guilfoyle and Miles, 2014). The arbitral tribunal (2014, para. 190), happily, was more expansive. It held that article 293(1) certainly contemplated secondary rules of the type discussed above. It then went on to note: 'In the case of some broadly worded or general [UNCLOS] provisions, it may also be necessary to rely on primary rules of international law other than the Convention in order to interpret and apply . . . the Convention' (para. 191).

This, however, could not turn Part XV into a means of adjudicating whether a treaty other than UNCLOS (such as the International Covenant on Civil and Political Rights) had been violated (para. 193). Nonetheless, the Tribunal found it could apply customary international law, including human rights standards, in judging the legality of a law-enforcement operation conducted under UNCLOS, at least where UNCLOS was silent or ambiguous (paras. 197–198). This could be described as giving article 293(1) a principled, but liberal, gap-filling role.

The arbitral tribunal (or, rather, the majority) in *Chagos MPA* relied on a different, more conservative interpretative technique. It applied the uncontroversial principle that a Part XV tribunal can have regard to other rules of international law to the extent UNCLOS incorporates them by reference. That is, a not uncommon drafting technique in UNCLOS is to provide for the filling in of certain provisions by 'rules of reference' which gain their content by referring out of the Convention (*renvoi*). For example, certain action in the territorial sea is only permissible where approved by the 'competent international organisation' (e.g. article 41(4)). This *renvoi* effectively incorporates rules made by the IMO from time to time into UNCLOS.

The problem in *Chagos MPA* was that it would have been difficult to meaningfully interpret the rights and obligations between the two parties without reference to the pre-decolonization Lancaster House Undertakings. Having decided those undertakings constituted legal obligations, the question arose for the Tribunal as to what effect they had on UNCLOS obligations. This squarely raised the 'regime interaction' issue. UNCLOS Part XV only acknowledges a limited jurisdiction over other related conventions, and even then only where they expressly provide for the application of Part XV dispute settlement (article 288(2)). Taken literally and *a contrario*, this could be taken to exclude all *pre*-UNCLOS agreements which naturally will not include a reference to Part XV dispute settlement. The Tribunal overcame this problem through a curious application of the *renvoi* technique.

A critical issue in the case was the extent of Mauritian fishing rights in waters around the Chagos archipelago as preserved in the Lancaster House Undertakings. The difficulty was, of course, that fisheries disputes in the EEZ are plainly excluded from Part XV dispute settlement. Nonetheless, the UNCLOS definition of the EEZ is that it starts seaward of the territorial sea (article 55). Therefore, the Tribunal reasoned, fisheries disputes within the territorial sea remain *within* Part XV. This was significant as in the territorial sea the coastal state's sovereign rights are to be 'exercised subject to this Convention and to other rules of international law' (article 2(3) UNCLOS). Somewhat circuitously, the Tribunal reached the conclusion that this had the effect of preserving situations where (quoting the International Law Commission), 'by reason of some special relationship, geographical or other, between two States, rights in the territorial sea of one of them are granted to the other in excess of the rights recognized in [the Convention]' (*Chagos MPA*, 2014, paras. 515–6). Thus it held article 2(3) was not only a *renvoi* incorporating general rules of international law but was also intended to preserve special bilateral legal relations pre-dating the Convention.

This was, at best, an odd approach. While not seeming to exclude the broader 'regime interaction' approach it is clearly much narrower. This left the *Philippines v China* tribunal with the question of what to say about the approach taken in *Chagos MPA*. Remarkably, the Tribunal in *Philippines v China* re-characterised the logic of the Tribunal in *Chagos MPA* and said instead the UK's reiteration of past undertaking to Mauritius fell 'within the ambit' of article 311. Article 311 allows States to conclude bilateral agreements that modify the application of UNCLOS between them. Logically, it only applies to agreements that post-date UNCLOS, which is presumably why the *Chagos MPA* tribunal did not attempt to bring the earlier 1965 Lancaster House Undertakings within its ambit. The *Philippines v China* tribunal instead appeared to take the view that UK's *later* reiteration of the Undertakings could attract the operation of article 311.

2.3 *The sovereignty question*

Questions of regime interaction may seem arcane when set against the question of sovereignty over territory. Two of the cases under discussion potentially involve this issue: *Chagos MPA* and *Philippines v China* (Klein, 2014). In both cases the respondent States sought to avoid the jurisdiction of the relevant arbitral tribunal through claiming the dispute was essentially a 'disguised' sovereignty dispute and as such was 'outside' UNCLOS. As noted, the Philippines legal strategy was to expressly disclaim it was inviting the Tribunal to rule on questions of sovereignty, and the Tribunal was unimpressed by Chinese claims that the Tribunal should decline jurisdiction on this ground. (The Tribunal further, perhaps conveniently, found the great majority of disputed maritime features were mere LTEs over which no claims of sovereignty were possible.)

Chagos MPA did, however, raise the question directly. Mauritius argued that the repeated use of the phrase 'the coastal State' in UNCLOS made it a question of law, not fact, which State was the coastal State in respect of the exercise of 'sovereign rights' in the archipelago's maritime zones. In part its case relied on the *a contrario* reading of article 298(1)(a)(i) mentioned above. The logic runs that as article 298 contains *optional* exclusions to the dispute settlement system and as article 298(1)(a)(i) is the only *express* instance where sovereignty disputes are ruled out, then Part XV should otherwise allow sovereignty disputes to be heard. It was an ambitious claim. Academic commentary on the issue is divided, but proponents of the idea that UNCLOS Part XV *might* cover *some* sovereignty disputes tend to be cautious (Buga, 2012; Treves, 2006). The usual argument is that the only sovereignty disputes that might fall within Part XV would be 'mixed' maritime boundary disputes: essentially cases where there is jurisdiction over a delimitation dispute but it cannot be resolved without incidentally determining (for example) sovereignty over a disputed island.

The alternative view is that such disputes – however limited – can never fall within Part XV. The arguments are, essentially:

- a structural argument: maritime zones presuppose sovereignty over territory, and therefore the question of who is sovereign over that territory is prior or anterior to the Convention;
- a textual presumption argument: article 298(1)(a)(i) sets up a conciliation mechanism as an alternative to binding dispute resolution and therefore only refers to sovereignty disputes for the avoidance of doubt. That is, sovereignty disputes are presumptively excluded from Part XV generally, and the drafting of article 298(1)(a)(i) ensures such

disputes are not 'let back in' through the conciliation procedure (*Chagos MPA*, para. 195); or

- an original intent argument: various statements in the negotiating history or the views expressed at the time by eminent academic commentators (who often participated in the negotiations for a particular State) make it plain that Part XV was never intended to encompass sovereignty disputes (see, e.g. the recollections in Adede, 1987, p. 132).

Unsurprisingly, the UK ran variations on all three arguments in *Chagos MPA*. Obviously, had the arbitral tribunal accepted either the Mauritian *a contrario* argument (all sovereignty disputes are potentially 'in') or any of the UK arguments (all sovereignty disputes are always 'out') a wide-ranging precedent could have been set. Instead, the Tribunal found that close examination of the 'negotiating records of the Convention provide no explicit answer regarding jurisdiction over territorial sovereignty' (*Chagos MPA*, para. 215). Nonetheless, the Tribunal considered that disputes as to sovereignty over territory are, by their nature, so sensitive that the drafters of a system of dispute resolution containing optional exceptions would clearly have included an opt-out for sovereignty disputes had they otherwise fallen within its scope (*Chagos MPA*, paras. 216–217). It thus upheld a version of the original intent argument: such disputes were not generally intended to fall within Part XV. Nonetheless, the Tribunal acknowledged the regime interaction argument discussed above: that article 288(1) may allow determination of issues of law 'ancillary' to a law of the sea dispute (*Chagos MPA*, para. 220). The Tribunal thus did 'not categorically exclude that in some instances a minor issue of territorial sovereignty could indeed be ancillary to a dispute concerning the interpretation or application of the Convention' (*Chagos MPA*, para. 221). On this basis the Tribunal held that the core of Mauritius' first claim was a pure sovereignty dispute, not an ancillary question to a dispute about the interpretation or application of UNCLOS. It was thus without jurisdiction to determine the claim. It did, however, clearly leave the door open to the possibility of future tribunals hearing some sovereignty disputes.

For Mauritius this was not necessarily a major setback. The determination that it had legally protected rights in the Chagos archipelago under the Lancaster House Undertakings represented a significant victory. It had the result that the UK's declaration of the Marine Protected Area around the archipelago was procedurally void for failure to adequately consult Mauritius and respect protected Mauritian interests.

2.4 *What impact on the UNCLOS system?*

One could conclude that these cases show only isolated examples of legal technique: be it *ad hoc* uses of textual *renvoi* or using an applicable law clause to take jurisdiction over a limited range of legal issues seemingly falling outside UNCLOS, strictly construed. Further, there is no hierarchy of courts in international law or doctrine of precedent. As a result, one might further conclude that it is too early to say if any such techniques will be applied to similar effect in subsequent cases. This, however, would likely underestimate the way the tide is running. Part of the practical context for the operation of UNCLOS dispute settlement is that there is only a limited pool of practitioners – international judges, litigators, and scholars – likely to be appointed to arbitral tribunals. To the extent that the International Court of Justice (ICJ) and ITLOS are also fora available under Part XV, it is notable that judges of the ICJ and ITLOS are themselves frequently appointed to Annex VII arbitral tribunals. Apart from the obvious potential for cross-fertilisation of thought, arbitrators who also hold judicial posts are likely to have in mind the consequences of excessively narrow or wide decisions about jurisdiction for their 'home' institution. That is, any time an arbitral panel decides an issue of jurisdiction those involved know that they will be establishing precedents (in the non-binding sense) which will later be quoted by parties to UNCLOS Part XV disputes heard before the ICJ and ITLOS. Thus, a supposedly isolated decision may well have systemic consequences. This result is all the more apparent if one considers not only the revolving door of international arbitrators and judges but also the limited community of international law advocates. There was, for example, as regards *Chagos MPA* and *Philippines v China* substantial overlap between the litigation teams for Mauritius and the Philippines, and one ITLOS judge (Judge Wolfrum) sat on both arbitrations.

3. Conclusions

There are two main issues to discuss following this brief examination of three complex cases. First, can small states succeed in law of the sea litigation against great powers – and if so, what will those victories be worth in practice? Second, what may be the systemic consequences of 'salami slice' litigation upon the integrity of the law of the sea as a system? Each is addressed in turn below, before a few comments on accusations of 'lawfare' are offered. Much of the discussion will focus on the most contentious of the examples studied, the South China Sea dispute.

3.1 Can smaller powers win against great powers in international litigation?

The short answer to this is: yes, so long as the objectives are limited. Let us consider each case. The Netherlands secured its principal objective in *MV Arctic Sunrise*: the release of the protestors. This may also have had something to do with a Russian desire to avoid bad publicity before the winter Olympics – but it would be hard to claim that the ITLOS proceeding played no role at all. The goal was to place pressure on Russia to achieve a result, and that worked. Better still (for the plaintiffs), the Netherlands achieved this goal through provisional measures proceedings, and the legitimacy of its 'win' was later cemented by the arbitration tribunal's award on the merits.

Mauritius obtained international recognition that is *has present legal rights* in the Chagos archipelago and not a mere promise that the United Kingdom would return the islands to it when they are no longer needed for defence purposes by the United States. It obtained a ruling that the United Kingdom's declaration of a marine protected area surrounding the islands without consulting it was a procedural violation of the Convention. This was significant for Mauritius as it constitutes a symbolic vindication of Maritius' position regarding the archipelago, at least in part.

Did Philippines win against China? On the legal issues, it did sweepingly well. The Tribunal's findings on the status of various maritime features and Chinese claims to historic rights kicks an irreparable hole in claims as to the legality of the nine-dash line. This can only further undermine the already shaky legitimacy of those claims. Extraordinarily, it has also ruled *de facto* that China is in illegal occupation of an artificial island within the Philippines' EEZ. What has all this achieved? At least three things:

- as noted, it has dealt a devastating blow to legal arguments supporting China's 'nine-dash line';

- it will favour the Philippines in any future delimitation case with China; and
- it will mean that Chinese claims to historic waters can only be maintained through a policy of force and without international legitimacy.

China's reaction to the Tribunal's various rulings tends to vindicate this view: it initially appeared rattled, uncertain, and unable to articulate a legal case (Ku, 2015) and has descended into bizarre *ad hominem* attacks against Tribunal members (Guilfoyle, 2016). While some have claimed following the ruling that this is an example of how great powers simply ignore international law as an irrelevance, the Chinese propaganda campaign against the Tribunal has not been an example of how States respond to an irrelevance. It has been how States respond to a grave threat. While China has in the past stated publicly that 60 States support its view that the Tribunal is without jurisdiction, only eight have been willing to step forward and be named, and others have repudiated the claim they do not support the Tribunal's jurisdiction (Page, 2016). The result is that China appears, at the least, diplomatically isolated on the issue.

Until now the long game for China was probably to maintain strategic ambiguity and multiple lines of semi-plausible legal argument, long enough for it to establish its position as a question of fact irrespective of law. Effectively, it hoped to could defer the legal question until its claimed 'special status' in the South China Sea became tacitly accepted and the ordinary legal question irrelevant. Instead, the Philippines' litigation forced China to reveal its hand: and, absent a policy of force, it does not have one. An alternative view might be that China appreciates that, in the long term, agreements must be struck over maritime delimitation in the South China Seas and it has to date been pursuing a maximalist position to set up the deal it wants. On this analysis, the Philippines' litigation may been seen as an attempt to reduce any great power 'premium' expected by China in a final deal and to bargain in the shadow of the law.

A key obstacle to constructive regional engagement with China over the South China Sea has been a lack of a common response by ASEAN. A legal win for the Philippines, even if it is largely symbolic, may serve as a rallying point for other regional States to reach a common diplomatic position supported by the law. Indeed, such a position may be crystallising with Indonesia recently expressing its dissatisfaction with China and openly contemplating legal action of its own (Bosco, 2015). The *Philippines v China* litigation has clearly played a role in beginning to shift the position of ASEAN States and other regional powers. (India and Vietnam are reported to have engaged in strategic dialogue on the issue: Press Trust of India, 2016.) If the Philippines is also seen as 'winning' under the final award it may encourage other affected States in the region to pursue similar litigation, effectively 'ganging up' on the regional superpower.

Generally, it is easier for great powers to achieve their purposes through a rules-based order rather than force (Simpson, 2004, pp. 6–10). A rules-based order may constrain great powers somewhat, but great powers will be in a position to have a disproportionate influence on rule-formation and shaping a system that serves their ends. Force is costly, and in territorial questions one must be prepared to commit to it over a very long time (as Iraq, Afghanistan, and the Ukraine show). However, while buying into a rules-based system – even if only to a limited extent – is an efficient means of great-power rule it necessarily opens up avenues for small players to exert pressure. Certainly, realists are right to suggest that international litigation alone seldom brings great powers to the table or gets small or medium powers everything they want (Crawford, 2014, p. 30). This, however, is a straw man: it assumes that the function of litigation in any context is to invariably subdue the powerful or secure the weak everything they want, and that this happens in practice in national legal systems. It is to deny what effect international law actually has through comparison with an exaggerated view of the effectiveness of national law (Crawford, 2014, pp. 27–49).

Ultimately, if a great power such as China wants to claim special privileges or status and have those claims acknowledged, its claims must be accepted as legitimate. A determination as to the legality of those claims cannot but affect their legitimacy and acceptance by other participants in the law-making process, even if it may not be solely determinative (Brunnée & Toope, 2010, p. 53). As above, this does not mean litigation will force China to abandon its manifestly excessive maritime claims, but there will obviously be expense incurred in maintaining them unilaterally in the absence of either widespread tacit acceptance or a negotiated settlement.

3.2 What might be the consequences of 'salami slice' litigation under UNCLOS?

Overall, this chapter has illustrated a number of pressures on the law of the sea dispute settlement system:

- its compulsory nature may make it very attractive to litigants (albeit that law of the sea litigation remains relatively limited);
- its numerous complex exceptions, however, invite respondent States to challenge the jurisdiction of a court or tribunal to hear a case – or make more credible the claim that there is so clearly no basis for jurisdiction that non-appearance is (politically if not legally) a plausible strategy (Ku, 2014); and
- the number of institutions that can hear UNCLOS cases – despite the fact that only a small pool of people will ever sit on such cases – may make the system more dynamic than expected.

To take the last point first: if a growing number of complex cases are heard by different bodies which are – as it were – competing for work this may itself affect the development of the law. If courts and tribunals are too conservative, they will have no work – as applicant States will stop bringing them cases. If they are too radical, there is a risk respondent States might decide that the Convention is too much of a burden and withdraw from it. Again, it does not affect this argument that most of the disputes are heard in practice by arbitral tribunals. Such panels invariably include at least two if not three ITLOS judges. The rules of jurisdiction before the panels are the same as before the Tribunal – when sitting as arbitrators such judges know they are helping develop what may very well become applicable law before ITLOS or, indeed, the ICJ.

Further, the duty of international judges or arbitrators in interpreting a treaty is potentially threefold: to interpret the text in front of them; to give effect to the intention of the parties who produced the text; and, to the extent this is a separate question, to promote the objects the parties had in mind (Pauwelyn, 2013, 450 ff). The difficulty with UNCLOS is that it is a huge text, negotiated by dozens of States and hundreds of individuals over nearly ten years. The idea that it embodies a single set of intentions is implausible. What judges are left with is a very complex text, and in complex texts there is always room for progressive interpretation. That of course does not mean *any* interpretation is possible. A natural brake on excessively liberal interpretation is the nature of the international legal system: one that is still very much grounded in the consent of States. Dispute settlement bodies will be cautious about upsetting States – especially major powers – but they will not necessarily be timid. Judges and arbitrators in the law of the sea appear to show some concern with what has been called elsewhere 'the responsibility of the jurist to create and maintain some form of "interiority" to law' (McVeigh, 2014, p. 490). That is, the judge or arbitrator is subject to an ethic of office whereby they must not only maintain the internal integrity of the law but also find 'the appropriate internal qualities' within that body of law 'to meet external realities' (McVeigh, 2014, p. 490). One might thus expect that, over time, the law may legitimately develop through progressive interpretation – though radical interpretations that risk disrupting the legal system are unlikely (compare Boyle, 2005). This chapter's observations on the three cases discussed would appear to bear that out.

3.3 UNCLOS: the rule of law or lawfare?

Lawfare in its ordinary sense describes the achievement of policy goals, usually in the context of armed conflict, through instrumental use of the law (Kittrie, 2016). It is usually a pejorative term, suggesting that recourse to law has occurred for improper purposes. Such 'bad faith' arguments have been made in some of the cases under consideration. China has done so expressly as regards the Philippines, and the arbitral tribunal gave the point short shrift. (And indeed went on to find that it was China that had acted in bad faith by taking measures that served to exacerbate the dispute: see *Philippines v China*, paras. 1133–5, 1172 and 1203(B)(16)). An implicit argument along similar lines was made by the UK against Mauritius, in suggesting that the entirety of Mauritius's case was simply dressing up a sovereignty dispute it knew to be non-justiciable as a law of the sea dispute. The accusation of lawfare is also perhaps implicit in some academic criticism of creative or 'unexpected' litigation under Part XV. The argument being that it may destabilise the UNCLOS regime if the dispute settlement system is extended to cover cases it is generally agreed the drafters never intended to be included (Klein, 2014).

I consider such concerns overblown. The function of litigation in the international community is that it affirms the formal equality of small States and great powers. When great powers accuse small States of destabilising the system through recourse to litigation the allegation seems somewhat farcical. What have great powers to fear? What they have to fear, other than embarrassment, is delegitimisation of their policies. Where policies are judged by an independent judicial body (according to the rules of the game as agreed in advance among the players) to be unlawful, they are unlikely to be perceived by the international community as legitimate.

The effectiveness of international litigation in constraining the ambition of great powers – and this chapter has only contended that that effectiveness is limited and of a particular sort – is most evident in the reaction of great powers when they lose. It is hard to believe the international litigation is of no consequence when it is treated by the targeted states as being a matter of such moment (Ku, 2015). At the end of the day, however, if UNCLOS dispute settlement is truly to be a system of law and not lawfare it requires the inculcation of rule of law values in great powers. The unwillingness of dispute settlement bodies to decline jurisdiction merely because great power respondent States refused to show up is one sign of the strength of that system and a step in the right direction. When a legal dispute exists, unless States submit to judicial settlement, 'the dispute remains and it cannot simply be wished away, even by the most powerful' (Crawford, 2014, p. 49).

References

The Arctic Sunrise Case (Kingdom of the Netherlands v. Russian Federation) (Provisional Measures) (International Tribunal for the Law of the Sea, Order 2013/3, 25 October 2013) Retrieved from http://www.itlos.org/.

The Arctic Sunrise Case (Kingdom of the Netherlands v. Russian Federation) (Award on the Merits) (Permanent Court of Arbitration, 14 August 2015) Retrieved from https://pca-cpa.org/en/cases/.

Adede, A. O. (1987). *The system for settlement of disputes under the United Nations Convention on the Law of the Sea: A Drafting History and a Commentary*. Martinus, Nijhoff: Leiden.

Allott, P. (1983). Power sharing in the Law of the Sea. *American Journal of International Law, 77*, 1–30.

Bosco, D. (2015). Indonesia hints at South China Sea litigation. Retrieved from https://www.lawfareblog.com/indonesia-hints-south-china-sea-litigation.

Boyle, A. & Chinkin, C. (2007) *The making of international law*. Oxford University Press: Oxford.

Boyle, A. E. (1997). Dispute settlement and the Law of the Sea Convention: Problems of fragmentation and jurisdiction. *International and Comparative Law Quarterly, 46*, 37–54.

Boyle, A. (2005). Further development of the Law of the Sea Convention: Mechanisms for change. *International and Comparative Law Quarterly, 54*, 563–584.

Brunnée, J. & Toope, S. J. (2010). *Legitimacy and legality in international law: An interactional account*. Cambridge University Press: Cambridge.

Buga, I. (2012). Territorial sovereignty issues in maritime disputes: A jurisdictional dilemma for Law of the Sea tribunals. *The International Journal of Marine and Coastal Law, 27*, 59–95.

Chagos Marine Protected Area Arbitration (Mauritius v. United Kingdom) (Award on the Merits) (Permanent Court of Arbitration, 18 March 2015) Retrieved from http://www.pcacases.com/web/allcases/.

Crawford, J. (2014). *Chance, order, change: The course of international law*. The Hague Academy of International Law: Maubeuge.

Guilfoyle, D. (2016). Philippines v China: first thoughts on the Award in the South China Seas Case. Retrieved from http://www.ejiltalk.org/philippines-v-china-first-thoughts-on-the-award-in-the-south-china-seas-case/.

Guilfoyle, D.J.A., & Miles, C. (2014). Provisional measures and the MV Arctic Sunrise. *American Journal of International Law, 108*(2), 271–287.

Kittrie, O. (2016.) *Lawfare: Law as a weapon of war*. Oxford: Oxford University Press.

Klein, N. (2005). *Dispute settlement in the UN Convention on the Law of the Sea*. Cambridge: Cambridge University Press.

Klein, N. (2014). The effectiveness of the UNCLOS dispute settlement regime: Reaching for the stars?. *American Society of International Law Proceedings, 108*, 359–364.

Ku, J. (2014). The Philippines' massive lawfare blunder in the South China Sea. Retrieved from http://nationalinterest.org/feature/the-philippines-massive-lawfare-blunder-the-south-china-sea-11837.

Ku, J. (2015). China launches op-ed rebuttal to Philippines' arbitration case. Retrieved from http://opiniojuris.org/2015/12/15/china-launches-op-ed-rebuttal-to-philippines-arbitration-case/.

McVeigh, S. (2014). Law as (more or less) itself: On some not very reflective elements of law. *UC Irvine Law Review, 4*, 471–491.

Official Records of the Third United Nations Conference on the Law of the Sea (1973–1982), Vol. V.

Page, J. (2016). Beijing's claims of South China Sea support may not hold water. Retrieved from http://www.wsj.com/articles/beijings-claims-of-south-china-sea-support-may-not-hold-water-1466138014.

Pauwelyn, J. & Manfred Elsig, M., (2013) The politics of treaty interpretation: Variations and explanations across international tribunals. In J. L. Dunoff, & M. A. Pollack *Interdisciplinary*

Perspectives an International Law and International Relations: The State of the Art (pp. 445–473). New York: Cambridge University Press.
Press Trust of India. (2016). India, Vietnam hold strategic dialogue; talk South China Sea. Retrieved from http://www.business-standard.com/article/pti-stories/india-vietnam-hold-strategic-dialogue-talk-south-china-sea-116080301473_1.html.
Republic of Philippines v. The People's Republic of China (Award on Jurisdiction and Admissibility) (Permanent Court of Arbitration, 29 October 2015) Retrieved from http://www.pcacases.com/web/allcases/.
Republic of Philippines v. The People's Republic of China, (Award) (Permanent Court of Arbitration, 12 July 2016) Retrieved from http://www.pcacases.com/web/allcases/.
Simpson, G. (2004). *Great powers and outlaw states: Unequal sovereigns in the international legal order*. Cambridge: Cambridge University Press.
Tanaka, Y. (2015). *The international law of the sea* (2nd ed.). Cambridge: Cambridge University Press.
Treves, T. (2006). What have the United Nations Convention and the International Tribunal for the Law of the Sea to offer as regards maritime delimitation disputes?. In R. Lagoni, & D. Vignes (Eds.), *Maritime delimitation* (pp. 63–78). Leiden: Brill.
United Nations. *Official Records of the Third United Nations Conference on the Law of the Sea* (1973–1982). Vol. V. Retrieved from http://legal.un.org/diplomaticconferences/lawofthesea-1982/lawofthesea-1982.html.
United Nations Convention on the Law of the Sea, opened for signature 10 December 1982, 1833 UNTS 3 (entered into force 16 November 1994).

12 Foreign Military Aid as Good Governance?

The Case of South Asia

Maziar M. Falarti and Syed Ali Abbas

India and Pakistan have had a heavy reliance on foreign military aid since 1947. This reliance is due to an interplay of political and economic events and influences, as well as regional rivalries. This chapter argues that the provision of foreign military aid to India and Pakistan by the United States (US), Soviet Union/Russia, and China has been a key factor in enabling both to develop a nuclear program and to uplift the financial burden associated with conventional warfare. Further, and more radically, we posit that the mutual threat of nuclear armament has resulted in better economic relations between India and Pakistan and a de-escalation of border tensions and disputes. This can be seen in an analysis of the Kargil War in 1999 and in India's implementation of the 'Cold Start' doctrine in the 'post Kargil' period.

The year 2017 marks 70 years since partition of the Indian sub-continent and creation of the *Islamic Republic of Pakistan* and the *Republic of India*. It also marks the beginning of regular political and border tensions, rivalry, and enmity between the two republics. The 1947 partition between India and Pakistan resulted in more than a million deaths and left approximately fifteen million homeless and stranded as refugees (Dalrymple, 2015). This began years of hostility between the two nations.

Since the partition, Pakistan and India have been two of the world's larger recipients of foreign military supplies and aid. Much of Pakistan's foreign military aid and supplies has, and continues to, come from the United States (US) and the Peoples Republic of China (Alavi, 1998; Cohen, 2007; Curtis, 2009; Paul, 2003), whereas India has traditionally received military supplies from the Soviet Union/Russia (Chenoy, 2008, 2010). For example, data from the US Overseas Loans and Grants report (the Greenbook) list Pakistan amongst the top-ten US military aid recipients since 1945 (U.S. Agency for International Development, 2014a; 2014b). Data collected by the Stockholm International Peace Research Institute (SIPRI) rank India highest in receiving military supplies from the Soviet Union/Russia since 1950 (Stockholm International Peace Research Institute (SIPRI), 2015). Little is known, however, about the precise amount and types of aid received annually by these two South Asian nations.

There are several definitions of the term *foreign military aid*. This chapter, however, adopts the definition of foreign military aid given by the US Agency for International Development (USAID) that defines military aid as "total bilateral military assistance loans and grants" given by the donor country in the form of training, education and hardware (Sullivan, et al., 2011; OECD redefines foreign aid to include some military spending, 2016). The aid provided includes weapons, counter-narcotics activities, anti-terrorism operations, de-mining, military education and training, and peace-keeping operations (Dunning, 2004; Grimmett, 2009;

Sullivan et al., 2011). Notably, a number of empirical studies and reports suggest that foreign military aid has also been provided to the armed forces, militia groups, and other non-government forces without consultation or coordination with the central governments of India and Pakistan (Sanjian, 1999; Jones et al., 2006; Rohde et al., 2007; Boschini & Olofsgard, 2007; Cohen, 2009; Dube & Naidu, 2010; O'Hanlon, 2010; Fair et al., 2010; Fellowship of Reconcilliation, 2010; Sullivan et al., 2011). As also pointed out by Umair Ghori in Chapter 16 on Pakistan, the provision of foreign military aid to the armed forces, without government knowledge, highlights the central role played by the military in the Indian and Pakistani political landscapes, and the significant power they hold.

This chapter argues that the attainment of foreign military aid and nuclear technology transfers to India and Pakistan have been key factors in enabling both nations to develop nuclear weapon programs. Rather than further destabilising relations between the two, this aid has served to improve relations and deter an escalation of tensions. We argue that varying deterrence theories assist in understanding why, over time, militarization has been helpful in promoting a weapon-controlled peace between the nuclear-capable India and Pakistan. Our empirical analysis of India–Pakistan relations will be derived from an analysis of the Kargil War of 1999 and its aftermath. This is because the Kargil War was the first and last major battle between nuclear-capable Pakistan and India.

1. Foreign military aid

It is difficult to be certain of the extent and type of aid directed and allocated for defence, including what is allocated to nuclear programs and weapons. Additionally, US, Chinese, and Soviet Union-Russia information and statistics on their foreign aid to South Asia are not clear (Fleck & Kilby, 2010; Lai, 2003; Meernik, Krueger, & Poe 1998; Mesquita & Smith, 2007; Wright & Winters, 2010). It does appear, however, that US military aid has been disbursed episodically and in a manner consistent with US geopolitical interests. These interests include containing communism during the Cold War, balancing the Indo-Russian defence alliance, and anti-terrorism strategies (Cohen, 2007; Meernik, Krueger, & Poe, 1998; Mueller, 2006; O'Hanlon, 2010; Sanjian, 1998; Talbott, 2005). Studies examining Pakistan's behaviour suggest that provision of foreign military aid by the US to Pakistan has continued despite Pakistan's long history of undeclared nuclear activity, including the test of nuclear devices and a warhead in 1998 (Cohen, 2007; Ibrahim, 2009; Jervis, 1984; Jones et al., 2006; Kapur, 2005; Knopf, 2002; Kristensen & Norris, 2013). Further, Pakistan is not a signatory to the nuclear Non-Proliferation Treaty (NPT). In our view, Pakistan is often in disagreement with the US on global political issues, for example, during the Cold War (Fleck & Kilby, 2010; Kapur, 2005; Sanjian, 1998; Sullivan et al., 2011) and in having economic, nuclear, and political relationships with countries such as North Korea or China (Bukhari & Rehman, 2011; Siddiqui, 1986; Squassoni, 2006). Despite these political differences, for much of its history, the Pakistani military has been useful to the US in its military operations against the Soviet Union/Russia and Al Qaeda in Afghanistan.

The overall arms imported from the US, China, and Soviet Union, as shown in Figure 12.1, are likely indicative of military aid contributions to Pakistan and India. Pakistan, as Figure 12.1 indicates, did not receive any US aid during the 1960s or during the decade prior to the Kargil War of 1999. The US stopped providing military aid to Pakistan in the 1960s because of Pakistan's decision to initiate a war with India. The blocking of military aid to

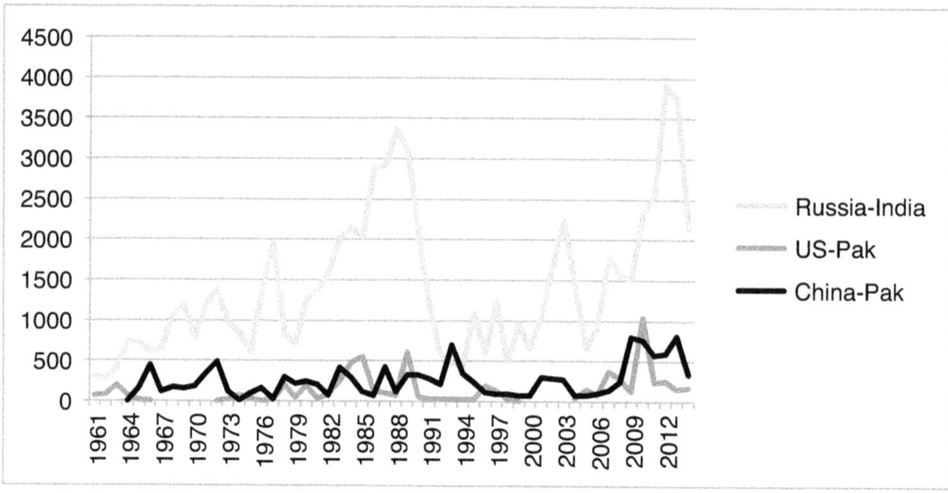

Figure 12.1 Value of arms imported annually by India and Pakistan, from 1961–2012, measured in USD millions. Imports from Russia, the US, and China are reported. Adapted from the "SIPRI Arms Trade Database" [Data file], Stockholm International Peace Research Institute. (2015), http://www.sipri.org/databases/armstransfers.

Pakistan in the 1990s was due to the 1990 implementation of the Pressler Amendment by the then US president George W. Bush (Ali, 1995; Hussain, 2005). The Pressler Amendment required the US president to certify that Pakistan did not possess and/or was not in the process of developing nuclear weapons in order for that nation to purchase or receive US military aid (Holmes, 1993). In 1990, Pakistan was not certified and therefore did not receive US military aid.

The resumption of US military aid to Pakistan since the early 2000s is attributed to the global changes and world order since the 9/11 attacks and the global impacts of the US War on Terror. This period also saw the removal of the Pressler Amendment and other sanctions that had previously been imposed on Pakistan by US president George W. Bush (Aguilar et al., 2011; Boutton & Carter, 2013; Fleck & Kilby, 2010; Hussain, 2005; Kronstadt, 2011). Pakistan is seen in the vanguard of the War on Terror, as well as an ally. This is because of a variety of factors, including its geopolitical and military influences in Afghanistan and the Muslim world (Chossudovsky, 2005; Buckley & Singh, 2006). Mueller (2006) argues that the US foreign military aid policy since 9/11 has moved towards countering terrorism threats in order to protect itself and its allies. Lake (2009) suggests that as part of protecting itself and its global allies, the US sees itself as responsible for ensuring stability of such allies, including Pakistan.

Figure 12.2 above outlines the spike in military spending by Pakistan during the increase in US military aid following the Soviet invasion of Afghanistan (1979–1989) during the Cold War era. Figure 12.2 also shows the sharp fall in military expenditures during the suspension of US economic and military aid to Pakistan in the 1990s, and the subsequent increase in spending corresponding with the resumption of US military aid following 9/11 and the beginning of the War on Terror (Aguilar et al., 2011; Fleck & Kilby, 2010; Hussain, 2005; Kronstadt, 2011; Boutton & Carter, 2013).

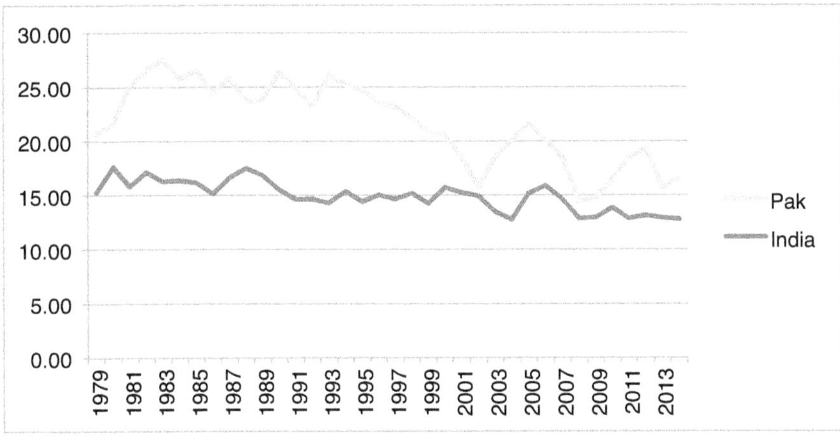

Figure 12.2 Defence expenditures in Pakistan and India from 1979–2013 as a percentage of their central government expenditures. Adapted from the Economic Surveys of India, 2007–2014; Pakistan–OECD [Data file]; Aid to Pakistan by the Numbers (n.d); State Bank of Pakistan Annual Reports 1999–2015 [Data file] and the "World DataBank: World Development Indicators" [Data file], World Bank. (2016), http://databank.worldbank.org/data/reports.aspx?source=world-development-indicators&preview=on.

India, when compared to Pakistan, did not receive as much US military aid. Instead, India began receiving military supplies from Soviet Union/Russia in the early 1960s. As Figure 12.1 indicates, Soviet Union/Russia contributions to the Indian military have been almost twice in dollar value that of the contributions of the US and China to Pakistan, except for in the early 1990s. Figure 12.2 also shows the fluctuations in aid provided to India and Pakistan generally run parallel to each other.

As occurs in Pakistan, provision of foreign military aid to India occurs despite India having yet to sign the NPT. India, since the end of the Cold War, has also had a clandestine and controversial nuclear program, which has included the purchase of uranium, and has engaged in technology transfer from Russia (Conley, 2000). India, however, has also cooperated, for a combination of technological, political, and economic reasons, with the US and its allies, particularly Australia, Israel, and France (Cohen, 2009; Ganguly 2013; India-Australia agreement complete, 2015; Kapur, 2009; Krishnan, 2002; Lai, 2003; Sanjian, 1998; Sarkar, 2014). One of these reasons was that the transfer of US civil nuclear technology to India alone intensified the power equation in South Asia by calling for greater Sino-Pak, as in Chinese and Pakistani, cooperation in nuclear, military, and economic matters. Pakistan, in response, demanded the same civil nuclear technology from the US but was refused. This refusal indicates the shift in US geopolitics since the Cold War, from strategic interests in Pakistan to economic and political interests in India. Notably, India has not been given a membership status of Nuclear Supplies Group (NSG) due to Chinese opposition, backed by Pakistani diplomacy.

Several academic and political commentators argue that rivalry between India and Pakistan led to each obtaining and maintaining nuclear technology and weapons programs (Conley 2000; Kapur, 2005; Krishnan, 2002; Lake, 2009; Lavoy, 2009; Nanavatty, 2009; Sanjian,

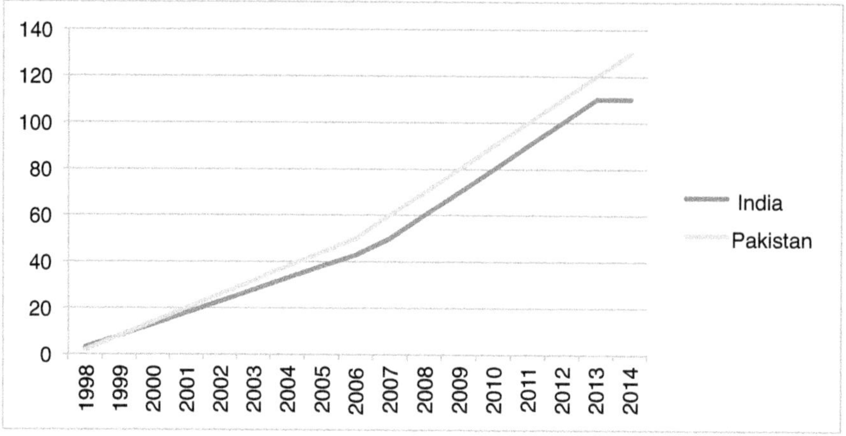

Figure 12.3 Stocks of nuclear weapons in India and Pakistan in 1998–2013. Adapated from "Global Nuclear Weapons Inventories: 1945–2013" by H. M. Kristensen, and R. S. Norris, 2013, *Bulletin of the Atomic Scientists, 69*(5), pp: 75–81.

1998; Singh, 1998; Tomar, 1980). Figure 12.3 indicates a steady stockpile of nuclear weapons by both India and Pakistan since successful tests of 1998. Each was concerned to deter the other. For example, India, a former ally of the Soviet Union, began its quest for nuclear weapons as deterrence against Pakistan and China, in the midst of the Cold War in the 1960s (Krishnan, 2002; Singh, 1998; Tomar, 1980). India successfully tested its first nuclear bomb, the *Smiling Buddha* (Pokhran I), in 1974 (Sanjian, 1998). Pakistan, allied with the US and China, and in the spirit of 'keeping up with India', established a nuclear program in the 1970s. However, Pakistan did not successfully test its nuclear weapon and devices until 1998 and only did so after India's second nuclear detonation (Pokhran II). This second detonation consisted of five nuclear devices (Chakma, 2005).

It is generally believed the Soviet Union/Russia was instrumental in India acquiring its nuclear technology (Conley, 2000). Pakistan's aquisition involved a prolonged combination of Chinese and North Korean involvement during, and after, the Cold War (Bukhari & Rehman, 2011; Siddiqui, 1986; Squassoni, 2006). The traditional definition of nuclear deterrence dates back to the Cold War era. The definition is premised on the idea that possession of nuclear weapons offers stability because a nuclear war amongst adversaries is not a viable option as it would destroy both parties (Lavoy, 2009). Jervis (1984) suggests that when "the military balance is stable at the level of all out nuclear war, it will become less stable at lower level of violence" (p. 31). In the specific case of Pakistani and Indian military, we suggest their mutual ability to utilize nuclear technology has acted as a deterrence against one another and has resulted in better relations and treaties of friendship between the two nations. For example, the historic Lahore Summit and Declaration in February 1999 took place only a matter of months after nuclear tests by Pakistan. It called on India and Pakistan to ensure mutual trust, responsibility, and cooperation in avoiding a nuclear conflict, in maintaining peace and order, and in preventing future conventional and non-conventional conflicts (Chen, 2015; Thornton, 2000). The Summit provided a 'political' platform to settle unresolved issues, particularly the future of the disputed Kashmir region (Maggsi, 2013). By way of further example, the threat of nuclear war also promoted a quick end to hostilities and a de-escalation of border tensions in the 1999 'Kargil War'.

2. The Kargil War of 1999

The Kargil War took place in 1999. The weak democratic government and independent nature of Pakistani military in taking unilateral action raised alarm and distrust in India. This was particularly so given that the Pakistani military had, a year earlier in 1998, successfully built and tested its first nuclear devices. The Kargil War, as well as political rhetoric from Pakistan and India on their willingness to resort to 'all options' to defend themselves, including the possibility of using nuclear weapons, was a major concern to the international community. The concern, unlike previous conventional wars and the frequent border clashes between the two nations, was that this conflict could escalate from a limited war into a nuclear one (Branch, 2009; Joeck, 2008; Lavoy, 2009; Tellis, Fair, & Medby, 2001). Additionally, the Pakistani military timing the intrusion into nuclear India less than a year after successfully testing its own nuclear capability appeared to be an act of sabotage to destroy the Lahore Declaration and peace initiative. This was controversial, both domestically and internationally (Kapur, 2009; Lavoy, 2009; Maggsi, 2013; Panday, 2011; Thornton, 2000). Many view the Kargil War as a tarnish on earlier peace initiatives for Kashmir as well, highlighting the mistrust between India and Pakistan (Kapur, 2005; Maggsi, 2013; Raghavan, 2001).

Following a combination of international pressures, including the threat of sanctions on Pakistan for intruding onto the demarcated Kargil border, diplomacy, and internal politics, the Kargil conflict remained limited and soon subsided. The Kargil War lasted less than two months, leaving behind about 1,500 deaths on both sides. The conflict finally ended when the Pakistani military fully retreated back to the defacto border known as the 'line of control' (LOC) shared between India and Pakistan since 1972 (Branch, 2009; Leghari & Moorthy, 2015). Pakistani military argued it was their right and 'honour' to reclaim the region as part of a free 'Kashmir'. India's heavy-handed military approach and persistence were viewed as acts of 'patriotism', with the military taking all measures necessary to counteract the Pakistani invasion (Joeck, 2008; Kapur, 2009; Kronstadt, 2011; Chen, 2015).

For India, the Kargil objectives were simple: push the Pakistani forces back to the LOC and inflict as much political, economic, and military damage on Pakistan as possible. For Pakistan, perspectives on the outcome of the Kargil War are not as clear and vary between the military and the political entities. Recent remarks by the chief architect of the 1999 Pakistani military attack, General Pervez Musharraf, suggest the Pakistani army "caught India by the throat" (Pak army caught India by the throat, 2015, para. 1) during the Kargil conflict and that, by the end of the conflict, all the objectives were met (Chen, 2015; Riedel, 2002). By contrast, the current Information Minister of Pakistan, Pervaiz Rashid, recently commented that Musharaf's actions in the 1999 attack have harmed the peaceful settlement of the Kashmir question (Pervez Musharraf harmed, 2015). These different viewpoints emphasize the dichotomy and complexity of understanding Pakistani dynamics and separation of its politics and the military. The autonomous nature, financial independence, and conduct of the Pakistani and Indian army, as well as their ability to influence the political process, the media, and international relations, are not unusual and have been studied elsewhere (Aguilar et al., 2011; Akhtar, 2008; Branch, 2009; Chakraborty & Natrajan, 1995; Chen, 2015; Grimmett, 2009; Joeck 2008; Ladwig,

2008; Ricchiardi, 2012; Sanjian, 1998; Talbott, 2005). What is intriguing here is the clandestine conduct of the Pakistani military and its timing for such a high-risk mission in Kargil, which could have been catastrophic at an international level, ruined future peace talks with India, restricted or stoppped foreign military aid, and jeopardised the existence of the nation and its peoples.

3. The Kargil War and the stability–instability paradox

To date, the Kargil War is one of only a few instances where two nuclear-capable adversaries went to war head on rather than by proxy, as occured during the Cold War. It also marks the first and last major battle between the newly nuclear-capable Pakistan and India. This is not to say, however, that the Kargil War has ended all small cross-border forms of conflict in the region. For example, New Delhi accused Islamabad of supporting Kashmiri militants attacking the Indian Parliament in 2001, and later for its role in the 2008 Mumbai attack, while Pakistan blames India for promoting insurgency in Balochistan (Ladwig, 2007/2008; Panday, 2011; Raghavan, 2010). Rather, in accordance with the *stability–instability paradox*, the possession of nuclear weapons by both parties has increased small-scale tensions but limited the possibility of a full-fledged war between India and Pakistan.

The stability–instability paradox, as posited by Jervis (2009), states that a strategic stability permits, if not creates, instability. This stability makes lower levels of violence relatively safe because it is too dangerous for the violence to escalate up the nuclear ladder. As Panday (2011) observed, South Asia, the region in which India and Pakistan are located, "will see low levels of violence for some time to come, but large-scale wars will likely be very uncommon" (p. 13). Further, since the Kargil War, both nuclear nations have maintained "peace despite two major terrorist attacks and other flare-ups in their relationship" (Panday, 2011, p. 13).

In their examinations of nuclear India and Pakistan, and the intensity of the Kargil conflict, Kumar (2008), Lavoy (2009), and Raghavan (2010) agree with and accept Jervis's stability–instability paradox argument. Other commentators, while not expressly using the term stability–instability paradox, agree that nuclear deterrence has resulted in peace in South Asia. For example, Hagerty and Ganguly (2006) argue that nuclear deterrence in South Asia has prevented further global disorder. In a later study, Ganguly (2013) reported on the Pakistani military and Musharaf prior to and during the Kargil War and concluded that Musharaf and the Pakistani military's intention in Kargil was always a conventional limited war with India, and nothing beyond. Similarly, Tellis, Fair, and Medby (2001) argue that having nuclear weapons was what prevented the Kargil War between Pakistan and India from escalating further.

There are, however, other scholars who view the issue differently. For example, Sagan (2001), responding to an early article in which Waltz (1981) argued that possessing nuclear weapons has deterred major catastrophic conflicts during the Cold War, used the Kargil War and the 1960s Cuban missile crisis to disagree. Sagan instead argued that reliance on nuclear deterrence to achieve global order is not tenable. Similarly, Cheema (2004) and Knopf (2002) suggest that the Kargil War is proof that long-time adversaries will always go to war, even if one or both nations possess nuclear weapons. Further, in his unpublished doctoral thesis, Wieninger (2004) suggests that nuclear weapons in South Asia or elsewhere are risky and will never bring peace.

In his study of the nuclear deterrence during and after the Cold War and in South Asia, Kapur (2005) makes a distinction between the Cold War era and Kargil conflict. He concedes that nuclear deterrence worked during the Cold War era, but with the caveat that not all nations possessed the same technology as during the Kargil conflict. Additionally, Kapur (2005) writes that nuclear Pakistan is not stable, lacks maturity, and suffers from a "significant degree of conventional insecurity" (pp. 129–130). Recently, the Nuclear Threat Initiative's (NTI) 2014 report has placed and identified Pakistan better in overall ranking than India in Nuclear Materials Security Index. Chari (2001) writes that possession of nuclear weapons was in fact the trigger for the Pakistani military to attack Kargil. Prior to the 1990s, Chari (2001) explains, the Pakistani army realised that its militarily had fallen behind India and that in a conventional war it would be easily overrun or defeated by India's forces. Joeck (2008), meanwhile, credits India with the resolution to the Kargil War. Similarly, Ladwig (2007/2008) focuses on the 'post Kargil' period and admires the implementation of the *Cold Start doctrine* by India as a step taken by its military to contain nuclear Pakistan and maintain the status quo. At the core of this new doctrine, Ladwig (2007/2008) argues, is the creation of a rapid military force with conventional capability to undertake limited retaliatory attacks against Pakistan without crossing the nuclear threshold. It can be argued that adoption of the Cold Start doctrine by India and its intention to quickly resolve a military crisis with Pakistan is reminiscent of the previously mentioned stability–instability paradox and positively signals the maturing of contending nuclear adversaries to keep any sudden forms of conflict limited.

In contrast, other scholars suggest de-escalation of the Kargil War and prevention of a nuclear war in South Asia had little to do with nuclear deterrence. For example, Leghari and Moorthy (2015) argue that a combination of rigorous international diplomacy, and India and Pakistan both being democracies, is actually what brought a peaceful end to the Kargil War. Further, a combination of American diplomacy, political pressure, and personal input by the then US president Bill Clinton for Pakistan to withdraw also explains the conclusion of the Kargil War (Branch, 2009; Riedel, 2002; Talbott, 2005).

4. Reflecting on the post-Kargil War era: economic relations

Reflecting almost two decades after the Kargil War, it appears that Jervis's (1984, 2009) argument of the stability–instability paradox is a sound one. Since Kargil, there have been fewer border tensions and reduced military conflict between Pakistan and India. Further, specific acts of violence, including by militant or separatist groups, and other forms of disputes post-Kargil have been resolved quickly between the two nations, and such incidences have remained limited and isolated. Additionally, since the Kargil War, the socio-economic relations between the two nations have surged remarkably (see Figure 12.4). Notably, this surge has not been discussed by any of the aforementioned studies, and it is this factor in particular that we seek to draw attention to. Despite visa restrictions and banking difficulties, many borders between India and Pakistan are now open for trade purposes, and the number of items allowed to be traded bewteen the two nations has risen sharply. For example, in early 2016, almost 6,000 items were allowed to be imported into Pakistan from India. This compares with fewer than 2,000 items two to three years ago (Sharma, 2016; Trade between India and Pakistan surges, 2013).

As can be seen in Figure 12.4, bilateral trade between India and Pakistan increased sharply following the Kargil War in 1999. Trade rose from approximately $300 million in 1999

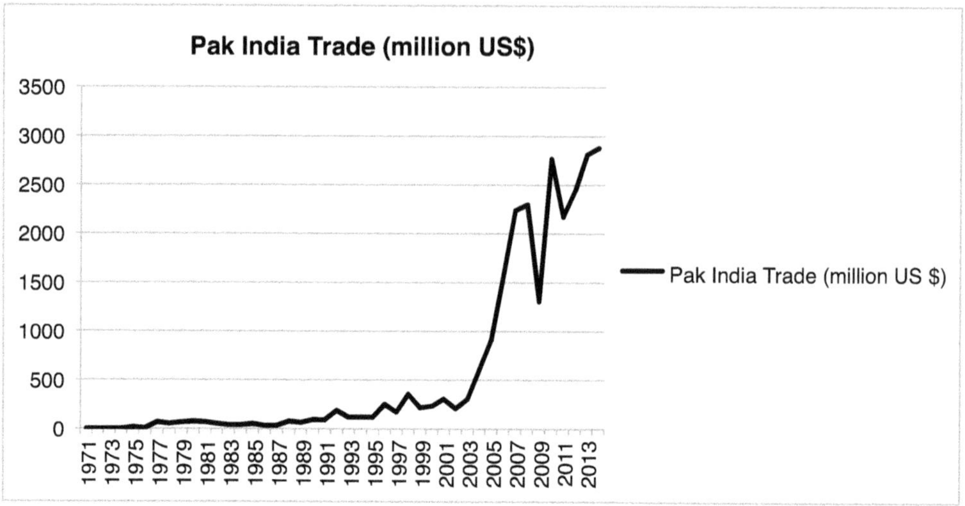

Figure 12.4 Annual trade between India and Pakistan from 1971–2012, measured in USD millions. Adapated from the Direction of Trade Statistics [Data file]. International Monetary Fund, Statistics Department, https://www.imf.org/external/pubs/cat/longres.aspx?sk=19305.0.

to about $2.3 billion five years later in 2004. The direct trade between the two nations remained steady at about $2–3 billion dollars in the 2010–2015 period (Sattar, 2015; Trade between India and Pakistan surges, 2013). Notably, informal trade between India and Pakistan through a third country or port, particularly Dubai, Singapore, and Hong Kong, is said to be much larger, with estimates ranging from $5–7 billion dollars (Nothing, 2011; Sharma, 2016; Taneja & Bimal, 2016). India and Pakistan have also made rigorous attempts to remove tariffs, ease travel restrictions, establish banks between the two nations, and stop informal or illegal trade via third party nations. Further, since 2010, both nations have taken the initiative to give each other 'Most Favoured Nation' (MFN) or 'Non Discriminatory Market Access' (NDMA) status (Nothing, 2011; Sattar, 2015).

In our view, these changes reflect extraordinary improvements in trade relations between India and Pakistan. Such improvements can be interpreted as the maturing of relations, which in turn can be attributed, at least in part, to the role of nuclear deterrence in the post-Kargil period. In this way, the post-Kargil period can act as an opportunity to test, assess, and observe the durability of the paradox and deterrence theory for South Asia.

The influence, independence, and power of the Indian and Pakistani militaries at a political level and their connection to nuclear deterrence and the Kargil War is a subject neglected by most academics. It is the military in both nations that are trusted with nuclear weapons, that have the capacity to escalate violence, intelligence, call to arms, and complex decisions such as whether to initiate a second strike in the event of a nuclear attack. There is, despite assertions to the contrary, little to support the suggestion that democracy in India and Pakistan was a motivating factor for peace during the Kargil conflict. Akhtar (2008) argues that, historically, Pakistan has been a political democracy in name only, and in reality it should be viewed as a *guided democracy*. Akhtar (2008) also argues that the "take over by the military four times in Pakistani history and the determination of leaders to stay in power as long as possible by manipulating political institutions has caused institutional decay that included the political parties" (p. 5). The important contribution of foreign military aid to the Indian and Pakistani militaries is also an area that has been discounted and not examined by any of the studies on the Kargil War. Foreign military, as has been explained, allowed the Pakistani and Indian militaries to enhance their secretive nuclear programs and conventional armies as well as expand their political clout and domestic presence.

5. Conclusion

We suggest Pakistan and India are capable of nuclear capability mainly due to the provision of military aid. In turn, the nuclear capabilities of Pakistan and India have actually brought order, rather than disorder, to India–Pakistan relations. The implementation of India's 'Cold Start doctrine' and the extraordinary rise in trade relations may suggest that, with time, a sense of responsibility, care, confidence, and maturity has developed between these two long-time adversaries. This is not to say that political, social, and other differences will disappear between the two nations. We simply suggest that a sense of tolerance, respect, and peaceful coexistence appears to be the unexpected by-product of the nuclear deterrence. The impacts of foreign military aid, Cold War rivalries, military power, 9/11, terrorism, and democracy are also other important factors that have influenced, shaped, and directed the development of Pakistan and India as individual nations and as competing neighbours. It can be argued that these influences have fueled militarisation across borders and ultimately transformed these countries into nuclear states, due to a consistent greater demand for high-tech conventional weapons along with nuclear support from external powers. However, it is difficult to speculate on the extent that foreign military aid has been used by India and Pakistan to develop their nuclear technology, conventional armies, and second strike capability. Nonetheless, the significance of military aid and the India–Pakistani rivalry are realities that have been intertwined with their creation and independence for the past seventy years and will continue to shadow their future relationship.

References

Aguilar, F., Bell, R., Black, N., Falk, S., Rogers, S., & Peritz, A. (2011). *An introduction to Pakistan's military*. Cambridge, MA: Harvard Kennedy School, Belfer Centre for Science and International Affairs. Retrieved from http://belfercenter.hks.harvard.edu/publication/21219/introduction_to_pakistans_military.html.

Aid to Pakistan by the Numbers. (n.d). Washington D.C., Centre for Global Development. Retrieved from http://www.cgdev.org/page/aid-pakistan-numbers.

Akhtar, N. (2008, July). *Pakistan's undemocratic political culture*. Paper presented at the 17th Biennial Conference of the Asian Studies Association of Australia, Melbourne. Retrieved from http://artsonline.monash.edu.au/mai/files/2012/07/nasreenakhtar.pdf.

Alavi, H. (1998). Pakistan-US military alliance. *Economic and Political Weekly*, *33*(25), 1551–1557.

Ali, M. M. (1995, December). Brown Amendment prepares way for arms delivery to Pakistan. *Washington Report on Middle East Affairs*, *38*, 119. Retrieved from http://www.wrmea.org/1995-december/brown-amendment-prepares-way-for-arms-delivery-to-pakistan.html.

Boschini, A., & Olofsgard, A. (2007). Foreign aid: An instrument for fighting communism? *International Studies Quarterly, 43*(4), 622–648.
Boutton, A., & Carter, B. D. (2013). Fair-weather allies? Terrorism and the allocation of US foreign aid. *Journal of Conflict Resolution, 58*(7), 1144–1173.
Branch, T. (2009). *The Clinton tapes, a President's secret diary, 1993–2001.* New York, NY: Simon & Schuster.
Buckley, M., & Singh, R. (Ed.). (2006). *The Bush Doctrine and the War on Terrorism: Global responses, global consequences.* London: Routledge.
Bukhari, S. S. H, & Rehman, A. (2011). Pakistan China nuclear deal and international fictions. *Berkeley Journal of Social Sciences, 1*(3), 1–14.
Chakma, B. (2005). Toward Pokhran II: Explaining India's nuclearisation process. *Modern Asian Studies, 39*(1), 189–236.
Chakraborty, A. K., & Natrajan, V. C. (1995). *Defence reporting in India: The communication gap.* Nolda: Trishul Publications.
Chari, P. R. (2001). Nuclear restraint, nuclear risk reduction, and the security–insecurity paradox in South Asia. In M. Krepon (Ed.), *Nuclear Risk Reduction in South Asia* (pp. 19–41). New York, NY: Palgrave MacMillan.
Cheema, Z. I. (2004). *Conflict, crisis and nuclear stability in South Asia, New challenges to strategic versus stability in South Asia.* Bradford: University of Bradford Press.
Chen, C. L. (2015, July 26). What you should be knowing about the Kargil War. *India Today.* Retrieved from http://indiatoday.intoday.in/.
Chenoy, A. M. (2008). India and Russia: Allies in the international political system. *South Asian Survey, 15*(1), 49–62.
Chenoy, A. M. (2010). India and Russia in the changing international setting. *International Studies, 47*(2–4), 435–47.
Chossudovsky, M. (2005). *America's War on Terrorism.* Canada: Global Research, Centre for Research in Globalization (CRG). Retrieved from http://ethosworld.com/library/Chossudovsky-America's-War-On-Terrorism-(2005).pdf.
Cohen, C. (2007). *A perilous course: US strategy and assistance to Pakistan.* A Report of the Post-Conflict Reconstruction Project.Washignton, DC: Center for Strategic and International Studies.
Cohen, S. M. (2009). Arms for the world. *Dissent,* (Fall), 69–74.
Conley, J. M. (2000). *Indo-Russian military and nuclear cooperation: Implications for US security interests* (Proliferation Series, INSS Occasional Paper 31). Colorado: USAF Institute for National Security Studies.
Curtis, L. (2009, May). China's military and security relationship with Pakistan. *The Heritage Foundation.* Retrieved from http://www.heritage.org/research/testimony/chinas-military-and-security-relationship-with-pakistan.
Dalrymple, W. (2015, June). The great divide. The violent legacy of Indian partition. *The New Yorker.* Retrieved from http://www.newyorker.com/magazine/2015/06/29/the-great-divide-books-dalrymple.
Direction of Trade Statistics [Data file]. International Monetary Fund, Statistics Department, https://www.imf.org/external/pubs/cat/longres.aspx?sk=19305.0.
Dube, O., & Naidu, S. (2010). *Bases, bullets, and vallots: The effect of U.S. military aid on political conflict in Colombia* (CGD Working Paper197). Washington, D.C.: Centre for Global Development. Retrieved from http://www.cgdev.org/content/publications/detail/1423498.
Dunning, T. (2004). Conditioning the effects of aid: Cold War politics, donor credibility, and democracy in Africa. *International Organization, 58,* 409–423.
Economic Surveys of India, 2007–2014. Retrieved from http://www.oecd.org/eco/surveys/economic-survey-india.htm.
Fair, C. C., Crane, K., Chivvis, S. C., Puri, S., & Spirtas, M. (2010). *Pakistan: Can the United States secure an insecure state?* Santa Monica, CA: RAND Project Air Force (PAF), United States Air

Force. Retrieved from http://www.rand.org/content/dam/rand/pubs/monographs/2010/RAND_MG910.pdf.

Fellowship of Reconcilliation, USA Archives. (2010). *Military assistance and human rights: Colombia, U. S. accountability, and global implications.* Retrieved from http://archives.forusa.org/content/report-military-assistance-human-rights-colombia-us-accountability-global-implications.

Fleck, K. R., & Kilby, C. (2010). Changing aid regimes? U.S. foreign aid from the Cold War to the war on terror. *Journal of Development Economics, 91*, 185–197.

Ganguly, S. (2001). *Conflict unending: India-Pakistan tensions since 1947.* New York: Columbia University Press.

Ganguly, S. (2013). Diverging Nuclear Pathways in South Asia. *The Nonproliferation Review, 20*(2), 381–387.

Geneva. The International Council on Human Rights Policy. (2011). Conflict, Media and Human Rights in South Asia: Report from a Roundtable. Retrieved from http://www.ichrp.org/files/assets/260/south_asia_roundtable_report.pdf.

Grimmett, R. F. (2009). *US arms sales to Pakistan* (Congressional Research Service Report RS22757). Retrieved from http://fas.org/sgp/crs/weapons/RS22757.pdf.

Hagerty, T. D., & Ganguly, S. (2006). *Fearful Symmetry: India-Pakistan crises in the shadow of nuclear weapons.* Washington, DC: University of Washington Press.

Holmes, A. S. (1993, November 27). Clinton Plans Change in the Law Banning Military Aid to Pakistan. *New York Times.* Retrieved from http://www.nytimes.com/.

Hussain, T. (2005). *U.S.-Pakistan Engagement: The War on Terrorism and Beyond* (special report: United States Institute of Peace). Retrieved from https://www.usip.org/sites/default/files/sr145.pdf.

Ibrahim, A. (2009). *US aid to Pakistan – US taxpayers have funded Pakistani corruption* (Discussion paper 2009–06). Cambridge, MA: Belfer Center for Science and International Affairs, John F. Kennedy School of Government, Harvard University.

India-Australia agreement complete. (2015, November 16). *World Nuclear News.* Retrieved from http://www.world-nuclear-news.org/NP-India-Australia-agreement-complete-1611157.html.

Jervis, R. (1984). *The Illogic of American Nuclear Strategy.* Ithaca, NY: Cornell University Press.

Jervis, R. (2009). Kargil, deterrence, and international relations theory. In P. R Lavoy. (Ed.), *Asymmetric warfare in South Asia the causes and consequences of the Kargil conflict* (pp. 377–397). Cambridge: Cambridge University Press.

Joeck, N. (2008). The Kargil War and nuclear deterrence. In S. Ganguly and S. P. Kapur (Eds.), *Nuclear proliferation in South Asia: Crisis behaviour and the bomb* (pp. 117–143). New York: Routledge.

Jones, G. S., Oliker, O., Chalk, P., Fair, C. C., Lal, R., & Dobbins, J. (2006). *Securing tyrants or fostering reform? U.S. internal security assistance to repressive and transitioning regimes.* Santa Monica, CA: RAND, National Security Research Division. Retrieved from http://www.rand.org/content/dam/rand/pubs/monographs/2006/RAND_MG550.pdf.

Kapur, S. P. (2005). India and Pakistan's unstable peace: Why nuclear South Asia is not like cold war Europe. *International Security, 30*(2), 127–152.

Kapur, S. P. (2009). *Dangerous deterrent: Nuclear weapons proliferation andconflict in South Asia.* Singapore: NUS Press.

Knopf, J. W. (2002). Recasting the proliferation aptimism–Pessimism debate. *Security Studies, 12*(1), 41–96.

Krishnan, A. G. (2002). Evolution of the Indian nuclear program. *Annual Review of Energy and the Environment, 27*, 369–395.

Kristensen, H. M., & Norris, R. S. (2013). Global nuclear weapons inventories: 1945–2013. *Bulletin of the Atomic Scientists, 69*(5), 75–81.

Kronstadt, K. A. (2011, October 21). *Pakistan–U.S. Relations: A Summary* (Congressional Research Service Report R41832). Retrieved from http://fpc.state.gov/documents/organization/178250.pdf.

Kumar, R. (2008). Revisiting the Kashmir insurgency, Kargil, and the Twin Peak Crisis: Was the stability/instability paradox at play? *The New England Journal of Political Science, 3*(1), 49–97.

Ladwig III, C. W. (2007/2008). A cold start for hot wars? The Indian army's new limited war Doctrine. *International Security, 32*(3), 158–190.

Ladwig III, C. W. (2008). India and military power projection: Will the land of Gandhi become a conventional great power? *Asian Survey, 50*(6), 1162–1183.

Lai, B. (2003). Examining the goals of U.S. foreign assistance in the post-Cold War period, 1991–1996. *Journal of Peace Research, 40*(1), 103–128.

Lake, D. A. (2009). *Hierarchy in international relations.* Ithaca, NY: Cornell University Press.

Lavoy, R. P. (Ed.). (2009). *Asymmetric warfare in South Asia: The causes and consequences of the Kargil conflict.* Cambridge: Cambridge University Press.

Leghari A. F., Moorthy, R. (2015). Nuclear deterrence: A complete failure at Kargil. *Research on Humanities and Social Sciences, 5*(2), 105–108.

Maggsi, A. A. (2013). *Lahore Declaration February, 1999: A major initiative for peace in South Asia. Pakistan Vision, 14*(1), 183–201.

Meernik, J., Krueger L. J., & Poe C. S. (1998). Testing models of U.S. foreign policy: Foreign aid during and after the Cold War. *Journal of Politics, 60*(1), 63–85.

Mesquita, B., & Smith, A. (2007). Foreign aid and policy concessions. *Journal of Conflict Resolution, 51*(2), 251–284.

Mueller, J. (2006). *Overblown: How politicians and the terrorism industry inflate national security threats, and why we believe them.* New York, NY: Free Press.

Nanavatty, K. R. (2009). Army media relations in sub-conventional conflict. *CLAWS Journal,* (summer), 132–146.

Nothing. (2011, February 3). Re: Pakistan imports $3b Indian goods via Dubai [Online forum comment]. Retrieved from http://defence.pk/threads/pakistan-imports-3b-indian-goods-via-dubai.91732/.

Nuclear Threat Initiative. (2014). *Nuclear Material Security Index: Building a framework for assurance, accountability, and action* (2nd ed.) Washington, D.C: Nuclear Threat Initiative.

OECD redefines foreign aid to include some military spending. (2016, February 20). *The Guardian.* Retrieved from https://www.theguardian.com/global-development/2016/feb/20/oecd-redefines-foreign-aid-to-include-some-military-spending.

O'Hanlon, M. E. (2010, March 23). Pakistan's war of choice. *New York Times.* Retrieved from http://www.nytimes.com/.

Pak army caught India by the throat during Kargil War: Musharraf. (2015, May 18). *The Indian Express.* Retrieved from http://indianexpress.com/.

Pakistan–OECD. [Data file]. Retrieved from https://data.oecd.org/searchresults/?q=pakistan.

Panday, A. (2011). The stability-instability paradox: The case of the Kargil War. *Penn State Journal of International Affairs,* (Fall), 7–14.

Paul, T. V. (2003). Chinese-Pakistani nuclear/ missile ties and balance of power politics. *The Nonproliferation Review, 10*(2), 21–29.

Pervez Musharraf harmed cause of Kashmir the most: Pakistan minister Pervaiz Rashid. (2015, July 12). *The Indian Express.* Retrieved from http://indianexpress.com/.

Raghavan, V. R. (2001). Limited war and nuclear escalation in South Asia. *The Nonproliferation Review, 8*(3), 82–98.

Raghavan, V. R. (2010, May 18). Kargil War & nuclear deterrence. *The Hindu.* Retrieved from http://www.thehindu.com/.

Rajagopalan, R. (2005). *Second Strike: Arguments about nuclear war in South Asia.* New Delhi. India: Viking.

Ricchiardi, S. (2012). *Challenges for independent news media in Pakistan* (Report to the Centre for International Media Assistance, National Endowment for Democracy). Retrieved from http://reliefweb.int/sites/reliefweb.int/files/resources/Challenges%20for%20Independent%20News%20Media%20in%20Pakistan_Ricchiardi.pdf.

Riedel, B. (2002). *American diplomacy and the 1999 Kargil Summit at Blair House.* (CASI Policy Paper Series 5). Retrieved from http://www.ciaonet.org/wps/rib02/rib02.pdf.

Rohde, D., Gall, C., Schmitt, E., & Sanger E. D. (2007, December 24). U.S. officials see waste in billions sent to Pakistan. *New York Times.* Retrieved from http://www.nytimes.com/.

Sagan, S. (2009). Nuclear instability in South Asia. In R. J. Art & K. Waltz (Eds.), *The use of force military power and international politics* (pp. 382–393). Plymouth, United Kingdom: Rowman & Littlefield Publishers.

Sanjian, G. S. (1998). Cold War imperatives and quarrelsome clients: Modelling U.S. and USSR arms transfers to India and Pakistan. *The Journal of Conflict Resolution, 42*(1), 97–127.

Sanjian, G. S. (1999). Promoting stability or instability? Arms transfers and regional rivalries, 1950–1991. *International Studies Quarterly, 43*(4), 641–670.

Sarkar, J. (2014, December 10). India and Israel's secret love affair. *The National Interest.* Retrieved from http://nationalinterest.org/blog/the-buzz/india-israels-secret-love-affair-11831.

Sattar, H. (2015, February 14). India–Pakistan: The curious case of the MFN status. *The Diplomat.* Retrieved from http://thediplomat.com/2015/02/india-pakistan-the-curious-case-of-the-mfn-status/.

Sharma, V. (2016, March 27). Traders want governments to open India-Pakistan trade routes. *The Economic Times.* Retrieved from http://articles.economictimes.indiatimes.com/2016–03–27/news/71849984_1_indian-traders-informal-trade-bilateral-trade.

Siddiqui, W. (1986). Sino-Pak nuclear accord. *Pakistan Horizon, 39*(4), 53–59.

Singh, J. (1998). Against nuclear apartheid. *Foreign Affairs, 77*(5), 41–52.

Squassoni, S. A. (2006). *Weapons of mass destruction: Trade between North Korea and Pakistan* (Congressional Research Service Report RL31900). Retrieved from http://fas.org/spp/starwars/crs/RL31900.pdf.

State Bank of Pakistan Annual Reports 1999–2015. [Data file]. Retrieved from http://www.sbp.org.pk/reports/annual/.

Stockholm International Peace Research Institute. (2015). *SIPRI arms trade database.* [Data file]. Retrieved from http://www.sipri.org/databases/armstransfers.

Sullivan L. P., Tessman, F. B., Li, X. (2011). US military aid and recipient state cooperation. *Foreign Policy Analysis, 7*, 275–294.

Talbott, S. (2005). *Engaging India: Diplomacy, democracy and the Bomb.* Washington, DC: Brookings Institution Press.

Taneja, N., & Bimal, S. (2016, January 14). India-Pakistan trade relations: Seizing golden opportunities. *The Financial Express.* Retrieved from http://www.financialexpress.com/article/fe-columnist/india-pakistan-trade-relations-seizing-golden-opportunities/193562/.

Tellis, A. J., Fair, C. C., & Medby, J. (2001). *Limited conflicts under the nuclear umbrella: Indian and Pakistani lessons from the Kargil crisis.* Santa Monica, CA: Rand Corporation. Retrieved from https://www.rand.org/.

Thornton, P. T. (2000). A long way to Lahore: India and Pakistan negotiate. In C. Baxter & C. H. Kennedy (Eds.), *Pakistan 2000* (pp. 62–78). Lanham: Lexington Books.

Tomar, R. (1980). The Indian nuclear power program: Myths and mirages. *Asian Survey, 20*(5), 517–531.

Trade between India and Pakistan surges 21% to $2.4 billion. (2013, May 14). *The Express Tribune.* Retrieved from http://tribune.com.pk/story/548768/trade-between-india-and-pakistan-surges-21-to-2–4-billion/.

U.S. Agency for International Development. (2014a). *U.S. overseas loans and grants: Obligations and loan authorizations, July 1, 1945–September 30, 2014.* Retrieved from https://explorer.usaid.gov/reports-greenbook.html.

U.S. Agency for International Development. (2014b). *U.S. overseas loans and grants: Obligations and loan authorizations, July 1, 1945–September 30, 2014.* [Data file]. Retrieved from https://www.usaid.gov/developer/greenbookapi.

Waltz, K. (1981). The spread of nuclear weapons: More may be better. *Adelphi Papers International, 21*(171), 1–32.

Wieninger A. W. (2004). *Nuclear deterrence: Neither necessary nor sufficient* (Unpublished doctoral dissertation). McGill University, Montreal, Canada. Retrieved from http://digitool.library.mcgill.ca/R/-?func=dbin-jump-full&current_base=GEN01&object_id=85030.

World Bank. (2016). *World DataBank: World development indicators.* [Data file]. Retrieved from http://databank.worldbank.org/data/reports.aspx?source=world-development-indicators&preview=on.

Wright, J., & Winters, M. (2010). The politics of effective foreign aid. *Annual Review of Political Science, 13*, 61–80.

13 The Obligation to Respect and to Ensure Respect for International Humanitarian Law

A Potential Source of Assistance in Combating Humanitarian Cross-border Challenges Created by Armed Conflict

Eve Massingham[1]

The obligation to 'respect and to ensure respect' for the provisions of international humanitarian law is a core legal obligation of every country in the world. The source of this obligation is found both in the Geneva Conventions of August 1949 and their Additional Protocols and in customary international humanitarian law. Although the obligation is well known, its interpretation has been the subject of some debate. Kalshoven (1999, p. 3) described this obligation as a 'ripening fruit' that had emerged from a 'tiny seed'. This chapter explores the continual 'ripening' of this 'fruit' with a view to further elucidating the meaning and scope of the obligation. It proposes that this obligation be viewed as relevant to notions of global order and disorder because it requires States to consider the cross-border impacts of the actions of other States. The faithful application of this obligation by States can reduce the occurrence of cross-border humanitarian issues created by armed conflict.

Mass movements of people fleeing armed conflict across international boundaries and the spill-over of conflicts into neighbouring States create significant humanitarian challenges. The body of law that regulates the conduct of armed conflict, international humanitarian law (IHL), seeks to protect those not, or no longer, taking part in the hostilities and to limit the means and methods of warfare. The Four Geneva Conventions of August 12, 1949 and their Additional Protocols of 1977 and 2005 are the central documents of IHL. These documents, in conjunction with customary IHL, establish a rule, applicable in both international and non-international armed conflict (GCI-V, AP I and AP III Article 1; Henckaerts and Doswald-Beck, 2005; Rule 139; *Nicaragua*, 1986, p. 220), whereby IHL must not only be respected but that States must also 'ensure respect' for IHL (Common art 1).

1 The author wishes to thank Professor Anthony Cassimatis, Professor Jonathan Crowe, Catherine Drummond and Annabel McConnachie for their most helpful comments on earlier drafts of this chapter. The editors Associate Professors Danielle Ireland-Piper and Leon Wolff have provided most useful editorial guidance. Any errors are those of the author alone.

The meaning and significance of this rule has been the subject of debate and evolution over the years (Boisson de Chazournes & Condorelli, 2000; Kalshoven, 1999; Focarelli, 2010; Henckaerts and Doswald-Beck, 2005). The key question in these debates is whether the intention behind Common Article 1 was to restate existing principles of international law (Focarelli, 2010) or create specific legal obligations (Meron, 1987; Sassoli, 2002). This chapter concludes that Common Article 1 imposes a specific legal obligation – both within a State and vis-à-vis third States and other actors – to respect and ensure respect for IHL. The chapter identifies that the obligation to respect IHL requires the good faith implementation of IHL by States. It argues that the scope of the obligation to 'ensure respect' will vary in each circumstance, depending on the capacity of the third State and its ability to influence the transgressor State or other actor. The Chapter outlines what actions Common Article 1 does and does not envisage and identifies what possible actions third States may take to ensure respect.

If States are able to support other States in ensuring respect for IHL then the likelihood of conflicts creating mass movements of populations, or of conflicts spreading to other States, is reduced. This chapter argues for the international community to give greater deference to the legal obligation created by Common Article 1. It proposes that Common Article 1 should be seen as a source of the obligation for States to assist other States in preventing the creation of these cross-border humanitarian issues.

1. The obligation to respect IHL

The Geneva Conventions and their Additional Protocols do more than set out the principles of IHL. They also impose specific duties on States to implement their terms, including:

- disseminating the texts of the Geneva Conventions (GC I art 47, GC II art 48, GC III art 127, GC IV art 144, AP I art 83, AP II art 19);
- protecting the Red Cross, Red Crescent, and Red Crystal emblems (GC I art 53, AP III);
- enacting legislation to provide effective penal sanction for breaches (GC I art 49, GC II art 50, GC III art 129, GC IV art 146, AP I art 86);
- ensuring that medical and religious personnel have adequate identification (such as a distinctive emblem and identity card) (GC I art 40);
- identifying potential hospital and safety zones (GC I art 23);
- identifying medical aircraft (GC I art 36, GC II art 39);
- ensuring that there is the capacity and process to create a national information bureau for prisoners of war and detained civilians (GC III art 122, GC IV art 137);
- ensuring that their armed forces comply with IHL when abroad (*Prosecutor v Dusko Tadic (Judgment)*, 1999) and that legal advisors of the armed forces are available to commanders in the field (AP I art 82); and
- reviewing new weapons technologies to check that they are compatible with the fundamental principles of IHL (AP I art 36).

States discharge the obligation to respect IHL by complying with these duties in good faith (Sandoz et al, 1987, p. 34; Dormann and Serralvo, 2015, p. 5). The obligation is one that applies in all circumstances (GCI-V, AP I and AP III art 1) – this includes in times of peace as well as war. Meeting these obligations necessitates the involvement of both government and civil society: town planners, educational institutions, hospitals, the press, Red Cross and Red Crescent societies, weapons manufacturers, civil defence, shipping and aircraft authorities, and environmental advisors (Durham, 2009). The implementing State needs significant expertise, resources, and commitment to meet these obligations, and they may request assistance from the international community (Durham, 2009) – including that which is required to give effect to Common Article 1. As such, while it is not necessarily a simple task for States to implement all of the aspects required to respect IHL, the parameters of the obligation are clearly discernible from the text of IHL itself. States need to direct greater efforts towards implementation of these obligations.

2. The obligation to ensure respect for IHL

The obligation to 'ensure respect' for IHL is directed to the actions States must take to help other States respect IHL (Sassoli, 2002, p. 421). In a recent article ICRC Chief Legal Officer Knut Dormann and his colleague Jose Serralvo (2015, p. 723) conclude that Common Article 1 goes beyond an entitlement for third States to take steps to ensure respect for IHL. It establishes not only a right to take action but also an international legal obligation to do so.

The texts of the Geneva Conventions do not provide guidance as to the scope of the obligation to ensure respect. What, then, must States do to discharge this obligation? The principles of treaty interpretation in the *Vienna Convention of the Law of Treaties* (VCLT) can be used to answer this question. This part looks at the subsequent practice in the application of the treaty (pursuant to Article 31(3)(b) VCLT), other relevant rules of international law applicable in the relations between the parties (pursuant to Article 31(3)(c) VCLT), and the drafting history of Common Article 1 (pursuant to Article 31(4) and Article 32 VCLT).

2.1. *Subsequent practice in the application of the treaty*

Most references to Common Article 1 and the phrase 'respect and ensure respect for IHL' are in the context of calls to warring parties to comply with their obligations to respect the principles of IHL (Henckaerts and Doswald-Beck, 2005). Security Council Resolutions often 'appeal to both parties strictly to abide by applicable rules of [IHL]' or appeal to 'leaders' to ensure their group or faction complies with IHL (Henckaerts and Doswald-Beck, 2005; Dormann and Serralvo, 2015). The Council of Europe (1992) has also adopted the approach of inviting member States to 'appeal' to warring parties to respect the Geneva Conventions. At the Teheran Conference on Human Rights in 1968, attended by 84 States, the notion of third States having responsibilities to ensure respect for the Conventions received support. Resolution XXIII of the Teheran Conference held that:

> States parties to the Red Cross Geneva Conventions sometimes fail to appreciate their responsibility to take steps to ensure the respect of these humanitarian rules in all circumstances by other States, even if they are not themselves directly involved in armed conflict.

Kessler (2001, p. 505) argues that, following the International Conference for the Protection of War Victims in 1993, 'no State can deny any longer the existence of a positive obligation under Common Article 1 to ensure that the Conventions are respected'. The Final

Declaration of the Conference specifically referenced Common Article 1 and included an undertaking by the participants to act in cooperation with the UN and in conformity with the UN Charter to ensure full compliance with international humanitarian law in the event of genocide and other serious violations of this law.

UN General Assembly Resolution on the Decade of International Law in 1993 reminded 'all States of their responsibility to respect and ensure respect for IHL in order to protect the victims of war'. The UN Sub-Commission on Human Rights (2000) adopted a resolution on the role of universal or extraterritorial competence in preventive action against impunity which specifically referenced Common Article 1. The Declaration of the Conference of High Contracting Parties to the Fourth Geneva Convention (2001) declared: 'The participating High Contracting Parties welcome and encourage initiatives by States Parties, both individually and collectively, according to art. 1 of the Convention and aimed at ensuring respect'. A Declaration made at the African Parliamentary Conference on International Humanitarian Law for the Protection of Civilians during Armed Conflict (2002) articulated the 'determination to do everything in our power in order that States and all parties to armed conflicts honour their duties as regard International Humanitarian Law'. SC Resolution 1502 of 2003 condemning violence against UN and humanitarian personnel in conflict zones reads: '[r]eiterating its primary responsibility for the maintenance of international peace and security and, in this context, the need to promote and ensure respect for the principles and rules of international humanitarian law'.

2.2. Other relevant rules of international law applicable in the relations between the parties

Pursuant to Article 31(3)(c) of the *Vienna Convention on the Law of Treaties*, other relevant rules of international law applicable in the relations between the parties may be considered in interpreting Common Article 1. Certain key international obligations (known as obligations *erga omnes*) are so important that their protection is the concern of all States (*Barcelona Traction* case (1970, [33]). These key international obligations include 'a substantial part of the rules of humanitarian character applicable in armed conflict' (Gasser, 1993, pp. 22–23). Meron (1987) notes that the *erga omnes* character of much of IHL implies that third States have not only the right to make appropriate representations, urging respect for these norms to States allegedly involved in violating them, but also a duty not to encourage others to violate the norms, and, perhaps, even to discourage others from violating them. As such it is clear that the concept of *erga omnes* supports a third State interpretation of 'ensure respect' in Common Article 1.

The ICJ has made two clear pronouncements on Common Article 1. Encouraging violations of IHL and the provision of advice on how to violate IHL have been held by the ICJ in *Military and Paramilitary Activities in and against Nicaragua* (1986, para. 220) to constitute a breach of the Common Article 1 obligation to ensure respect for IHL. In the *Wall Advisory Opinion* (*Legal Consequences of the Construction of a Wall in the Occupied Palestinian Territory*, 2004, para. 158) the ICJ held 'that every State party to [the Geneva Conventions], whether or not it is a party to a specific conflict, is under an obligation to ensure that the requirements of the instruments in question are complied with'. The ICJ has also implied that customary international law obligations are not limited by jurisdiction (*Application of the Convention on the Prevention and Punishment of the Crime of Genocide (Bosnia and Herzegovina v. Serbia and Montenegro) (Preliminary objections)* [1996] ICJ Rep [31].

The other relevant rule of international law is the principle of due diligence (Barnidge, 2006; Tzevelekos, 2013; Max Plank Encyclopedia, 2010). The principle requires a State to 'demonstrate that it did everything that was possible to fight wrongfulness' and to 'suitably use the pertinent means at their disposal' (Tzevelekos, 2013, p. 73). The application of this principle is different depending on the nature of the primary rule (Pisillo-Mazzeschi, 1992; Barnidge, 2006) to which the principle is being applied and the capacity of the State with the due diligence obligation. As Tzevelekos (2013, p. 73) points out, 'we are only now starting to understand how this principle can find application in a wide range of areas of international law'. Barnidge (2006, p. 121) observes that the questions of 'how, whether, and with what breadth the due diligence principle is applied, however, remain one[s] of political will'. The due diligence principle has been particularly adopted by certain fields of international law including international environmental law and cultural property law and with regard to the duty to safeguard the security of aliens.

The focus of the work of Pisillo-Mazzeschi (1992, p. 45) is distinguishing between the concepts of obligations of *conduct* (what the state does) and obligations of *result* (what actually eventuates from the conduct). He concludes, 'it is logical that international law may only impose on the State the obligation "to make every effort" to reach [a] result; that is, only an obligation of diligent conduct'. In further unpacking the scope of the rule, Pisillo-Mazzeschi (1992, p. 45) contends that the standard to which due diligence is required is 'the average general standard of behaviour by the "civilized" or "well-organized" State'.

Hessbruegge (2004, p. 306) urges caution when applying due diligence to weak States. He argues that '[t]he law cannot indefinitely set off the relocation of functions to the non-state sector by burdening weak States with increased duties of due diligence and an ever-increasing ambit of state responsibility'. Although his discussion was in the context of preventing terrorism, his warning also applies to Common Article 1. The European Court of Human Rights has also held that due diligence obligations must not impose an 'impossible or disproportionate burden on the authorities' (*Case of Osman v The United Kingdom*, 1998, para. 116).

This raises the issue of what a State must do to meet its due diligence obligations under Common Article 1. The ICRC, in its discussion of Common Article 1, has adopted the approach of Pisillo-Mazzeschi to construing the 'duty of diligent conduct' as part of broader international obligations (Dormann and Serralvo, 2015). Dormann and Serralvo (2015) specifically consider the scope of the due diligence obligation in Common Article 1, submitting that it depends on the specifics of the case. States are required to do what is reasonable to ensure respect. The 'capacity to influence' and the 'seriousness of the potential violation' are two key considerations in testing reasonableness (Dormann and Serralvo, 2015, p. 725). For example, a small, non-influential State, removed from the conflict region, would have a due diligence obligation to ensure respect that would include supporting UN General Assembly resolutions calling on parties to respect IHL. By contrast, 'a State with close political, economic and/or military ties (for example, through equipping and training of armed forces or joint planning of operations) to one of the belligerents has a stronger obligation to ensure respect for IHL by its ally' (Dormann and Serravlo, 2015, p. 724).

The ICJ decision in the *2007 Genocide Case* (*Case concerning application of the Convention on the prevention and punishment of the crime of genocide (Bosnia and Herzegovina v Serbia and Montenegro)*, para. 430) provides guidance on how States must 'make every effort'. The Court held that the relevant due diligence standard depends on 'the capacity to influence effectively the action of persons likely to commit, or already committing, genocide'. Capacity, in turn, depends on factors including 'geographical distance', 'strength of political [and other] links', and 'legal position'. The parameters of due diligence, therefore, are case-specific (Barnidge, 2006, p. 188).

2.3. *Drafting history*

Article 31 of the VCLT provides that '[a] special meaning shall be given to a term if it is established that the parties so intended'. The intended meaning of Common Article 1 was not clearly articulated by the Diplomatic Conference of 1949. Kalshoven (1999, p. 27) observes 'how conspicuously little time and energy the Diplomatic Conference of 1949 spent on draft Article 1'. As such it is not possible to argue that a special meaning was intended by the parties in respect of this provision.

However, Article 32 of the VCLT entitles recourse to the drafting history of a treaty provision to clarify its interpretation. Subsequent practice in the application of Common Article 1 shows that its meaning today is 'unanimously understood as referring to violations by other States' (Sassoli, 2002, p. 421). The drafting history of Common Article 1, too, demonstrates that, by the time of the 1977 Additional Protocols, it was accepted that this obligation was one which concerned third States.

Common Article 1's predecessor – Article 25 of the Convention for the Amelioration of the Condition of the Wounded and Sick in Armies in the Field of 27 July 1929 and Article 82 of the Convention relative to the Treatment of Prisoners of War of 27 July 1929 – provided that the Conventions were to 'be respected by the High Contracting Parties in all circumstances'. Shortly before the April 1947 conference of government experts meetings in anticipation of the Diplomatic Conference of Geneva of 1949, ICRC staff lawyer Claude Pilloud authored an internal note proposing (apparently for the first time) that each of the four Conventions include the requirement of respect and ensuring respect for the Conventions in all circumstances (Final Record of the Diplomatic Conference, 1949). Draft Common Article 1 was adopted without modification following only short consideration by the Diplomatic Conference (9th meeting, 25 May 1949). Maresca, representing Italy, made a prescient comment raising concern over the lack of clarity of 'undertake to ensure respect' – noting this was either a redundant provision 'or introduced a new concept into international law' (7th meeting, 17 May 1949 and 9th meeting, 25 May 1949). This, however, was not further discussed.

The original Commentaries to the Geneva Conventions were published in the 1950s and 1960s by the ICRC. The Commentary on Common Article 1 (Pictet, 1952, p. 26) clearly introduces the notion that third States may and should play a role in the promotion of respect for the Convention by asserting that: 'in the event of a Power failing to fulfil its obligations, the other Contracting Parties (neutral, allied or enemy) may, and should, endeavour to bring it back to an attitude of respect for the Convention'. The original approach to AP I, in drafts prepared by the ICRC, was that it was not necessary to reaffirm the general principles common to the Geneva Conventions in AP I. Rather, AP I would be supplementary to the Geneva Conventions. Common Article 1, however, became the focus of discussions relating to the nature of armed conflict – specifically the plan to extend the scope of Additional Protocol to cover wars of national liberation. The end result was that this issue was dealt with in Article 2, but that Common Article 1 would indeed be included in AP I. Commentary on why this occurred is, again, sparse and uninformative (Focarelli, 2010; Kalshoven, 1999). Additional Protocol II of the Conventions did not include a corollary of Common Article 1. This is telling: if Common Article 1 was entirely about ensuring respect within a States' boundaries, then logically it should be included in Additional Protocol II.

The Commentary to AP I equates the good faith obligation in Article 26 of the VCLT with the obligation to respect. The 'ensure respect' obligation was said to require States to 'endeavour to bring [a State in breach of the Conventions] back to an attitude of respect for the Convention' (Sandoz et al, 1987, pp. 35–36). Article 7 and 89 of AP I provided for mechanisms to facilitate this inter-State support (Sandoz et al, 1987).

Additional evidence that no State had any concerns about the ICRC interpretation comes almost three decades later when the international community adopted AP III with the same wording in Article 1(1) as the Conventions and AP I. The Commentaries to AP III state of Common Article 1 that it is taken *verbatim* from the earlier Conventions and 'no specific comments are called for in the context' of the AP III (ICRC, 2007).

The ICRC is currently undergoing a project to update the Commentaries on the Geneva Conventions and their Additional Protocols. The ICRC update aims to 'reflect the experience gained in applying the Conventions and Protocols during the last few decades' (Henckaerts, 2012). The ICRC specifically identified the commentary on Common Article 1 as needing updating because '[t]he international community's understanding of the obligation . . . has significantly expanded since the 1950s' (Henckaerts, 2012). The first volume of the new Commentary was released in March 2016 and includes the ICRC's current thinking on Common Article 1. The institutional view is reflective of the views of Dormann and Serralvo (2015), referenced throughout this chapter.

3. Actions encapsulated (and not encapsulated) by the Common Article 1 ensure respect obligation

Clearly, States are not obliged to take *all possible and imaginable measures* to induce transgressor States, or other actors, to comply (Focarelli, 2010, p. 167). This is implausible and inconsistent with State practice. To read Common Article 1 this way would result in 193 breaches of Common Article 1 every time the Conventions are breached (Focarelli, 2010). Moreover, Common Article 1 does not render lawful otherwise unlawful action, such as unilateral military action to 'ensure respect' for the Conventions (Gasser, 1993; Kalshoven, 1999; Kessler, 2001; Palwankar, 1994). This would be in breach of the prohibition on the use of force in Article 2(4) of the United Nations Charter.

However, a State which is in conflict cannot legitimately accuse a third State of acting unlawfully in interfering (through lawful measures) to ensure respect for IHL (Benvenuti, 1989–90). The International Criminal Tribunal for Former Yugoslavia has held that armed conflict constitutes a threat to international peace and security and, therefore, actions relating to armed conflict (including non-international armed conflict) are not the internal affairs of a State (*Prosecutor v. Dusko Tadic (Judgment)*, 1999). Inaction by third States, in response to such threats to international peace and security, are neither the intention nor the custom in today's world. Third State responsibility is increasingly a clear part of the modern day legal, if not always political, landscape.

A number of authors have considered the measures a State can take to ensure that a third State respects the Geneva Conventions – both in times of peace and conflict (Gasser, 1993; Kalshoven, 1999; Palwankar, 1994; Kessler, 2001). In peace time, States' actions include:

- providing legal advisors to assist in developing or adapting national legislation and penal codes for effective implementation of IHL;
- training legal advisors within the armed forces;
- teaching IHL as part of military co-operation;

- holding regional and international seminars with the participation of States to discuss the issues; and
- helping set up regional databanks on various aspects related to national measures and their implementation (Palwankar, 1994; Gasser, 1993).

The ICRC Customary Law Study (Henckaerts and Doswald-Beck, 2005, p. 512) concludes that state practice 'shows an overwhelming use of (i) diplomatic protest and (ii) collective measures through which States exert their influence, to the degree possible, to try and stop violations of [IHL]'.

States can also help to 'ensure respect' by offering humanitarian assistance. The Geneva Conventions require States in receipt of such assistance to facilitate relief operations (Kessler, 2001; GC IV art 23). Geneva Convention IV requires States to 'allow the free passage' of relief consignments, and 'agree to relief schemes . . . and . . . facilitate them' (GC I art 23, GC II art 59(3), GC III art 61(3), GC IV arts 70(2), 70(3)). Article 69 of AP I and Article 18 of AP II add to these provisions, although State consent for the relief activities is required where civilians are suffering undue hardship in situations of non-international armed conflict (Schindler, 1994). For example, Security Council Resolution 668 (1990) and General Assembly Resolution 45/170 (1990) condemned the refusal of humanitarian assistance by Iraq, from both humanitarian organisations and, in the case of the General Assembly resolution, from the Government of Kuwait. Article 64 of AP I, which deals with civilian civil defence organisations of neutral or other States, requires that the Parties to the conflict receiving assistance under this provision 'should facilitate international cooperation'.

Some provisions of the Conventions are themselves mechanisms for ensuring respect for IHL. Examples include Article 7 of AP I which provides for meetings to be convened addressing concerns about the application of the Protocol, Article 89 AP I pertaining to joint or individual action in cooperation with the UN in situations of serious violations of the Conventions, and Article 90 AP I pertaining to the establishment of an International Fact Finding Commission.

There is no checklist for States in implementing Common Article 1. States need to exercise both good faith and due diligence. Appropriate actions depend on the relevant circumstances. States must also ensure that they 'clearly explain, convincingly justif[y] and properly carr[y] out [any] action [so it] is not misunderstood as improper interference in the internal affairs of a sovereign State' (Gasser, 1993, p. 27).

The ICRC sees a broad role for Common Article 1. In his 60th Anniversary of the Geneva Conventions address Dr Jakob Kellenberger (2009), then President of the ICRC, observed

> it has always been the view of the ICRC that all States have an obligation not only to respect, but also to ensure respect for international humanitarian law, as stated in common Article 1 of the Geneva Conventions. One way of doing so is through diplomatic means, whether through quiet diplomacy or in the intergovernmental bodies just mentioned. The ICRC sees great potential in making common Article 1 more operational and there are encouraging developments in this regard . . .

Humanity remains a long way from achieving universal respect for the Geneva Conventions. The ongoing suffering in much of the world affected by armed conflict makes this very evident. Clearly the challenge is convincing States to take their 'ensure respect' obligations seriously. The existence of a legal obligation does not always result in action. Many of the principles of IHL have long been sold to military personnel on the basis that compliance is in their self-interest. Military personnel comply with IHL so as to benefit from combatant privilege (immunity from criminal sanctions from killing the enemy, and prisoner of war status). With the mass movement of populations and the spillover of armed conflicts into neighbouring States alarming the international community, now is a good time for the promotion of Common Article 1 in the self-interest of States.

4. Conclusion

This chapter has argued that 'respect and ensure respect for IHL' is not mere exhortation. It is a legal obligation (Cassese, 2005; Dormann and Serralvo, 2015). The scope of this obligation can be found in the provisions of the Geneva Conventions themselves and in the capacity of third States to ensure respect by other States or other actors. This is evident from an analysis of State practice, a discussion of comparable international legal developments, and an evaluation of the drafting history of the provision.

The obligation is not for States to take any *set* measures or *specific* steps in relation to violations of the Geneva Conventions by other States or other actors. Rather, it is to take those measures required by due diligence and that are within their capacity and influence. Common Article 1 provides a basis for a range of actions, both domestically and vis-à-vis other States, to achieve this. The obligation to ensure respect for the Geneva Conventions can therefore be seen as providing a source of obligation for States to assist others in achieving compliance with the Geneva Conventions. In doing so, Common Article 1 can help to combat humanitarian cross-border challenges such as the mass movement of populations and the spillover of armed conflict into neighbouring States.

Common Article 1 provides scope for third States to play a role as a force for good in the international community to prevent violations of IHL. Although the 'indeterminacy' of Common Article 1 cannot be overlooked just by giving the concept pre-eminent status (Focarelli, 2010, p. 170), the potential power of Common Article 1 as the source of an obligation for States to improve humanitarian outcomes is clear. States that engage in activities that are consistent with the notion of respecting and ensuring respect for the Geneva Conventions have an opportunity to prevent breaches of IHL and to prevent the impacts of armed conflict spreading throughout the world, including to their part of the world.

References

Treaties

Geneva Convention for the Amelioration of the Condition of the Wounded and Sick in Armed Forces in the Field, 12 August 1949, 75 UNTS 31 (entered into force 21 October 1950).

Geneva Convention for the Amelioration of the Condition of Wounded, Sick and Shipwrecked Members of Armed Forces at Sea, 12 August 1949, 75 UNTS 85 (entered into force 21 October 1950).

Geneva Convention relative to the Protection of Civilian Persons in Time of War, 12 August 1949, 75 UNTS 287 (entered into force 21 October 1950).

Geneva Convention relative to the Treatment of Prisoners of War, 12 August 1949, 75 UNTS 135 (entered into force 21 October 1950).

Protocol Additional to the Geneva Conventions of 12 August 1949, and relating to the Protection of Victims of International Armed Conflicts, 8 June 1977, 1125 UNTS 3 (entered into force 7 December 1978).

Protocol Additional to the Geneva Conventions of 12 August 1949, and relating to the Protection of Victims of Non-International Armed Conflicts, 8 June 1977, 1125 UNTS 609 (entered into force 7 December 1979).

Protocol additional to the Geneva Conventions of 12 August 1949, and relating to the Adoption of an Additional Distinctive Emblem, 8 December 2005, 2404 UNTS 261 (entered into force 14 January 2007).

Vienna Convention on the Law of Treaties, opened for signature 23 May 1969, 8 ILM 679 (entered into force 27 January 1980).

Cases

Application of the Convention on the Prevention and Punishment of the Crime of Genocide (Bosnia and Herzegovina v Serbia and Montenegro) (Preliminary objections) [1996] ICJ Rep, p 595.

Barcelona Traction, Light and Power Company, Limited (Belgium v Spain) (Second Phase, Judgment) [1970] ICJ Rep.

Case concerning application of the Convention on the prevention and punishment of the crime of genocide (Bosnia and Herzegovina v Serbia and Montenegro) (Judgement) [2007] ICJ Rep, p. 243.

Case of Osman v The United Kingdom [1998] Eur Court HR.

Legal Consequences of the Construction of a Wall in the Occupied Palestinian Territory (Advisory Opinion) [2004] ICJ Rep, p. 136.

Military and Paramilitary Activities in and against Nicaragua (Nicaragua v. United States of America), Merits, (Judgment) [1986] ICJ Rep, p. 14.

Prosecutor v Dusko Tadic (Judgment) (ICTY, Appeals Chamber, Case No. IT-94-1, 15 July 1999).

Documents

Council of Europe, Parliamentary Assembly Res 984 (30 June 1992).

Declaration made at the African Parliamentary Conference on International Humanitarian Law for the Protection of Civilians during Armed Conflict, Held in Niger (18-20 February 2002).

Declaration of the Conference of High Contracting Parties to the Fourth Geneva Convention, Held at Geneva (5 December 2001).

Final Declaration of the International Conference for the Protection of Victims of War, Geneva (30 August – 1 September 1993).

Final Record of the Diplomatic Conference convened by the Swiss Federal Council for the Establishment of the International Conventions for the Protection of War Victims and Held at Geneva (21 April – 12 August 1949).

GA Res 45/170 (18 December 1990).

International Conference on Human Rights, Held in Teheran, Iran from (22 April – 13 May 1968).

SC Res 1502, UN SCOR, 4814th mtg, UN Doc S/RES/1502 (26 August 2003).

SC Res 681, UN SCOR, 2970th mtg, UN Doc S/RES/681 (20 December 1990).

SC Res 668, UN SCOR, 2941th mtg, UN Doc S/RES/668 (20 September 1990).

UN Human Rights Committee. General Comment No. 31: Nature of the General Legal Obligation Imposed on States Parties to the Covenant (29 March 2004).

Secondary Sources

Barnidge, R. (2006). The due diligence principle under international law. *International Community Law Review, 8,* 81–121.

Benvenuti, P. (1989–90). Ensuring observance of international humanitarian law: Function, extent and limits of the obligations of third states to ensure respect for IHL. *Yearbook of International Law, 30,* 27–55.

Boisson de Chazournes, L., & Condorelli, L. (2000). Common Article 1 of the Geneva Conventions revisited: Protecting collective interests. *International Review of the Red Cross, 837,* 67–86.

Cassese, A. (2005). *International law* (10th ed). Oxford University Press.

Dormann, K., & Serralvo, J. (2015). Common Article 1 to the Geneva Conventions and the obligation to prevent international humanitarian law violations. *International Review of the Red Cross, 96*(895/896), 707–736.

Durham, H. (2009). From paper to practice: The role of treaty ratification post conflict. In B. Bowden, H. Charlesworth and J. Farrall (Eds.), *The role of international law in rebuilding societies after conflict* (pp. 177–197). Cambridge: Cambridge University Press.

Focarelli, C. (2010). Common Article 1 of the 1949 Geneva Conventions: A soap bubble?. *The European Journal of International Law, 21*(1), 125–171.

Gasser, H.P. (1993). Chapter 2 ensuring respect for the Geneva Conventions and Protocols: The role of third states and the United Nations. In H. Fox and M. Meyer (Eds.). *Effecting compliance: armed conflict and the new law* (Vol 2) (pp. 15–49). London: British Institute of International and Comparative Law.

Henckaerts, J.M. (2012). Bringing the commentaries on the Geneva Conventions and their Additional Protocols into the 21st Century. *International Review of the Red Cross, 94*(888), 1551–1555.

Henckaerts, J.M., & Doswald-Beck, L. (Eds.) (2005). *Customary international humanitarian law* (Vol. 1) Cambridge: Cambridge University Press.

Hessbruegge, J.H. (2004). The Historical development of the doctrines of attribution and due diligence in international law. *New York University Journal of International Law and Politics, 36,* 265–306.

ICRC, Commentary on Protocol additional to the Geneva Conventions of 12 August 1949, and relating to the Adoption of an Additional Distinctive Emblem (Protocol III), 8 December 2005 (ICRC, 2007).

International Commission on Intervention and State Sovereignty, *The responsibility to protect report* (International Development Research Centre, Canada, 2001).

Kalshoven, F. (1999). The undertaking to respect and ensure respect in all circumstances: From tiny seed to ripening fruit. *Yearbook of International Humanitarian Law 2* (3–4), 3–61.

Kellenberger, J. (2009, September 26). *Ensuring respect for international humanitarian law in a changing environment and the role of the United Nations,* speech delivered at Ministerial Working Session, Geneva. Retrieved from: https://www.icrc.org/eng/resources/documents/statement/geneva-conventions-statement-260909.htm/.

Kessler, B. (2001). The duty to 'ensure respect' under Common Article 1 of the Geneva Conventions: Its implications on international and non-international armed conflicts. *German Yearbook of International Law, 44,* 498–516.

Meron, T. (1987). The Geneva Conventions as customary law. *American Journal of International Law, 81(2),* 348–370.

Oxford University Press, *Max Planck Encyclopaedia of Public International Law* (at February 2010) 'Due Diligence'. Retrieved from: http://opil.ouplaw.com/view/10.1093/law:epil/9780199231690/law-9780199231690-e1034.

Palwankar, U. (1994). Measures available to states for fulfilling their obligation to ensure respect for international humanitarian law. *International Review of the Red Cross, 298,* 9–26.

Pictet, J. (1952). Commentary on the Geneva Conventions of 12 August 1949. Geneva: International Committee for the Red Cross.
Pisillo-Mazzeschi, R. (1992). The due diligence rule and the nature of the international responsibility of States. *German Yearbook of International Law, 35*, 9–51.
Sandoz, Y., Swinarski, C., & Zimmerman, B. (Eds.). (1987). *Commentary on the Additional Protocols of 8 June 1977 to the Geneva Conventions of 12 August 1949.* Geneva: International Committee of the Red Cross.
Sassoli, M. (2002). State responsibility for violations of international humanitarian law. *International Review of the Red Cross, 846*, 401–434.
Schindler, D. (1994). Humanitarian assistance, humanitarian interference and international law. In Macdonald, R.(Ed.), *Essays in honour of Wang Tieya* (pp. 690–701). Dordrecht: Martinus Nijhoff Publishers.
Tzevelekos, V.P. (2013). Revisiting the humanisation of international law: Limits and potential. *Erasmus Law Review, 6*(1), 62–76.

14 International Criminal Law as a Regulatory Tool

Jodie O'Leary

International criminal law has become the preferred regulatory tool for addressing certain organized violent behaviour. However, the growth of international criminal law has not improved global order. Indeed, the opposite is the case with recent increases in the levels of organized violence. This Chapter examines the crimes and modes of participation justiciable before judicial mechanisms used to respond to three conflicts: East Timor, Chad and the former Yugoslavia. In addition to those judicial mechanisms, the Chapter considers the International Criminal Court. The Chapter argues that, although the International Criminal Court has played an important role in advancing specificity of standards, the polycentric nature of international criminal law and the resulting regulatory pluralism creates incoherence in overall regulatory design. The Chapter further contends that to improve global order international criminal law would benefit from adding further principle-based standards to the current rules that address organized violent behaviour.

In 2014, Kofi Annan (2014) lamented that "instead of the new world order, we have growing disorder . . . Whether it is in peace and security, climate change, international justice or global trade, there has been little progress". This Chapter argues that Annan's observations on the lack of progress towards global order also apply to international criminal law. To advance this claim, this Chapter equates global order with stability and peace throughout the world – a world free of armed conflict, in which people live free from serious human rights abuses. Global disorder, by contrast, is marked by an increase in violence, conflict, death and displacement. Further, although order is often associated with law (and disorder with lawlessness), the presence of law does not necessarily lead to order. International criminal law was introduced with a view to minimising conflict and human rights abuses; it does not suffer from an absence of "law". However, there is no evidence linking the development of international criminal law to an improvement in global order.

Is it reasonable, then, to have 'faith' in international criminal law as a means of increasing global order? To contextualise this question, this Chapter first discusses the extent to which organized conflict is currently a characteristic of the world in which we live and, therefore, evidence of 'disorder'. Second, to explore the theoretical nexus between international criminal law and global order, the Chapter submits that international criminal law should be considered a means of regulation. This justifies the Chapter drawing on regulatory theory to explain and evaluate the role international criminal law plays in global order. Third, the Chapter explores three criteria by which regulatory effectiveness could be judged – impact, compliance and transparency – and submits that, in the case of international criminal law, transparency is the most apposite. Fourth, the Chapter then applies the criteria of transparency to:

- international criminal law generally;
- the specific crimes of genocide, torture, crimes against humanity, war crimes and aggression; and
- the modes of participation in international crimes.

Three international conflicts serve as case studies for this analysis: East Timor (1975–1999), Chad (1982–1990) and the former Yugoslavia (1991–). In addition to applying the principles of transparency to the law and practice of courts created or used to respond to these conflicts, this part also considers the International Criminal Court (ICC) whose jurisdiction post-dates these conflicts. This is because the ICC was created, in part, to address the limitations of these courts.

The Chapter concludes that international criminal law, as a diffused body of jurisprudence and practice, *has* succeeded in transmitting clear normative standards. However, like the cha-cha, it has taken steps forward, back and to the side. This legal dance has meant that progress in eradicating global violence has been slow. Like Cassimatis in Chapter 2, this Chapter sees reason for both hope – and despair – in the future relationship between international criminal law and global order.

1. Context: international crime and global disorder

The prevalence of armed conflict around the globe suggests that we live in a current world 'disorder'. So much is evident from empirical data on State-based armed conflict compiled by the Uppsula Conflict Data Program (UCDP) (Melander, 2015), a world-renowned provider of data on organized violence world-wide. (In addition to State-based conflict, the UCDP also reports on conflict between non-State actors and one-sided killing of civilians.) 'State-based armed conflict' includes any "contested incompatibility that concerns government and/or territory where the use of armed force between two parties, of which at least one is the government of a State, results in at least 25 battle-related deaths in one calendar year" (*Definitions*, n.d). State-based armed conflict can be interstate (between two or more countries), intrastate (occurring within State borders), internationalized (conflicts in which States contributed troops to one or both sides of a conflict) or extra-State (conflict between a State and a non-State group outside its own territory).

Over the last twenty years, fatalities from organized violence peaked in 2014. Approximately 126,000 people were killed (Melander, 2015, p. 1).[1] The upturn in overall levels of organized violence has been particularly dramatic over the last five years (Melander, 2015). Over the past ten years, purely State-based conflicts have evinced an "uneven, yet clearly visible, upward trend in armed conflicts" with a "growing number of internationalized armed conflicts" (Pettersson & Wallensteen, 2015, p. 536). The figures become even more horrific if we count those who died as an indirect consequence of armed conflict as well as those who were injured or displaced among the victims of organized violence (see, Bassiouni, 2010, p. 11).

1 However, twenty years ago, the Rwandan Genocide caused an even larger number of fatalities.

The three regions of the world that have suffered the highest levels of organized violence in the past 25 years are the Middle East, Africa and Central and South Asia. More recently, with the developments in Syria and Iraq, the Middle East has emerged as the most violent region (see Table 14.1). Although Africa has averaged the highest levels of violence over the last twenty-five years, it has witnessed significant declines recently (Melander, 2015, 1, pp. 4–7). Yet, taken as a whole, the UCDP data, both in terms of raw numbers and geographical distribution, make it clear that disorder is widespread across the world.

2. Theory: international criminal law as regulation

2.1 The rise of international criminal law

International criminal law refers to the body of law concerned with the prosecution of individuals for international crimes, whether in international, hybrid, foreign or domestic courts.

Traditionally, responsibility for, and attribution of, acts unlawful under international law was confined to States. This position has shifted lately as part of what Sikkink (2011) has coined "the justice cascade". The justice cascade includes the rise of international criminal law. The early 1990s saw the institution of *ad hoc* tribunals for the former Yugoslavia and Rwanda and a proposal for an international criminal court, culminating in the entry into force of the *Rome Statute of the International Criminal Court* (*Rome Statute*) in 2002. On 3 March 2016, with the deposit of its instrument of accession, El Salvador became the 124th State Party to the *Rome Statute.* As such, in early 2016, 65 per cent of the States that were either member States or observer States of the United Nations were also States Party to the *Rome Statute.*

According to Teitel (2011, p. 104), international criminal justice offers "a promising basis for the globalizing order". International criminal law exemplifies what she perceives as a move away from the original ordering framework of international law based on State sovereignty to an alternative model in which individuals are placed at the centre (Teitel, 2011, p. 104). Individuals are not only the subject of the protective scope of international criminal law; increasingly, too, they are also the *object* of international obligations (see, for example, Cogan, 2011). Therefore, individuals can be prosecuted – and not only by their own State – for their role in the commission of international crimes against other individuals. Although this represents a significant shift, the spectre of sovereignty still looms large in international criminal law. Having tethered the negotiations of the *Rome Statute*, sovereignty is now hampering international criminal prosecution, thereby stifling the possibilities of international criminal law in effecting necessary global – and local – order.

One of the defining strengths of international criminal law is its normative role (see, for example, Damaška, 2008). International criminal law sets standards about what qualifies as unacceptable behaviour, including organized violence in intra-state and transnational conflicts (the subject of this Chapter). Although, according to regulatory studies, standard-setting is not the only mechanism for achieving regulatory goals, the scholarly consensus is that it is of central importance in international criminal law (see, for example, Sang-Hyun Song, 2014). This suggests that international criminal law may be evaluated for its effectiveness in securing global order through the lens of its norm-creating function.

To justify this approach, this part conceptualises international criminal law as a field of regulation; identifies the key mechanisms in general regulatory design; and traverses the academic literature on why standard-setting is of particular significance in international criminal justice.

2.2 *Applying Regulatory Studies to international criminal law*

Regulatory studies, as Simm (2011, p. 476) explains, "offers a way of thinking about law that does not understand law as the primary or only solution to regulatory problems". Rather, law is just one strand in a regulatory web (Parker, Scott, Lacey & Braithwaite, 2004, p. 1). In this Chapter, regulation refers to the

> focused attempt to alter the behaviour of others according to defined standards or purposes with the intention of producing a broadly defined outcome or outcomes, which may involve mechanisms of standard-setting, information gathering and behaviour-modification (Black, 2002, p. 26).

To reiterate, according to Black, regulation involves three mechanisms: (a) standard-setting, (b) information gathering and (c) behaviour-modification (Black, 2002, p. 26).[2]

Lacey (2004, p. 148) has identified that criminal law (in its domestic incarnation) engages all three mechanisms.[3] For example:

- *Standard-setting* in criminal law involves determining appropriate behaviour, often by way of negative association. Particular conduct is designated as criminal and, as such, behaviour that does not involve such conduct is permitted. The standards of criminal conduct are set officially either by legislation or, in some States, by the common law. (Courts' decisions in individual cases can also result in setting or clarifying standards.)
- *Information gathering* (domestically) is largely the vestige of the police or other similar criminal investigation authorities. When investigations reveal breaches of official standards, the third task involves enforcement by prosecution in a State court, adjudication of guilt and, if relevant, determination of a sentence.
- *Behavioural change* is attempted through sentencing – specifically by way of deterrence. Sentencing can also achieve behavioural change by inculcating norms in potential offenders' minds. Further, behaviour may be modified not because of courts' decisions but instead due to the prospect of monitoring.

As Charlesworth and Chinkin (2004, p. 246) observe, international law "delivers on each of [the regulatory] criteria in a different way from national legal systems". Thus, international law differs from domestic systems insofar as:

1 There is no central law-making power;
2 Standards are generally set by the primary objects of the law, the States;
3 There is limited compulsory jurisdiction and no centralized enforcement mechanisms;
4 Compliance monitoring involves broad State discretion; and
5 Enforcement is weaker and more porous (Charlesworth & Chinkin, 2004, p. 246).

An important difference between international law and international criminal law is that the primary object in international criminal law is the individual. Further, since States set the

2 Parker et al (2014, 1) advance a model involving (a) standard-setting, (b) monitoring compliance and (c) enforcement.

3 Strictly speaking, Lacey (2014) reaches this conclusion by equating monitoring with information gathering, and enforcement with behaviour-modification.

standards in international criminal law, it might be tempting to conclude that international criminal law is more akin to domestic criminal law than international law. Yet this ignores the character of many of the crimes falling with the ambit of international criminal law. Those crimes, by their collective nature, often involve State actors. In any event, many of the other distinguishing features of regulation Charlesworth and Chinkin (2004, p. 246) identify in international law apply to international criminal law.

As an emerging body of jurisprudence and practice, international criminal law has largely avoided the gaze of regulatory scholars. Yet its conceptualization as a field of regulation is compelling. In the definition of regulation adopted here, the focus is on behavioural change (Black, 2002, p. 26) where the identity of the regulator is irrelevant. This means that regulatory studies can apply to State-centred, de-centred and even polycentric regulation. Polycentric regulation, with different regulators both within and apart from the State, is a defining characteristic of international criminal justice. For example, regulation of organized violence can take place at the international, supranational, national or even sub-national levels (within domestic institutions). Thus, the ICC is an international regulator; the Extraordinary African Chambers (EAC), a supranational regulator; and domestic courts, national regulators. Sikkink (2009, p. 121) argues that international criminal law – by holding individuals accountable for their international crimes as well as affording redress to individual victims – is an advance on international law created and enforced only by regulating States. For example, the atrocities in the Balkans and Rwanda occurred notwithstanding the existence of various human rights treaties and monitoring regimes (Sikkink, 2009, p. 124); adding individual criminal accountability to the existing regulatory regime of State accountability has resulted in increased enforcement levels of human rights (Sikkink, 2009, p. 125). Key to this success is the global nature of international criminal law enforcement: although the majority of trials occurred in domestic systems, "the existence of international and foreign trials make the overall decentralized system more effective and less open to regulatory capture" (Sikkink, 2009, p. 128).

The *Rome Statute* – which created the ICC and vested it with complementary jurisdiction over the four core international crimes of genocide, crimes against humanity, war crimes and the crime of aggression – has, at its heart, the goal of avoiding regulatory capture or regulatory vacuum. *Regulatory capture* results where an industry directs regulation "away from the public interest and towards the interests of the regulated industry" (Carpenter & Moss, 2014, p. 13). *Regulatory vacuum* exists where there is State inaction (Carpenter & Moss, 2014, p. 12). Thus, where a State with jurisdiction does not investigate or prosecute a sufficiently grave crime within the ICC's jurisdiction or where any investigation, prosecution or trial was not genuinely conducted with the intention to afford justice to the perpetrators, that matter can be admissible before the ICC (*Rome Statute*, arts 17, 20). This potential for vertical intervention, by an international body, into otherwise sovereign space may prompt State action (Kleffner, 2003). However, as this Chapter will demonstrate, it is partly the regulatory pluralism that exists in international criminal law that impedes some of its goals.

2.3 *Standard-setting in international criminal regulation*

In her study of the international legal framework for regulating sex crimes committed by peacekeepers, Simm (2011) submits that international law's particular strength lies in standard-setting. This is despite the absence of a central power and the potential for States to capture the standards set due to the self-regulatory nature of international law. The potential sites for standard-setting in international criminal law include treaties, which may or may not have had criminalization of conduct as their original aim, or declaration of custom by courts. Standards can also be implemented and interpreted differently in different domestic jurisdictions. It is the behaviour prohibited by virtue of the crimes articulated in these sources that constitute the standards pertinent for this Chapter.

Like Simm's view of international law, standard-setting, too, is the most important function of international criminal law. This is the view both of its judicial members (see, for example, Justice Sang-Hyun Song, 2014) and academic experts (see Damaška, 2008). As Drumbl (2007, p. 174) elaborates, "punishment [for international crimes] internalizes – and even reinforces – social norms among the public and, thereby, from the expressivist perspective promotes law-abiding behaviour". More recently, other eminent scholars have stressed the importance of the standard-setting task of international criminal law, not confined to the standards set by judicial decisions. In particular, Akhavan (2013, p. 532) writes that the ICC's role in catalysing international norms "in domestic systems may be less sensational than trials at The Hague. But in the long term, it is a far more important and far-reaching contribution to eradicating impunity". Luban (2013, p. 511) similarly argues that the process of acculturation is vital: "[e]ven an under-enforced domestic law against war crimes can be effective if it becomes part of military training. It matters too when that law gets built into the process by which operational military lawyers approve operations". Given the importance of standard-setting in international criminal law, this Chapter will focus on this aspect of regulation.

3. Criteria for evaluating the regulatory effectiveness of international criminal law

Freiberg (2010, p. 263) explains that "good regulatory design should conform to general principles of justice, administrative law and good government". Drawing on Diver's classical analysis of administrative rules (see Diver, 1983), Scott (2010, p. 108) identifies transparency – along with congruence and accessibility – as a preferred regulatory design principle for standard-setting.

3.1 Why transparency?

This Chapter adopts the principle of transparency as the primary criteria for evaluating the regulatory effectiveness of international criminal law. Transparency, after all, is an accepted aim of criminal law (see, for example, Hassemer, 2014, p. 195); moreover, international law is shifting towards transparency (Peters, 2013).

Transparency, however, is not the only evaluative criteria for testing the robustness of the regulatory design of international criminal law. One alternative is *impact* – that is, whether or not developments in international criminal justice have correlated with an increase in global order. Another is *compliance* – that is, whether, according to publicly available databases of State or institutional reports and policies, there is documentary evidence of a shift in practice in response to developments in international criminal law. Both these criteria have significant drawbacks.

3.2 Why not impact?

Impact is difficult to substantiate. As early as 1998, the year the *Rome Statute* was adopted creating the ICC alongside already-existing *ad hoc* tribunals, claims have been made that international criminal law has reduced violence and improved global order. (Meron (1998b,

p. 463), for example, submitted that international criminal law was beginning to produce deterrent effects, modifying the prevailing or potentially problematic behaviour of its regulatory targets.) Yet the evidence of such impact is largely anecdotal. In 2012, for instance, the ICC Prosecutor Fatou Bensouda argued that behavioural change had occurred within those institutions often implicated in international crimes, attributing this to the influence of international criminal law especially since the ICC's inception:

> The Court will only do a few cases, but each case can have an exponential impact, to reach beyond the confines of the courtroom . . . there is now a large 'shadow of the Court', referring to the impact of the Court or a single Court ruling, extending to State Parties, and even beyond, to reach non-State Parties. It is affecting the behaviour of Governments and political leaders; armies all over the world are adjusting their operational standards . . . The shadow of the court is what really matters (Bensouda, 2012, pp. 442–443).

However, it is unclear what evidence she was drawing on to substantiate these observations. More recently, in 2014, the then president of the ICC, Justice Sang-Hyun Song, remarked that, although deterrence was difficult to empirically confirm, he had spoken to persons in the Democratic Republic of the Congo who relayed that, during elections, Congolese candidates were acutely aware of their behaviour, given the proceedings faced by Kenyan politicians in the ICC (Sang-Hyun Song, 2014).

Empirical evidence of change, however, *does* exist. For example, there are data pointing to less repression in States where human rights prosecutions have occurred (Sikkink, 2011). Nevertheless, it is by no means clear that prosecution of individuals for their role in international crime is correlated to ameliorating problematic behaviour. Recalling the UCDP's data, the past ten years has actually seen a *rise* in the number of armed conflicts, with 2014 recording the highest number of fatalities over the last twenty years. This is *despite* the operation of the ICC. Therefore, just as Sikkink (2009, p. 124) notes that the atrocities in the Balkans and Rwanda occurred despite the human rights regime aimed at States, the same could now be said about atrocities occurring subsequent to the development of international criminal law.

Looking at the UCDP's data in more depth (see Table 14.1), approximately 64 per cent of the deaths in 2014 occurred in or at the hands of non-State parties to the ICC. As such, it follows that the ICC's shadow (and that cast by international criminal law more generally) is not extending to non-State parties. To be fair, the situation might improve over time and with larger numbers of ratifications of the *Rome Statute*. Equally, however, the majority of the remaining deaths, approximately one-third, occurred in States that were named in situations before the ICC (that is, the Democratic Republic of the Congo, Central African Republic, Kenya, Uganda, Mali, Libya and Sudan) or States subject to preliminary examination by the Office of the Prosecutor of the ICC (Afghanistan, the Ukraine, Iraq, Colombia and Nigeria). Therefore, the Court's message has been ineffective in terms of behaviour modification. And even though the levels of death from organized violence in Africa are undoubtedly less than the time of the Rwandan genocide and less also than the early 2000s, the numbers are again on the rise (see Melander, 2015)

3.3 Why not compliance?

An alternative yardstick by which to evaluate the effectiveness of international criminal law is compliance. This can be verified by documentary research into State and

Table 14.1 Organized violence and the ICC in 2014

Conflict State	*Deaths (best estimate) in 2014*	*Situation before/Subject to ongoing preliminary examination before the ICC*	*State Party*
AFRICA			
Algeria	107	No	No
Cameroon/Chad/ Nigeria	3783	Nigeria subject to preliminary examination	Chad Yes, Cameroon and Nigeria No
Central African Republic (CAR)	2672	Yes	Yes
CAR/Democratic Republic of Congo	37	Yes	Yes
Democratic Republic of Congo	286	Yes	Yes
Djibouti/Kenya/ Somalia	274	Kenya before the ICC	Kenya, Djibouti Yes, Somalia No
Ethiopia	25	No	No
Kenya	122	Yes	Yes
Libya	1457	Yes (SC referral)	No
Mali	251	Yes	Yes
Nigeria	5922	Yes	Yes
Somalia	1140	No	No
South Sudan	2397	No	No
Sudan	1909	Yes (SC referral)	No
THE AMERICAS			
Colombia	113	Yes	Yes
Mexico	1583	No	Yes
United States of America	103	No	No
Uganda	864	Yes	Yes
ASIA			
Afghanistan	12551	Yes	Yes
India	626	No	No
India/Pakistan	37	No	No
Myanmar	228	No	No
Pakistan	3470	No	No
Philippines	470	No	Yes
Thailand	103	No	No
MIDDLE EAST			
Egypt	236	No	No
Iraq	12662	Yes	No
Iraq/Syria	4186	No	No
Israel	1665	No	No
Lebanon	162	No	No
Lebanon/Syria	67	No	No
Syria	59832	No	No
Yemen	1189	No	No

Conflict State	*Deaths (best estimate) in 2014*	*Situation before/Subject to ongoing preliminary examination before the ICC*	*State Party*
EUROPE			
Azerbaijan	46	No	No
Russia	167	No	No
Ukraine	4398	Yes (by virtue of article 12(3) declaration	Yes

NB: The data on deaths were compiled from: Sundberg, Eck & Kreutz (2012); Eck & Hultman (2007); and UCDP Battle-Related Deaths Dataset v.5-2015 (2015, June).

institutional responses to developments in international criminal law. A number of information tools exist for this purpose. For example, the International Committee of the Red Cross (ICRC) maintains a customary international humanitarian law database and international humanitarian law national implementation database. These databases incorporate information contained in military training manuals or in relevant legislation of the associated State (ICRC, *Databases on International Humanitarian Law*). The information can be searched at points of time when new behaviour is criminalized. This type of research should reveal whether or not – and, if so, when – the military, for example, normalizes or undermines obedience to international humanitarian law. Further, the State responses to committee reports and various United Nations' monitoring bodies may disclose the rules and policies of some relevant institutions, allowing insight into whether behaviour that might amount to crimes against humanity or genocide has been prohibited or not.

The inferences that may be drawn from such database research, however, may not be particularly strong. For example, according to the ICRC's customary international humanitarian law database, Indonesia issued a *Decree on the Implementation of IHL and Human Rights in State Defence* in 2002 following the conflict in East Timor. That Decree stated "that the administration of State Defence shall always be guided by humanitarian law, customary international law, and national human rights law, as well as by universal international law" (ICRC, *Databases on International Humanitarian Law*, 2015). Even if the decree was a *bona fide* expression of Indonesia's intent to formally comply with requisite standards, this does not necessarily signify behavioural transformation (see, for example, Muñoz-Rojas & Frésard, 2004, p. 196). That is, words and practice may be disconnected. Indeed, one of the institutions responsible for international crimes in the conflict in East Timor, the Indonesian military, continues to perpetrate similar conduct in other Indonesian provinces despite this decree (see, for example, International Center for Transitional Justice & KontraS, 2011, p. 80). Therefore, although policies exist, there is no compelling evidence that necessary standards or norms have translated into practice. In any event, the causal determination for the introduction of the decree is difficult to pinpoint. It followed a number of trials in the Special Panel for Serious Crimes (SPSC) and the adoption of the *Rome Statute,* to which Indonesia is not a party. However, it preceded the *Rome Statute* coming into force and the first trials in the Indonesian *ad hoc* Court, the only court to conduct trials of Indonesian military members. Any transformation then cannot necessarily be attributed to the regulatory force of international criminal law. This is also true even when the connection between the legal development and the institution or State response is obvious and immediate – such as when, coinciding with Chad's ratification of the *Rome Statute* in 2006, Chad's security forces amended its *Instructor's Manual* the same year, prohibiting torture and acknowledging it to be a war crime. This is not evidence of actual behavioural change.

4. Applying the criterion of transparency to evaluate international criminal law

Preferable as an evaluative criterion to both impact and compliance, therefore, is transparency. Although not without its limitations, transparency provides better explanations for the regulatory effectiveness (or otherwise) of international criminal law. This part then applies this criterion to (a) international law generally, (b) specific international crimes and (c) modes of participation in international crimes.

The international conflicts in East Timor (1975–1999), Chad (1982–1990) and the former Yugoslavia (1991–) serve as case studies for this analysis. In the East Timor case study, where the majority of organized violence was committed by militia members or members of the Indonesian armed forces, this part considers the law and practice of the hybrid SPSC in East Timor and the *ad hoc* Human Rights Court in Indonesia. In the Chad case study, evidence is drawn from the domestic courts in Chad, foreign domestic courts (such as Belgium and Senegal) and the EAC. And in the case study on the former Yugoslavia, the focus is on the International Criminal Tribunal for the Former Yugoslavia (ICTY) and the domestic jurisdictions of Kosovo (specifically its Special Chambers) and Bosnia and Herzegovina. This part also takes into account the role and jurisprudence of the ICC.

4.1 International criminal law generally

How transparent is international criminal law as a body of law? According to Scott (2010, p. 108), transparency requires comprehensibility or clarity of the standard. Disagreement exists over what amounts to clarity. This is attributable to the uneasy marriage between international law and human rights standards on the one hand and, on the other, criminal law (van Sliedregt, 2012a, p. 8; Robinson, 2008). Although international lawyers prefer broad, aspirational standards, criminal lawyers seek specificity (because of the legality principle) (Ashworth, 2009, p. 63; see also *Veeber v Estonia (No 2)*, 2004, para. 31). Without specificity, regulatory targets would not know clearly what behaviour needed to be changed to avoid breaking the law (Gardner, 2008).

Specificity is equally important to international criminal law. Trial Chamber II in the ICTY, in *Prosecutor v Vasiljević* (2002, para. 193), stressed the requirement for specificity in eventually acquitting the accused of two war crimes counts, stating:

> it would be wholly unacceptable for a Trial Chamber to convict an accused person on the basis of a prohibition which, taking into account the specificity of customary international law and allowing for the gradual clarification of the rules of criminal law, is either insufficiently precise to determine conduct and distinguish the criminal from the permissible, or was not sufficiently accessible at the relevant time. A criminal conviction should indeed never be based upon a norm which an accused could not reasonably have been aware of at the time of the acts, and this norm must make it sufficiently clear what act or omission could engage his criminal responsibility.

However, as a regulatory tool, international criminal law standards can be criticized for lack of specificity. This was especially so prior to the *Rome Statute* coming into force. Van Schaack (2009, p. 101) has stated that "international criminal law tribunals boldly apply new norms to past conduct". She argues that resort to customary international law was had where positive law gaps were extant (van Schaack, 2009, p. 102). International criminal law's reliance on custom undermined its specificity.

A strong message as to the standards *should* be expected once a crime reaches the status of customary international law. But is this true in reality? Consider the case of the conflict in the former Yugoslavia. Customary international law applied to the crimes committed during this conflict. (Indeed, most offences within the purview of international criminal law were part of customary international law prior to the introduction of the *Rome Statute.*) Thus, the ICTY was vested with subject-matter jurisdiction (United Nations Secretary-General, 1993, para. 34; *Prosecutor v Vasiljević*, 2002, paras. 197–198). As Van Schaack (2009, p. 103) argues, "between analogous prohibitions contained in domestic penal law, extant international law, and the human rights treaties, anyone in the Former Yugoslavia . . . was capable of honestly attempting to conform his or her behaviour to the law". However, the nature of customary international law means that many persons would not comprehend its criminality until it is declared – and maybe not even then. It would depend on accessibility to courts' judgments directly or indirectly (such as where audiences are educated by external bodies). Yet individuals do not typically investigate the practice and *opinio juris* of States to seek guidance on prohibited conduct. Some might rely on training by others – civil society actors or States; others may receive no training at all. Even for those who are trained, their understanding of the law will only be as good as the information they receive. As Celermajer and Grewal (2013, p. 248) note, much human rights training "draws on a common pool of circulating materials". Although the impact of the use of such materials is not clear, it is reasonable to speculate that generic materials may exacerbate a lag in the infiltration of new legal standards.

4.2 *International crimes*

Even if a potential perpetrator is on notice that certain conduct is criminal, the exact nature of the prohibited behaviour may remain unclear. The crimes of genocide, torture, aggression, crimes against humanity and war crimes are analysed below to determine whether it is clear what the prohibited behaviour entails.

4.2.1 *Genocide and Torture: Transparent*

Standards prohibiting genocide are clear. The *Convention on the Prevention and Punishment of the Crime of Genocide* (*Genocide Convention*) states that genocide is a crime under international law, requiring both punishment of those involved as well as enactment by State Parties of legislation with appropriate penalties. The courts and tribunals created in response to the conflicts in the three case studies, East Timor, Chad and the former Yugoslavia, to the extent that they were vested with jurisdiction over genocide, incorporated the definition of genocide directly from the *Genocide Convention* art 2 (*Rome Statute,* art 6; *Statute of the ICTY,* art 4; *Statute of the EAC,* art 5; *On the Establishment of Panels with Exclusive Jurisdiction Over Serious Criminal Offences,* s 4; *Act Establishing the Ad Hoc Human Rights Courts*, art 8; *Belge Code Penal,* art 136 *bis*; *Senegal Penal*

Code, art 431; *Criminal Code of Bosnia and Herzegovina,* art 171; *Criminal Code of the Republic of Kosovo,* art 148). This evidence shows that international criminal law –at least for the crime of genocide – has achieved good regulatory design by delivering transparency. Indeed, this is not only so in the three case studies, but also more widely, because a number of other jurisdictions have adopted the relevant provisions on genocide following the *Rome Statute.*

The prohibition against torture is also clear. The *Convention Against Torture (CAT)* (arts 4, 7), like the *Genocide Convention*, requires the criminalization of torture in domestic jurisdictions of State Parties. The prohibition against torture, as defined in the *CAT*, has been determined to be customary international law (see *Filártiga v Peña-Irala*, 1980, para. 882; *Prosecutor v Furundžija*, 2000, para. 111). Although the ICTY, ICC and the Specialist Chamber in Kosovo do not have jurisdiction over torture as a separate crime, they can punish torture as a separate crime against humanity and as a war crime (*Statute of the ICTY*, arts 2(b), 5(f); *Rome Statute,* arts 7(1)(f), 8(2)(a)(ii), 8(2)(c)(i); *Law on Specialist Chambers*, arts 13(1)(f), 14(1)(a)(ii), 14(1)(c)(i)). Torture is a separate crime within the subject-matter jurisdiction of the EAC (*Statute of the EAC,* art 4(d)) and the SPSC (*On the Establishment of Panels with Exclusive Jurisdiction Over Serious Criminal Offences*, s 1.3(f)), respectively. Apart from Chad and Indonesia, domestic law criminalizes torture as a separate crime (*Belge Code Penal,* art 417 *bis; Criminal Code of Bosnia and Herzegovina*, art 190; *Criminal Code of the Republic of Kosovo,* art 199; *Senegal Penal Code,* art 295.) Indonesia includes torture as conduct that may amount to a crime against humanity in its domestic *Act Concerning Human Rights Courts* (art 9(f)); but, otherwise, has been criticized by the UN Committee against Torture for not including a crime with the definition of torture in its Penal Code (Committee against Torture, 2008, p. 4). Chad, although reportedly lacking domestic legislation criminalizing torture in 2009 (Committee against Torture, 2009, p. 3), has a new draft Criminal Code art 314 that criminalizes torture in the manner prescribed in the *CAT* (Human Rights Committee, 2013, para. 137). The definition of torture in the *Statute of the EAC* (art 8) is identical to that in the *CAT.* The definition in the Regulations establishing the SPSC is broader in that it does not require any link to a public official or person acting in an official capacity (*On the Establishment of Panels with Exclusive Jurisdiction Over Serious Criminal Offences*, s 7). The same link is removed for the Crime Against Humanity and War Crime of torture in the *Rome Statute* (arts 7(1)(f), 8(2)(a)(ii), 8(2)(c)(i)).

The standards prohibiting genocide and torture are consistent: in convention, custom, the founding documents of the international criminal tribunals, and domestic statutes. International criminal law, therefore, has succeeded in increasing the transparency of standards for these crimes. Cutting against this conclusion is the inclusion of a broader conception of the crimes, such as in the SPSC and the *Rome Statute*; this may create some confusion. However, the number of cases considering these crimes of genocide and torture, by virtue of their articulation as international crimes, may serve to clarify expected standards of behaviour.

4.2.2 Crimes against humanity, war crimes, aggression: questionable transparency

Although international criminal law has successfully made genocide and torture transparent crimes, its clarity with respect to other international crimes is much more questionable. As Bassiouni (2011, p. 297) argues, there is uncertainty "as to the specific contents of crimes against humanity, the elements of that crime, as well as several aspects of the general part, namely responsibility and defences". Uncertainty also infects the contents and elements (or the specific parts) of war crimes and aggression. So much is evident in the law relating to the three case studies of East Timor, Chad and the former Yugoslavia.

Rules governing the laws of war (international humanitarian law) are articulated in a web of treaties that make war crimes the most regulated of international crimes. Although the rules are many, it is mainly the *Geneva Conventions* (1949) that oblige criminalization and only of their grave breaches (*Geneva Convention (I),* art 49; *Geneva Convention (II),* art 50; *Geneva Convention (III),* art 129; and *Geneva Convention (IV),* art 146). The ICTY (whose statute was apparently declarative of customary international law) had jurisdiction over grave breaches of the *Geneva Conventions,* which apply to international armed conflicts (see *Prosecutor v Tadić,* 1995, para. 71, 84), and a non-exhaustive list of violations of the laws or customs of war which was, not without criticism, found to apply in certain circumstances to international and non-international armed conflicts (*Prosecutor v Tadić,* 1995, para. 137; *Statute of the ICTY,* arts 2–3). Article 7 of the *Statute of the EAC* also criminalizes grave breaches and provides a non-exhaustive list of other serious violations, taken almost verbatim from *Additional Protocol II,* art 4, which relates to non-international armed conflicts. Williams (2013) has expressed concern about this provision, suggesting that it may not have emerged as custom until the early 1990s, predating the commission of the conduct under consideration in the EAC. She went on to explain that:

> similarly, Article 7(2) includes three crimes (collective punishment, acts of terrorism and outrages on personal dignity) that are included in the ICC Statute as crimes in an international armed conflict (Article 8(2)(c) ICC Statute), but not included in the ICC Statute as crimes in a non-international armed conflict (Article 8(2)(e) ICC Statute). The EAC will have to determine whether these crimes were criminalized as a matter of customary international law in non-international armed conflicts by 1982 (Williams, 2013, p. 1158).

An important difference evident in the war crimes provision of the *Rome Statute* (art 8) is that it provides an exhaustive and extensive list of war crimes. While there is much similarity, the list of crimes differs depending upon whether the crimes occur in the context of a non-international or an international armed conflict. Items were only included on the list if they were considered by the drafters of the *Rome Statute* to be definitively prohibited in customary international law (see Dörmann, 2003, p. 341). This clarification arguably increases transparency. This trend of listing war crimes has filtered into domestic legislation regarding international crimes, especially in those States that have adhered to the *Rome Statute* – for example, Senegal (*Senegal Penal Code,* art 431–3), Belgium (*Belge Code Penal,* art 136 *quater*), and Kosovo (*Criminal Code of the Republic of Kosovo,* arts 150–159; *Law on Specialist Chambers,* art 14).

Crimes against humanity and aggression have had very different trajectories as international crimes. Both were criminalized (albeit in different forms to those now familiar in international criminal law) in the *Nuremberg Charter,* which purported to be declarative of existing international law (Bassiouni, 2011, p. 307). Aggression in the *Nuremberg Charter* was described as a Crime Against Peace (*Nuremberg Charter,* art 6(a)). Whether these offences amounted to customary international law at the time has been questioned (Bassiouni, 2011, chps. 3, 5; Brownlie, 1963, pp. 159–166).

Crimes against humanity are indisputably now a feature of customary international law (see Bassiouni, 2011, chp. 5). However, the definition has had a chequered history. For conduct to amount to a crime against humanity under the ICTY's statute, it had to be committed in an armed conflict (*Statute of the ICTY*, art 5). This connection was abandoned in the International Criminal Tribunal for Rwanda's (ICTR) statute despite no evidence that customary international law had changed "between the adoption of the ICTY statute in 1993 and the ICTR's adoption in 1994" (Bassiouni, 2011, pp. 348–349). The *Rome Statute* (art 7) continued in this vein but outlined a wider variety of conduct that may amount to crimes against humanity than had been articulated in the *ad hoc* tribunals. Except Chad, all the jurisdictions examined include crimes against humanity in their associated legislation (*On the Establishment of Panels with Exclusive Jurisdiction Over Serious Criminal Offences*, ss 1.3(c), 5.1; *Statute of the EAC*, arts 4(b), 6; *Act Concerning Human Rights*, art 9; *Belge Code Penal*, art 136; *Criminal Code of Bosnia and Herzegovina*, art 172; *Criminal Code of the Republic of Kosovo*, art 149; *Law on Specialist Chambers*, art 13; and *Senegal Penal Code*, arts 431–2). According to Bassiouni (2011, pp. 660–662), fifty-five States have criminalized crimes against humanity.

Although Chad has ratified the *Rome Statute* and enacted law to that effect, it has not incorporated legislation specifically criminalizing the conduct domestically. As such, Chad would be "able to surrender persons charged with crimes against humanity to the ICC" but would not be able to prosecute them domestically (Bassiouni, 2011, pp. 663–664). As of 2011 there were 58 other States in this position (Bassiouni, 2011, p. 663). Further, some of the statutory documents again restrict the prohibited conduct. For example, the *Statute of the EAC* (art 6) does not include imprisonment or other severe deprivation of physical liberty, nor persecution, as conduct that can amount to a crime against humanity.

The crime of aggression too is now thought of as part of customary international law (see Dinstein, 2005, p. 121). Its status, though, is still open to question. This is evident by the lack of original consensus as to its definition, delaying its inclusion within the ICC's jurisdiction and explaining its absence in many of the jurisdictions involved in the East Timor, Chad and the former Yugoslavia conflicts. One exception to this is Kosovo, which criminalizes the instigation of a war of aggression (*Criminal Code of the Republic of Kosovo*, art 162). Aggression has now been defined in the *Rome Statute*, and the requisite number of ratifications/acceptances has been reached. As such, if a two-thirds majority decision of the Assembly of State Parties is taken to activate the ICC's jurisdiction after January 2017, that conduct will be criminalized.

The uncertainty of standards for the crimes of crimes against humanity, war crimes and aggression is attributable to the polycentric nature of international criminal law and the resulting regulatory pluralism. Mixed messages between jurisdictions may stifle comprehension, particularly where, as Black (2008a, p. 140) states, there is not a "body whose role it is to act as the lead interpreter of the regimes' rules or principles". Burke-White (2003–2004, p. 970) recognizes the potential for conflicting messages, noting "the potential for fragmentation with differing lines of jurisprudence, over-specialization, irreconcilable holdings and conflicting obligations is real". However, he argues that inter-judicial dialogue helps to combat potential fragmentation. Although the ICC may be regarded as having the role of lead interpreter, it is not bound by its own precedent, and other jurisdictions would be free to ignore any interpretation proffered by it (or other international criminal law tribunals). So while such dialogue is undeniable in some instances, there are examples where this dialogue is plainly absent. For example, in the SPSC's early years, it was reported that "there was limited reliance on substantive jurisprudence or procedure from the ICTY or ICTR" (Reiger & Wierda, 2006, p. 23).

4.2.3 Modes of participation

These mixed messages are not only evident in the specific part but also, and importantly in international criminal law, as to what sort of participation may result in criminal responsibility (the general part). Although some argue that international criminal law should aim to achieve consistency with respect to this general part (Ambos, 2006), the contrasting view is that doing so may fragment the criminal justice systems at the domestic level (Greenawalt, 2011, p. 1068). This is because domestic courts might have to apply certain forms of participation for those charged with international crimes and different forms for offenders who participate in domestic crimes, regardless of any similarity of the underlying conduct (such as rape or murder).

There is currently a significant level of incoherence surrounding modes of responsibility. Traditional modes of responsibility had to be stretched to confront the evidentiary challenge of holding more influential figures within a collective responsible for conduct directly perpetrated by another (van Sliedregt, 2012b, p. 1173). For example, the ICTY did this when it read the concept of Joint Criminal Enterprise into art 7 of its *Statute* (*Prosecutor v Tadić*, 1999, paras. 190–191). Its reasoning was initially based on statutory interpretation principles, supported by the justification that "international criminal rules of common purpose are substantially rooted in, and to a large extent reflect, the position taken by many States of the world in their national legal systems" (*Prosecutor v Tadić*, 1999, para. 193). This new form of individual liability plays a part in standard-setting. However, the ICTY's approach has been criticised (see the 'Symposium: Guilty by Association: Joint Criminal Enterprise on Trial', 2007, pp. 67–226). By contrast, the system of participation in the *Rome Statute*, particularly under art 25, has been described as more precise (Manacorda & Meloni, 2011, p. 163; see also Werle, 2007, p. 953). However, as Sadat and Jolly (2014, p. 756) explain, the article takes "on a different meaning depending on the underlying legal training, tradition, and even policy-orientation of those seeking to interpret it". In the *Prosecutor v Lubanga* (2007, paras. 330–341), the ICC read the control of crime doctrine into the *Statute*, and it has been applied subsequently (see, Manacorda & Meloni, 2011, pp. 163–165). This interpretation may suffer against the principle of legality (see Sadat & Jolly, 2014, p. 757, discussing the separate opinion of Judge Fulford in *Prosecutor v Lubanga* (2012)). The defence made such an argument in *Prosecutor v Lubanga* (2014, para. 456), but the appeal was ultimately unsuccessful. Even so, there may be mixed messages caused as domestic jurisdictions may retain their existing modes of liability and only overlay the crimes from the *Rome Statute* into their jurisdictions.

Conclusion

The *Rome Statute* deserves credit for promoting transparency in international criminal law. Individuals – at least from State Parties – could hardly complain in the ICC that they had insufficient notice as to prohibited conduct and (since the exposition and subsequent confirmation of the control of the crime doctrine of responsibility by the ICC) the participation in prohibited conduct that may attract criminal responsibility. The *Rome Statute* (art 22.1) also expressly provides for the *nullem crimen sine lege* principle – persons cannot be criminally responsible, within the ICC's jurisdiction, for conduct that was not a crime at the time of its commission. Although the *Rome Statute* does not restrict prosecution of conduct to that defined within it, this is apparent when art 22.1 is read with other provisions. For example, art 24 limits criminal responsibility to conduct committed subsequent to the *Statute's* entry into force.

Further, the *Rome Statute* is more specific as to prohibited conduct than under former international criminal law. This is due to the codification of the conduct and the requirement that the definitions of the crimes be "strictly construed" and not "extended by analogy" (*Rome Statute*, art 22.2). Unless the conduct is outlined in arts 5–8 *bis*, it cannot be prosecuted in the ICC. Those provisions are exhaustive. For example, rather than suggesting that war crimes "include, but are not limited to", a list of behaviours, the *Rome Statute* names those behaviours, leaving no room for additional categories of conduct. To further achieve specificity, the Assembly of State Parties adopted the Elements of Crimes. The Elements of Crimes clearly set out the requirements for behaviour to amount to a crime under the *Rome Statute* and give notice as to how some of the potentially unclear words or terms used in the crimes will be interpreted. In addition, the judges are directed in their reasoning to give precedence to the Statute, the Elements of Crimes and the Rules of Procedure and Evidence (*Rome Statute*, art 21). As such, other sources of law take a backseat, leaving less room for judges to resort to material that may be even less clear and accessible for regulatory targets.

However, whether this transparency in the ICC has produced greater transparency in the standards required in international criminal law more generally is questionable. For example, some States, like Indonesia, are not party to the *Rome Statute*. If such States criminalize international criminal behaviour, they do not necessarily do so with the same level of specificity as in the *Rome Statute*. This dissonance exacerbates the potential for incoherence as to the standards that apply, especially since customary international law is not always clear.

Although not obligatory, State Parties have adopted the practice of implementing the crimes under the *Rome Statute* into domestic legislation (Triggs, 2003, p. 507). Without criminalizing conduct in similar terms to the *Rome Statute*, States risk losing their option of retaining primary jurisdiction over persons involved in international crimes due to the operation of art 17. Among the jurisdictions considered in the three case studies, Senegal, Belgium, Kosovo and East Timor have domestically legislated crimes that look very similar to those in the *Rome Statute*. Here, the domestic and international systems (under the *Rome Statute*) send a unified message as to required standards – at least with respect to the prohibited criminal behaviour. However, those standards could risk losing their clarity as courts in the domestic systems start to interpret the crimes. The specificity garnered in the ICC by virtue of judicial recourse to the *Rome Statute* and to the Elements of Crime as a priority will not necessarily translate the same way in domestic systems. It will depend upon the content of the inter-judicial conversation that Burke-White (2003–2004) suggests is an important protection against fragmentation and whether the context of the domestic system and requirement of consistency within that system necessitates departure from a position advanced elsewhere.

Some State Parties have either enlarged or restricted the definitions of international crimes when implementing the *Rome Statute*. For example, Bosnia and Herzegovina included additional conduct that can potentially amount to war crimes, such as forced conversion to another nationality or religion (*Criminal Code of Bosnia and Herzegovina*, art 173(1)(d)) and failed to include other conduct (such as enlisting or conscripting children into the armed forces) that is criminalized as a war crime in the *Rome Statute* (Terracino, 2007, p. 426). Such a practice may also result in confused messages about standards and allow individuals to justify practices by delegitimizing either the international or the State system (depending on which is more favourable to them).

Other State Parties have not incorporated the *Rome Statute's* crimes at all into their domestic legislation (Terracino, 2007, p. 426; Coalition for the International Criminal Court, 2012). Chad is one of those States. According to research by the Coalition for the ICC (2012, p. 32) "[n]ational experts affirm that none of the international treaties and human rights instruments ratified by Chad have ever been incorporated into national law". So while there is no conflicting definition in the domestic system, there is no supporting definition either. This is not a regulatory vacuum; however, the silence in the domestic system sends a confused message by competing with the clearly articulated international message.

Whether international criminal law has become more specific is debatable. In a polycentric international criminal law regime, the specificity in the *Rome Statute* creates less certainty and transparency of standards. This reduction of transparency may then be a reason for international criminal law's ineffectiveness in regulating to improve global order.

Empirical research, however, contradicts the need for specificity to achieve effective regulation (see Scott, 2010, at p. 111 discussing Braithwaite & Braithwaite, 1995). Greater specificity may result in targets complying with the letter of the law, while ignoring its spirit. McBarnet (2001) describes this as "creative compliance". For example, to avoid the shadow of international criminal law and its associated evidentiary burdens, leaders in the former Yugoslavia took great care in perpetrating offences to refer to the "'enemy populations' in the most indirect and euphemistic way" (Meron, 1998a, p. 1). Similarly, in its attack on Balibo in East Timor, the Indonesian army dressed in civilian clothes in what Saul (2009, p. 90) argued was an effort to disguise Indonesia's involvement in the attack – an apparent effort to avoid the application of international humanitarian law.

Conversely, where the standards are kept broad, this allows regulatees a significant level of discretion. However, as Black (2008b, p. 456) notes, this requires "a high degree of trust" to be credible and effective. Some regulatory scholars have avoided taking a position on specificity, instead suggesting that both the narrow and broad conceptions have their problems and their place (Scott, 2010, p. 111; Braithwaite, 2002). Braithwaite, for example, hypothesizes that rules (the more specific standards) regulate with greater certainty than principles (the broader standards) "when the type of action to be regulated is simple, stable (not changing unpredictably across time) and does not involve huge economic interests"; but as phenomena become more complex in a changing environment "where large economic interests are at stake[,] principles are more likely to enable legal certainty than rules" (Braithwaite, 2002, pp. 52–53). Braithwaite's hypothesis goes further than this, noting that ultimately a combination of rules and principles delivers more consistency.

When regulating internationally criminal behaviour, the action to be regulated is not simple. The individual action is usually couched in a much larger collective context. This regulation then is complex, and it may be difficult to pinpoint specifically which individual is responsible for what behaviour (Braithwaite, 2002, p. 53).

Further, the prohibited behaviour being regulated cannot be considered stable. While the core prohibitions regulated by international criminal law are fairly well established, and could not be sensibly contested, the outer limits of prohibited behaviour should not be closed. The development of the prohibitions within the *Geneva Conventions* and their additional protocols are instructive in this regard. The experience of atrocious behaviour was responsively prohibited in these documents. In 1950, when the *Geneva Conventions* came into force, the concern was largely with war crimes committed in the context of international armed conflict; but with the subsequent escalation in the incidence of internal armed conflicts, a new document, *Additional Protocol II*, was drafted to cover behaviour committed in that context. From biological warfare to drones, new technology for weaponry and warfare advances causes previously unforeseen harmful behaviour. As such, some flexibility needs to surround these outer limits. Flexibility is much more restricted under the *Rome Statute*, which stipulates an exhaustive list of crimes.

Lastly, Braithwaite's hypothesis ties the usefulness of rules or principles to the economic interests of the regulated at stake. Braithwaite (2002, p. 53) explains that the larger the economic interest, the more likely that otherwise rational decisions to desist from prohibited behaviour will be ignored. Some individuals may be involved in international criminal behaviour due to large economic interests at stake, direct or indirect. For example, with power comes wealth, and some individuals may be motivated to commit crimes against humanity to obtain or retain their power. Sometimes, though, the interest at stake is not economic – yet still significant: nationalism and identity, for example. This would similarly drive some to criminally prohibited behaviour. Therefore, applying the logic of Braithwaite's hypothesis, where there are large interests at stake (regardless of their nature), rules will be less effective and principles should be favoured.

Braithwaite's hypothesis suggests that, given that international criminal law has had mixed success in achieving transparency, it should be regulated at a broader, more principled level in the future. But, of course, it would be unpalatable to afford too much trust to offenders prone to committing international crimes. Braithwaite's suggestion of combining rules and principle-based standards offers a better solution. International criminal law, straddling, as it does, criminal law and international law, would seem in the unique position to take this dual approach to regulation. Incorporating aspirational principles into international criminal law, such as those already articulated in international conventions to which States are bound (and in addition to those in the preamble to the *Rome Statute*), may seem unusual. This is especially so given the *Rome Statute*'s exhaustive approach to defining international crimes. But it has promise. It may go some way towards assuring greater consistency of standards in a polycentric regime, as well as combating creative compliance concerns and changing attitudes. Such a scheme requires much thought; but the rate of movement in international criminal law and the importance of peace, security and global order justify such labours.

References

Secondary Sources

Akhavan, P. (2013). The rise, and fall, and rise, of international criminal justice. *Journal of International Criminal Justice, 11*(3), 527–536.

Ambos, K. (2006). Remarks of the General Part of International Criminal Law. *Journal of International Criminal Justice, 4*(4), 660–673.

Annan, K. (2014). The New World Disorder: Challenges for the UN in the 21st Century. Andrew Carnegie Distinguished Lecture on Conflict Prevention (23 October 2014). Retrieved June 2, 2016 from http://www.kofiannanfoundation.org/speeches/"the-new-world-disorder-challenges-for-the-un-in-the-21st-century/.

Ashworth, A. (2009). *Principles of criminal law.* (6th ed.). Oxford and New York: Oxford University Press.

Bassiouni, M.C. (2010). Assessing conflict outcomes: Accountability and impunity. In M. Cherif Bassiouni (Ed.), *The pursuit of international criminal justice: A world study on conflicts, victimization, and post-conflict justice: Volume I* (pp. 3–39). Antwerp: Intersentia.

Bassiouni, M.C. (2011). *Crimes against humanity: Historical evolution and contemporary application.* New York, NY: Cambridge University Press.

Bensouda, F. (2012). Looking back, looking ahead – Reflections from the Office of the Prosecutor of the ICC. *Washington University Global Studies Law Review, 11*(2), 437–444.

Black, J. (2002). Critical reflections on regulation. *Australian Journal of Legal Philosophy, 27*, 1–35.

Black, J. (2008a). Constructing and contesting legitimacy and accountability in polycentric regulatory regimes. *Regulation and Governance, 2*(2), 137–164.

Black, J. (2008b). Form and paradoxes of principles-based regulation. *Capital Markets Law Journal, 3*(4), 425–457.

Braithwaite, J., & Braithwaite, V. (1995). The politics of legalism: Rules versus standards in nursing-home regulation. *Social and Legal Studies, 4*, 307–341.

Braithwaite, J. (2002). Rules and principles: A theory of legal certainty. *Australian Journal of Legal Philosophy, 27*, 47–82.

Brownlie, I. (1963). *International law and the use of force by States.* Oxford, New York: Oxford University Press.

Burke-White, W.W. (2003–2004). International legal pluralism. *Michigan Journal of International Law, 25*(4), 963–979.

Carpenter, D., & Moss, D. (Eds.). (2014). *Preventing regulatory capture: Special interest influence and how to limit it.* Cambridge: Cambridge University Press.

Celermajer, D., & Grewal, K. (2013). Preventing human rights violations "from the inside": Enhancing the role of human rights education in security sector reform. *Journal of Human Rights Practice, 5*(2), 243–266.

Charlesworth, H., & Chinkin, C. (2004). Regulatory frameworks in international law. In C. Parker, C. Scott., N. Lacey., & J. Braithwaite (Eds.), *Regulating law* (pp. 246–268). Oxford: Oxford University Press.

Coalition for the International Criminal Court. (2012). *Global advocacy campaign for the International Criminal Court: Chart on the status of ratification and implementation of the Rome Statute and the Agreement on Privileges and Immunities (APIC).* Retrieved June 2, 2016 from http://www.coalitionfortheicc.org/documents/Global_Ratificationimplementation_chart_May2012.pdf.

Cogan, J.K. (2011). The regulatory turn in international law. *Harvard International Law Journal, 52*(2), 321–372.

Damaška, M. (2008). What is the Point of International Criminal Justice. *Chicago-Kent Law Review, 83*(1), 329–365.

Definitions. (n.d.). Retrieved March 13, 2016 from http://www.pcr.uu.se/research/ucdp/definitions/.

Dinstein, Y. (2005). *War, Aggression and Self-Defence.* (4th ed.). New York: Cambridge University Press.

Diver, C. (1983). The optimal precision of administrative rules. *Yale Law Journal, 93*(1), 65–109.

Dörmann, K. (2003). War Crimes under the Rome Statute of the International Criminal Court, with a special focus on the negotiations on the elements of crimes. *Max Planck UNYB, 7*, 341–407.

Drumbl, M. (2007). *Atrocity, punishment and international law.* Cambridge, New York: Cambridge University Press.

Eck, K,. & Hultman, L. (2007). One-sided violence against civilians in war: Insights from new fatality data. *Journal of Peace Research 44*(2), 233–246; UCDP One-sided Violence Codebook, Version 1.4 – September 2015, updated by Therése Pettersson (2012).

Freiberg, A. (2010). *The tools of regulation*. Sydney: The Federation Press.
Gardner, J. (2008) Introduction. In HLA Hart (Eds.), *Punishment and responsibility*. (2nd ed.). (pp. xiii–liii). Oxford: Oxford University Press.
Greenawalt, A. K. A. (2011). Pluralism of international criminal law. *Indiana Law Journal, 86*(3), 1063–1130.
Hassemer, W. (2014). The harm principle and the protection of 'legal goods' (*Rechtsgüterschutz*): A German perspective. In A.P. Simester., A. Du Bois-Pedain, U. Neumann (Eds.), *Liberal criminal theory: Essays for Andreas Von Hirsch*. Oxford: Hart Publishing.
Instructor's Manual. (2006). Droit international humanitaire, Manuel de l'instructeur en vigueur dans les forces armées et de sécurité, Ministère de la Défense, Présidence de la République, Etat-major des Armées, Edition 2006.
International Center for Transitional Justice & KontraS. (2011). *Derailed: Transitional justice in Indonesia since the fall of Soeharto*.
International Committee of the Red Cross. (2015). *Databases on International Humanitarian Law*. Retrieved December 4, 2015 from https://www.icrc.org/eng/resources/ihl-databases/index.jsp.
Kleffner, J. K. (2003). The impact of complementarity on national implementation of substantive international criminal law. *Journal of International Criminal Justice, 1*(1), 86–113.
Lacey, N. (2004). Criminalization as regulation: The role of criminal law. In C. Parker., C. Scott., N. Lacey., & J. Braithwaite (Eds.), *Regulating law* (pp. 144–167). Oxford: Oxford University Press.
Luban, D. (2013). After the honeymoon: Reflections on the current state of international criminal justice. *Journal of International Criminal Justice, 11*(3), 505–515.
Manacorda, S., & Meloni, C. (2011). Indirect perpetration versus joint criminal enterprise: Concurring approaches in the practice of international criminal law? *Journal of International Criminal Justice, 9*(1), 159–178.
McBarnet, D. (2001). *When compliance is not the solution but the problem: From changes in law to changes in attitude*. Working Paper No 18. The Australian National University Australian Tax Office: Centre for Tax System Integrity.
Melander, E. (2015). *Organized violence in the world 2015: An assessment by the Uppsala Conflict Data Program*. UCDP Paper No. 9. Uppsala: Uppsala Conflict Data Program.
Meron, T. (1998a). Crimes and accountability in Shakespeare. *American Journal of International Law, 92*(1), 1–40.
Meron, T. (1998b). War crimes law comes of age. *American Journal of International Law, 92*(3), 462–468.
Muñoz-Rojas, D,. & Frésard, J.J. (2004). The roots of behaviour in war: Understanding and preventing IHL violations. *International Review of the Red Cross, 86*(853), 189–206.
Parker, C., Scott, C., Lacey, N,. & Braithwaite, J. (2004). Introduction. In C. Parker., C. Scott., N. Lacey, & J. Braithwaite (Eds.), *Regulating law* (pp. 1–12). Oxford: Oxford University Press.
Peters, A. (2013). Towards transparency as a global norm. In A. Bianchi., & A. Peters (Eds.), *Transparency in international law*. Cambridge: Cambridge University Press.
Pettersson, T., & Wallensteen, P. (2015). Armed conflict, 1946–2014. *Journal of Peace Research, 52*(4), 536–550.
Reiger, C., & Wierda, M. (2006). *The serious crimes process in Timor-Leste: In retrospect*. New York: International Center for Transitional Justice.
Robinson, D. (2008). The identity crises of international criminal law. *Leiden Journal of International Law, 21*(4), 925–963.
Rothe, D.L., & Collins, V.E. (2013). The International Criminal Court: A pipe dream to end impunity. *International Criminal Law Review, 13*, 191–209.
Sadat, L.N., & Jolly, J.M. (2014). Seven canons of ICC treaty interpretation: Making sense of Article 25's Rorschach Blot. *Leiden Journal of International Law, 27*(3), 755–788.
Sang-Hyun, S. (2014, October). *Preventative potential of the International Criminal Court*. Paper presented at the Foreign Policy Distinguished Speaker Series, Cornell Law School.

Saul, B. (2009). Prosecuting war crimes at Balibo under Australian Law: The killing of five journalists in East Timor by Indonesia. *Sydney Law Review, 31*(1), 83–120.
Scott, C. (2010). Standard-setting in regulatory regimes. In R. Baldwin., M. Cave, & M. Lodge (Eds.), *The Oxford handbook of regulation* (pp.104–119). Oxford: Oxford University Press.
Sikkink, K. (2009) From state responsibility to individual criminal accountability: A new regulatory model for core human rights violations. In W. Mattli., & N. Woods (Eds.), *The politics of global regulation* (pp. 121–150). Princeton: Princeton University Press.
Sikkink, K. (2011). *The justice cascade: How human rights prosecutions are changing world politics.* New York: WW Norton & Company.
Simm, G. (2011). International law as a regulatory framework for sexual crimes committed by peacekeepers. *Journal of Conflict and Security Law, 16*(3), 473–506.
Sundberg, R., Eck, K., & Kreutz, J. (2012). Introducing the UCDP non-state conflict dataset. *Journal of Peace Research, 49*, 351–362; Non-State Conflict Codebook Version 2.5–2015 updated by Therése Pettersson (2014).
Symposium: Guilty by Association: Joint Criminal Enterprise on Trial (2007). *Journal of International Criminal Justice, 5*(1), 67–226.
Teitel, R. (2011). *Humanity's law.* New York: Oxford University Press
Terracino, J.B. (2007). National implementation of ICC crimes: Impact on national jurisdictions and the ICC. *Journal of International Criminal Justice, 5*(2), 421–440.
Triggs, G. (2003). Implementation of the Rome Statute for the International Criminal Court: A quiet revolution in Australian Law. *Sydney Law Review, 25*(4), 507–534.
UCPD Battle-Related Deaths Dataset v.5–2015 (2015, June). Uppsala Conflict Data Program. www.ucdp.uu.se. Uppsala University. UCDP Battle-Related Deaths Dataset Codebook: Version 5.0–2015 updated by Therése Pettersson (2014).
van Schaack, B. (2009). Legality and International Criminal Law. In the principle of legality in international criminal law. *American Society of International Law Proceedings*, 101–104.
van Sliedregt, E. (2012a). *Individual Criminal Responsibility in International Law.* Oxford, New York: Oxford University Press.
van Sliedregt, E. (2012b). The Curious Case of International Criminal Liability. *Journal of International Criminal Justice, 10*(5), 1171–1188.
Werle, G. (2007). International criminal responsibility in Article 25 ICC Statute. *Journal of International Criminal Justice, 5*(4) 953–975.
Williams, S. (2013). The extraordinary African Chambers in the Senegalese Courts: An African solution to an African problem? *Journal of International Criminal Justice, 11*(5), 1139–1160.

Cases

Filártiga v Peña-Irala, 630 F 2d 876 (1980).
France et al v Goering et al, Judgment and Sentences (International Military Tribunal – Nuremberg, 1947) 41 AJIL 172.
Prosecutor v Furundžija, Judgment (International Criminal Tribunal for the Former Yugoslavia, Appeals Chamber, Case No IT-95–17/1-A, 21 July 2000).
Prosecutor v Lubanga, Decision on the Confirmation of Charges (International Criminal Court, Pre-Trial Chamber I, Case No ICC-01/04–01/06, 29 January 2007).
Prosecutor v Lubanga, Judgment pursuant to Article 74 of the Statute (International Criminal Court, Trial Chamber I, Case No (ICC-01/04–01/06, 14 March 2012).
Prosecutor v Lubanga, Judgment on the Appeal of Mr Thomas Lubanga Dyilo against his Conviction (International Criminal Court, Appeals Chamber, Case No ICC-01/04–01/06 A 5, 1 December 2014).
Prosecutor v Tadić, Decision on the Defence Motion for Interlocutory Appeal on Jurisdiction (International Criminal Tribunal for the Former Yugoslavia, Appeals Chamber, Case No IT-94–1-A, 2 October 1995).

Prosecutor v Tadić, Judgment (International Criminal Tribunal for the Former Yugoslavia, Appeals Chamber, Case No IT-94–1-A, 15 July 1999).
Prosecutor v Vasiljević, Judgment (International Criminal Tribunal for the Former Yugoslavia, Trial Chamber, Case No IT-98–32-T, 29 November 2002).
Veeber v Estonia (No 2) (2004) 29 EHRR 6.

Conventions/Statutes

Act Establishing the Ad Hoc Human Rights Courts (Indonesia) Act No. 26 of 2000 [English Translation <https://www.icrc.org/applic/ihl/ihl-nat.nsf/xsp/.ibmmodres/domino/OpenAttachment/applic/ihl/ihl-nat.nsf/B30917E8E5443532C1257D90004DC6C5/TEXT/Indonesia%20-%20Act%20on%20the%20Human%20Rights%20Courts,%202000%20%5BEng%5D.pdf.>]
Belge Code Penal (Belgium) (1867) as amended in 2003.
Charter of the International Military Tribunal, Annex to the Agreement for the Prosecution and Punishment of the Major War Criminals of the European Axis, 82 UNTC 280 (adopted 8 August 1945) (*'Nuremberg Charter'*).
Convention on the Prevention and Punishment of the Crime of Genocide, opened for signature 9 December 1948, 78 UNTS 277 (entered into force 12 January 1951) ('*Genocide Convention'*).
Convention against Torture and Other Cruel, Inhuman or Degrading Treatment or Punishment, opened for signature 10 December 1984, 1465 UNTS 85 (entered into force 26 June 1987) ('*CAT*').
Criminal Code of Bosnia and Herzegovina, Official Gazette of Bosnia and Herzegovina 3/03, (2003) as amended in 2015.
Criminal Code of the Republic of Kosovo, Code No. 04/L-082–2011 (Promulgated 22 June 2012).
Geneva Convention (I) for the Amelioration of the Condition of the Wounded and Sick in Armed Forces in the Field, opened for signature 12 August 1949, 75 UNTS 31 (entered into force 21 October 1950) ('*Geneva Convention (I)*').
Geneva Convention (II) for the Amelioration of the Condition of Wounded, Sick and Shipwrecked Members of the Armed Forces at Sea, opened for signature 12 August 1949, 75 UNTS 85 (entered into force 21 October 1950) ('*Geneva Convention (II)*').
Geneva Convention (III) Relative to the Treatment of Prisoners of War, opened for signature 12 August 1949, 75 UNTS 135 (entered into force 21 October 1950) ('*Geneva Convention (III)*').
Geneva Convention (IV) Relative to the Protection of Civilian Persons in Time of War, opened for signature 12 August 1949, 75 UNTS 287 (entered into force 21 October 1950) ('*Geneva Convention (IV)*').
Law on Specialist Chambers and Specialist Prosecutor's Office, Assembly of the Republic of Kosovo, Law No. 05/L-053 (3 August 2015) ('*Law on Specialist Chambers*').
On the Establishment of Panels with Exclusive Jurisdiction Over Serious Criminal Offences, UNTAET Regulation 2000/15, UN Doc UNTAET/REG/2000/15 (6 June 2000).
Protocol additional to the Geneva Conventions of 12 August 1949, and relating to the protection of victims of non-international armed conflicts, opened for signature 8 June 1977, 1125 UNTS 609 (entered into force 7 December 1978) ('*Additional Protocol II*').
Rome Statute of the International Criminal Court, opened for signature 17 July 1998, 2187 UNTS 90 (entered into force 1 July 2002) ('*Rome Statute*').
Senegal Penal Code 1965 as amended in 2007.
Statute of the Extraordinary African Chambers within the Courts of Senegal created to Prosecute International Crimes Committed in Chad between 7 June 1982 and 1 December 1990 (adopted 30 January 2013), Unofficial Translation by Human Rights Watch available at http://www.hrw.org/news/2013/09/02/statute-extraordinary-african-chambers ('*Statute of the EAC*').
Statute of the International Criminal Tribunal for the Former Yugoslavia, annexed to Resolution 827, SC Res 827, UN SCOR, 48th sess, 3217th mtg, UN Doc S/RES/827 (1993) ('*Statute of the ICTY*').

Other International Law Materials

Committee against Torture, 'Concluding Observations of the Committee against Torture: Indonesia' (2 July 2008) CAT/C/IDN/CO/2.
Committee against Torture, 'Concluding Observations of the Committee Against Torture: Chad' (4 June 2009) CAT/C/TCD/CO/1.
United National Human Rights Committee, 'Second Periodic Reports of States Parties: Chad' (28 January 2013) CCPR/C/TCD/2.
United Nations Secretary-General, *Report of the Secretary-General Pursuant to Paragraph 2 of Security Council Resolution 808*, UN Doc S/25704 (3 May 1993).

Courts

15 Access to Courts by Public Interest Groups Seeking to Challenge Government Decisions

A Comparative Analysis of the Modern Position in Canada and Australia

Lisa J. Bonin and Narelle Bedford

In an era marked by increasing government regulation, one method of challenging government decisions is for citizens and public interest groups within society to seek access to the courts. Although there are other avenues, such as through the political process or media pressure, the legal process is attractive because courts can grant effective remedies and their decisions carry weight due to the authority and independence of the judiciary. Judicial review by the courts provides an effective mechanism for review of government decisions. However, the first step – gaining access to the courts – can be a barrier. Citizens have increasingly sought access to the courts to redress broad social and political issues. Courts have responded by gradually granting access to some public interest groups, carefully ensuring a credible, predictable basis for this access. This chapter will map how the courts have widened access to public interest groups. It will adopt a comparativist approach by considering cases in a variety of different interest areas in Canada and Australia. The chapter argues that meaningful redress of wrongs through public interest litigation in domestic courts can – and should – remain a useful strategy for securing global justice.

Although the phrase 'global order and disorder' evokes perceptions of internationality, global order need not depend only on international enforcement and accountability. To the contrary, in our submission, meaningful redress of wrongs through public interest litigation – by ordinary citizens and community organisations in domestic courts – can, and should, be a material piece of the global order puzzle. This is most obvious in cases challenging government policy that has international ramifications, such as overseas military activities (eg, *Amnesty International Canada v Canada (Canadian Forces)*, 2007) (*'Amnesty International'*) or trade (eg, *Animals' Angels*, 2014). But it can also be used to hold domestic governments accountable to international standards, such as those in human rights (Forster & Jivan, 2008). More subtly, public interest litigation is increasingly seeking to influence State action in policy fields such as health, gender, the environment, housing, land and education (Gloppen, 2008, p. 343). Further, these causes can attract the interest, and sponsorship, of international nongovernmental organisations (NGOs) and networks (Gloppen, 2008, p. 343) and so move the issue into a larger domain with deeper support. As issues arise that transcend individual disputes and remain unsatisfactorily resolved through traditional political processes, public interest access to courts has a legitimate and vital role to play either alone or as part of a broader campaign of mobilisation (see, eg, Durbach et al, 2014).

A comparison of the Australian and Canadian experience provides a useful lens through which to explore the utility and potential impact of public interest litigation and in particular the threshold issue of gaining access to courts called 'standing' (or more traditionally referred to as locus standi). Review of government decisions and actions by courts (specifically in both Canada and Australia) is effective for two main reasons. The first is that principles of judicial independence are traditionally widely accepted by the community (Brennan, 1996). The second is that courts are an effective forum in which to seek redress because, generally speaking, they have power to quash invalid government decisions (in Canada this power is inherent and derived from the common law while in Australia it is entrenched in section 75(v) of the Australian Constitution). Under the separation of powers doctrine, one of the roles of the judiciary is to ascertain where the executive has exercised power illegally and to declare such exercises of power invalid. The latter provides a very focused, effective and practical outcome for those seeking to control the exercise and limits of government power.

The exercise of judicial review, however, is not without difficulty. Gaining the necessary legal approval to access the courts (the concept of 'standing') has its own requirements, and, in practice, across many jurisdictions, this has presented barriers to citizens seeking to initiate public interest litigation (see, eg, Bigwood, 2006). In Australia, for example, in the past the courts tended to view public interest standing with scepticism and caution ([Australian Law Reform Commission, ALRC], 1985). Now, in Australia, public interest standing depends upon a multifactorial, context-specific analysis underpinned by the concept of 'interest' ([*Australian Conservation Foundation, ACF] No. 1*, 1980 and *North Coast Environmental Council, NCEC]*, 1994). By contrast, Canadian courts employ a purposive and principled test, due to a concern to ensure that excesses of government power do not escape judicial scrutiny: *Canada (Attorney General v Downtown Eastside Sex Workers United Against Violence Society*, 2012) ('*DESWUAVS*').

Born of the same common law origins, Canada and Australia are also similar in that both operate under written constitutions providing for a federal system of government where power is divided between central and provincial governments. Nonetheless there are, of course, constitutional differences between the two nations. Canada, for example, has the *Charter of Rights and Freedoms*, whereas Australia has a strict, formalised separation of powers between the three branches of government (parliament, executive and judiciary) in chapters I, II, and III of its *Constitution*. Australia is further differentiated by the absence of any national, overarching human rights law. Recognising their similarities and differences, it remains that these two nations are an appropriate and useful choice for comparative analysis because, despite their similarities, each has developed different approaches to standing for public interest litigation. A comparative study of this divergence enables us to draw conclusions about possible reasons for the divergence and which approach to standing is preferable and, ultimately, whether standing tests for public interest litigation are useful for furthering global order.

Areas related to public interest standing that are beyond the scope of this chapter include public interest litigation funding (such as litigation funds and crowd-sourced funding); the nexus between claims for public interest standing and potentially negative costs orders (Campbell, 1998); and the possible future impact of private legal professionals' commitment to pro-bono services being utilised in public interest litigation matters.

1. The role of standing

The question of standing serves three primary purposes. It ensures the economical use of scarce judicial resources; it respects the adversarial nature of the judicial process; and it maintains the role of the judiciary as arbiter of disputes and not policy-maker (Bailey, 2011, p. 259; *DESWUAVS*). In this way, the rules of standing act as the gatekeeper, controlling who has access to the courts and for what issues. Traditionally, the role of pursuing the public interest was left to the Attorney General (Sossin, 2008, p. 216) with individuals having standing only in those matters that directly affected their private rights. Generally, under the common law of both jurisdictions, the requirement for a private right evolved to include 'interests' in the greater public sphere. This evolution took the form of 'public interest standing' in Canada and development of the 'special interest' test in Australia.

2. The Canadian position

2.1 Background to and development of public interest standing in Canada

Until the mid-1970s, standing to challenge the validity of legislation was limited to those "placed in jeopardy by its provisions or . . . affected . . . in a manner different from the ordinary citizen" (*Mercer*, 1972, citing *Smith v Attorney General of Ontario*, 1924). However, in a trilogy of cases beginning with *Thorson v Attorney General of Canada* ('*Thorson*') in 1975, this restrictive view of standing was relaxed by the introduction of what has become known as discretionary public interest standing. Underlying this relaxation was a concern that public wrongs not be shielded from judicial review by the rules of standing.

In granting Thorson standing to challenge the constitutionality of the *Official Languages Act*, the Supreme Court of Canada (SCC) expressly recognised that the traditional rules of standing could operate to preclude judicial scrutiny of public wrongs and bar access to justice. The government argued that Thorson lacked standing because he was not personally affected by the impugned legislation. The Court disagreed, reasoning that to deny standing in such circumstances would have the effect of immunising legislation from constitutional review, an outcome that the Court found "alarming" (*Thorson*, p. 145).

Subsequently, in *Nova Scotia Board of Censors v McNeil* (1975) ('*McNeil*'), a member of the public was granted public interest standing to challenge the wide powers of the Nova Scotia Board of Censors, the administrative body tasked with carrying out the province's censorship laws. The film exchanges, theatre owners and cinematograph operators, although directly affected and, therefore, entitled to commence proceedings, were not motivated to challenge the breadth of the Board's jurisdiction because they still had to do business under the administrative scheme and feared less favourable treatment might result from such a challenge. In granting McNeil public interest standing, the Court recognised also that the directly affected entities did not necessarily share the public interest represented by McNeil, namely, the interest in determining what members of the public could and could not view in the theatre.

Finally, in *Canada (Minister of Justice) v Borowski* (1981) ('*Borowski*'), the SCC granted standing to an anti-abortion activist seeking to challenge the therapeutic abortion provisions in the Criminal Code. In so doing, the Court articulated three principles governing the exercise of discretion to grant public interest standing:

1. there must be a serious issue to be tried;
2. the party bringing the case must have a personal stake in the matter or a genuine interest in the validity of the legislation; and
3. there must be no other reasonable or effective way to bring the issue before the court (*Borowski*, p. 598).

Commonly referred to as the *Borowski* test, these three elements guard against abuses of judicial process by limiting access to public interest standing to genuinely interested parties seeking resolution of serious issues for which no other or more appropriate avenue of redress is available. In this way, a balance may be struck "between ensuring access to the courts and preserving judicial resources" (*Canadian Council of Churches,* 1992, p. 35).

In the decades following its articulation, the *Borowski* test has been considered in hundreds of cases by all levels of courts. In fact, a search for 'public interest standing' in a leading Canadian case law database returned 625 results. The trend in the ensuing jurisprudence, however, was to apply the third branch of the test restrictively, following the SCC pronouncements in *Canadian Council of Churches* and *Hy and Zels Inc., et al., v Ontario (Attorney General)* (1993) ('*Hy and Zels*'), that public interest standing should not be granted where the impugned measure could be challenged by a private litigant. In short, if there were other means to bring the matter before the court, scarce judicial resources could be put to better use (*Hy and Zels*, p. 16). Though perhaps unintended, the combined effect of *Canadian Council of Churches* and *Hy and Zel's* was to elevate the third criterion to the status of a pre-condition. Invoking these precedents, the mere existence of private litigants directly affected by a challenged measure was often sufficient for courts to deny public interest standing, irrespective of the reasonableness of requiring those private litigants to bring a case or their real capacity to do so (Bowal & Cranwell, 1994; Ross, 1995). In *Canadian Council of Churches* itself, the Court concluded that individual refugee claimants could challenge the impugned legislation and therefore public interest standing was unwarranted (1992, p. 42). This conclusion appears to completely ignore the fact that most refugees do not have the resources (or frankly the desire) to engage in complex and lengthy constitutional litigation.

Despite the more restrictive approach, several public interest litigants were successful in obtaining standing in the ensuing years. In *Chaoulli v Quebec (Attorney General)* (2005) ('*Chaoulli*'), a doctor and a patient were granted public interest standing to challenge a province's prohibition on private health insurance. Finding that access to medical care was a concern for all residents and recognising that the issues raised were systemic and not limited to a particular claimant, the Court reasoned that there was in fact no other class of persons more directly affected by the prohibition that could be expected to undertake the lengthy and costly litigation (*Chaoulli*, p. 189).

Notwithstanding the minority of successful public interest litigants, the trend in the jurisprudence after *Canadian Council of Churches* was generally regarded as restrictive (Bailey, 2011, p. 264). Recognising the limitations of such a restrictive interpretation, the SCC recently re-cast the third branch of the test in a more purposive and flexible light. In its reformulation, the Court emphasised the need for a 'purposive approach' to standing, taking into account:

> whether the proposed action is an economical use of judicial resources, whether the issues are presented in a context suitable for judicial determination in an adversarial setting and whether permitting the proposed action to go forward will serve the purpose of upholding the principle of legality (*DESWUAVS*, p. 50).

The Court also stressed that these factors do not admit of a mechanistic "binary, yes or no, analysis" (*DESWUAVS*, p. 50); nor should the test be considered a "checklist" (*DESWUAVS*, p. 36) of freestanding "hard and fast requirements" (*DESWUAVS*, p. 20). Instead, the various elements of the test should be seen as interrelated considerations to be weighed and assessed cumulatively in light of the purposes of limiting standing, which are then applied "in a flexible and generous manner that best serves those underlying purposes" (*DESWUAVS*, pp. 20, 36).

Applying the reformulated test, the Court concluded that the Downtown Eastside Sex Workers United Against Violence Society did have standing to challenge the constitutionality of Canada's prostitution laws, notwithstanding that a similar case brought by the sex workers themselves was already pending in another province. In granting standing, the Court noted that waiting for a criminal case was not necessarily a more reasonable or effective alternative (*DESWUAVS*, p. 69). Indeed, requiring the issue to be resolved in individual criminal cases may result in many challenges being brought to many different courts; combined with the unpredictability of criminal trials, this prospect makes a comprehensive declaratory judgement more effective and less taxing on limited judicial resources (*DESWUAVS*, p. 70).

Though it is still early days, the effect of the reformulated test appears to be a more flexible and holistic approach to public interest standing. Thus, we see, for example, public interest standing being granted to the Fédération des parents francophones de Colombie-Britannique to challenge a province's failure to meet its constitutional obligations in respect of minority language education rights, notwithstanding that the claim was originally instituted by 35 individual plaintiffs, 33 of whom were directly affected because they were entitled to have their children schooled in French (*Fédération des parents francophones de Colombie-Britannique v British Columbia (Attorney General)*, 2012) ('*Fédération de parents francophones*'). The British Columbia Court of Appeal, applying the reasoning in *DESWUAVS*, concluded that even though the litigation could proceed in the absence of the Fédération, the Fédération nevertheless had a genuine contribution to make and could assist the other plaintiffs in ensuring a complete perspective was presented to the Court (*Fédération de parents francophones*, p. 34). The Court further found that judicial efficiency was also better served by granting public interest standing (*Fédération de parents francophones*, pp. 35–36).

2.2 *Use of public interest standing to challenge administrative action*

As a concept originally developed in relation to constitutional challenges, the question arises as to whether public interest standing is available to challenge administrative decisions.

Although administrative action often is concerned with individual decisions, there can be circumstances in which administrative decision makers are called upon to make decisions that transcend the immediate import of the individual claimant before them. The SCC in *DESWUAVS* recognised that individual litigants do not always share an identity of interest with the common good (*DESWUAVS*, p. 64). Moreover, the rights and interests of vulnerable groups within society are far more likely to be assessed and determined within the administrative context than within the judicial system (Sossin, 2008, p. 212).

Historically, under the prerogative writs, standing to challenge administrative action was limited to those individuals directly affected by the impugned action (Sossin, 2008, p. 216). Although it generally remains the case that an individual must be 'affected' by the impugned decision or action to obtain standing, discretionary public interest standing has also been granted to enable challenges to administrative decisions in the general public interest. Thus, in *Finlay v Canada (Minister of Finance)* (1986) ('*Finlay*'), the Court granted standing to an individual to challenge the federal government's failure to impose penalties on the province of Manitoba for breach of conditions related to social welfare benefits. Neither the federal nor the provincial government had an interest in compelling application of the penalty;

but, as a recipient of social assistance, Finlay had a genuine interest in challenging the legality of the government's inaction. Allowing Finlay standing ensured that the government action (or inaction, in this case) would not be immunised from judicial review simply because neither of the governments 'directly affected' wished to pursue the case.

Public interest standing, therefore, plays an important role in ensuring access to the courts to challenge entrenchment of systemic injustice. In such cases, those directly affected by legislative or administrative decisions may have no interest in challenging the status quo. Such was the case in *McNeil.* Public interest standing in the judicial review of administrative action is also necessary in circumstances where those directly affected are unable to bring proceedings, as in *Amnesty International.* In granting Amnesty International standing to seek judicial review of the "conduct of the Canadian Forces with respect to detainees held by the Canadian Forces in Afghanistan, and the transfer of [those] individuals to Afghan authorities" (*Amnesty International*, 2007, p. 1), the Federal Court recognised that the directly affected individuals had no meaningful ability to mount a challenge in Canada regarding their treatment by the Canadian Forces in Afghanistan. This was so, notwithstanding that the family of one deceased Afghani had commenced proceedings in an Ontario Court (*Amnesty International*, 2007, pp. 47–50).

The discussion so far speaks to the utility of public interest standing in the context of judicial review. However, judicial review of administrative action requires an originating challenge. Thus, an issue arises as to whether public interest standing may be invoked at first instance in the administrative process. The answer to this question is yes, though it is qualified by some additional restrictions. Significantly, whereas the courts derive their authority to grant public interest standing from their inherent jurisdiction, administrative decision makers have no such jurisdiction. Administrative decision makers are jurisdictionally confined by the terms of their enabling legislation (*Douglas/Kwantlen Faculty Association*, 1990, p. 37).

Many attempts to seek public interest standing at the tribunal level have been thwarted by statutory terms limiting standing to specifically enumerated classes of individuals. For example, the British Columbia Environmental Appeal Board interpreted the *Water Act*'s enumeration of "licensee, riparian owner or applicant for a licence" to be determinative of the class of objectors permitted to file an appeal under the Act (*Allied Tsimshian Tribes Assn v BC (Min of Environment, Lands and Parks)*, 1995). Similarly, the Alberta Environmental Appeals Board declined to grant public interest standing to three concerned environmental groups to challenge a licence amendment relating to the provisioning of water resources (*Water Matters Society of Alberta (Re)*, 2012). In the same vein, various human rights tribunals, concerned as they are with the infringement of individual rights, have repeatedly denied public interest standing due to lack of statutory authority (see, eg, *D'Orazio*, 2014; *Locke*, 2004; *AA v New Brunswick*, 2011).

However, where the enabling legislation is found not to foreclose tribunal discretion with respect to standing, the same test as is applied by the courts is applied by tribunals to determine the issue. Most, however, have tended to follow the Supreme Court of Canada's example in *Canadian Council of Churches* in interpreting the last step of the public interest standing test narrowly. Thus, for example, the British Columbia Environmental Appeal Board denied standing on the basis that other individuals, including adjacent landowners, had a more direct and substantial interest and could have appealed the decision (*Columbia River*, 1996, pp. 23–26). The Ontario Labour Relations Board also denied standing to an employer to challenge the conduct of a representation vote. The employer asserted that the failure to translate ballots discriminated against Chinese and Punjabi employees. Applying the test for public interest standing, the Board concluded that the issue raised was not sufficiently serious, that the employer did not have a genuine interest in the outcome, and that the employees directly affected could sufficiently raise the issue if they wished (*Maple Leaf Consumer Foods Inc*, 2006). In a similar vein, the British Columbia Labour Relations board denied public interest standing to a union because the issue raised did not transcend the private interests of the affected parties (*Dunoon Contracting*, 2014, pp. 23–26).

It is unclear to what extent the more relaxed test articulated in *DESWUAVS* will impact public interest standing at the tribunal level. However, if *Platinum Produce Co v Ontario (Ministry of the Environment)* (2014) ('*Platinum Produce*') is any indication, the more purposive and flexible *DESWUAVS* test is likely to enlarge the potential for public interest standing at the tribunal level (at least in those circumstances where the enabling legislation does not foreclose such standing). In that case, the Ontario Environmental Review Tribunal granted standing to Platinum Produce to challenge the approval of a wind turbine project on the basis that the project posed a serious harm to human health and violated its employees' *Charter* guaranteed right to security of the person. Applying the public interest factors purposively and flexibly, the Tribunal held that:

> the Appellant, on behalf of its employees, has raised a serious justiciable issue in regards to alleged harm to human health; the Appellant and the employees have a real stake or a genuine interest in the employees' health and well-being; and, in all the circumstances, the proposed *Charter* challenge, in the context of the unique circumstances of this case where the seasonal employees live and work in close proximity to industrial wind turbines and their employer has brought a renewable energy approval appeal under the *EPA*, is a reasonable and effective way to bring the issue before the Tribunal (*Platinum Produce*, 2014).

Thus, we see in Canada an evolution of standing from the domain of the purely private to the realm of the public interest. The growing acceptance of public interest litigation as a practical means of challenging governmental decisions suggests its utility in facilitating order.

In Canada, it has long been accepted that, to have legitimacy, public institutions must rest on legal foundations (*Reference re Secession of Quebec*, 1998, pp. 67–68). Adherence to the rule of law and to the principal of legality underpin the exercise of public power and constrain its arbitrary use. (*Roncarelli*, 1959; *Re Manitoba Language Rights Act*, 1985). Adherence to the rule of law also imports an element of fairness in the form of the "just exercise of power" (*Canada (Attorney General) v Mavi*, 2011, pp. 39, 42). Public interest standing furthers the rule of law, legality and legitimacy by ensuring that government decisions are held to account, even in circumstances where the traditional rules of standing would preclude judicial review.

3. The Australian position

Similar to Canada, Australia also traditionally adopted an approach to standing that was permissive to only those with a private interest in the matter, mirroring the historical approach in the United Kingdom ([Australian Law Reform Commission ALRC], 1985, p. 121). This approach was reinforced by the formal role of the Attorney-General as the first law officer with the ability and duty to commence actions on behalf of the public and the public interest (ALRC, 1985, p. 55). Notwithstanding this, and as Carney (1997, p. 6) observes, the role of guardian of the public interest is in reality and theory a shared one between all vested with the sovereign power of the people – the parliament, executive and judiciary.

In Australia, at common law, the requirement for a private interest was gradually expanded to recognise other relevant types of rights. The test the courts applied to cover all of these circumstances was the "special interest" test (*ACF No. 1*, 1980). This test accorded with the requirements associated particularly with the equitable remedies of injunction and declaration (Aronson & Groves, 2013).

As in Canada, the judiciary have given indications that a relatively low threshold for standing may apply in respect of legal action which challenges the constitutional validity of legislation. In the High Court case of *Combet v Commonwealth* (2005), Justices McHugh and Kirby (in separate judgments) considered whether a peak trade union office holder or a shadow Attorney-General had standing to question the validity of government legislation on industrial/workplace relations. Both justices concluded that the shadow Attorney-General would have standing, while Justice Kirby speculated that it was likely the trade union office holder also would have standing. The other justices of the Court did not find it necessary to determine the standing issue given the resolution of other issues raised in the case. The position of who may have standing in respect of specific, individual decisions (as opposed to challenging constitutional validity of legislation) will be considered in the remainder of this analysis.

In addition to common law judicial review of government decisions, the Australian Parliament passed legislation in 1977 to confer a statutory right of judicial review as an alternative option to proceeding under the common law. The new act, the *Administrative Decisions (Judicial Review) Act 1977* (Cth) ('ADJR Act') introduced many reforms into judicial review. This statutory model both drew on, and refined, the common law position on judicial review (Administrative Review Council, 2012). In respect of standing, the new legislative test (sections 5, 6 and 7) required a "person aggrieved", and this phrase was further defined in section 3(4) of the Act as a person whose "interests were adversely affected" by the decision/conduct under review. Cassimatis (1995) has explored whether the statutory test for standing in Australia was in fact wider than that at common law. He concluded that no court had been prepared to positively state it was so, and this blurred position continues to exist in Australia. Therefore, it is instructive to review the leading case authorities on standing in public interest litigation in Australia, regardless of whether the action was commenced under the statute or relying on the common law.

The traditional common law approach to standing was at issue in 1980 through a judicial review application made by the national environmental group, the Australian Conversation Foundation, to challenge a pending government decision to grant foreign exchange permission for funding to develop a tourist resort without compliance with environmental protection legislation. In *Australian Conservation Foundation Inc v Commonwealth (ACF)* the High Court explained that "the action was not brought by the [ACF] to assert a private right. It is brought to prevent what is alleged to be a public wrong" (*ACF No. 1*, p. 526).

Gibbs J (as he then was) held that the special interest required for standing must amount to more than "a mere intellectual or emotional concern". He continued that: "belief, however strongly felt . . . does not suffice to give its possessor locus standi, if that were not so the rules requiring special interest would be meaningless. Any plaintiff who felt strongly enough to bring an action could maintain it" (*ACF No. 1*, p. 526). The ACF was held not to have a special interest and standing was accordingly refused. The impact of this reasoning has continued to resonate throughout all subsequent cases where public interest standing was raised as an issue. It remains a strong precedential authority and is relied on as the current test for public interest standing.

Chronologically, the next significant High Court decision occurred the following year. In *Onus v Alcoa* (1981), the High Court considered an application by two indigenous women to challenge a planning decision which permitted the construction of an aluminium smelter on land containing Aboriginal cultural relics. Gibbs CJ confirmed the test as laid out in *ACF No. 1* and explained the argument both for and against a generous approach to public interest standing:

> On the one hand it may be thought that in a community which professes to live by the rule of law the courts should be open to anyone who genuinely seeks to prevent the law from being ignored or violated. On the other hand, if standing is accorded to any citizen to sue to prevent breaches of the law by another, there exists the possibility not only that the processes of the law will be abused by busybodies and cranks and persons attenuated by malice, but also that persons or groups who felt strongly enough about an issue will be prepared to put some other citizen . . . to very great cost and inconvenience in defending the legality of his actions (*Onus*, 1981, p. 35).

Gibbs CJ (at 35) stated that the principle developed in *ACF No. 1* "does attempt a reconciliation between these considerations". His Honour found that the special interest rule was "obviously a flexible one, since as was pointed out in that case, the question of what is a sufficient interest will vary according to the nature of the subject matter of the litigation" (at 36).

Gibbs CJ then held (at 36), and other members of the High Court also separately agreed, that:

> It seems to me that the appellants have an interest in the subject matter of the present action which is greater than that of other members of the public . . . the appellants . . . would be more particularly affected than other members of the Australian community by the destruction of the relics.

Stephen J cautioned though that the criterion of special interest supplies "no rule of thumb, capable of mechanical application" (*Onus*, 1981, p. 42). The High Court granted standing to the appellants, but Stephen J opined that it would not have been granted to Aboriginal people in general, as the connection to the relics was experienced only by a particular Aboriginal group/tribe (*Onus*, 1981, p. 42).

In contrast to the outcome in *ACF No. 1*, in 1989 the ACF was granted standing this time by a single judge of the Federal Court of Australia, in *Australian Conservation Foundation Inc v Minister for Resources* (*ACF No. 2*, 1989). This case demonstrates the flexibility in the special interest test – as an organisation that had been denied standing previously, but that was seeking to challenge a government decision in different circumstances, was able to establish a special interest sufficient to warrant the grant of standing. Davies J said that *ACF No. 1* was not an authority for the proposition that ACF could never obtain standing in a public interest litigation matter (specifically concerning the environment), and given the nature of the requirement that there be a special interest, logically that test must be applied on a case-by-case basis (*ACF No. 2*, p. 74). Davies J took into account the fact that ACF was by then a peak national body about which the community had developed an expectation of activity on issues such as wood chip licences and which had a history of engagement and official recognition on the particular issue:

> The ACF is not just a busybody in this area. It was established and functions with governmental financial support to concern itself with such an issue, it is pre-eminently the body concerned with that issue. If the ACF does not have a special interest in the South East Forests, there is no reason for its existence (1989, p. 74).

Subsequently, there were a string of cases that considered standing in public interest litigation, each following this context-specific approach. Often there appeared to be a lack of predictability about whether standing would be granted. For instance, in *Ogle v Strickland* (1987) public interest standing was granted to religious office holders, but in *Right to Life Association (NSW) v Secretary Department of Human Services and Health* (1995) it was refused for the Right to Life Association. Both of these cases involved "moral issues", where the question of who represents the public interest is often contested and the outcomes in these cases stand in stark contrast to each other.

In the face of the evolving contextual approach to public interest standing, in 1994 a single judge of the Federal Court undertook an innovation in *North Coast Environmental Council Inc v Minister for Resources* (NCEC), when a comprehensive, multifactorial approach to the consideration of special interest was applied. NCEC were seeking standing to apply for reasons (under judicial review legislation) in a decision by the Minister to grant a woodchip export licence. Sackville J noted that a special interest could arise from a multiplicity of issues that all should be taken into consideration (at p. 512). For example, in that case, relevant factors included: NCEC's organisational structure in the area where the concerned decision would have its impact; official recognition by the Commonwealth government, which included regular modest financial grants; official recognition by the NSW government; active record of participation and engagement and a past history of engagement on the specific issue that was the subject of the challenged decision (at pp. 512–513). His Honour concluded (at p. 514) that NCEC's interests were more than "mere intellectual or emotional interests" and that it was "well placed to put forward the conservation viewpoint as a counter to the economic activities proposed and undertaken by [the licencees]. On the evidence there is no other conservation body with a greater interest or commitment to the issue raised by the grant of export licences".

Unlike the multifactorial approach adopted in Canada around the same time period, the approach applied by Sackville J was highly contextual and fact-specific; he did not seek to distil a range of general criteria. Indeed, the criteria applied in *NCEC* can be criticised as not being sufficiently adaptable to general application. A highly contextual approach would not necessarily assist in any liberalisation in public interest litigation standing, which would thereby meet the goals of increased government accountability and improved access to justice. To take a specific example, the elements of organisational recognition by government and receipt of government funding could unintentionally limit access to the courts. It may advantage those bodies garnering favour with the current government and operate to exclude bodies desiring to remain independent of government and not reliant upon the same for financial support. Such organisations might receive funding from generous private sector benefactors, for instance, or through broad-based community fund raising activities. In our submission, these entities have as much, if not more, legitimacy to further the goals of order and increase governmental accountability than those in receipt of the government's fiscal support. These 'independent' bodies, therefore, should have equal access to the judicial review system for public interest litigation as those whom the government of the day views favourably. This is in recognition that judicial review exists because sometimes governments overstep when exercising their powers. If only those entities supported by government could gain access, then that would just reinforce a lack of accountability in the system.

In 1998, three justices of the High Court expressed their opinion about the general approach to standing (*Bateman's Bay*, 1998) noting that the common law resulted in "an unsatisfactory weighting of the scales in favour of defendant public bodies" (1998, p. 258) and that the special interest test should be "construed as an enabling, not restrictive" requirement (1998, p. 261). Despite the promise of a possible wider approach to standing indicated by these words, subsequent changes in the composition of the Court has meant that the High Court has not re-expressed such views thus leading to *Bateman's Bay* (1988) being distinguished on its facts.

Both the Federal Court and the State and Territory Supreme Courts have been the site of innovation by single judges in judicial approaches to standing. A prime example is Chesterman J of the Queensland Supreme Court, who proposed a new test in *North Queensland Conservation Council Inc v Executive Director, Queensland Parks and Wildlife Service* (2000). He preferred that public interest standing be widened to permit any litigant who was not seeking to abuse the processes of the courts rather than a test based on the concept of 'interests'. This approach received some judicial consideration in subsequent cases, including by Dutney J, also of the Queensland Supreme Court, in *Save Bell Park Group v Kennedy* (2002). Both these cases concerned applications for judicial review under the Queensland *Judicial Review Act* (1991), which is almost identical in its terms to the Commonwealth ADJR Act. The abuse of process test for standing was also cited by Crispin J of the ACT Supreme Court in *Save the Ridge Inc v Australian Capital Territory* (2004), who also noted that it was beyond the scope of previous authorities.

However, all the cases examined above remain as single instance decisions and have not been widely cited with approval by superior courts. It is therefore timely that the High Court and the Full Court of the Federal Court should re-consider the issue of standing in public interest litigation. There have been some recent decisions of interest that signal a slow, evolutionary development in the expansion of standing in Australia, which would correspond with the widely perceived convergence (Aronson & Groves, 2013) between the common law and statutory standing tests in Australia – all centred on the concept of 'interest'. In 2014, the High Court decision in *Argos Pty Ltd v Minister Environment & Sustainable Development* held that an economic interest, which was able to be demonstrated in financial terms, was sufficient to amount to a special interest. In this case, the High Court delivered three separate judgments, although in respect of the point about financial interests being sufficient to form a special interest, all were agreed. French CJ and Keane J observed that "in the present case, once it was shown, on the balance of probabilities . . . [the appellant] would suffer a not insignificant loss of profitability in their business, no further inquiry as to directness or remoteness was required" (2014, p. 197). Hayne and Bell JJ noted that "none of these expressions is, or should be, used as if it were a term of art having a single fixed meaning" (2014, p. 201). Gaegler J adopted the broadest approach to standing as he was prepared to grant standing to the second appellant to whom the other judges did not grant standing. He stated: "the effect of the decision on the economic interests . . . to be both real and of an intensity and degree well above the effect of the decision on an ordinary member of the public" (2014, p. 206).

This case is significant, however, in that it was not concerned with the public interest in the broad sense, but rather it was confined to the economic interests of the parties opposed to a development application. Although it represents a broadening of the scope of standing with its confirmation that economic interests can be sufficient, it does not touch on the issue where an organisation is seeking to challenge a government decision on behalf of the broader community or public interest.

Notably, in the same year, the Full Court of the Federal Court handed down *Animals' Angels v Secretary, Department of Agriculture* (2014). The applicant in this case was an international animal welfare organisation seeking judicial review of a failure to issue a show cause notice under the legislation regulating live animal export trade from Australia. At first instance, Edmonds J held that Animals' Angels did not have standing under either the statutory test of a person aggrieved or the common law test of special interest. He said that the factors utilised in *NCEC* were too fact-specific to give the applicant a "leg-up" (*Animals' Angels*, p. 123). Edmonds J remarked that both parties had embraced a multi-factorial approach to standing, noting that:

> It is not just the nature of the factors to be considered, but the weight to be attached to each, individually and together; some will carry great weight; at the other end of the spectrum, some will be negative, while others neutral (*Animals' Angels*, p. 123).

However, the Full Court of the Federal Court disagreed on the existence of standing. Kenny and Robertson JJ held that "the matters relied on by the primary judge do not, in our respectful opinion, adequately convey the duration and quality of the appellant's involvement in the live animal export trade from Australia" (*Animals' Angels*, p. 119) and concluded that "we accept that standing requires a sufficient interest, not one that is a unique interest or the strongest interest compared with others who may have an interest" (*Animals' Angels*, p. 121). Pagone J concurred entirely with the joint judgment, thus resulting in unanimity on the Full Court on this point. Although not a decision by a court at the apex of the Australian judicial system, this decision is nonetheless significant as it stands as a precedent for all lower courts to apply in public interest litigation matters.

Turning now from judicial approach to standing to consider a possible legislative approach, it is possible that the relevant statute under which the original decision was made may contain express provisions concerning standing, and these will prevail over the common law or a general judicial review statute (*Sinclair*, 1975 and *Truth About Motorways*, 2000). However, such cases are not instructive for this analysis because they turn on their own unique legislative criteria. However, they do suggest that individual legislative reform would create a patchwork effect of potentially differing approaches without an underlying, comprehensive rationale.

Separate from judicial developments, the Australian Law Reform Commission (ALRC) has issued two reports on the topic of standing (1985 and 1996). Another specialist advisory body, the Administrative Review Council (ARC), has also considered the issue of standing in its review of federal judicial review in Australia (2012). These reports all considered arguments for and against widening the standing test, including its full extension to allow so-called "open standing", whereby any concerned person may commence action provided it is not frivolous or vexatious and does not impact on third party rights. Despite the various recommendations for reform of standing made by these expert bodies, the proposed reforms all remain unimplemented by various governments. Both the ALRC and the ARC are statutory creations who act on terms of reference provided by the government. Despite their statutory mandate, the inherent limitation on the effectiveness of these official advisory bodies is that the legislation that establishes these bodies does not contain a statutory requirement that the government make an official response to the recommendations within a set time-frame. Thus, alongside the seeming reluctance of the Australian judiciary to further develop the common law or interpretation of statutory requirements for standing, the Australian Parliament is equally hesitant to embark on comprehensive reform in this area.

Therefore, the ambivalence in Australia towards adopting a more generous approach to public interest standing is not limited to the courts but also extends to the Australian Government (both the executive and legislative branches). This is despite access to justice clearly remaining a concern and priority for the executive, as evidenced by the government decision to issue a referral to the Australian Productivity Commission on 'Access to Justice Arrangements' (2014).

4. Conclusions and implications

In an era where the courts are out of the financial reach of most private litigants and there is unmet legal need (Australian Productivity Commission, 2014, p. 87), public interest standing has a very real role to play in ensuring maintenance of legality in government decision making and more broadly in upholding the foundational doctrine of the rule of law. As Gleesons of the Australian High Court observed in a 2001 speech:

> The importance of the rule of law lies partly in the power it denies to people and to governments, and in the discipline to which it subjects all authority. That denial, and that discipline, are conditions of the exercise of power, which in a democracy, comes from the community which all government serves.

The three-step test adopted in Canada ensures that the courts do not become the domain of the busy-body litigant, while at the same time allowing deserving cases to be heard. Frivolous challenges are thwarted by requiring a serious justiciable issue brought by a party with a genuine interest. The foregoing analysis demonstrates that Canada has been more liberal in granting public interest litigants standing whereas both the judiciary and the government have been more cautious in Australia.

Within the administrative context, however, different considerations make the role of public interest standing more contentious. Concerned as they are with individual decision making, it may not be desirable or practical to permit broad public interest standing. After all, governments must continue to function and should not necessarily face the spectre of continued litigation/challenge based on some esoteric claimed public interest. Moreover, basing decisions that affect individual rights, interests and privileges on some perceived greater public good seems contrary to the liberal individual rights embodied in our society and the general autonomy-based underpinnings of our politico-legal system. Given the costs associated with the legal process, public interest litigation can be at risk of becoming dominated by those who can afford to commence legal action, and their interests may not necessarily align with the disadvantaged or marginalised members of society (Durbach et al, 2013, p. 223).

Implicit in the very existence of judicial review and underpinning all of the decisions in both Canada and Australia on public interest standing is the idea that democratic processes alone fail to ensure against abuses of power. In a free and democratic society, public interest standing can serve to uphold the rule of law and to improve government accountability. This does not equate to public interest standing being the only avenue for achieving these goals, as there remain many challenges in this area. One future constraint may be the particular context of an administrative action where the relevant enabling legislation for the original decision does not permit public interest standing. This would be a rare occurrence though, and most often the enabling legislation would be silent. Thus, the current systems underline the critical role exercised by superior courts which retain an inherent jurisdiction to scrutinise government decisions. If it is not possible to reconcile the public interest into our current paradigms and institutions, then perhaps the judiciary need to adopt a reformist approach to change.

Arguments against public interest standing are often reduced to the concern of 'floodgates' and an inundation of litigants into an already burdened court system. Experience in Canada does not give credence to this concern, despite adoption of a broader, more welcoming test for public interest standing. The spectre of idle, busy-body litigants seems divorced from the reality of modern litigation, which has been described by the Ontario Law Reform Commission as an arduous and uncertain ordeal which individuals would prefer to avoid (1989, p. 46). In reality, administrative tribunals and courts in Canada have not been flooded with vexatious public interest litigants. Instead, Canadian law provides public interest litigants recourse to the courts to challenge legitimate cases of injustice from unauthorised decision making. By so doing, they seek justice for the public interest (which may not be aligned with private interests). Thus, it is concluded that Canada's liberal approach has not led to the floodgates fear in standing, whilst Australia's more restrictive approach is unnecessarily inhibiting.

Public interest issues that have been the subject of prominent public interest litigation include the environment (see, eg, *Platinum Produce, 2014; ACF No. 1*, & *ACF No. 2*) and animal welfare rights (see, eg, *Reece v Edmonton (City)*, 2011 & *Animals' Angels*, 2014). Municipal planning (where planning decisions disadvantage already disadvantaged groups within society) may also be a source of future avenues for justice through public interest litigation. These are all issues which are inherently beyond the narrow domain of individual interests – these types of administrative decision makers deal with issues of public importance/significance beyond simply issuing a licence to drive or determining how much one owes in taxes or whether one can put up a fence or require her neighbour to cut down a nuisance tree.

Despite the disadvantages of public interest litigation – that it is slow, time consuming, expensive, demanding (in the sense of resource-intensive) and risky, especially in organisations with scarce financial and people resources – public interest standing is, and will continue to be, particularly important in those circumstances where the law or action at issue reinforces systemic biases and disadvantages. In such cases, those directly benefitted may have no interest at all in seeing the decision reversed. The impact of public interest litigation should also be assessed in terms of its ability to attract media and community interest in matters not previously exposed to broad scrutiny and its ability to operate as part of a campaign to raise awareness and mobilise increased participation in the democratic processes available within our society – conceived on both a domestic and global scale.

Ultimately, the broader point is that public interest litigation has a central role in ensuring the continuation of both global and domestic order because each influences and informs the other. Relaxing public interest restrictions on standing as a threshold requirement, therefore, will be an effective way to secure the public interest and ensure justice in public policy terms. The cases of *Amnesty International* and *Animals' Angels* are exemplars of the potential for a judicial relaxation of standing in domestic public interest litigation to have impact beyond the domestic sphere. In two very different sets of circumstances, the actions of a domestic government that had consequences beyond its domestic borders were able to be held accountable by a domestic court. More widely, it builds robustness in public policy-making processes; subjects governments to account for their policy agendas; and can apply pressure on State action in important – and globally significant – fields of social and economic policy (eg, Durbach et al, 2014 and Gloppen, 2008).

References

AA v New Brunswick (Department of Health) [2011] NBHRBID No 2.
Administrative Decisions (Judicial Review) Act 1977 (Cth).
Administrative Review Council. (2012). *Federal judicial review in Australia* (No. 50). Canberra.
Allied Tsimshian Tribes Assn v BC (Min of Environment, Lands and Parks) [1995] BCEA No 42.
Amnesty International Canada v Canada (Canadian Forces) [2007] FCJ No 1460, [2007] AFC no 1460.
Animals' Angels v Secretary, Department of Agriculture (2014) 141 ALD 158.
Animals' Angels v Secretary, Department of Agriculture (2014) 228 FCR 35.
Argos Pty Ltd v Minister Environment & Sustainable Development (2014) 254 CLR 394.
Aronson, M. & Groves, M. (2013). *Judicial review of administrative action* (5th ed.). Australia: Thomson Reuters.
Australian Conservation Foundation Inc v Commonwealth (ACF No. 1) (1980) 146 CLR 493.
Australian Conservation Foundation Inc v Minister for Resources (ACF No. 2) (1989) 19 ALD 70.
Australian Law Reform Commission. (1985). *Standing in public interest litigation* (No. 27). Canberra.
Australian Law Reform Commission. (1996). *Beyond the door-keeper: Standing to sue for public remedies* (No. 78). Canberra.
Australian Productivity Commission. (2014). *Access to justice arrangements* (No. 72). Canberra.
Bailey, J. (2011). Reopening law's gate: Public interest standing and access to justice. *University of British Columbia Law Review, 44*, 255–285.
Bateman's Bay Local Aboriginal Land Council v Aboriginal Community Benefit Fund Pty Ltd (1998) 194 CLR 247.
Bigwood, R. (Ed.). (2006). *Public interest litigation: New Zealand experience in international perspective*. Wellington: LexisNexis.
Bowal, P & Cranwell, M. (1994). Case comment: Persona non grata: The Supreme Court of Canada further constrains public interest standing. *Alberta Law Review, 33*, 192.
Brennan, G. (1996). Judicial independence (Speech delivered at the Australian Judicial Conference, University House, Australian National University, Canberra, 2 November 1996).
Campbell, E. (1998). Public interest costs orders. *Adelaide Law Review, 20*, 245–264.
Canada (Attorney General) v Downtown Eastside Sex Workers United against Violence Society [2012] SCC 45, [2012] 2 SCR 524.
Canada (Attorney General) v Mavi [2011] 2 SCR 504.
Canada (Minister of Justice) v Borowski [1981] 2 SCR 575.
Canadian Council of Churches v Canada (Minister of Employment and Immigration) [1992] 1 SCR 236.
Carney, G. (1997). Comment – The role of the Attorney-General. *Bond Law Review, 9*, 1.
Cassimatis, A. (1995). Judicial review in Queensland: standing under the Judicial Review Act. *Queensland Lawyer, 16*, 27–33.
Chaoulli v Quebec (Attorney General) [2005] SCC 35 [2005] 1 SCR 791.
Columbia River & Property Protection Society and East Kootenay Environmental Society v British Columbia (Ministry of Environment, Lands and Parks) [1996] BCEA No 37.
Combet v Commonwealth [2005] 224 CLR 494.
D'Orazio v Ontario Human Rights Commission [2014] OHRTD No 665, [2014] HRTO 654.
Douglas/Kwantlen Faculty Association v Douglas College [1990] 3 SCR 570, [1990] SCJ No 124.
Dunoon Contracting Ltd. (Re) [2014] BCLRBD No 47.
Durbach, A., McNamara, L., Rice, S., & Rix, M. (2014). Public interest litigation: making the case in Australia. *Alternative Law Journal, 38*(4), 219–223.
Fédération des parents francophones de Colombie-Britannique v British Columbia (Attorney General) [2012] BCCA 422.

Finlay v Canada (Minister of Finance) [1986] 2 SCR 607.
Forster, C. M. & Jivan, V. (2008). Public interest litigation and human rights implementation: The Indian and Australian experience. *Asian Journal of Comparative Law 3*, 143–172.
Gleeson, M. (2001). Courts and the rule of law (Speech in the Rule of Law Series, delivered at Melbourne University, 7 November, 2001).
Gloppen, S. (2008). Public Interest Litigation, Social Rights, and Social Policy. In Dani, A. A. & de Hans, A. (Eds.), *Inclusive States. Social Policy and Structural Inequalities* (pp. 343–367). Washington: World Bank.
Hy and Zel's Inc., et al., v Ontario (Attorney General) [1993] 3 SCR 675, [1993] SCJ No. 113.
Judicial Review Act 1991 (Qld).
Locke v Ontario (Minister of Community and Social Services) [2004] OHRTD No 12, [2004] HRTO 12.
Maple Leaf Consumer Foods Inc [2006] OLRD No 2901.
Mercer v AG of Canada [1972] 24 DLR (3d) 758, [1972] AJ No. 136.
North Coast Environmental Council Inc v Minister for Resources (NCEC) [1994] 55 FCR 492.
North Queensland Conservation Council Inc v Executive Director, Queensland Parks and Wildlife Service [2000] QSC 172.
Nova Scotia Board of Censors v McNeil [1975] 2 SCR 265.
Official Languages Act, RSC 1985, (4th Supp), c 31.
Ogle v Strickland [1987] 13 FCR 306.
Ontario Law Reform Commission (1989). *Report on the law of standing.* Toronto: Publication Services.
Onus v Alcoa [1981] 149 CLR 27.
Platinum Produce Co v Ontario (Ministry of the Environment) [2014] OERTD No 8, 84 CELR (3d) 106.
Reece v Edmonton (City) [2011] ABCA 238.
Reference re Secession of Quebec [1998] 2 SCR 217.
Re Manitoba Language Rights Act [1985] 1 SCR 721.
Right to Life Association (NSW) v Secretary Department of Human Services and Health [1995] 56 FCR 50.
Roncarelli v Duplessis [1959] SCR 121.
Ross, J. (1995). Standing in charter declaratory actions. *Osgoode Hall Law Journal, 33,* 151–201.
Save Bell Park Group v Kennedy [2002] QSC 174.
Save the Ridge Inc v Australian Capital Territory [2004] ACTSC 3.
Sinclair v Maryborough Mining Warden [1975] 132 CLR 473.
Smith v Attorney General of Ontario [1924] SCR 331.
Sossin, L. (2008). Access to administrative justice and other worries. In Flood, C. M. & Sossin, L. (Eds.), *Administrative Law in Context* (pp. 391–409). Toronto: Emond Montgomery.
Thorson v Attorney General of Canada [1975] 1 SCR 138.
Truth About Motorways Pty Ltd v Macquarie Infrastructure Investment Ltd [2000] 200 CLR 591.
Water Act, SBC 1979, c 29.
Water Matters Society of Alberta (Re) [2012] AEABD No 14.

16 Military Courts in Pakistan

A Critical Analysis

Umair Ghori

Pakistan is a frontline state against the global war on terrorism. In December 2014, an attack on a school in Peshawar, Pakistan killed more than 130 students. In response, the Government of Pakistan established military courts to conduct trials of those suspected of terrorism-related offences. This measure may be viewed as a necessary evil – a temporary measure to speed up the trial process. On the other hand, it breaches human rights guarantees such as the right to a fair trial and undermines the separation of judicial power. Therefore, it cannot be a desirable long-term solution to terrorism. From a global perspective, the issue confronting Pakistan is one shared by other States confronting the scourge of terrorism: should national security and public safety trump other human rights? Even so, should the Pakistani government continue on its path of prioritising national security at the expense of civil liberties and various constitutional rights? And, if so, are there controls and a system of checks and balances over the powers of the government security organisations? Ultimately, I argue that the establishment of military courts is justified, albeit an 'antibiotic' solution to larger systemic deficiencies in the justice system.

The 9/11 attacks in the US mark a grim point in recent history. In response, the US initiated the global 'War on Terror' which has forever changed the global security landscape. The resulting global military efforts to curtail terrorism have seen invasions of Afghanistan in 2001 and Iraq in 2003. The displacement of the ruling regimes in both Afghanistan and Iraq have created a severe power vacuum that has been exploited by various groups with often conflicting agendas, not necessarily aligned with the US and Western interests.

Pakistan is deeply implicated in these events. Indeed, the war in neighbouring Afghanistan has serious repercussions for Pakistan. Data show that Pakistan ranks amongst the top targets of terrorists attacks post-9/11. For example, The Economist ("Fear and Loathing", 2012) cites data from the Institute for Economics and Peace showing that between 2002 and 2011, Pakistan was the second most targeted country after Iraq. Similarly, the South Asia Terrorism Portal (SATP) recorded 436 suicide bombings in Pakistan from 2002 to May 2016, resulting in more than 20,000 casualties (SATP, 2016). This is in addition to the death toll from other terrorist attacks. While Iraq and Afghanistan have struggled to rebuild and maintain stable governments following the US invasion, Pakistan's challenge is to maintain the integrity of its domestic system while providing security to its population. This makes Pakistan a unique case study: a densely populated country situated at a geo-strategic crossroads struggles with its religious ideological identity and the global imperative to counter the menace of terrorism.

Those keeping an eye on events in Pakistan may have noticed the recent changes in Pakistan's struggle against extremist elements and terrorist groups. The foremost change was the establishment of military courts to try terror suspects as a complementary measure to the ongoing military operation against the terrorist elements. The decision to establish military courts is deeply unpopular amongst civil society, political parties with liberal agendas and the judiciary (Dawn, 2014a, 2014b, 2015). Even though the decision to establish military courts is a result of numerous discussions and consultations, the mainstream liberal narrative concludes that soldiers, as administrators of justice, are an aberration of the country's judicial system. The military, on the other hand, states that the countermeasures taken are more than skin deep (Manan, 2014; Reuters, 2016; ICJ, 2016; Kine, 2015). The military's narrative is that 'reforms' essential for military courts to function such as amendments to enhance the ambit of laws pertaining to military discipline are a reflection of substantive developments that embody a plan for the future of Pakistan's anti-terrorism strategy (Government of Pakistan, 2015; Kine, 2015; Manan, 2014). Military courts are a central component of Pakistan's *National Action Plan* to confront the spectre of terrorism. While the measure of establishing military courts in order to speed up the trial process of terror suspects may appear short-sighted, it is in line with a deeply ingrained popular ethos of just deserts and vengeance. The popular public opinion (reinforced by reports and data cited later in this chapter) is that perpetrators of terrorism are rarely brought to justice and that the only solution is to either eliminate terror suspects in action by the military/law enforcement agencies or, if they are captured, either tried by the military (because the judicial system and the police have proven incapable of dealing with the problem) or enrolled in counter-radicalisation programmes (for example *the Sabaoon* programme established after the military cleared the Swat Valley from militant influence). Horgan terms this initiative as "unique not just because of the success it has had but also because it is specifically aimed at rehabilitating children which, to my knowledge, is the only such programme in the world" (quoted in Dawn, 2015d).

The nature of Pakistan's security environment and the ever-present danger of extremist groups pose several uncomfortable questions concerning the stability of Pakistan and the region more broadly: Should military dispense justice in the first place? If the military courts prove a "successful" solution to the problem of terrorism in Pakistan, will they become a permanent feature? In the alternative, for how long will police and judicial reforms be postponed? Finally, and most importantly, should a society barter precepts of fundamental human rights with security?

There are no easy answers to these questions. While the State is primarily responsible for protecting its people and prosecuting those accused of threatening peace and security, the challenge is compounded if State organs responsible for public security are failing to discharge their functions. Where such failure occurs, those functions may automatically shift elsewhere. In considering this automatic shift within the context of Pakistan, the question is: are military courts a suitable vehicle to dispense justice as a response to terrorism where conventional mechanisms for dispensing justice are ineffective?

Various human rights bodies, members of the legal profession and the civil society disagree over the move to establish military courts (AHRC, 2015; [International Crisis Group ICG], 2010; ICG, 2015; Khan, 2015; [International Commission of Jurists ICJ], 2016). Their collective argument is that military courts are an ineffective vehicle in delivering security to the populace and that the Constitutional Amendments breach several provisions of the *International Covenant on Civil and Political Rights* (ICCPR) (Dawn, 2015b; ICG, 2015; ICJ, 2016). The ICCPR is a human rights treaty carrying universal effect, which has been ratified by Pakistan. Even though the ICCPR makes room for suspension of some rights in times of national emergencies, it does not allow for suspension of protective rights against torture or cruel, inhuman, or degrading treatment or punishment, or arbitrary deprivation of right to life provided for in Articles 6(1), 7, 9 and 17 of the ICCPR. Khan (2015) observes that military courts established under the 21st Constitutional amendment do not satisfy the obligations under the ICCPR because the accused have minimal rights before the military courts, yet face capital punishment in view of evidence that may be extracted through torture or other degrading treatment. Justice Tariq Mehmood, a former Supreme Court Bar Association (SCBA) president, criticises military courts on the grounds that they bypass the constitutional guarantee of a fair trial under Article 10A of the Constitution of the Islamic Republic of Pakistan (hereinafter the "1973 Constitution") (Dawn, 2015b). Another Advocate of the Supreme Court of Pakistan, Ali Zafar, discredits the widespread perception that only military courts are able to convict terrorists, and to do so, secrecy must be maintained in order to protect witnesses and prosecutors (Dawn, 2015b). However, he cautions, punishments without judgments will create doubts in the minds of the people (Dawn, 2015b). In other words, the argument taken by legal experts in Pakistan is that any non-transparent mechanisms that override separation of powers and violate constitutional rights in the name of providing security, are not only undemocratic but also violate the international human rights standards as enunciated in the ICCPR.

Pakistan may be described as a praetorian State where constitutional changes "are effected and sustained by the military, and the army frequently intervenes in the government" (Perlmutter, 1969, p. 383). The military, therefore, plays a dominant role in political structures and institutions (Perlmutter, 1969, p. 383). The military's role in developing countries is not a phenomenon limited to Pakistan only. Several commentators have focussed on praetorianism in the developing world. Mahmud (1993, p. 1229) cites Dowse (1969, pp. 213–227), who discusses how prevailing developmental conditions give rise to "power vacuums" that eventually pave the way for military takeover. Pye (1962, pp. 69–87) notes various developmental roles that are played by the military during transition periods in developing countries. Huntington (1968, pp. 194–208) views the militaries of newly decolonised States as an instrument of modernisation and change.

Broken down to its basics, Pakistan's problem is similar to any developing country facing typical governance challenges, where governmental bodies primarily tasked with maintaining law and order have failed to do so and, in turn, have left a power vacuum. This vacuum then prompts the emergency response from the State in the form of military intervention.

More recently, the International Crisis Group (ICG) forwarded its counter-terrorism recommendations to Pakistan (ICG, 2015). These recommendations repeat what is a commonly known truth in Pakistan: the need for police and judicial reforms. The question, however, is: who will undertake this important task? Political parties have consistently dragged their feet in reforming the judiciary and the police by depoliticising it. Police reforms have long been debated in Pakistan as one of the solutions to the rule of law problem. The police departments in each of the four provinces have often seen accusations of non-transparency, politically motivated recruitment policies, inefficiency and lack of departmental accountability (Express Tribune, 2015). Rustam Shah Mohmand, a former interior secretary, declares that Pakistan had the lowest conviction rate of 3.5% in the world due to incomplete and faulty investigation by the police (Express Tribune, 2015). While the policymakers and legislature delay implementing police and judicial reforms, the regulatory vacuum continues to persist. The solution to the problem posed by the regulatory vacuum in law enforcement, security and the legal process is temporarily bandaged through the military courts.

Military courts are not the long-term solution to Pakistan's challenges. This is because the operation of military courts conflicts with several provisions of the 1973 Constitution and international law instruments such as the ICCPR. But they are a necessary stop-gap.

Military courts are justified by the extraordinary prevailing circumstances that threaten not only the peace and security in the region but also the integrity of the country. Until the State can design and implement solutions to long-standing problems to its legal and judicial institutions, the military courts, despite their shortcomings, meet an immediate need.

To develop this argument, this chapter is divided into four parts. Part 1 briefly introduces Pakistan's anti-terror laws along with a concise overview of its current legal and constitutional system. Part 2 of this chapter summarises the common critique of the military courts by civil society groups, human rights bodies and international observers such as the ICG. Part 3 attempts a partial defence of military courts. It argues that military courts are a necessary short-term solution. When the State fails to govern, due to institutional failure, it may be forced to hand over some of its State functions to its *de facto* sovereign. In Pakistan's case, the institutional failure is the ineffectiveness of current laws and legal institutions to respond to the scourge of terrorism; the *de facto* sovereign is the Pakistani military; and the institutional manifestation of the hand-over of State power is the establishment of military courts to try non-military personnel. However, as the chapter concludes, military courts are not a desirable, long-term solution; at best, they are a temporary measure along the lines of an antibiotic prescription. It should only remain in place until such time as the State can effect necessary reforms to the police and judicial system.

1. Military courts: historical and legal context

The military acting as an arbiter of justice raises concerns as to the separation of powers. This is because the military is traditionally understood as part of the executive arm of government. And it is a fundamental tenet of the rule of law that executive action be subject to review by an independent judicial system (see, generally, Scharpf, 1966; Engdahl, 1971; Peck, 1975; Meeks, 1975).

The involvement of the military in civil affairs, however, has a long history internationally. In his historical study of military troops in civil disorders in the US, for example, Engdahl (1971, p. 28) refers to the declaration of martial law in 1775 by General Gage in Boston during the American Revolution. This deployment of military, rather than civilian, measures against dissident citizens was what "most roused the mass of Americans to arms". The lesson learned was that "soldiers . . . are never to be used against their civilian countrymen, no matter how expedient their utilization might seem" (Engdahl, 1971, p. 28). Meeks (1975, pp. 86–93), too, identifies times during American history when civilian authorities requisitioned services from the local military units to enforce civil laws such as taxation, control industrial action or the arrest of offenders. Meeks (1975, pp. 121–123) also cites the *Jaramillo* case (*US v Jaramillo* 380 F. Supp 1375 510 F.2d 808 8th Circuit 1975) where the court complimented a serving US military officer in an advisory role as "unreservedly reasonable". Even so, the presiding judge acquitted the accused simply because employment of a military officer in the case violated congressional prohibitions against the use of military in civil law enforcement matters.

However, in Pakistan, the military's participation in domestic governance is not consigned to history. Due to the cumulative effect of several constitutional provisions, discussed further below, the military can still be "elevated" to exercise some powers of the judiciary and the executive, provided the Federal Government directs the armed forces to act in "aid of civil power". The most recent example of this was the April 2016 security operation against the notorious *Chottu Gang* bandit group in the south Punjab riverine region. The military was called in following several failed police actions (Express Tribune, 2016).

Article 245(1) of the 1973 Constitution defines the role of the armed forces of Pakistan to defend "Pakistan against external aggression or threat of war". To eliminate any ambiguities, Article 256 of the 1973 Constitution forbids "private armies" and any organisation capable of functioning as a military organisation. Additionally, Article 245(1) specifies a secondary role for the armed forces of Pakistan whereby it can "act in aid of civil power when called upon to do so" by the Federal Government. Article 245(2) provides for immunity against legal challenge in any court when it does so. Further reinforcement comes from Article 237 of the 1973 Constitution, which allows the Parliament to indemnify actions of "any person in the service of the Federal Government or a Provincial Government, or any other person, in respect of any act done in connection with the maintenance or restoration of order in any area in Pakistan".

Although Article 8 of the 1973 Constitution renders void any law inconsistent with, or in derogation of, fundamental rights, Article 8(3)(a) of the 1973 Constitution crucially provides that this does not apply to any law relating to members of the armed forces, or of the police or of such other forces that are "charged with the maintenance of public order, for the purpose of ensuring the proper discharge of their duties or the maintenance of discipline among them". In effect, it provides the military – and therefore the executive arm of government – with an immunity from constitutional human rights obligations. The constitutional immunity does not come without oversight. In the case of *Sh. Liaquat Hussain v Federation of Pakistan* (PLD 1999 SC 504), the Supreme Court of Pakistan held that any law that vests armed forces with the power to try civilians for non-military related matters is not immune from scrutiny under Article 8(3)(a) of the 1973 Constitution. This case came in the aftermath of the military takeover by General Parvez Musharraf in October 1999. In addition to this limitation on immunity, later regulations enabling action by armed forces in aid of civil power in the Northwest regions of Pakistan specifically include a provision that deals with "misuse of force during actions in aid of civil power" (see Regulation 5(1) of the Actions (in Aid of Civil Power) Regulation, 2011) (hereinafter referred to as the "2011 Regulations"). However, the Asian Human Rights Commission (AHRC) observes that the 2011 Regulations allow the military to detain suspects indefinitely if they fear a court may order their release or acquittal (AHRC, 2015). For example, military authorities may seek to convict suspects on the basis of electronic evidence and computer forensics (such as computer transmission data and e-mails). However, past experience has shown that any electronic/computer evidence collected by security agencies from combat zones are not admissible in courts, which then leads to acquittals for want of evidence (AHRC, 2015).

The 1973 Constitution authorises legislation prescribing the role of the Pakistan army as the largest branch of the armed forces of Pakistan. The primary law in the area is the *Pakistan Army Act 1952* (PAA). This Act is supplemented by the *Pakistan Army Rules 1954* (PAR). For long, the combined effect of the PAA and PAR was to regulate service in the Pakistan army. However, under the 21st Constitutional Amendment, these regulations have been enhanced to enable the formation and operation of military courts in the country.

The Statement of Objects accompanying the 21st Constitutional Amendment recognises the "extraordinary situation and circumstances" that demand "special measures" for speedy trial of offences relating to terrorism, waging of war or insurrection against Pakistan and prevention of acts threatening the security of Pakistan. The Statement of Objects further provides that since there is "grave and unprecedented threat to the territorial integrity of Pakistan by miscreants, terrorists and foreign funded elements", it is "expedient that an appropriate amendment is made in the Constitution". The effects of the 21st Constitutional Amendment is that the PAA, along with its sister statutes of *Pakistan Airforce Act 1953*,

Pakistan Navy Ordinance 1961 and the more recent *Protection of Pakistan Act 2014*, are not invalidated even if they are inconsistent with or in derogation of fundamental rights. This is because they are included in the First Schedule, which lists all federal and provincial legislative instruments that are exempt from the application of Articles 8(1) and (2) of the 1973 Constitution.

Once inured from constitutional scrutiny under the umbrella of the First Schedule, the operative amendments necessary for PAA to be used for trying terror suspects in military courts were enacted through the *Pakistan Army (Amendment) Act 2015* (the "2015 Act"). The 2015 Act amended Section 2 of the PAA, which lists the category of persons subject to the PAA (in addition to the officers and other military personnel). The amended Section 2(1)(d)(iii) expands the scope of application of the PAA to include:

> any person who is or claims or is known to belong to any terrorist group or organization using the name of religion or a sect and raises arms or wages war against Pakistan or attacks the Armed Forces of Pakistan and law enforcement agencies, or attacks any civil or military installations in Pakistan or kidnaps any person for ransom or causes death of any person or injury, or is in possession, storage, fabrication or transport of explosives, fire-arms, instruments, articles, suicide jackets or vehicles designed to be used for terrorist acts, or receives or provides funding from any foreign or local sources for such illegal activities and acts or does any act to overawe the state or any section of the public or a sect or a religious minority or to create terror or insecurity in Pakistan or attempts to commit any of the said acts, within or outside Pakistan shall be punished under this Act.

The 2015 Act clarifies that, for the purposes of Section 2(1)(d)(iii), the word "sect" denotes a sect of religion and does not include any religious or political party regulated under the *Political Parties Order 2002*. Ostensibly, this was done to gain the support of reluctant political parties for the 21st Constitutional Amendment. Political parties were originally apprehensive about military courts targeting their activists (The News, 2015), but, after extended debates, agreed to pass it through both Houses of Parliament (Dawn, 2014a).

The 2015 Act also introduced new Section 2(1)(d)(iv) within the PAA 1952 which states:

> any person who is or claims or is known to belong to any terrorist group or organization using the name of religion or a sect, commits an offence mentioned at serial Nos. (i), (ii), (iii), (v), (vi), (vii), (viii), (ix), (x), (xi), (xii), (xiii), (xv), (xvi), (xvii) and (xx) in the Schedule to the Protection of Pakistan Act, 2014.[1]

1 The *Protection of Pakistan Act 2014* (PPA 2014) is Pakistan's anti-terrorism legislation. It stands alongside the more procedural *Anti-Terrorism Act 1997* (which provides for trial of terrorism suspects). The PPA 2014 provides for "protection against waging war against Pakistan and the prevention of acts threatening the security of Pakistan". The Schedule to the PPA 2014 lists offences that fall within its ambit. The provisions mentioned hereinabove are as follows:

> "(i) crimes against ethnic, religious and political groups or minorities including offences based on discrimination, hatred, creed and race;
>
> (ii) use of arson, fire-bombs, suicide bombs, biological weapons, chemical weapons, nuclear arms, plastic explosives and other materials capable of exploding or creating bombs employed to kill or cause hurt to persons or destroy property;

It also introduced new Section 2(4) of the PAA 1952, which gives the Federal Government the power to transfer any proceedings in respect of any persons who commit offences under Sections 2(1)(d)(iii)[2] and (iv) for trial through the military courts. Section 1(3) of the 2015 Act provides that the military courts set under the current system will be active for an initial period of two years.

2. Criticisms of military courts

Domestic civil society (see, for example, Express Tribune, 2015; The Asia Society, 2012) and international groups (see, for example, ICG, 2008, 2015, pp. 25–29) have strongly criticised the establishment of military courts in Pakistan. Principal among the concerns is that military courts violate fundamental human rights (both domestically and internationally). This includes fundamental rights under Article 8 of the 1973 Constitution and the

---

(iii) use of arson and bombs on public places, government premises, sites of worship, historical places, business concerns, or other places, and risking or causing death or hurt to any person therein;
(v) killing, kidnapping, extortion, assault or attack on officers and employees of Pakistan including armed forces and law enforcement agencies;
(vi) killing, kidnapping, extortion, assault or attack on foreign officials, official guests, tourists, foreign visitors, or internationally protected persons etc;
(vii) killing, kidnapping, extortion, assault or attack on social or welfare workers, including health personnel, aid workers, and volunteers;
(viii) destruction of or attack on communication and interaction lines, devices, grids of stations, or systems etc;
(ix) destruction of or attack on energy facilities including dams, power generating and distributing systems including stations, lines and poles;
(x) destruction of or attack on aircrafts and airports, attack on flight crew with any weapon or endangering human life by means of weapons on aircrafts;
(xi) destruction of or attack on gas or oil pipelines and liquid or natural gas facilities and other means of their transport including tankers;
(xii) destruction of or attack on of national defense materials, premises, utilities, and installations including check posts, prisons and other fixtures;
(xiii) destruction of or attack on educational institutions, police stations and security organizations etc.
(xv) wrecking, disrupting or attacking mass transport systems including trains, buses, cats and their stations and ports;
(xvi) violence or attack against maritime navigation, maritime fixed platforms, shipping and port installations and other maritime fixtures;
(xvii) violence against nuclear arms, sites or any other related installations;
(xviii) hostage taking, or attempting to take hostage any person;
(xx) illegally crossing national boundaries in connection with Scheduled offence"

2 Section 2 (1) (d) (iii) of the PAA 1952 mentions a series of offences. These include the following:

"(a) raise arms or wage war against Pakistan, or attack the Armed Forces of Pakistan or law enforcement agencies, or attack any civil or military installations in Pakistan; or
(b) abduct any person for ransom, or cause death of any person or injury; or
(c) posses, store, fabricate or transport the explosives, fire arms, instrument, articles, suicide jackets; or
(d) use or design vehicles for terrorist acts; or
(e) provide or receive funding from any foreign or local source for the illegal activities under this clause; or
(f) act to over-awe the state or any section of the public or sect or religious minority; or
(g) create terror or insecurity in Pakistan or attempt to commit any of the said acts within or outside Pakistan, shall be punished under this Act"

protections against torture or cruel, inhuman, or degrading treatment or punishment, or arbitrary deprivation of right to life, as provided in Articles 6(1), 7, 9 and 17 of the ICCPR.

Furthermore, military courts adopt an inquisitorial system under which the presumption of innocence does not operate. Salman Raja, a senior lawyer in Pakistan, comments that the military courts operate at a lower evidentiary threshold compared to civil courts. This means that the arrest of any person accused of terrorism amounts to *prima facie* evidence of guilt (Al Jazeera, 2015). The Human Rights Commission of Pakistan (HRCP) was amongst the first groups to voice their concerns against the use of military courts soon after the Peshawar carnage. The HRCP has unequivocally condemned the decision to establish military courts because this move undermines the judiciary (Human Rights Watch, 2015). The International Commission of Jurists declares in its 2016 brief on Pakistan that the "military justice" system is "an affront to human rights" (ICJ, 2016). The brief notes that trials through military courts are conducted in secret with no written reasoned judgment available (ICJ, 2016; Dawn, 2015a). ICG (2015) echoes similar observations on the risk of miscarriage of justice. According to the ICG Report, even though there is a right of legal defence, convictions are relatively straightforward due to secret trials and the absence of public oversight. Therefore, the ICG concludes, the potential for abuse far outweighs any potential benefits (ICG, 2015, p. 22).

The ICG (2015) further criticises the appellate process under which appeal hearings are headed by a senior military officer. However, these concerns were addressed by the Supreme Court of Pakistan's decision on 5 August 2015. The Supreme Court held that any order passed, decision taken or sentence awarded by the military courts is subject to judicial review by superior judiciary on the grounds of being "*coram non judice*, being without jurisdiction or suffering from *mala fides* including malice in law" (Supreme Court of Pakistan, 2015).

One criticism might be that the military is a judge in its own cause and, therefore, inherently biased against those accused of terror offences. In other words, those accused or suspected of terrorism cannot be expected to receive a fair trial because of the inherent bias in the trial by military court system.

Finally, some have sought to challenge military courts on the grounds they offend the basic structure of the Constitution. Originally expounded in India (see, generally, Mate, 2010), the 'basic structure' doctrine holds that Constitutions have certain basic features that cannot be amended by the parliament, including federalism, adoption of a particular State religion or secularism, or enshrining certain fundamental rights. Petitioners maintained that, similar to India, the 1973 Constitution has a basic structure that cannot be altered by the Parliament through amendments (Supreme Court of Pakistan, 2015). However, the Supreme Court of Pakistan did not endorse this submission. The Chief Justice of Pakistan observed that "there are no limitations, express or implied on the powers of the Parliament to amend the Constitution and the amendments brought about in exercise of such power are not liable to be challenged on any ground whatsoever before any Court" (Supreme Court of Pakistan, 2015).

3. Partial defence of military courts

3.1 Military courts as antibiotics

Legally and constitutionally, military courts are valid. So much is clear from the Supreme Court of Pakistan's judgment of 5 August 2015 where the Court upheld both the validity of the 21st Constitutional Amendment as well as the amendments to the PAA 1952 and other applicable laws pertaining to the formation and operation military courts (Supreme Court of Pakistan, 2015). However, the lead judgment of Justice Sheikh Azmat Saeed (Supreme Court, 2015, para 180(f)) provides some grounds for a broader defence of military courts. His Honour wrote:

> The 21st Constitutional Amendment and the Pakistan Army (Amendment) Act, 2015 accumulatively provide, **a temporary measure** for the trial of terrorists accused of offences including waging war against Pakistan by a forum already constituted under the law and consistent with a recognized procedure already available for and applicable to personnel of the Pakistan Army. The **enlargement of the jurisdiction of such forum is subject to due compliance with an ascertainable criteria constituting a valid classification having nexus with the defence of Pakistan** and does not abrogate, repeal, or substantively alter the Salient Features of the Constitution. The provisions of the 21st Constitutional Amendment as such are intra vires the Constitution. The provisions of the Pakistan Army (Amendment) Act, 2015, are not ultra vires the Constitution. *(emphasis added)*

The judgment has three notable features. First, it describes military courts as "temporary" measures that are a necessary response to the "war against Pakistan". Second, it implicitly recognises that the country's legal system has failed to adapt to the threat of terrorism. In other words, the inability of the police and the judiciary to respond effectively to the security challenges posed by terrorists constitutes regulatory failure of the State. And third, it "enlarges" the jurisdiction of military courts, an already existing "forum", and legitimates this by its "nexus with the defence of Pakistan". This third element is the *raison d'etre* behind formation of military courts. Such courts are intended to deter terrorism expeditiously by suspending constitutional rights and adopting inquisitorial hearings that nullify the presumption of innocence. They are a short-term, stop-gap measure to compensate for the failures of traditional courts to mete out justice.

This chapter agrees with this defence of military courts. Importantly, it is a *partial* defence. Military courts, this chapter argues, are like antibiotics. Just as antibiotics are prescribed to cure disease and infection when the human body's immune system proves insufficient, so, too, military courts are fulfilling a role that traditional courts are failing to serve. However, antibiotics have two limitations: first, they may have side effects; and, second, they are always prescribed in controlled quantities and discontinued after the disease and infection is controlled. These metaphorical limitations apply with equal force to military courts: Their "side effects" are that they are stunting and undercutting the development of an efficient justice system. Therefore, they should be deployed in "controlled" circumstances and discontinued as soon as possible.

Military courts, for anti-terrorist activities, should not be ends in themselves. The government must embark upon a comprehensive programme of systematic judicial and police reforms. This not only accords with the wishes of the general public, civil society and the legal profession (see, for example, Express Tribune, 2015; The Asia Society, 2012) but is also in line with the recommendations of the ICG in its 2008 and 2015 reports (see ICG, 2008, 2015, pp. 25–29). If the current government embarks upon this process, then any reformed judicial and police system must be ready by the time the term of military courts expires in two years' time. However, this looks highly unlikely since there is no evidence of any police or judicial reforms programme in place. This could mean that either the term of the military courts would have to be extended or the institutional failures of the judicial and police will return. To return to the antibiotics analogy, if the original "prescription" is not resolving the malaise then either the potency of antibiotics needs to be increased or the prescription changed. In Pakistan's case, policymakers confront the challenge of devising a new "medical plan" for Pakistan's terrorism problem if military courts fail to "cure" the low conviction rates or if the "body" (that is, the judiciary, the executive or society at large) continues to reject and question the "prescription" of the military courts as the solution.

Although we can at best speculate at the possible fallout of discontinuing military courts in the wake of pressure from civil society, international rights groups and the judiciary, one thing is clear: the lacklustre performance of the Anti-Terrorism Courts (ATCs). The operational failures of the ATCs, the immediate precursors to military courts, highlight the failings of the police and the traditional judiciary to the threat of terrorism. Established under the *Anti-Terrorism Act 1997* (ATA 1997) with the aim of speeding up the trial process of terror suspects, the ATCs, after nearly two decades of operation, have proven ineffective despite procedural relaxations and lower evidentiary requirements.

For example, two anti-terrorism courts in the city of Rawalpindi heard 205 cases but convicted only ten of the accused (Dawn, 2014a). In Islamabad, no convictions were recorded for the same period (Dawn, 2014a). In the Punjab provision, the largest and most populous in Pakistan, only 506 cases had been heard as of 2013, with 307 acquittals and 136 convictions (Shaukat, 2014). One thousand and fifteen cases are pending (Shaukat, 2014). According to the Centre for Public Policy and Governance (CPPG) at the Forman Christian College, Lahore, Pakistan had 1,717 terror attacks in 2013 resulting in 2,400 deaths (Shaukat, 2014). Two thousand terrorists accused have been freed because of lack of evidence, incomplete investigation or intimidation tactics (Wall Street Journal, 2015). In one such case, a leading government prosecutor with a conviction rate of 70% was forced to seek asylum in the US because of the threats to himself and his family (Wall Street Journal, 2015). The CPPG Report concludes that the entire criminal justice system must be reformed because of the compromising effect of factors such as incomplete investigation, poor prosecution and the performance of the criminal justice system (Shaukat, 2014; similar recommendations were made by ICG, 2010, 2015). The CPPG Report also notes that an unusually large number of acquittals is primarily due to the witnesses withdrawing their statements against the accused (Shaukat, 2014).

This ATC experience demonstrates that the fault lies in the underlying legal system. For example, the definition of "terrorism" under Section 6(1) and (2) of the ATA 1997 is so broad that literally all violent crime qualifies. Section 6(2) lists crimes such as causing damage to property; doing anything that causes death; kidnapping for ransom; inciting violence or sectarian hatred; burning of vehicles; and extortion. However, the ATA 1997 does not provide any distinguishing criteria of when such criminal actions were committed by a "terrorist" or when these were committed by an ordinary criminal. Therefore, the ATCs were soon overwhelmed by cases. Further, due to the "speedy" nature of the proceedings, several convictions were overturned on appeal due to lack of evidence or other procedural deficiencies.

Fast forward 17 years, and the PPA 2014, successor to the ATA 1997, adopts a similar approach, carving terrorism out of the mainstream legal system and converting it into a "special" category of crime that merits its own legal standards, procedure and process. The PPA, however, attempted to distinguish when violent crime became a terror-related crime by specifying in the Schedule a list of criminal actions that, upon closer inspection, bear resemblance to the standards enumerated in the ATA 1997. The distinction is the addition of the proviso "if committed with the purpose of waging war or insurrection against

Pakistan or threatening the security of Pakistan". Thus, the message is that the law is that whether or not a crime (say, kidnapping for ransom or arson) amounts to a terrorist act depends on whether national security is implicated. If the answer to the query is yes, then a different legal process applies. The aim of this legal process is to achieve a conviction, because the underlying objective of the PPA 2014, like the ATA 1997 it succeeds, is to ensure punishment to deter future challenges to the national security of Pakistan.

3.2 Judicial and legal system failure as underlying "infection"

For military courts to be an effective "anti-biotic", it has to address an "infection" in the current system. To what extent do military courts rectify institutional failures in Pakistan's legal and judicial response to terrorism?

Pakistan has consistently relied on its military for support when the administrative machinery of the executive breaks down or is incapable of discharging its intended function. Thus, the 1973 Constitution provides for the armed forces of Pakistan to act in aid of civil power (see Part 1). The provisions for acting in aid of civil power are intended for inward diversion of the military resources to supplement the operation of law enforcement agencies. However, the provisions (and the power of immunity) have been used in the past to quell insurrections and civil disturbances and to cover actions of martial law regimes. Similar to the concept of acting in aid of civil power, the military courts are, in effect, acting in "aid of judicial authority" because the original judicial authorities that were charged to adjudicate terrorism cases have, for reasons outlined above, failed to do so.

On closer examination, the aim of the military courts is beyond conventional notions of punishment and deterrence. The procedural shortcuts, reduced evidentiary standards and presumption of an arrest as *prima facie* evidence of guilt all point out to its true aim – to enhance certainty of conviction. Upon securing a conviction, the State then can seek retribution for past crimes and deter future terrorist actions. The establishment of military courts is, therefore, a testament to the impotency of the regular courts in achieving certainty, retribution and deterrence.

Retribution and deterrence are recurring themes in the establishment of military courts in Pakistan. Retribution is to "get even" with the terrorists. This is effected by punishment by State organs, whether the judiciary or the military. Retributivists (Dolinko, 1991) provide a theoretical definition, although there is some variance in their approaches. "Negative" retributivists argue that the punishment for past crimes must not be undeserved and the conduct of a criminal is supposed to provide a necessary, but not sufficient, condition for punishment. "Positive" retributivists argue that punishment is justified only to the extent of being deserved and criminal conduct is a sufficient condition for punishment (Duff, 1999, p. 48). Brooks (2012, p. 35), for example, terms retribution as a "backward looking" theory of punishment in the sense that it aims to punish injustices/wrongs committed in the past.

But why does the crime of terrorism deserve the *strongest* possible retribution or punishment? It is to ensure deterrence – retribution or punishment communicates to potential terrorists and criminals the possible consequences of their actions. The criminal law of the State constitutes the regulatory tool of communicating the consequences of spreading terror (or even committing non-terror-related offences). Criminal law is an umbrella term for a set of rules that typically defines the prohibition of conduct considered "wrong" in a society, the applicable rules of procedure used to hold the "wrongdoer" accountable, and finally, the consequences of committing a "wrong". In essence, the aim of the criminal justice system is to prevent crime and criminals from committing further crimes. Additionally, some criminal law systems may bring in additional aims of reform and rehabilitation of criminals.

Several commentators have discussed the concept of deterrence and their effects on criminal activity. For example, according to Brooks (2012, p. 35), deterrence is a "forward looking" concept of punishment. Effective deterrence within a criminal justice system enables prevention of future crime which, according to Freiberg (2010, p. 211), projects to potential criminals the need for "avoidance of a given action through fear of perceived consequences". Freiberg (2010, p. 214), citing Schneider et al. (2001), argues that deterrence is a paradoxical concept: individuals who are likely to be deterred are in the least need of it while those that need to be deterred are least likely to be deterred. People who are likely to commit crimes are the ones who need to be deterred, but their criminal activity informs them of the actual chances of detection and punishment (Freiberg, 2010, p. 214). Other commentators classify deterrence into two categories: special and general (Von Hirsch et al., 1999, p. 5). Special deterrence deals with already identified offenders while general deterrence covers potential offenders (Von Hirsch et al., 1999).

The effects of deterrence further subdivide into two categories (Von Hirsch et al., 1999): initial deterrence and marginal deterrence. Initial deterrence deals with the effects of prohibiting conduct that was previously regarded as permissible. Marginal deterrence, on the other hand, is the altered deterrence (either increased or decreased) that may result from enforcement of policies against punishable conduct (Von Hirsch et al., 1999). The main issue for legislatures and policymakers is always marginal deterrence, because criminal conduct is already prohibited (Von Hirsch et al., 1999). Therefore, if criminal conduct is already prohibited, the issue arises as to how can deterrence be enhanced through changes in law? Such changes must enhance the "likelihood of apprehension and conviction and/or in the severity of punishment" (Von Hirsch et al., 1999, p. 5).

This scholarship on deterrence is relevant to explaining why Pakistan chose using military courts to deter terrorists. Effective marginal deterrence cannot be achieved through change in policies or enhancing severity of the penalties. Freiberg (2010, p. 211) states that successful marginal deterrence regimes require understanding the "subjective disutilities of offenders". Therefore, potential offenders must perceive benefits and consequences of penalised actions for marginal deterrence policies to succeed (Freiberg, 2010, pp. 211–212). If the consequences of crime outweigh the benefits of committing crime, most criminals may desist from committing crimes. Deterrence is effective only where the deterrence factors such as the severity of punishment, heightened probability of detection and assured punishment outweigh the "benefit" of committing criminal actions (Freiberg, 2010, p. 212; Von Hirsch et al., 1999, pp. 45–50).

Von Hirsch et al. (1999, p. 6) list five preconditions for marginal deterrence regimes to become effective:

1 The potential offenders must realise that the probability of conviction or the severity of punishment has changed.
2 The potential offenders must take altered risks into account when deciding whether to offend.
3 The potential offenders must believe that there is a greater than negligible likelihood of being caught.
4 The potential offenders must believe that the altered penalty will apply to them if caught.
5 The potential offenders must be willing to alter their choices regarding offending in the light of perceived change in certainty or severity of punishment.

To apply this criteria to Pakistan's legal response to terrorism, let us retrace our steps to the ATA 1997 – the first concerted legislative and judicial answer to the rise in sectarian terrorism in Pakistan during the 1990s. The essence of the ATA 1997 was that terrorism is a unique type of crime. The severity of terrorism and the threat it poses to the society at large must attract a response from the government. The response was to establish a separate court mechanism designed to speed up terrorist cases through the judicial system. However, the system failed because the underlying systemic shortcomings were not addressed – for example, police investigations were incomplete, the public prosecutor made defective presentations of evidence to court; judicial officers and witnesses were intimidated. Moreover, the crime of terrorism was defined in such broad terms that virtually all types of violent crime amounted to terrorism (see Part 2). The systemic shortcomings were further compounded by the fact that on appeal, several cases were dismissed due to faulty and incomplete investigations or lack of evidence.

In short, with terrorism unabated, the ATA 1997 system lacked deterrent effect. Applying Von Hirsch et al.'s (1999, p. 6) five-point criteria, it is clear that the ATA 1997 failed on several points; for example, offenders did not appreciate the change in probability of conviction and did not alter their calculation of risk when deciding to offend. The result was that many notorious and well-known individuals involved in sectarian terrorism escaped convictions. One well-known case was that of Malik Ishaq, the head of the Al-Qaeda-linked Lashkar-e-Jhangwi group. Ishaq was killed in a shootout with the police in July 2015 when the police party that was escorting him to a site where arms and ammunition were reportedly concealed was ambushed by militants attempting to free him (The Guardian, 2015). Ishaq escaped conviction by reading out the names of the children of the trial judge, thereby making it clear the risks of convicting him (The Guardian, 2015). Ishaq was also on the US State Department list of "specially designated global terrorists" (US Department of State, 2014). The inability of the courts established under the ATA 1997 to convict hardened terrorists such as Ishaq illustrates the ineffectiveness of the ATA 1997 regime. The ineffectiveness further projects the message to the criminals and terrorist elements that the judicial system remains malleable, thereby diminishing the deterrence value of the courts established under the ATA 1997.

Upon realising the ineffectiveness of the courts established under the ATA 1997, the government and the policymakers in Pakistan embarked upon yet another "quick fix" venture. The new solution was the PPA 2014 and the establishment of military courts under the 2015 Act (see Part 1). Put simply, the idea behind the military court process was to speed up the primary trial court stage. The military courts would operate under an altered standard that enables easy convictions for those accused of terrorist offences. Convictions can be appealed to a military appellate court. Thereafter, convictions can be appealed to the provincial High Courts and finally, the Supreme Court of Pakistan. The Supreme Court of Pakistan was at pains to explain that it still retained the discretion to review the judgments issued by the military courts. Herein lays the vulnerability of the military courts solution. Under the current constitutional structure, any exceptional court would have to "feed" into the existing appellate structures. This may potentially dilute the speedy nature of the military courts when judgments issued by military courts conflict with procedural requirements. For example, the Supreme Court of Pakistan recently halted the execution of two individuals – Ali Rehman and Taj Mohammad, convicted as facilitators in the Peshawar carnage by the military courts (Dunya News, 2016). The Supreme Court of Pakistan held that the military courts must issue a reasoned judgment (Dunya News, 2016). Yet the presiding officers of military courts are not trained judicial officers. Requiring them to submit written judgments justifying the legal grounds for conviction will clearly delay the trial process. At the same time, appellate courts are under constitutional duties to ensure no miscarriage of justice occurs. The outcome of the Ali Rehman and Taj Mohammad appeal case had not been decided at the time of writing this chapter, but it is clear that these cases are litmus tests on how the military courts system integrates with the existing judicial system.

4. Conclusion: antibiotics for a "sick" judicial system

The establishment of military courts is analogous to the prescription of antibiotics. The use of antibiotics is often necessary to cure diseases, even when their use may mean enduring unpleasant side effects. Long-term use of antibiotics, however, is harmful for the body. Similarly, long-term use of military courts is not the solution for Pakistan's terrorism problem. This is because it stunts the development of the judicial system of the country.

The powers of military courts, however, appear to be contained through the appeal process. The Supreme Court of Pakistan and the Provincial High Courts have entertained several appeals where due process has not been followed. In addition to staying the executions of Ali Rehman and Taj Mohammad (Dunya News, 2016) (see Part 3), the Supreme Court stayed the execution of three more individuals accused of carrying out terrorist acts in the country in May 2016 (Express Tribune, 2016). The counsel for the accused argued that no opportunity to engage a legal counsel was given to the accused and that the accused were not informed of the allegations against them (Express Tribune, 2016). It appears, therefore, that the Supreme Court of Pakistan is staying true to its word of retaining the discretion to review the decisions passed by the military courts. In turn, though, this then creates another problem where hardened terrorists may yet capitalise on the weakness of the system by exploiting the "magnanimity" of the Supreme Court of Pakistan. Theoretically, terrorists could challenge expedited military court processes, citing procedural unfairness; the Supreme Court of Pakistan will be constrained to order retrial, thereby defeating the very purpose of establishing military courts in the first place.

The establishment of the military courts in Pakistan has had an interesting side-effect. This is illustrated by the recent hanging of Mumtaz Qadri, who was convicted of assassinating Salman Taseer, the provincial governor of Punjab province. Qadri was serving as Taseer's bodyguard when he assassinated Taseer. Taseer had expressed open willingness to reform the country's controversial blasphemy laws and showed support for Aasia Bibi (a Christian woman accused of blasphemy). Qadri gunned down Taseer in broad daylight and proudly confessed his crime in the court. He was tried and convicted by an ATC established under the ATA 1997. Commenting anonymously on the hanging and the government's decision to follow through with the judicial sentence, one analyst observes: "With military courts regularly disposing of cases of hardened militants, passing and implementing on death sentences, the civilian side (executive & judiciary) was under even more pressure to take responsibility" (Dawn, 2016). Qadri's execution drew loud protests from hardline political groups. Yet Qadri's conviction in October 2011 to execution in March 2016 took roughly four and a half years, while Qadri's counsel exhausted all possible legal avenues. Contrast Qadri's case with that of Saulat Mirza (a notorious hitman for a political party) who was suspected to have been involved in several politically motivated murders. Mirza was convicted in May 1999 for his murder of Shahid Hamid (the managing director of the Karachi Electrical Supply Corporation) by the ATC established under the ATA 1997 in the city of Karachi (Dawn, 2015c). Mirza managed to dodge execution for 17 years, taking full advantage of the moratorium on the death penalty since 2008 while slowly exhausting all appellate forums (Dawn, 2015c). Mirza also allegedly handled his group of assassins from within the jail in Karachi, and he is thought to have arranged the assassination of a jail official (Amanullah Niazi) who tried to check his activities (Dawn, 2015c). Mirza was transferred to the remote jail in Macch (Balochistan) to disrupt his network (Dawn, 2015c). He was later executed in May 2015 for his crimes.

These two contrasting cases illustrate the importance of exceptional measures when State institutions fail. In an ideal judicial environment, the police arrest an accused person and the judiciary sentences the accused only if he or she is found guilty. The accused is then punished in accordance with the law. Where the police and the judiciary fail to discharge their respective functions, security in society is undermined. Society might feel insecure, and certain segments of society may even resort to self-help measures such as vigilantism. The failure of State organs such as the police and the judiciary leaves an institutional vacuum. Ideally, this should be addressed by focusing on the real problem: ***undertaking police and judicial reforms.***

However, where successive governments fail to address the underlying problems (whether due to lack of political will or incompetence), the institutional gap not only widens but may also manifest further problems (such as a general rule of law problem). In this light, the establishment of military courts is an antibiotic (unpleasant but necessary). It is unpleasant because it violates the norms of basic justice and human rights. Critics of the military courts and civil rights groups are taking this line of argument. The unpleasant measures are, however, necessary because the real solution of comprehensive police and judicial reforms has so far not materialised. The malaise of instability and insecurity will course through the body of the State unless the long-term solution is pursued with vigour and perseverance.

Therefore, the establishment of military courts represents a plug to an institutional gap in the legal infrastructure. The State always rules and has the public right to do so. When the State fails to deter criminals and terrorists through established legal avenues, other methods are required. Modern States often place checks and balances on their powers through declaratory measures such as the constitution of a country or a basic charter of human rights. Such instruments outline the State's behaviour in relation to people's rights (for example, the right of movement, speech, assembly or conduct of business). Therefore, what makes State action legitimate is whether that action is backed by sovereign authority which, in turn, may be dependent upon several factors such as public support, adherence to the precepts of fairness and rule of law. Where public dissatisfaction with State action to the point it becomes ineffective, then the State must search for an alternative solution. If the State fails to find or implement the solution, then it undercuts its own sovereignty. If allowed to continue, the State's sovereignty degenerates to the point where the people withdraw their support. Quite often this leads to violent upheavals, rebellions or bloody revolutions. In Pakistan's case, the military is often called upon to assist the civilian machinery of the State in various roles and functions. In the past, such assistance spanned aid activities, disaster relief, internal security operations, supervision of elections and even the conduct of census. Ordinarily, the State relies on government ministries to organise such activities. Where systemic governance problems lead to institutional failure, however, a governance shift occurs whereby the State surrenders part of its sovereignty to a *de facto* sovereign – in Pakistan's case, this is the military.

However, no State can continue on *de facto* terms for long. This necessitates the need for law reform by implementing judicial and police reforms, which must be ready by the time the effects of the "antibiotics" wear off, bearing in mind that the term of the military courts expires in two years' time. Failure to do so would mean perpetuation of an institutional vacuum that may eventually lead to the demise of the State.

References

Are military courts the best way to fight terror? (2015, January 17). *Human Rights Watch*. Retrieved from https://www.hrw.org/news/2015/01/17/are-military-courts-best-way-fight-terror.

Army Courts to Try Pakistan Terror Suspects (2015, January 11). *Al Jazeera*. Retrieved from http://www.aljazeera.com/indepth/features/2015/01/army-courts-try-pakistan-terror-suspects-201511017364652679l.html.

Asia Society (2012). *Stablizing Pakistan through police reform* (Report by the Independent Commission on Pakistan Police Reforms). Retrieved from http://asiasociety.org/files/pdf/as_pakistan_police_reform.pdf.

Bringing them home: Pakistan's child deradicalisation centre offers second chance (2015d, September 23). *Dawn*. Retrieved from http://www.dawn.com/news/1208602.

Brooks, T. (2012). *Punishment*. Routledge.

Chottu surrenders with 175 gang members (2016, April 20). *Express Tribune*. Retrieved from http://tribune.com.pk/story/1088434/chottu-surrenders-with-175-gang-members/.

Conviction rate slow in anti-terrorism courts in Pindi, Islamabad (2014a, December 18). *Dawn*. Retrieved from http://www.dawn.com/news/1151583.

Dolinko, D. (1991). Some Thoughts About Retributivism. *Ethics, 101*, 537.

Dowse, R.E. (1969). The military and political development. In C. Leys (Ed.), *Politics and change in developing countries* (pp. 213–246). Cambridge: Cambridge University Press.

Duff, R.A. (1999). Punishment, communication and community. In M. Matravers (Ed.), *Punishment and political theory* (pp. 48–68). Oxford: Hart Publishing.

Engdahl, D.E. (1971). Soldiers, riots and revolution: The law and history of military troops in civil disorders. *Iowa Law Review, 57(1)*, 1–73.

Fear and Loathing: Terrorists Attack Mapped Around the World (2012, December 4). *The Economist*. Retrieved from http://www.economist.com/blogs/graphicdetail/2012/12/daily-chart-0.

Freiberg, A. (2010). *The tools of regulation*. Sydney: Federation Press.

Government of Pakistan (2015). National Action Plan. Retrieved from http://infopak.gov.pk/InnerPage.aspx?Page_ID=46.

Huntington, S.P. (1968). *Political order in changing societies*. New Haven: Yale University Press.

International Commission of Jurists (2016). Pakistan: "Military justice" system an affront to human rights – new analysis brief. Retrieved from http://www.icj.org/pakistan-military-justice-system-an-affront-to-human-rights-new-analysis-brief/.

International Crisis Group (2008). *Reforming Pakistan's police*. (Asia Report No 157).

International Crisis Group (2010). *Reforming Pakistan's criminal justice system*. (Asia Report No 196).

International Crisis Group (2015). *Revisiting counter-terrorism strategies in Pakistan: opportunities and pitfalls*. (Asia Report No 271).

Khan, L.A. (2015, January 13). Militarisation of Pakistan Constitution. *The World Post*. Retrieved from http://www.huffingtonpost.com/liaquat-ali-khan/militarization-of-pakista_b_6452304.html.

Kine, P. (2015, January 17). Are military courts the best way to fight terror? *The Express Tribune*. Retrieved from http://tribune.com.pk/story/822903/are-military-courts-the-best-way-to-fight-terror/.

Mahmud, T. (1993). Praetorianism and common law in post-colonial settings: Judicial responses to constitutional breakdowns in Pakistan. *Utah Law Review*, *4*, 1225–1305.

Manan, A. (2014, December 25). Fight against terrorism: Defining moment. *The Express Tribune*. Retrieved from http://tribune.com.pk/story/811947/fight-against-terrorism-defining-moment/.

Mate, M. (2010). Two paths to judicial power: The basic structure doctrine and public interest litigation in comparative perspective. *San Diego International Law Journal, 12*, 175–222.

Meeks, C.I. (1975). Illegal law enforcement: Aiding civil authorities in violation of the Posse Comitatus Act. *Military Law Review*, *70*, 83–135.

Military courts to try terror suspects: Political parties thrash out consensus after marathon meeting (2014b, December 25). *Dawn*. Retrieved from: http://www.dawn.com/news/1153062.

Military courts' secrecy unnerves experts (2015b, April 4). *Dawn*. Retrieved from http://www.dawn.com/news/1173841.

Pakistan terrorist leader killed in police shootout (2015, July 29). *The Guardian*. Retrieved from http://www.theguardian.com/world/2015/jul/29/pakistan-terrorist-leader-maliq-ishaq-killed-police-shootout.

Pakistan: Military courts continue to extend their tentacles (2015, August 26). *Asian Human Rights Commission (AHRC)*. Retrieved from http://www.humanrights.asia/news/ahrc-news/AHRC-STM-140-2015/?searchterm=.

Pakistan's new military courts challenged over abuse claims (2016, June 27). *Reuters*. Retrieved from http://www.reuters.com/article/us-pakistan-military-courts-insight-idUSKCN0ZD2ZI.

Peck, D.L. (1975). The justices and the generals: The Supreme Court and judicial review of military activities. *Military Law Review, 70*, 1–81.

Perlmutter, A. (1969). The Praetorian state and the Praetorian army: Toward a taxonomy of civil military relations in developing polities. *Comparative Politics, 1*, 382–383.

Prosecutors in Pakistan face routine threats in terror cases (2015, January 20). *Wall Street Journal*. Retrieved from http://www.wsj.com/articles/prosecutors-in-pakistan-face-routine-threats-in-terror-cases-1421713991.

Pye, L.W. (1962). Armies in the process of political modernization. In J. J. Johnson (Ed.), *The role of the military in underdeveloped countries* (pp. 69–90). Princeton: Princeton University Press.

Qadri's execution was govt's only option (2016, March 1). *Dawn*. Retrieved from http://www.dawn.com/news/1242739/qadris-execution-was-govts-only-option.

Roundtable: Depoliticise police, say experts (2015, January 30). *Express Tribune*. Retrieved from http://tribune.com.pk/story/829940/roundtable-depoliticise-police-say-experts/.

Saulat Mirza executed at Balochistan's Machh Jail (2015c, May 12). *Dawn*. Retrieved from http://www.dawn.com/news/1181322.

Scharpf, F.W. (1966). Judicial review and the political question: A functional analysis. *Yale Law Journal, 75*(4), 517–597.

Schneider, F., Braithwaite, V., & Reinhart, M. (2001). Individual behaviour in Australia's shadow economy: Facts, empirical findings and some mysteries. *ANU/ATO Centre for Tax System Integrity*. Working Paper No 19 cited in Freiberg (2010).

Security for military court judges and prosecutors (2015a, February 25). *Dawn*. Retrieved from http://www.dawn.com/news/1165793.

Shaukat, A. (2014, May 29). Low conviction rate: Report seeks reforms in criminal justice system. *The Express Tribune*. Retrieved from http://tribune.com.pk/story/714690/low-conviction-rate-report-seeks-reforms-in-criminal-justice-system/.

South Asia Terrorism Portal (2016). Attacks in Pakistan. Retrieved from http://www.satp.org/satporgtp/countries/pakistan/database/Fidayeenattack.htm#.

Supreme Court halts execution of two APS convicts (2016, February 10). *Dunya News*. Retrieved from http://dunyanews.tv/en/Pakistan/321904-Supreme-Court-halts-execution-of-two-APS-convicts.

Supreme Court of Pakistan (5 August 2015). *Constitutional Petition Nos. 12, 13, 18, 20-22, 31, 35-36, 39, 40, 42-44 OF 2010*. Retrieved from http://www.supremecourt.gov.pk/web/page.asp?id=2001.

Top court stays execution of three military court convicts (2016, May 10). *Express Tribune*. Retrieved from http://tribune.com.pk/story/1100489/top-court-stays-execution-of-three-military-court-convicts/.

US Department of State (2014). Terrorist designations of Lashkar I Jhangvi and Malik Ishaq. Retrieved from http://www.state.gov/r/pa/prs/ps/2014/02/221398.htm.

US v Jaramillo 380 F. Supp. 1375 (D. Neb. 1974) (510 F.2d 808 (8th Circuit 1975)).

Von Hirsch, A., Bottoms, A.E., Burney, E., & Wikstrom, P.O. (1999). *Criminal Deterrence and Sentence Severity*. Oxford: Hart Publishing.

Index

For Product Safety Concerns and Information please contact our EU
representative GPSR@taylorandfrancis.com
Taylor & Francis Verlag GmbH, Kaufingerstraße 24, 80331 München, Germany

www.ingramcontent.com/pod-product-compliance
Ingram Content Group UK Ltd.
Pitfield, Milton Keynes, MK11 3LW, UK
UKHW050051200926
475702UK00019B/2773
* 9 7 8 0 3 6 7 5 9 3 5 6 8 *